Distributed Relational Database Architecture

Connectivity Guide

For book and bookstore information

http://www.prenhall.com

Prentice Hall PTR, Upper Saddle River, NJ 07458

Editorial/Production Supervision: Lisa Iarkowski
Acquisitions Editor: Michael Meehan
Manufacturing Manager: Alexis R. Heydt

 © 1995 Prentice Hall PTR
Prentice-Hall, Inc.
A Paramount Communications Company
Upper Saddle River, NJ 07458

The publisher offers discounts on this book when ordered in bulk quantities. For more information, contact:

Corporate Sales Department, PTR Prentice Hall, One Lake Street, Upper Saddle River, NJ 07458, Phone: 800-382-3419, FAX: 201-236-7141 e-mail: corpsales@prenhall.com

Printed in the United States of America
10 9 8 7 6 5 4 3 2 1

ISBN 0-13-398306-4

Fourth Edition (June 1995)

This edition replaces and makes obsolete the previous edition, SC26-4783-02. The technical changes for this edition are summarized under "Summary of Changes," and are indicated by a vertical bar to the left of a change.

This edition and applies to current versions and releases of IBM distributed relational database products (DB2 for MVS/ESA, DB2 for VM and VSE, DB2 for OS/400, DB2 for AIX, DB2 for OS/2). Consult the latest edition of the applicable IBM bibliography for current information on the product.

Order publications through your IBM representative or the IBM branch office serving your locality. Publications are not stocked at the address below.

A form for readers' comments is provided at the back of this publication. If the form has been removed, address your comments to:

IBM Corporation, Department J58
P.O. Box 49023
San Jose, CA, 95161-9023
United States of America

When you send information to IBM, you grant IBM a nonexclusive right to use or distribute the information in any way it believes appropriate without incurring any obligation to you.

Contents

Notices

References in this publication to IBM products, programs, or services do not imply that IBM intends to make these available in all countries in which IBM operates. Any reference to an IBM product, program, or service is not intended to state or imply that only IBM's product, program, or service may be used. Any functionally equivalent product, program, or service that does not infringe any of IBM's intellectual property rights may be used instead of the IBM product, program, or service. Evaluation and verification of operation in conjunction with other products, except those expressly designated by IBM, is the user's responsibility.

IBM may have patents or pending patent applications covering subject matter in this document. The furnishing of this document does not give you any license to these patents. You can send license inquiries, in writing, to the IBM Director of Commercial Relations, IBM Corporation, Purchase, NY 10577, U.S.A.

Online Publications

For online versions of this book, we authorize you to:

1. Copy, modify, and print the documentation contained on the media, for use within your enterprise, provided you reproduce the copyright notice, all warning statements, and other required statements on each copy or partial copy; and

2. Transfer the original unaltered copy of the documentation when you transfer the related IBM product (which may be either machines you own, or programs, if the program's license terms permit a transfer). You must, at the same time, destroy all other copies of the documentation.

You are responsible for payment of any taxes, including personal property taxes, resulting from this authorization.

THERE ARE NO WARRANTIES, EXPRESSED OR IMPLIED, INCLUDING THE WARRANTIES OF MERCHANTABILITY AND FITNESS FOR A PARTICULAR PURPOSE.

Some jurisdictions do not allow the exclusion of implied warranties, so the above exclusion may not apply to you.

Your failure to comply with the terms above terminates this authorization. Upon termination, you must destroy your machine readable documentation.

IBM may have patents or pending patent applications covering subject matter in this document. The furnishing of this document does not give you any license to these patents. You can send license inquiries, in writing, to the IBM Director of Licensing, IBM Corporation, 500 Columbus Avenue, Thornwood, NY 10594, U.S.A.

Trademarks

The following terms, denoted by an asterisk (*) at their first occurrence in this publication, are trademarks of the IBM Corporation in the United States or other countries or both:

ACF/VTAM	IBM
AIX	IMS/ESA
AIX/6000	MVS/ESA
APPN	MVS/XA
AS/400	NetView
Advanced Peer-to-Peer Networking	Operating System/400
AnyNet	OS/2
CICS	OS/400
CICS/ESA	QMF
CICS/VSE	RACF
DATABASE 2	RISC System/6000
DB2	SAA
DB2/2	S/370
DB2/6000	S/390
DRDA	SQL/DS
Distributed Database Connection	SQL/400
Services/2	Skill Dynamics
Distributed Relational Database	Systems Application Architecture
Architecture	VM/ESA
ES/3090	VM/XA
ES/4381	VSE/ESA
ES/9370	VTAM
Extended Services	3090
Extended Services for OS/2	

Other company, product, and service names, which may be denoted by a double asterisk (**), may be trademarks or service marks of others.

Windows is a trademark of Microsoft Corporation.

UNIX is a registered trademark in the United States and other countries licensed exclusively through X/Open Company Limited.

Foreword

It's over! The days of exclusive centralized, host-centric computing are over. Distributed, client/server systems are deployed today and are the predominant computing paradigm for the foreseeable future. Such systems clearly better match the business processes and organizational structures of companies today and tomorrow. Small or large, local or worldwide, companies need the flexibility, greater productivity and responsiveness of the client/server computing models.

However, the data in today's distributed systems is not well organized or easily accessible for efficient client/server processing. Many environments include a significant amount of data on various hardware platforms managed by database management systems supplied by more than one vendor. The business requirement is to access all of this data as painlessly (and cost effectively) as possible. Standards-based, open-systems solutions to these client/server data access requirements are needed.

As a result, one of the key challenges for vendors is to provide network facilities that allow an application program executing at one site in a network to access data being managed by another site. Various database vendors have responded to this challenge with products that implement proprietary data access protocols and application gateways. Unfortunately, to meet heterogeneous data access needs, these approaches typically require customers to install, manage, and administer a multitude of mechanisms. Thus, these solutions tend to be complicated and expensive.

The simplest and most cost-effective solution is a single, well-defined data access protocol that all vendors can implement. IBM's published Distributed Relational Database Architecture (DRDA) is designed to meet these requirements for open, client/server data access in an unlike, or heterogeneous, systems environment. DRDA was developed by IBM and enhanced in consultation with the multi-vendor DRDA Implementers' Advisory Council. Products implementing the DRDA protocols are available from a growing number of vendors and across the IBM product line, and they are widely deployed by businesses in production systems around the world.

Through DRDA, more data is available, on more servers, accessible by more client environments, and through products sold by more vendors, than through any other single data-access protocol in the world. All other solutions are single-vendor proprietary offerings. Each is, in its own right, arguably worthy of consideration, but none of them is capable of interoperation with each other.

The popularity of DRDA-based systems has grown steadily over the last three years, to the point where DRDA is the de facto standard for open, heterogeneous data access. DRDA can help you establish the linkages necessary to connect your distributed data to make your information more valuable across your enterprise. The DRDA Connectivity Guide can help businesses set up distributed relational databases to facilitate enterprise computing. This book covers both the database and networking technologies required to implement a distributed system so that applications can access data stored in remote databases, in addition to data stored locally.

Happy distributed, and open, client/server computing.

Sincerely,

Steve Mills   Chris Arnold

General Manager   General Manager
IBM Software Solutions   IBM Santa Teresa Laboratory
                                      Vice President Data Solutions

Preface

This book helps you implement a distributed relational database network.

The information in this book is not intended as a specification of the interfaces provided by any IBM* products discussed in this book. For more detailed information about the programming interfaces provided by any of the products discussed in this book, see the Publications section of the IBM Programming Announcement for the product in question.

About This Book

This book focuses on establishing a network of distributed relational databases that use *Distributed Relational Database Architecture** (DRDA*). DRDA specifies the protocols and conventions that provide connectivity among relational database management systems (RDBMSs). DRDA allows relational database information to be shared between multiple computer systems in a network.

This book contains the following parts:

Part 1, "DRDA Implementation," includes detailed descriptions of how to connect different products in a distributed relational database system.

Part 2, "Spiffy Network Scenarios," gives examples of several different distributed relational database scenarios.

Part 3, "Network and DRDA Concepts," gives background information on communication and DRDA concepts.

Also included in this book are appendixes containing:

VTAM* considerations
Information on how to set up interactive SQL utilities
Character conversion values

A bibliography and a glossary are at the back of the book.

Prerequisite Knowledge: Distributed relational database systems use both database and telecommunication technologies. Because most technical professionals do not specialize in both of these technologies, a certain degree of cross-training is necessary. This book is intended to help database administrators, system administrators, communication administrators, and system programmers understand distributed relational database concepts. As such, you should be familiar with at least one of the following relational database products:

- IBM DATABASE 2* for MVS/ESA* (DB2* for MVS/ESA)

- IBM DATABASE 2 for VM and VSE (DB2 for VM and VSE)

---

* Trademark of IBM Corporation

- IBM DATABASE 2 for OS/400* (DB2 for OS/400)

- IBM DATABASE 2 for AIX* (DB2 for AIX) with AIX Distributed Database Connection Services/6000 (DDCS for AIX) Connection Services/2 (DDCS/2)

- IBM DATABASE 2 for OS/2* (DB2 for OS/2)

In addition, you should have some knowledge of the operating system of the RDBMS, Systems Network Architecture (SNA), and structured query language (SQL). Part 3 of this book provides terminology and concepts of networking and DRDA that you need to know.

Summary of Changes to This Book

This is the fourth version of the Connectivity Guide. This version contains the following additions and updates:

- IBM product name terminology has changed. The following terms now refer to the IBM family of relational database products:

  DB2 for MVS/ESA (formerly DB2)
  DB2 for VM and VSE (formerly SQL/DS*)
  DB2 for OS/400 (formerly OS/400 DATABASE MANAGER)
  Communications Manager for OS/2 V1.1 (formerly OS/2 COMMUNICATIONS MANAGER or OS/2 EXTENDED SERVICES*)
  DB2 for OS/2 (formerly DB2/2*)
  DB2 for AIX (formerly DB2/6000*)
  DDCS for OS/2 (formerly DDCS/2)
  SNA Server for AIX (formerly SNA SERVICES/6000)

- With the Version 2 release of DB2 for OS/2 and DB2 for AIX, both products support the Application Server function in a DRDA compliant network.

- Chapter 5 outlines how the IBM DB2 products for OS/2, AIX, and other UNIX**-based systems implement DRDA.

- Chapter 19 outlines how to configure DDCS for OS/2.

- Chapter 20 outlines how to configure DDCS for AIX.

- Chapters 21 and 22 outline how to configure DB2 for OS/2 and DB2 for AIX as DRDA Application Servers.

Distributed Relational Database Education

IBM Education and Training offers the following classes to meet your Distributed Relational Database training needs:

---

* Trademark of IBM Corporation

** Trademark of Unix System Laboratories, Inc.

Distributed Relational Database Fundamentals and Planning (course code U4100)

This two-day class is a distributed database primer appropriate for planners, managers, developers, and programmers planning to implement a distributed relational database system. The course describes DRDA and how database products support DRDA. Distributed database planning, staffing, and product requirements are also discussed.

Distributed Database Design and Implementation Workshop (course code U4140)

This 3.5 day course teaches you how to design and implement distributed Client/Server Database solutions. The workshop provides a product independent view of Client/Server and distributed database technology and focuses on data placement. It can help the distributed database designer produce a data distribution model recognizing appropriate access, availability, management, and security requirements.

Distributed Relational Database Implementation (course code U4110)

This four-day course provides the database professional with information to configure and administer Client/Server distributed relational databases using DRDA and product specific implementations. Application programming and preprocessing techniques required to access distributed relational data are discussed. Classroom exercises reinforce the lecture material.

Distributed Database Workshop, DDCS/6000 to DB2 MVS/ESA (course code U4122)

This four-day course trains the database professional to install, design, configure, and administer AIX/6000* clients using DRDA. Using machine labs, students configure network and communication definitions, install DDCS for AIX, and define DB2 for AIX and DB2 for MVS/ESA directory entries to enable DRDA connections. Students also preprocess and bind applications, implement security, learn ways to improve performance, and resolve problem determination issues.

Distributed Database Workshop, DDCS/2 to DB2 MVS/ESA (course code U4120)

This four-day class teaches the database professional to install, design, configure, and administer OS/2 to DB2 for MVS/ESA Client/Server distributed relational databases using DRDA. Students install DDCS for OS/2, preprocess and bind applications, and deal with security, performance, application, and problem determination issues.

For more information, or to enroll in any IBM class, call 1-800-IBM-TEACh (1-800-426-8322). For locations outside the United States, see your IBM representative.

Navigating the Related Publications

Figure 1 on page xx shows a map to using the publications needed (both required and optional) when connecting IBM systems. Refer to the bibliography on page 456 for more details on each publication shown.

You can order manuals either through an IBM representative or by calling 1-800-879-2755 in the United States or any of its territories. You can pay with MasterCard, Visa, American Express, or an IBM account number.

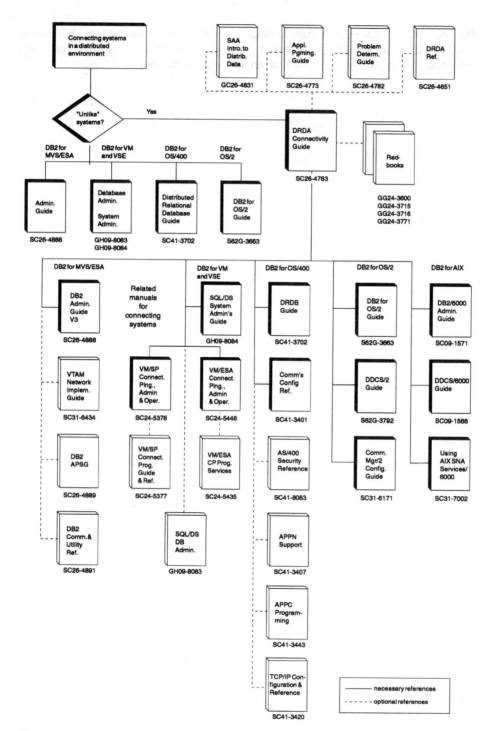

Figure 1. Map to Publications Referenced in this Manual

Part 1. DRDA Implementation

This part gives the details for connecting five different platforms in a distributed relational database system. The first chapter, Chapter 1, "Introducing DRDA Connectivity," describes the DRDA functions that a product must provide. The remaining chapters give details for specific products:

Chapter 2, "Connecting DB2 for MVS/ESA in a DRDA Network" on page 15 describes how to connect unlike DRDA systems to DB2 for MVS/ESA.
Chapter 3, "Connecting DB2 for VM and VSE in a DRDA Network" on page 49 describes how to connect unlike DRDA systems to DB2 for VM and VSE.
Chapter 4, "Connecting DB2 for OS/400 in a DRDA Network" on page 88 describes how to connect unlike DRDA systems to DB2 for OS/400.
Chapter 5, "Connecting DB2 for OS/2 or AIX in a DRDA Network" on page 103 describes how to connect unlike DRDA systems to DB2 for OS/2, AIX, and other UNIX-based systems.

Chapter 1. Introducing DRDA Connectivity

The information in this chapter is the basis for each of the product-specific implementations of DRDA presented later in the book. After reading this chapter, use the product-specific chapters that follow to learn how to connect products that support DRDA. For example, if you want to connect a DB2 for OS/2 application requester to a DB2 for MVS/ESA application server, you can use the book as follows:

1. Review "Product Levels Required to Support DRDA" on page 4 to be sure you have the required product levels.

2. Read Chapter 19, "DB2 for OS/2 and Other DRDA Servers" on page 304 to get specific details about how DRDA functions are implemented on OS/2, and what must be done to define the Application Requester to the network.

3. Then read "Setting Up the Application Server" on page 37 to get specific details about how to implement DB2 for MVS/ESA as a DRDA Application Server.

A DRDA Network

A distributed relational database consists of tables that can be stored at different locations and managed by different database management systems. DRDA is a set of potocols that coordinates communications between the systems. DRDA describes two levels of architecture: *remote unit of work* and *distributed unit of work*. All DRDA products support remote unit of work. With remote unit of work, you can access one remote relational database manager with multiple requests within one unit of work. For more information about the concepts of DRDA see Chapter 25. The two DRDA functions that are currently implemented are the *application requester* and the *application server* functions.

The Application Requester

The application requester allows end users and application programs to access remote database resources. Figure 2 shows the components that make up the Application Requester.

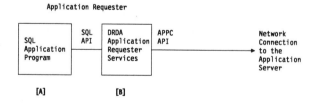

Figure 2. Application Requester Components

[A] The SQL application program running at the Application Requester issues SQL statements to request database services. This is identical to the way SQL application programs request database services in a nondistributed database system.

[B] The DRDA Application Requester services accept the SQL statements and convert them into messages to send to the application server. The content and meaning of each of these messages is defined by DRDA. The DRDA messages representing the application program's SQL statements are passed to the network by the Application Requester.

DRDA does not require the Application Requester to perform any local functions because DRDA does not require a local database management system (DBMS) at the application requester.

Some IBM products allow the Application Requester to run independently from the local DBMS. DB2 for VM and VSE is an example of an implementation in which the Application Requester can operate when the local database manager is not active. In other IBM products, the Application Requester is integrated into the local database manager and cannot run when the local database manager is unavailable. DB2 for MVS/ESA is an example of this implementation. DB2 for OS/400 is also an example of a product whose Application Requester support cannot function without the local database manager.

The Application Server

The application server performs database operations for the application requester. Figure 3 shows the components that make up the application server.

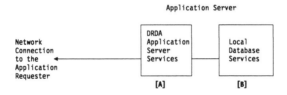

Figure 3. Application Server Components

[A] The communication network delivers the DRDA messages sent by the Application Requester. The DRDA messages describe the SQL operations to be performed, and they are transmitted using the DRDA application support protocols.

Each data object included in the DRDA messages contains a descriptor indicating the internal representation of the data. DRDA specifies that the system sending a data object is allowed to transmit data using its own internal data representation. If the data object is in a format that is not acceptable to the receiver, the receiver must perform any required data conversions. For example, DRDA allows machines using ASCII character representation to send messages to machines using EBCDIC character representations. When this occurs, the system receiving the message is responsible for performing the correct data conversion.

[B] When the DRDA messages are interpreted, the application server performs the requested SQL operations at the local database and sends the results back to the Application Requester.

Some application server products support connections to other servers using a *private* protocol. The private protocol implementations do not conform to the DRDA model and are limited to connections between like products (for example, DB2 for MVS/ESA connecting to other DB2 for MVS/ESA servers). Refer to the product implementation information in this book to determine whether the implementation you are using provides connections from the application server to other servers.

The Network Connection

DRDA defines LU 6.2 protocol for communication between the application requester and the application server in an SNA network. LU 6.2 protocol is also known as *advanced program-to-program communication (APPC)*. See Chapter 24, "LU 6.2 and APPC: Concepts" on page 399 for more details.

If you have TCP/IP users who want to access APPC applications in addition to TCP/IP applications, you should consider the IBM AnyNet[*] Product Family. AnyNet is a family of software products designed to allow you to choose the application that meets the needs of your business, regardless of what transport protocol is used in your central or remote sites. AnyNet products on MVS/ESA, OS/2, AIX/6000, OS/400, and Windows[**] enable APPC applications to run over TCP/IP, without changing applications or modifying hardware. See *IBM AnyNet Product Family* for more information.

Product Levels Required to Support DRDA

The following lists the *minimum* software product levels that support DRDA.

On MVS (application requester and application server functions)

- DB2 Version 2 Release 3 (remote unit of work level of DRDA)
- DB2 Version 3 Release 1 (distributed unit of work level of DRDA)
- MVS/XA[*] or MVS/ESA[*]
- VTAM Version 3 Release 3

On VM (application requester and application server functions)

- SQL/DS (DB2 for VM) Version 3 Release 3
- VM/SP Release 6 or VM/ESA[*] Release 1
- RSCS Networking Version 1 Release 2 (needed for ISQL printing)
- VTAM Version 3 Release 2

  VTAM V3R3 is required for the already verified conversation level security.

On VSE (application server function only)

- SQL/DS (DB2 for VSE) Version 3 Release 4
- VSE/ESA Version 1 Release 3
- CICS/VSE[*] Version 2 Release 2

[**] Trademark of Microsoft Corporation

[*] Trademark of IBM Corporation

- ACF/VTAM* Version 3 Release 3

On OS/400 (application requester and application server functions):

OS/400 Version 2 Release 1 Modification Level 1

On AIX/6000 (application requester and application server functions)

- DDCS for AIX Version 1
- DB2 Client Support/6000 Version 1 (for remote client support)
- SNA Services for AIX Version 1 Release 2
- AIX/6000 Version 3 Release 2

Host servers must be DB2 for MVS/ESA V3R1, DB2 for VM and VSE V3R4, and OS/400 V2R3. Down-level versions must have PTFs applied.

On OS/2 (application requester and application server functions)

- DDCS for OS/2 Version 1.0

  - Single-User version requires either Extended Services for OS/2* or Extended Services with Database Server for OS/2
  - Multi-User version requires Extended Services with Database Server for OS/2

- DDCS for OS/2 Version 2.0

  - Extended Services or Communications Manager/2
  - Single-User version requires either DB2 for OS/2 Single-User version or DB2 for OS/2 Client/Server version
  - Multi-User Gateway version requires DB2 for OS/2 Client/Server version

- Operating system (any of the following):

  - OS/2 Standard Edition Version 1 Release 3 (refresh level 1.30.1)
  - OS/2 Extended Edition Version 1 Release 2 (refresh level 1.30.1)
  - OS/2 Version 2.0

---

* Trademark of IBM Corporation

To use DRDA protocol over TCP/IP between OS/2 and MVS you need:

- On MVS

  - VTAM Version 4 Release 2
  - VTAM Version 4 Release 2 AnyNet Feature
  - TCP/IP for MVS Version 2 Release 2.1

- On OS/2

  - AnyNet/Version2 or
    AnyNet/2 workstation code downloaded from AnyNet Feature of VTAM V4R2
    AnyNet Feature
  - IBM TCP/IP for OS/2 Version 1.2.1 CSD 34109 or later
  - Communications Manager/2 Version 1.0 or later

Setting Up the Application Requester

This section gives a general description of the steps needed to set up an application requester function. For communication networking and DRDA terminology used in this section, you can refer to Part 3 of this manual.

Provide Network Information

Much of the processing in a distributed database environment requires messages to be exchanged with other locations in your network. For this processing to be successful, you need to do the following:

Define the local system

Define the remote systems

Supply information to the communication subsystem

Select request unit (RU) sizes and pacing

Defining the Local System

You must perform the following tasks to define your local system to the network:

- Select the NETID.LUNAME value used by your Application Requester and record this value using the system definition process supplied by the Application Requester. (In some cases, you need to work with your system programmer or communications administrator when choosing the NETID.LUNAME value.)

  Each program in the network is assigned a NETID and an LU name. The NETID.LUNAME value is a unique name used for network routing.

- Register the NETID.LUNAME value with your local communication subsystem.

  To enable your application requester to connect to other programs in the network, you must define this value in the local communication subsystem. Because the application server never routes distributed database requests to the Application Requester, you do not need to provide definitions at the application server to allow it to route requests back to the Application Requester.

- If your Application Requester runs under the control of a database management system, you must assign an RDB_NAME for your local database.

  The RDB_NAME value is a 1- to 18-character name that uniquely identifies your database. The SQL application can use the RDB_NAME to route SQL statements to the local system.

Defining the Remote Systems

You must register RDB_NAMEs and their corresponding network parameters for the Application Requester to route SQL requests to the correct network destinations. The registered information allows the Application Requester to determine the following:

- The RDB_NAMEs supplied by the SQL application program that are valid. Because each valid RDB_NAME is registered with the Application Requester, the Application Requester can inform the SQL application program when an RDB_NAME is not known.

- The correct NETID.LUNAME value for each RDB_NAME, allowing the communication subsystem to correctly route requests through the network.

- The transaction program name (TPN) value associated with the application server at the destination NETID.LUNAME. In some application server implementations, a given NETID.LUNAME can have more than one application server. When this occurs, the TPN is used by the communication subsystem to route the request to the correct application server. The DRDA TPN default is X'07F6C4C2'.

- The network security level required by the application server. This allows the Application Requester and the communication subsystem to supply the correct level of security for each partner application server. In some Application Requester implementations, this information is recorded in the communication subsystem. In others, this information is recorded within the Application Requester.

The Application Requester is also able to define mode names and conversation limits for each destination RDB_NAME.

Provide Information to the Communication Subsystem

You need to supply several pieces of information to the communication subsystem:

- Each of the NETID.LUNAME values for the destination application server systems.

- The mode names and session limits for each destination. The mode name identifies the SNA session characteristics to be used on the conversation. One of the session characteristics is the class of service (COS) name, which is roughly equivalent to a network priority rating. In some products, the Application Requester is able to choose mode names based on the application or end user issuing the request. This allows the system administrator to assign different network transmission priorities to the end users and applications. For example, the system administrator can choose to:

  - Assign a low priority to batch applications that habitually transmit very large amounts of data. This minimizes the impact of the large applications on smaller, online applications.

  - Assign a high priority to requests issued by the system administrators and operators. This maximizes their ability to diagnose problems when the system is heavily loaded.

- How the messages are to be broken into RUs for data transmission, how many RUs can be transmitted at a time, and how much network buffer space can be devoted to this effort. See "Selecting RU Sizes and Pacing" on page 9 for more information.

- Information to properly route the request to the final destination. This can involve defining the network node that ultimately contains the application server, or it can be as simple as identifying a gateway able to route the request to the final destination.

- The network security parameters used when communicating with the application server. See "Provide Security" on page 10 for more details on this subject.

- The SNA synchronization level. For remote unit of work, SYNCLEVEL=NONE must be selected. For two-phase commit, SYNCLEVEL=SYNC must be selected.

Selecting RU Sizes and Pacing

When you define your local system's connection to the network, you probably must select an RU size and a pacing window size. Both of these parameters have a big impact on the amount of storage required to transmit DRDA messages to and from your Application Requester.

RU Size

Many factors influence the choice for the RU size parameter:

Performance: Generally speaking, smaller RU sizes increase the processor overhead and add to the overall network transmission delay time. This occurs because the communication subsystem must break the data messages into smaller packets, and it must send and receive more network packets.

Storage: When using a large RU size, the communication subsystem and the various network controllers on the network path require more storage. Although this additional storage does not often pose a problem, the storage parameters in an existing network need to be adjusted to accommodate an application with large RU sizes. This is a consideration any time the RU size is larger than the storage values currently being used in the network.

Hardware limitations: Many hardware products limit the size of message they can support. For example, some LAN adapter cards support a maximum RU size of 1920 bytes. Another example is the 3174 control unit, which has a maximum RU size of 256 bytes when it is connected remotely to a network control program. (Some newer models can have a maximum RU size of 512 bytes.)

Consult your communications administrator to make sure you choose an RU size that fits into your network's hardware and software configuration.

Pacing Window Size

In most network applications, a relatively small amount of data is exchanged in each data transmission. Because the data volume is small, it is difficult for these applications to send more data than the receiver can process.

In a distributed database system, the amount of data transmitted in the network can be substantially larger than other network applications. The large data volumes can lead to problems, especially if the sending application produces data faster than the receiving application can process it. When this occurs, the network is forced to hold the excess data temporarily. When the amount of data being temporarily stored is very large, it can have an adverse effect on the entire network, because the network buffers that store the data are shared by all network applications.

You should always activate the SNA pacing support for your distributed database connections. This ensures your network traffic does not place an excessive strain on the rest of the network. Normally, the pacing window size is a relatively small number, where the choice is made based on how much buffer area you want to devote to your Application Requester. For example, a pacing window size of 2 means that you want to use enough buffer storage to hold two path information units (PIUs).

Review your network buffer usage with your communication administrator. Choose a reasonable value to begin your testing. For example, use a pacing window size of 2 and RU size of 4K for all systems, unless the OS/2 system needs to use a smaller RU size due to hardware requirements.

Provide Security

When a remote system performs distributed database processing for an SQL application, the system must be able to satisfy the security requirements of the Application Requester, the application server, and the network connecting them. These requirements fall into one or more of the following categories:

Selection of end user names
Network security parameters
Database manager security
Security enforced by an external security subsystem

End User Names

End users are assigned a *user ID*. This user ID value must be unique within a particular operating system, but might not be unique throughout the SNA network. For example, there is a user named JONES on the NEWYORK system, and another user named JONES on the DALLAS system. If these two users are the same person, no conflict exists. However, if the JONES in DALLAS is not the same person as the JONES in NEWYORK, the SNA network (and consequently the distributed database systems within that network) cannot distinguish between JONES in NEWYORK and JONES in DALLAS. If you do not correct this situation, JONES in DALLAS can use the privileges granted to JONES at the NEWYORK system.

To eliminate naming conflicts, distributed database systems often support *name translation* schemes:

Outbound name translation allows the Application Requester to translate the end user's name before sending the name to the destination in the SNA network.

Inbound name translation allows the application server to translate the end user's name it receives from its SNA partner.

Consider the previous example with the user named JONES. You might want to give JONES in NEWYORK a different name (NYJONES) when JONES makes distributed database requests. You can do this in two ways:

Outbound translation—Whenever JONES issues an SQL request to DALLAS, the NEWYORK system can change the name JONES to NYJONES before transmitting the user ID. The DALLAS system administrator must register this new name (NYJONES) so the DALLAS system can accept the name.

Inbound translation—Another approach is to allow DALLAS to translate names it receives from NEWYORK. In this case, DALLAS changes JONES to NYJONES.

Network Security

After the Application Requester selects the end user name to represent the remote application, the Application Requester must provide the required network security information.

Because the application server is responsible for managing the database resources, it dictates which network security features are required of the Application Requester. The requester must have some mechanism to record the security features required by each server and send the correct parameters when accessing the server. This mechanism can require security definitions in any or all of the following:

- The application requester
- The communication subsystem
- The security subsystem

The security information is validated by the application server before any database processing occurs. In some DRDA implementations, the communication subsystem validates security information before passing the request to the database management system. If the database management system is not directly involved in the security validation process, errors detected during the validation (for example, an expired password) are not described in the database management system's audit trace records. Instead, these failures are reported by the communication subsystem or the security subsystem.

Database Manager Security

The Application Requester can have authorization mechanisms that control access between the Application Requester and application server. These security mechanisms can include any of the following:

- Authorizing system-wide access to specific servers
- Authorizing end users to bind packages to a particular server
- Authorizing end users to run applications that use packages at a given server

Security Subsystem

The role of the security subsystem is dependent on both the database management system and the operating system. The security subsystem can be involved in making the following decisions:

- Which network nodes the Application Requester can access
- Which end users are allowed to access a particular application server (network node)
- What network security information is sent to a given application server

Represent Data

Different systems or products represent data in different ways. When data is moved from one system to another, data must sometimes be converted. Products supporting DRDA automatically perform any necessary conversions at the receiving system.

Both numeric data and character data might require conversion. All numeric conversions are built into the database products. However, because of the large number of possible character conversions, not all character conversions are supported by the database products.

Character sets, code pages, and encoding schemes are identified by coded character set identifiers (CCSIDs). Each system or product has an associated CCSID value. The tables in Appendix C, "CCSID Values" on page 448 describe the CCSID and conversions provided by the database products.

You should ensure that the CCSIDs used by the application server and the application requester are compatible (that is, each system can convert from the other's CCSID into its own CCSID). If the CCSIDs are not compatible, then the two systems will not connect successfully.

Setting Up the Application Server

This section gives a general description of the steps needed to set up an application server function. For communication networking and DRDA terminology used in this section, you can refer to Part 3 of this manual.

Provide Network Information

For the application server to properly process distributed database requests, you must take the following steps:

- Define the application server to the local communication subsystem.

- Review the existing network definitions to make sure the distributed database system does not adversely impact the existing network. See "Selecting RU Sizes and Pacing" on page 9 for more information.

Defining the Application Server

For the application server to receive distributed database requests, it must be defined to the local communication subsystem and be given a unique RDB_NAME. For information on the DRDA naming conventions for RDB_NAMEs, see the *Distributed Relational Database Architecture Reference*. Take the following steps to define the application server:

1. Select the NETID.LUNAME value to be used by the server and record it using the system definition process supplied by the server.

2. Register the NETID.LUNAME value with the local communication subsystem.

3. Register the NETID.LUNAME value for the server with each Application Requester requiring access so the requester can route SNA requests to the server. You must do this even in cases where the requester can perform dynamic network routing, because the requester must know the NETID.LUNAME before dynamic network routing can be used.

4. Assign a transaction program name (TPN) for the server. Register it with the local communication subsystem, so the communication subsystem can route requests to

the server. Also provide this value to each requester, so the requester can specify it on its distributed database requests. The default DRDA TPN is X'07F6C4C2'. However, each product or installation chooses a TPN for its application server, which does not necessarily match the default DRDA TPN.

5. Select an RDB_NAME for the application server, and provide this value to all end users and Application Requesters that might connect to the server.

6. Create the mode definitions required by the local communication subsystem, and create any definitions required in the server to use the modes. Also give these mode names to each requester requiring access.

7. Define the default session limits for the requesters that connect to the server.

8. Define the synchronization level for the application server.

Provide Security

When an Application Requester routes a distributed database request to the application server, the following security considerations can be involved:

- Come-from checking
- Selection of end user names
- Network security parameters
- Database manager security
- Security enforced by an external security subsystem

Come-From Checking

The application server might need to restrict the end user names received from a given application requester. This can be done with *come-from* checking. Come-from checking allows the server to specify a given user ID that can be used only by specific partners. For example, the NEW_YORK server can restrict JONES to "come from" DALLAS. If another requester (other than DALLAS) attempts to send the name JONES to the server (NEWYORK), the server can reject the request, because the name did not come from the correct network location.

End User Names

As stated in "Provide Security" on page 10, the user ID passed by the Application Requester might not be unique throughout the entire SNA network. The application server translates inbound names to create unique end user names throughout the SNA network.

Network Security

As the owner of the database resources, the application server can dictate the network security parameters that the Application Requester must provide.

DRDA provides three major network security features:

Session level security
Conversation level security
Encryption

The server typically provides a registration mechanism that allows the system administrator to specify which security features are supported for connections between the requester and the server.

Database Manager Security

As the owner of the database resources, the application server provides all the required database security. The application server can individually authorize users to:

Bind packages

This allows the end user at the Application Requester to create new distributed database applications. Additionally, the user ID identified by the Application Requester must have authority to access the SQL objects referenced in any static SQL statements contained in the package.

Run packages

This allows the end user at the requester to execute SQL statements contained in the package stored at the server.

Any static SQL statements contained in the package are automatically executable by each end user given authority to run the package. Thus, the end user does not necessarily need access to the SQL objects referenced by static SQL statements.

If the package contains dynamic SQL, the user ID sent by the Application Requester must have authority to issue the SQL statements issued dynamically. The user ID must also have access to the SQL objects referenced by those statements.

Security Subsystem

The role of the security subsystem is dependent on both the DBMS and the operating system. The security subsystem can be involved in making the following decisions:

- Which network nodes (application requesters) can access the server
- Which end users at those nodes are allowed to access the server
- What network security information is required from a given requester

Chapter 2. Connecting DB2 for MVS/ESA in a DRDA Network

DB2 for MVS/ESA is the IBM relational database management system for MVS/XA and MVS/ESA systems. DB2 for MVS/ESA Version 2 Release 3 is the first release of DB2 for MVS/ESA able to share distributed relational data with other DBMSs supporting DRDA protocols. This chapter describes how DB2 for MVS/ESA provides support for distributed relational database systems.

The information in the rest of this chapter is in the same general format as the information in Chapter 1, "Introducing DRDA Connectivity" on page 2. The primary emphasis is on connecting unlike DRDA systems to DB2 for MVS/ESA. For information about connecting two DB2 for MVS/ESA systems, or more detailed information describing how to define DRDA connections to DB2 for MVS/ESA, see the discussion of connecting distributed database systems in the *IBM Database 2 Administration Guide*.

With the AnyNet Feature of VTAM Version 4 Release 2, you can run APPC over a TCP/IP network. The AnyNet Feature consists of AnyNet/MVS, which runs in a host, and AnyNet/2, which runs in a workstation and is downloaded from the host. Any APPC application is accessible to end users in a TCP/IP network without change to the application. Using APPC over TCP/IP, an application program on MVS/ESA can communicate with another APPC application program running with AnyNet APPC over TCP/IP on MVS/ESA, OS/2, AIX/6000, OS/400, or Windows. See *VTAM AnyNet Feature for V4R2 Guide to SNA over TCP/IP* for more information.

Use Table 1 on page 16 to find other information in this manual to help you with the specific type of connection you are interested in.

Table 1. Where to Find Additional Information on DB2 for MVS/ESA Connections

Type of Connection	Also Read
DB2 for MVS/ESA and DB2 for VM and VSE	Chapter 3, "Connecting DB2 for VM and VSE in a DRDA Network" on page 49
	Chapter 6, "DB2 for MVS/ESA and DB2 for VM via CTC" on page 129
	Chapter 7, "DB2 for MVS/ESA and DB2 for VM via Channel-Attached NCP" on page 138
	Chapter 8, "DB2 for MVS/ESA and DB2 for VM via Link-Attached NCP" on page 148
DB2 for MVS/ESA and DB2 for OS/400	Chapter 4, "Connecting DB2 for OS/400 in a DRDA Network" on page 88
	Chapter 9, "DB2 for OS/400 and DB2 for MVS/ESA via SDLC" on page 160
DB2 for MVS/ESA and DB2 for AIX	Chapter 11, "DB2 for AIX and DB2 for MVS/ESA, DB2 for VM and VSE, or DB2 for OS/400 via Token Ring" on page 173
	Chapter 12, "DB2 for AIX and DB2 for MVS/ESA via SDLC" on page 189
	Chapter 20, "Configuring DDCS for AIX" on page 330
DB2 for MVS/ESA and DB2 for OS/2	Chapter 14, "DB2 for OS/2 and DB2 for MVS/ESA via Token Ring" on page 211
	Chapter 17, "DB2 for OS/2 and Multiple Hosts" on page 272
	Chapter 18, "DB2 for OS/2 and DB2 for MVS/ESA or DB2 for VM and VSE via 3174 Controller" on page 288
	Chapter 19, "DB2 for OS/2 and Other DRDA Servers" on page 304

DB2 for MVS/ESA

Figure 4 shows an MVS system running a single copy of DB2 for MVS/ESA. It is also possible to run multiple copies of DB2 for MVS/ESA on a single MVS system. To identify copies of DB2 for MVS/ESA within a given MVS system (or copies of DB2 for MVS/ESA within an MVS/JES complex), each DB2 system is given a *subsystem name*, a one- to four- character string unique within an MVS/JES complex. In Figure 4, the DB2 for MVS/ESA subsystem name is *xxxx*. Three of the MVS address space names are prefixed by the DB2 for MVS/ESA subsystem name. These three address spaces make up the DB2 for MVS/ESA product.

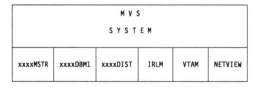

Figure 4. MVS Address Spaces Used by DB2 for MVS/ESA

Figure 4 shows the MVS address spaces involved in distributed database processing with DB2 for MVS/ESA. These address spaces work together to allow DB2 for MVS/ESA users to access local relational databases and communicate with remote DRDA systems. The purpose of each address space is as follows:

xxxxMSTR The system services address space for the DB2 for MVS/ESA product responsible for starting and stopping DB2 for MVS/ESA, and controlling local access to DB2 for MVS/ESA.

xxxxDBM1 The database services address space responsible for accessing relational databases controlled by DB2 for MVS/ESA. This is where the input and output to database resources is performed on behalf of SQL application programs.

xxxxDIST The portion of DB2 for MVS/ESA that provides distributed database capabilities; also known as the *Distributed Data Facility* (DDF). When a distributed database request is received, DDF passes the request to *xxxx*DBM1, so that the required database I/O operations can be performed. This book describes DDF in detail.

IRLM The lock manager used by DB2 for MVS/ESA to control access to database resources.

VTAM The SNA Communications Manager for the MVS system. DDF uses VTAM to perform distributed database communications on behalf of DB2 for MVS/ESA.

NETVIEW* The network management focal point product on MVS systems. When errors occur during distributed database processing, DDF records error information (also known as *alerts*) in the NetView hardware monitor database. System administrators can use NetView to examine the errors stored in the hardware monitor database, or provide automated command procedures to be invoked when alert conditions are recorded.

NetView can also be used to diagnose VTAM communication errors. For more information, see the *Distributed Relational Database Architecture Problem Determination Guide*.

Figure 4 on page 16 does not show any SQL application programs. When an application program uses DB2 to issue SQL statements, the application program must attach to the DB2 for MVS/ESA product in one of the following ways:

TSO Batch jobs and end users logged on to TSO are connected to DB2 for MVS/ESA through the TSO attach facility. This is the technique used to connect SPUFI and most QMF* applications to DB2 for MVS/ESA.

CICS/ESA* When a CICS/ESA application issues SQL calls, the CICS/ESA product uses the CICS* attach interface to route SQL requests to DB2 for MVS/ESA.

---

* Trademark of IBM Corporation

IMS/ESA[*]	Transactions running under the control of IMS/ESA use the IMS attach interface to pass SQL statements to DB2 for MVS/ESA for processing.
DDF	The Distributed Data Facility is responsible for connecting distributed applications to DB2 for MVS/ESA.
CAF	The call attachment facility allows user-written subsystems to connect directly to DB2 for MVS/ESA.

DB2 for MVS/ESA Implementation

DRDA defines types of distributed database management system functions. DB2 for MVS/ESA V2R3 supports remote unit of work. With remote unit of work, an application program executing in one system can access data at a remote DBMS using the SQL provided by that remote DBMS. DB2 for MVS/ESA V3R1 supports distributed unit of work. With distributed unit of work, an application program executing in one system can access data at multiple remote DBMSs using SQL provided by remote DBMSs. For more information on the types of distribution defined by DRDA, see "Types of Distribution" on page 413.

As shown in Figure 5 on page 19, DB2 for MVS/ESA supports three configurations of distributed database connections using two access methods:

[1] *System-directed access* allows a DB2 for MVS/ESA requester to connect to one or more DB2 for MVS/ESA servers. The connection established between the DB2 for MVS/ESA requester and server does not adhere to the protocols defined in DRDA and cannot be used to connect non-DB2 for MVS/ESA products to DB2 for MVS/ESA. This type of connection is established by coding three-part names or aliases in the application.

[2] *Application-directed access* allows a DB2 for MVS/ESA or non-DB2 for MVS/ESA requester to connect to one or more DB2 for MVS/ESA or non-DB2 for MVS/ESA application servers using DRDA protocols. The number of application servers that can be connected to the application requester at one time depends on the level of DB2 for MVS/ESA of the application requester. If the application requester is DB2 for MVS/ESA V2R3, then only one application server can be connected at a time. This type of connection is established by coding SQL CONNECT statements in the application. If the application requester is DB2 for MVS/ESADB2 V3R1, then one or more application servers can be connected at a time.

[3] Application-directed and system-directed access can be used together to establish connections.

The term *secondary server* describes systems acting as servers to the application server.

If all systems in a configuration support two-phase commit, then distributed unit of work (multiple-site read and multiple-site update) is supported. If not all systems support two-phase commit, updates within a unit of work are either restricted to a single site that does not support two-phase commit, or to the subset of sites that support two-phase commit.

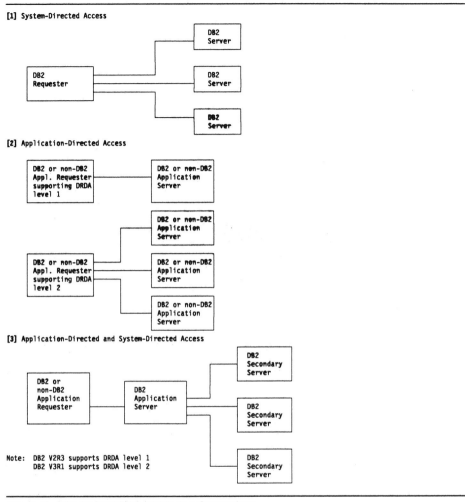

[1] System-Directed Access

[2] Application-Directed Access

[3] Application-Directed and System-Directed Access

Note: DB2 V2R3 supports DRDA level 1
DB2 V3R1 supports DRDA level 2

Figure 5. DB2 for MVS/ESA Distributed Connections

Table 2 compares the DB2 for MVS/ESA distributed database connection types.

Table 2. Comparison of DB2 for MVS/ESA Distributed Database Connections

[1] System-Directed Access	[2] Application-Directed Access (with all systems having two-phase commit)	[3] Application-Directed and System-Directed Accesses
All partners must be DB2 for MVS/ESA systems	Can interconnect any two DRDA systems	Application requester can be any DRDA system; servers must be DB2 for MVS/ESA systems
Can connect directly to many partners	Can connect directly to many partners	Application requester connects directly to application servers; application servers can connect to many DB2 for MVS/ESA secondary servers
Each SQL application can have multiple APPC conversations with each server	Each SQL application has one APPC conversation with each server	SQL application has one APPC conversation with each server; DB2 for MVS/ESA application server can establish many APPC conversations to each server for the application
Can access both local and remote resources in one commit scope	Can access both local and remote resources in one commit scope	Application requester and application server can access local and remote data
More efficient at large queries and multiple concurrent queries	More efficient at SQL statements that are executed very few times in one commit scope	Application requester-application server connection behaves like [2]; secondary server connections behave like [1]
Can support static or dynamic SQL, but server dynamically binds static SQL the first time it is executed in a commit scope	Can issue static or dynamic SQL	Application requester and application server can issue static or dynamic SQL; secondary servers support static or dynamic SQL, but dynamically bind static SQL the first time it is executed in a commit scope
Limited to SQL INSERT, DELETE, and UPDATE statements, and to statements that support SELECT	Can use any statement supported by the system that executes the statement	Application servers supports any SQL; secondary servers support only DML SQL (for example, CREATE or ALTER)

Setting Up the Application Requester

DB2 for MVS/ESA implements the DRDA application requester support as an integral part of the DB2 for MVS/ESA Distributed Data Facility (DDF). DDF can be stopped independently from the local DB2 for MVS/ESA database management facilities, but it cannot run in the absence of the local DB2 for MVS/ESA database management support.

When DB2 for MVS/ESA acts as an Application Requester, it can connect to a DB2 for MVS/ESA application server or any other product that supports the DRDA architecture.

For the DB2 for MVS/ESA Application Requester to provide distributed database access, you need to do the following:

- "Provide Network Information" on page 21—The Application Requester must be able to accept RDB_NAME values and translate these values into SNA NETID.LUNAME values. DB2 for MVS/ESA uses the *DB2 for MVS/ESA communications database* to register RDB_NAMEs and their corresponding network parameters. The communications database allows the DB2 for MVS/ESA Application Requester to pass the required SNA information to VTAM when making distributed database requests.

- "Provide Security" on page 31— For remote database requests to be accepted by the application server, the Application Requester must provide the security information required by the server. DB2 for MVS/ESA uses the communications database and RACF[*] to provide the required network security information.

- "Represent Data" on page 36—You must ensure that the CCSID of the application requester is compatible with the application server.

Provide Network Information

Much of the processing in a distributed database environment requires exchanging messages with other locations in your network. For this processing to be performed correctly, you need to do the following:

Define the local system
Define the remote systems
Define the communications
Set RU sizes and pacing

Defining the Local System

Each program in the network is assigned a NETID and an LU name, so your DB2 for MVS/ESA Application Requester must have a NETID.LUNAME value when it connects to the network. Because the DB2 for MVS/ESA Application Requester is integrated into the local DB2 for MVS/ESA database management system, the Application Requester must also have an RDB_NAME. In the DB2 for MVS/ESA publications, DB2 for MVS/ESA refers to the RDB_NAME as a *location* name.

Define the DB2 for MVS/ESA Application Requester to the SNA network as follows:

1. Select an LU name for your DB2 for MVS/ESA system. The NETID for your DB2 for MVS/ESA system is automatically obtained from VTAM when DDF starts.

2. Define the LU name and location name in the DB2 for MVS/ESA *bootstrap data set* (BSDS). (DB2 for MVS/ESA restricts the location to 16 characters.)

3. Create a VTAM APPL definition to register the selected LU name with VTAM.

Configuring the DDF BSDS: DB2 for MVS/ESA reads the BSDS during startup processing to obtain system installation parameters. One of the records stored in the BSDS is called the *DDF record*, because it contains the information used by DDF to connect to VTAM. This information consists of the following:

- The location name for the DB2 for MVS/ESA system
- The LU name for the DB2 for MVS/ESA system
- The password used when connecting the DB2 for MVS/ESA system to VTAM

You can supply the DDF BSDS information to DB2 for MVS/ESA in two ways:

---

[*] Trademark of IBM Corporation

- Use the DDF installation panel DSNTIPR when you first install DB2 for MVS/ESA to provide the required DDF BSDS information. Many of the install parameters are not discussed here because it is more important to know how to connect DB2 for MVS/ESA to VTAM. Figure 6 on page 22 shows how to use the installation panel to record location name SYDNEY, the LU name LUDBD1, and password PSWDBD1 in the DB2 for MVS/ESA BSDS.

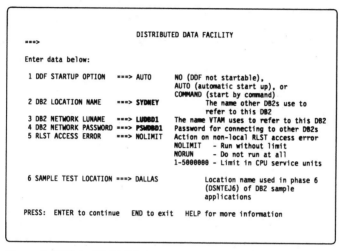

```
                        DISTRIBUTED DATA FACILITY
 ===>

 Enter data below:

 1 DDF STARTUP OPTION    ===> AUTO      NO (DDF not startable),
                                        AUTO (automatic start up), or
                                        COMMAND (start by command)
 2 DB2 LOCATION NAME     ===> SYDNEY       The name other DB2s use to
                                           refer to this DB2
 3 DB2 NETWORK LUNAME    ===> LUDBD1    The name VTAM uses to refer to this DB2
 4 DB2 NETWORK PASSWORD  ===> PSWDBD1   Password for connecting to other DB2s
 5 RLST ACCESS ERROR     ===> NOLIMIT   Action on non-local RLST access error
                                        NOLIMIT   - Run without limit
                                        NORUN     - Do not run at all
                                        1-5000000 - Limit in CPU service units

 6 SAMPLE TEST LOCATION ===> DALLAS        Location name used in phase 6
                                           (DSNTEJ6) of DB2 sample
                                           applications

 PRESS:  ENTER to continue    END to exit   HELP for more information
```

Figure 6. DB2 for MVS/ESA Installation Panel DSNTIPR

- If DB2 for MVS/ESA is already installed, you can use the change log inventory utility (DSNJU003) to update the information in the BSDS.

  Figure 7 on page 23 shows how to update the BSDS with location name SYDNEY, the LU name LUDBD1, and password PSWDBD1.

```
//SYSADMB JOB ,'DB2 2.3 JOB',CLASS=A
//*
//*        CHANGE LOG INVENTORY:
//*        UPDATE BSDS WITH
//*             - DB2 LOCATION NAME FOR SYDNEY
//*             - VTAM LUNAME (LUDBD1)
//*             - DB2/VTAM PASSWORD
//*
//DSNBSDS EXEC PGM=DSNJU003
//STEPLIB  DD  DISP=SHR,DSN=DSN230.DSNLOAD
//SYSUT1   DD  DISP=OLD,DSN=DSNC230.BSDS01
//SYSUT2   DD  DISP=OLD,DSN=DSNC230.BSDS02
//SYSPRINT DD  SYSOUT=*
//SYSUDUMP DD  SYSOUT=*
//SYSIN    DD  *
  DDF    LOCATION=SYDNEY,LUNAME=LUDBD1,PASSWORD=PSWDBD1
//*
```

Figure 7. Sample Bootstrap Data Set DDF Definition

When DDF is started (either automatically at DB2 for MVS/ESA startup or by the DB2 for MVS/ESA START DDF command), it connects to VTAM, passing the LU name and password to VTAM. VTAM recognizes the DB2 for MVS/ESA system by checking the LU name and password (if a VTAM password is required) with the values defined in the DB2 for MVS/ESA VTAM APPL statement. The VTAM password is used to verify that DB2 for MVS/ESA is authorized to use the specified LU name on the VTAM system. The VTAM password is not transmitted through the network, and it is not used to connect other systems in the network to DB2 for MVS/ESA.

If VTAM does not require a password, omit the PASSWORD= keyword on the change log inventory utility. The absence of the keyword indicates that no VTAM password is required.

Creating a VTAM APPL definition: After you define the VTAM LU name and password to DB2 for MVS/ESA, you need to register these values with VTAM. VTAM uses the APPL statement to define local LU names. Figure 8 on page 24 shows how to define the LU name LUDBD1 to VTAM.

Chapter 2. Connecting DB2 for MVS/ESA in a DRDA Network   **23**

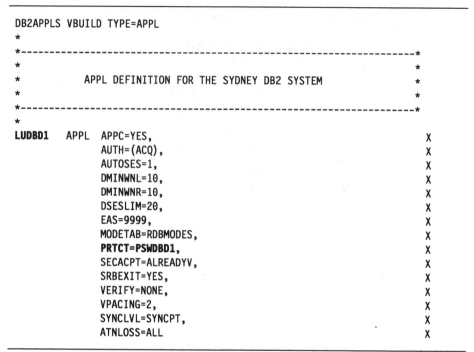

```
DB2APPLS VBUILD TYPE=APPL
*
*-----------------------------------------------------------------*
*                                                                 *
*           APPL DEFINITION FOR THE SYDNEY DB2 SYSTEM             *
*                                                                 *
*-----------------------------------------------------------------*
*
LUDBD1   APPL  APPC=YES,                                          X
               AUTH=(ACQ),                                        X
               AUTOSES=1,                                         X
               DMINWNL=10,                                        X
               DMINWNR=10,                                        X
               DSESLIM=20,                                        X
               EAS=9999,                                          X
               MODETAB=RDBMODES,                                  X
               PRTCT=PSWDBD1,                                     X
               SECACPT=ALREADYV,                                  X
               SRBEXIT=YES,                                       X
               VERIFY=NONE,                                       X
               VPACING=2,                                         X
               SYNCLVL=SYNCPT,                                    X
               ATNLOSS=ALL                                        X
```

Figure 8. Sample DB2 for MVS/ESA APPL Definition

Many keywords are available on the VTAM APPL statement. The meaning of the keywords is discussed in detail in the *DB2 Administration Guide*. The only keywords discussed here address topics in this book. The keywords of interest in Figure 8 are described as follows:

LUDBD1

VTAM uses the APPL statement label as the LU name. In this case, the LU name is LUDBD1. The APPL syntax does not allow room for a complete NETID.LUNAME value. The NETID value is not specified on the VTAM APPL statement, because all VTAM applications are automatically assigned the NETID for the VTAM system.

AUTOSES=1

The number of SNA contention winner sessions that start automatically when an APPC Change Number of Sessions (CNOS) request is issued. A nonzero value must be supplied with AUTOSES to inform DB2 for MVS/ESA in all cases when VTAM CNOS processing fails.

You do not have to automatically start all the APPC sessions between any two distributed database partners. If the AUTOSES value is less than the contention winner limit (DMINWNL), VTAM delays starting the remaining SNA sessions until they are required by a distributed database application.

See Chapter 24, "LU 6.2 and APPC: Concepts" on page 399 for more information on the CNOS process and how it relates to the number of LU 6.2 conversations that two distributed database systems can support.

DMINWNL=10

The number of sessions on which this DB2 for MVS/ESA system is the contention winner. The DMINWNL parameter is the default for CNOS processing, but can be overridden for any given partner by adding a row to the SYSIBM.SYSLUMODES table in the DB2 for MVS/ESA communications database.

DMINWNR=10

The number of sessions on which the partner system is the contention winner. The DMINWNR parameter is the default for CNOS processing, but can be overridden for any given partner by adding a row to the SYSIBM.SYSLUMODES table in the DB2 for MVS/ESA communications database.

DSESLIM=20

The total number of sessions (winner and loser sessions) you can establish between DB2 for MVS/ESA and another distributed system for a specific mode group name. The DSESLIM parameter is the default for CNOS processing, but can be overridden for any given partner by adding a row to the SYSIBM.SYSLUMODES table in the DB2 for MVS/ESA communications database.

If the partner cannot support the number of sessions requested on the DSESLIM, DMINWNL, or DMINWNR parameters, the CNOS process negotiates new values for these parameters that are acceptable to the partner.

EAS=9999

An estimate of the total number of sessions that this VTAM LU requires.

MODETAB=RDBMODES

Identifies the VTAM MODE table where each DB2 for MVS/ESA mode name exists. See "Creating a VTAM Mode Table" on page 437 for information on how to create a VTAM MODE table.

PRTCT=PSWDBD1

Identifies the VTAM password to use when DB2 for MVS/ESA attempts to connect to VTAM. If the PRTCT keyword is omitted, no password is required, and you should omit the PASSWORD= keyword from the DB2 for MVS/ESA change log inventory utility.

SECACPT=ALREADYV

Identifies the highest SNA conversation-level security value accepted by this DB2 for MVS/ESA system when it receives a distributed database request from a remote system. The ALREADYV keyword indicates this DB2 for MVS/ESA system can accept three SNA session security options from other DRDA systems that request data from this DB2 for MVS/ESA system:

- SECURITY=SAME (an already-verified request that contains only the requester's user ID).

- SECURITY=PGM (a request containing the requester's user ID and password).

- SECURITY=NONE (a request containing no security information). DB2 for MVS/ESA rejects DRDA requests that specify SECURITY=NONE.

It is best to always specify SECACPT=ALREADYV, because the SNA conversation security level for each DB2 for MVS/ESA partner is taken from the DB2 for MVS/ESA communications database (the USERSECURITY column of the SYSIBM.SYSLUNAMES table). SECACPT=ALREADYV gives you the most flexibility in selecting values for USERSECURITY.

VERIFY=NONE

Identifies the level of SNA session security (partner LU verification) required by this DB2 for MVS/ESA system. The NONE value indicates that partner LU verification is not required.

DB2 for MVS/ESA does not restrict your choice for the VERIFY keyword. In a nontrusted network, VERIFY=REQUIRED is recommended. VERIFY=REQUIRED causes VTAM to reject partners that cannot perform partner LU verification. If you choose VERIFY=OPTIONAL, VTAM performs partner LU verification only for those partners that provide the support. "Session-Level Security" on page 441 describes the steps you must take to implement partner LU verification in VTAM and RACF.

For a more detailed description of partner LU verification, see "LU 6.2 Security" on page 409.

VPACING=2

Sets the VTAM pacing count to 2. See "VTAM Pacing" on page 433 for more information on VTAM pacing considerations.

SYNCLVL=SYNCPT

Indicates that DB2 for MVS/ESA is able to support two-phase commit. VTAM uses this information to inform the partner that two-phase commit is available. If this keyword is present, DB2 for MVS/ESA automatically uses two-phase commit if the partner can support it.

ATNLOSS=ALL

Indicates that DB2 for MVS/ESA needs to be informed each time a VTAM session ends. This ensures that DB2 for MVS/ESA performs SNA resynchronization when required.

DSESLIM, DMINWNL, and DMINWNR allow you to establish default VTAM session limits for all partners. For partners that have special session limit requirements, the SYSIBM.SYSLUMODES table can be used to override the default session limits. For example, you might want to specify VTAM default session limits that are appropriate for your OS/2 systems. For other partners, you can create rows in the SYSIBM.SYSLUMODES table to define the desired session limits. Consider these sample values:

```
DSESLIM=4,DMINWNL=0,DMINWNR=4
```

These parameters allow each partner to create up to four sessions with DB2 for MVS/ESA, where the partner is the contention winner on each of the sessions. Because OS/2 creates the LU 6.2 conversations with DB2 for MVS/ESA, by making OS/2 the contention winner on the sessions, you gain a small performance advantage. If OS/2 has an available contention winner session, it does not have to ask for permission to start a new LU 6.2 conversation.

Defining the Remote Systems

When a DB2 for MVS/ESA application requests data from a remote system, DB2 for MVS/ESA searches the communications database tables to find information about the remote system, including a search on:

- The LU name and TPN
- The network security information required by the remote site
- The session limits and mode names used to communicate with the remote site

The communications database is a group of SQL tables managed by the DB2 for MVS/ESA system administrator. As the DB2 for MVS/ESA system administrator, you must use SQL to insert rows in the communications database to describe each potential DRDA partner. The communications database consists of five tables:

1. **SYSIBM.SYSLOCATIONS**

    This table allows DB2 for MVS/ESA to determine the LU name and TPN value for each RDB_NAME selected by a DB2 for MVS/ESA application. The columns are:

    LOCATION   The RDB_NAME of the remote system. DB2 for MVS/ESA limits the RDB_NAME value to 16 bytes, which is two bytes shorter than the 18-byte limit defined in DRDA.

    LOCTYPE   Currently not used; it must be blank.

    LINKNAME   The LU name of the remote system.

    LINKATTR   The TPN of the remote system. If the remote system is a DB2 for MVS/ESA system or the remote system uses the default DRDA TPN value (X'07F6C4C2'[1]), an empty string can be used to specify the TPN because DB2 for MVS/ESA automatically chooses the correct value.

                              If the remote system requires a TPN value other than the default TPN value, you must supply this value here.

2. **SYSIBM.SYSLUNAMES**

    This table defines the network attributes of the remote systems. The columns are:

    LUNAME   The LU name of the remote system.

---

[1] This TPN value *currently* applies to DB2 for VM and VSE.

SYSMODENAME   The VTAM logon mode name used to establish the DB2 for MVS/ESA-to-DB2 for MVS/ESA *intersystem* conversations for the DB2 for MVS/ESA secondary server support (system-directed access). A blank value in this column indicates IBMDB2LM should be used for DB2 for MVS/ESA system conversations.

USERSECURITY   The network security acceptance options required of the remote system when this DB2 for MVS/ESA system acts as a server for the remote system (*inbound security* requirements).

ENCRYPTPSWDS   Whether passwords exchanged with this partner are encrypted. Encrypted passwords are only supported by DB2 for MVS/ESA requesters and servers.

MODESELECT   Determines whether the SYSIBM.SYSMODESELECT table is used to select a VTAM logon mode entry (mode name) based on the end user and application making the request. If this column contains a 'Y', the SYSIBM.SYSMODESELECT table is used to obtain the mode name for each outbound distributed database request.

If MODESELECT contains anything other than a 'Y', the mode name IBMDB2LM is used for system-directed access requests, and the mode name IBMRDB is used for DRDA requests.

The MODESELECT column allows you to prioritize distributed database requests by specifying a VTAM class of service (COS) associated with the mode name.

USERNAMES   The level of come-from checking and user ID translation required. This column also specifies the security parameters this DB2 for MVS/ESA subsystem uses when requesting data from the remote partner (*outbound security* requirements). USERNAMES can have the value I, O, or B.

3. **SYSIBM.SYSLUMODES**

This table is used to define LU 6.2 session limits (CNOS limits) for each partner system. The columns are:

LUNAME   The LU name of the remote system.

MODENAME   The name of the VTAM logon mode whose limits are being specified. A blank value in the MODENAME column defaults to IBMDB2LM.

CONVLIMIT   The maximum number of active conversations between the local DB2 for MVS/ESA and the remote system for this logon mode. This value is used to override the DSESLIM parameter in the VTAM APPL definition statement for this logon mode, which supplies the default VTAM session limits for DB2 for MVS/ESA.

The value selected in CONVLIMIT is used during CNOS to set the DMINWNR and DMINWNL values to CONVLIMIT/2.

AUTO   Whether CNOS processing and preallocation of sessions are initiated automatically at DDF startup or deferred until the first reference to the LU name via this logon mode.

4. **SYSIBM.SYSMODESELECT**

This table allows you to specify different mode names for individual end users and DB2 for MVS/ESA applications. Because each VTAM mode name can have an associated class of service (COS), you can use this table to assign network transmission priorities to distributed database applications based on a combination of AUTHID, PLANNAME, and LUNAME. "Creating a VTAM Mode Table" on page 437 gives an example of using the COS parameters to establish a high priority mode (RDBHIGH) and a low priority mode (RDBLOW). The columns are:

AUTHID   The DB2 for MVS/ESA user's authorization ID (user ID). The default is blank, indicating the specified logon mode name applies to all authorization IDs.

PLANNAME   The plan name associated with the application requesting access to a remote database system. The default is blank, indicating that the specified logon mode name applies to all plan names. The plan name used for the BIND PACKAGE command is DSNBIND.

LUNAME   The LU name associated with the remote database system.

MODENAME   The name of the VTAM logon mode to use when routing a distributed database request to the indicated remote system. The default is blank, indicating that IBMDB2LM should be used for system-directed access conversations and IBMRDB should be used for DRDA conversations.

5. **SYSIBM.SYSUSERNAMES**

This table is used to manage end user names by providing passwords, name translations, and come-from checking. DB2 for MVS/ESA refers to the end user's name as an authorization ID. Most other products refer to this name as a user ID.

With this table, you can use name translation to force different values to be used for the SNA user ID and the DB2 for MVS/ESA authorization ID. The name translation process is allowed for requests to a remote system (*outbound* requests) and for requests coming from a remote system (*inbound* requests). If passwords are not encrypted, this table is the source of the end user's password when both user ID and password are sent to a remote site. The columns are:

TYPE   The description of how the row is to be used (whether it is a row describing name translations for outbound or inbound/come-from checking requests).

AUTHID	For outbound name translation, this is the DB2 for MVS/ESA authorization ID to translate. For inbound name translation, this is the SNA user ID to translate. In either case, a blank AUTHID value applies to all authorization IDs or user IDs.
LUNAME	The LU name of the remote system to which this row applies. If blank, the NEWAUTHID value applies to all systems.
NEWAUTHID	The new end user name (either SNA user ID or DB2 for MVS/ESA authorization ID). Blank specifies that you do not need to translate the ID.
PASSWORD	The password used on the allocate conversation, if passwords are not encrypted (ENCRYPTPSWDS = 'N' in SYSIBM.SYSLUNAMES). If passwords are encrypted, this column is ignored.

Defining Communications

VTAM is the communication subsystem for MVS systems. VTAM accepts LU 6.2 verbs from DB2 for MVS/ESA and converts these verbs into LU 6.2 data streams you can transmit over the network. For VTAM to communicate with the partner applications defined in the DB2 for MVS/ESA communications database, you need to provide VTAM with the following information:

- The LU name for each server.

  When DB2 for MVS/ESA communicates with VTAM, DB2 for MVS/ESA is allowed to pass only an LU name (not NETID.LUNAME) to VTAM to identify the desired destination. This LU name must be unique within the LU names known by the local VTAM system, allowing VTAM to determine both the NETID and LU name from the LU name value passed by DB2 for MVS/ESA. When LU names are unique throughout an enterprise's SNA network, it greatly simplifies the VTAM resource definition process. However, this might not always be possible. If LU names within your SNA networks are not unique, you must use VTAM LU name translation to build the correct NETID.LUNAME combination for a nonunique LU name. This process is described in "Resource Name Translation" in the *VTAM Network Implementation Guide*.

  The placement and syntax of the VTAM definitions used to define remote LU names are highly dependent on how the remote system is logically and physically connected to the local VTAM system. See "VTAM Remote System Connections" on page 440 for information describing the VTAM definition statements used to describe remote system connections.

- The RU size, pacing window size, and class of service for each mode name. Create an entry in the VTAM mode table for each mode name specified in the communications database. You also need to define IBMRDB and IBMDB2LM. See "Creating a VTAM Mode Table" on page 437 for information on how to perform these tasks.

- The VTAM and RACF profiles for the LU verification algorithm, if you intend to use partner LU verification. See "Session-Level Security" on page 441 for more details.

Setting RU Sizes and Pacing

The VTAM mode table entries you define specify RU sizes and pacing counts. Failure to define these values correctly can have a negative impact on all VTAM applications. See "VTAM Pacing" on page 433 for information on how to specify this information in your VTAM definitions.

After choosing RU sizes, session limits, and pacing counts, it is extremely important to consider the impact these values can have on the existing VTAM network. You should review the following items when you install a new distributed database system:

- For VTAM CTC connections, verify that the MAXBFRU parameter is large enough to handle your RU size plus the 29 bytes VTAM adds for the SNA request header and transmission header. MAXBFRU is measured in units of 4K bytes, so MAXBFRU must be at least 2 to accommodate a 4K RU.

- For NCP connections, make sure that MAXDATA is large enough to handle your RU size plus 29 bytes. If you specify an RU size of 4K, MAXDATA must be at least 4125.

  If you specify the NCP MAXBFRU parameter, select a value that can accommodate the RU size plus 29 bytes. For NCP, the MAXBFRU parameter defines the number of VTAM I/O buffers that can be used to hold the PIU. If you choose an IOBUF buffer size of 441, MAXBFRU=10 processes a 4K RU correctly because 10*441 is greater than 4096+29.

- "VTAM Buffer Pools" on page 428 describes how to assess the impact your distributed database has on the VTAM IOBUF pool. If you use too much of the IOBUF pool resource, VTAM performance is degraded for all VTAM applications.

Provide Security

When a remote system performs distributed database processing on behalf of an SQL application, it must be able to satisfy the security requirements of the Application Requester, the application server, and the network connecting them. These requirements fall into one or more of the following categories:

Selection of end user names
Network security parameters
Database manager security
Security enforced by an external security subsystem
Data representation

Selecting End User Names

On MVS systems, end users are assigned a 1 to 8-character *user ID*. This user ID value must be unique within a particular MVS system, but might not be unique throughout the SNA network. For example, there can be a user named JONES on the NEWYORK system, and another user named JONES on the DALLAS system. If these two users are the same person, no conflict exists. However, if the JONES in DALLAS is a different person than the JONES in NEWYORK, the SNA network (and consequently the distributed database systems within that network) cannot distinguish between JONES in NEWYORK and JONES in DALLAS. If you do not correct this situation, JONES in DALLAS can use the privileges granted to JONES at the NEWYORK system.

To eliminate naming conflicts, DB2 for MVS/ESA provides support for end user name translation. When an application at the DB2 for MVS/ESA Application Requester makes a distributed database request, DB2 for MVS/ESA performs name translation if the communications database specifies that *outbound name translation* is required. If outbound name translation is selected, DB2 for MVS/ESA always forces a password to be sent with each outbound distributed database request.

Outbound name translation in DB2 for MVS/ESA is activated by setting the USERNAMES column in the SYSIBM.SYSLUNAMES table to either 'O' or 'B'. If USERNAMES is set to 'O', end user name translation is performed for outbound requests. If USERNAMES is set to 'B', end user name translation is performed for both inbound and outbound requests.

Because DB2 for MVS/ESA authorization is dependent on both the end user's user ID and the user ID of the DB2 for MVS/ESA plan or package owner, the end user name translation process is performed for the end user's user ID, the plan owner's user ID, and the package owner's user ID.[2] The name translation process searches the SYSIBM.SYSUSERNAMES table in the following sequence to find a row that matches one of the following patterns (TYPE.AUTHID.LUNAME):

1. O.AUTHID.LUNAME—A translation rule for a specific end user to a specific partner system.
2. O.AUTHID.blank—A translation rule for a specific end user to any partner system.
3. O.blank.LUNAME—A translation rule for any user to a specific partner system.

If no matching row is found, DB2 for MVS/ESA rejects the distributed database request. If a row is found, the value in the NEWAUTHID column is used as the authorization ID. (A blank NEWAUTHID value indicates the original name is used without translation.)

Consider the example discussed earlier. You want to give JONES in NEWYORK a different name (NYJONES) when JONES makes distributed database requests to DALLAS. In the example, assume that the application used by JONES is owned by DSNPLAN (the DB2 for MVS/ESA plan owner), and you do not need to translate this user ID when it is sent to DALLAS. The SQL statements required to supply the name translation rules in the communications database are shown in Figure 9 on page 33.

---

2 If the request is being sent to a DB2 for MVS/ESA server, name translation is also performed for the package owner and plan owner. Package and plan owner names never have passwords associated with them.

```
INSERT INTO SYSIBM.SYSLOCATIONS
    (LOCATION, LOCTYPE, LINKNAME, LINKATTR)
  VALUES ('DALLAS', ' ', 'LUDALLAS', '');

INSERT INTO SYSIBM.SYSLUNAMES
    (LUNAME, SYSMODENAME, USERSECURITY, ENCRYPTPSWDS, MODESELECT, USERNAMES)
  VALUES ('LUDALLAS', ' ', 'A', 'N', 'N', '0');

INSERT INTO SYSIBM.SYSUSERNAMES
    (TYPE, AUTHID, LUNAME, NEWAUTHID, PASSWORD)
  VALUES ('0', 'JONES', 'LUDALLAS', 'NYJONES', 'JONESPWD');

INSERT INTO SYSIBM.SYSUSERNAMES
    (TYPE, AUTHID, LUNAME, NEWAUTHID, PASSWORD)
  VALUES ('0', 'DSNPLAN', 'LUDALLAS', ' ', 'PLANPWD');
```

Figure 9. SQL for Outbound Name Translation

The resulting communications database tables are shown in Figure 10:

NEWYORK.SYSIBM.SYSLOCATIONS			
LOCATION	LOCTYPE	LINKNAME	LINKATTR
DALLAS		LUDALLAS	

NEWYORK.SYSIBM.SYSLUNAMES					
LUNAME	SYSMODENAME	USERSECURITY	ENCRYPTPSWDS	MODESELECT	USERNAMES
LUDALLAS		A	N	N	0

NEWYORK.SYSIBM.SYSUSERNAMES				
TYPE	AUTHID	LUNAME	NEWAUTHID	PASSWORD
0	JONES	LUDALLAS	NYJONES	JONESPWD
0	DSNPLAN	LUDALLAS		PLANPWD

Figure 10. Outbound Name Translation

Network Security

After the Application Requester selects the end user names to represent the remote application, the Application Requester must provide the required LU 6.2 network security information. As discussed in "LU 6.2 Security" on page 409, LU 6.2 provides three major network security features:

- Session-level security, which is controlled by the VERIFY keyword on the VTAM APPL statement. See the discussion following Figure 8 on page 24 for a description of how to specify session-level security options.

- Conversation-level security, which is controlled by the contents of the SYSIBM.SYSLUNAMES table.

- Data encryption, which is supported only for VTAM 3.4 and later releases of VTAM.

Because the application server is responsible for managing the database resources, the application server dictates which network security features are required of the Application Requester. You must record the conversation-level security requirements of each application server in the SYSIBM.SYSLUNAMES table by setting the USERNAMES column of the SYSIBM.SYSLUNAMES table to reflect the application server's requirement.

The possible SNA conversation security options are:

SECURITY=SAME

This is also known as already-verified security because only the end user's user ID is sent to the remote system (no password is transmitted). Use this level of conversation security when the USERNAMES column in SYSIBM.SYSLUNAMES does not contain 'O' or 'B'.

Because DB2 for MVS/ESA ties end user name translation to outbound conversation security, it does not allow you to use SECURITY=SAME when outbound end user name translation is activated.

SECURITY=PGM

This causes the end user's ID and password to be sent to the remote system for validation. Use this security option when the USERNAMES column of the SYSIBM.SYSLUNAMES table contains either an 'O' or 'B'.

Depending upon options specified in the SYSIBM.SYSLUNAMES table, DB2 for MVS/ESA obtains the end user's password from two different sources:

- Unencrypted passwords are obtained from the PASSWORD column of the SYSIBM.SYSUSERNAMES table. DB2 for MVS/ESA extracts passwords from the SYSIBM.SYSUSERNAMES table when the ENCRYPTPSWDS column in SYSIBM.SYSLUNAMES is not set to 'Y'. Passwords obtained from this source can be transmitted to any DRDA application server.

Figure 11 defines passwords for SMITH and JONES. The LUNAME column in the example contains blanks, so these passwords are used for any remote system SMITH or JONES attempts to access.

```
INSERT INTO SYSIBM.SYSUSERNAMES
    (TYPE, AUTHID, LUNAME, NEWAUTHID, PASSWORD)
    VALUES ('O', 'JONES', ' ', ' ', 'JONESPWD');

INSERT INTO SYSIBM.SYSUSERNAMES
    (TYPE, AUTHID, LUNAME, NEWAUTHID, PASSWORD)
    VALUES ('O', 'SMITH', ' ', ' ', 'SMITHPWD');
```

Figure 11. Sending Passwords to Remote Sites

- Encrypted passwords are sent to the remote site when the ENCRYPTPSWDS column of SYSIBM.SYSLUNAMES contains 'Y'. Encrypted passwords are extracted from RACF (or a RACF-equivalent product), and can only be interpreted by another DB2 for MVS/ESA system. When communicating with a non-DB2 for MVS/ESA system, do not set ENCRYPTPSWDS to 'Y'.

  DB2 for MVS/ESA searches the SYSIBM.SYSUSERNAMES table to determine the user ID (NEWAUTHID value) to transmit to the remote system. This translated name is used for the RACF password extraction. If you do not want to translate names, you must create rows in SYSIBM.SYSUSERNAMES that cause names to be sent without translation. Figure 12 allows requests to be sent to LUDALLAS and LUNYC without translating the end user's name (user ID).

```
INSERT INTO SYSIBM.SYSUSERNAMES
    (TYPE, AUTHID, LUNAME, NEWAUTHID, PASSWORD)
  VALUES ('O', ' ', 'LUNYC', ' ', ' ');

INSERT INTO SYSIBM.SYSUSERNAMES
    (TYPE, AUTHID, LUNAME, NEWAUTHID, PASSWORD)
  VALUES ('O', ' ', 'LUDALLAS', ' ', ' ');
```

Figure 12. Sending Encrypted Passwords to Remote Sites

SECURITY=NONE

This option is not supported by DRDA, so DB2 for MVS/ESA has no provision for this security option.

Database Manager Security

One way the Application Requester can participate in distributed database security is through outbound name translation, as stated earlier in "Selecting End User Names" on page 31. You can use outbound name translation to control access to each application server, based on the identity of the end user making the request and the application making the request. Other ways the DB2 for MVS/ESA Application Requester contributes to the distributed system security are:

Binding remote applications

End users bind remote applications at the application server with the DB2 for MVS/ESA BIND PACKAGE command. DB2 for MVS/ESA *does not* restrict the use of the BIND PACKAGE command at the requester. However, an end user cannot use a remote package until the package is included in a DB2 for MVS/ESA plan. DB2 for MVS/ESA *does* restrict the use of the BIND PLAN command. An end user cannot add the remote package to a plan unless the end user is given either the BIND or BINDADD privilege with the DB2 for MVS/ESA GRANT statement.

When you bind a package, use the ENABLE/DISABLE option to specify whether the package is to be used by TSO, CICS/ESA, IMS/ESA, or a remote DB2 for MVS/ESA subsystem.

Executing remote applications

For the DB2 for MVS/ESA end user to run a remote application, the end user must have authority to run the DB2 for MVS/ESA plan associated with that application. The DB2 for MVS/ESA plan owner automatically has authority to run the plan. Other end users can be given authority to run the plan with the DB2 for MVS/ESA GRANT EXECUTE statement. In this way, the owner of a distributed database application can control use of the application on a user-by-user basis.

Security Subsystem

The external security subsystem on MVS systems is provided by RACF and other products that provide an interface compatible with RACF. The DB2 for MVS/ESA Application Requester does not have any direct calls to the external security subsystem, with the exception of the encrypted password support described in "Network Security" on page 33. However, the external security subsystem is used indirectly at the Application Requester in the following situations:

- The product responsible for attaching the end user to DB2 for MVS/ESA uses the external security subsystem to validate the end user's identity (user ID and password). This occurs before the end user is attached to DB2 for MVS/ESA. As stated earlier, CICS/ESA, TSO, and IMS/ESA are examples of products that attach end users to DB2 for MVS/ESA.

- If you use SNA session-level security (via the VERIFY keyword on the DB2 for MVS/ESA VTAM APPL statement), the external security subsystem is invoked by VTAM to validate the identity of the remote system.

Represent Data

DB2 for MVS/ESA is shipped with a default installation coded character set identifier (CCSID) of 500. This default is probably *not* correct for your installation.

When installing DB2 for MVS/ESA, you must set the installation CCSID to the CCSID of the characters generated and sent to DB2 for MVS/ESA by the input devices at your site. This CCSID is generally determined by the national language you use. If the installation CCSID is not correct, character conversion will produce incorrect results. See Appendix C, "CCSID Values" on page 448 for a list of the supported CCSIDs for each country or national language.

You must ensure that your DB2 for MVS/ESA subsystem has the ability to convert from each application server's CCSID to your DB2 for MVS/ESA subsystem's installation CCSID. DB2 for MVS/ESA provides conversion tables for the most common combinations of source and target CCSIDs, but not for every possible combination. You can add to the set of available conversion tables and conversion routines if you need to. See the *DB2 Administration Guide*, for more information about DB2 for MVS/ESA character conversion.

Setting Up the Application Server

The application server support in DB2 for MVS/ESA allows DB2 for MVS/ESA to act as a server for DRDA application requesters. The Application Requester connected to a DB2 for MVS/ESA application server can be:

- A DB2 for MVS/ESA requester
- A DB2 for AIX requester
- A DB2 for OS/2 requester
- A DB2 for OS/400 requester
- An DB2 for VM and VSE requester
- Any product that supports the DRDA Application Requester protocols

For any Application Requester connected to a DB2 for MVS/ESA application server, the DB2 for MVS/ESA application server supports database access as follows:

- The Application Requester is permitted to access tables stored at the DB2 for MVS/ESA application server. The Application Requester must create a package at the DB2 for MVS/ESA application server before the application can be run. The DB2 for MVS/ESA application server uses the package to locate the application's SQL statements at execution time.

- The Application Requester can inform the DB2 for MVS/ESA application server that access must be restricted to read-only activities if the DRDA requester-server connection does not support the two-phase commit process. For example, a DB2 for MVS/ESA V2R3 requester with a CICS front end would inform the DB2 for MVS/ESA application server that updates are not allowed.

- The Application Requester can also be permitted to access tables stored at other DB2 for MVS/ESA systems in the network using system-directed access. System-directed access allows the application requester to establish connections to multiple database systems in a single unit of work.

Provide Network Information

For the DB2 for MVS/ESA application server to properly process distributed database requests, you must take the following steps:

- Define the application server to the local communication subsystem.
- Define each potential secondary server destination so the DB2 for MVS/ESA application server can reroute SQL requests to their final destination.
- Provide the necessary security.
- Provide for data representation.

Defining the Application Server

For the application server to receive distributed database requests, it must be defined to the local communication subsystem and have a unique RDB_NAME. You must take the following steps to properly define the application server:

1. Select the LU name and RDB_NAME to be used by the DB2 for MVS/ESA application server. The process to record these names in DB2 for MVS/ESA and VTAM is the same process described in "Defining the Local System" on page 21.

The RDB_NAME you choose for DB2 for MVS/ESA must be supplied to all end users and Application Requesters that require connectivity to the application server.

2. Register the NETID.LUNAME value for the DB2 for MVS/ESA application server with each Application Requester requiring access, so the Application Requester can route SNA requests to the DB2 for MVS/ESA server. This is true even in cases where the Application Requester is able to perform dynamic network routing, because the Application Requester must know the NETID.LUNAME before dynamic network routing can be used.

3. Provide the DRDA default TPN (X'07F6C4C2') to each Application Requester because DB2 for MVS/ESA automatically uses this value.

4. Create an entry in the VTAM mode table for each mode name that is requested by an Application Requester. These entries describe the RU sizes, pacing window size, and class of service for each mode name. See "Creating a VTAM Mode Table" on page 437 for information on how to perform this task.

5. Define session limits for the Application Requesters that connect with the DB2 for MVS/ESA application server. The VTAM APPL statement defines default session limits for all partner systems. If you want to establish unique defaults for a particular partner, you can use the SYSIBM.SYSLUMODES table of the communications database (CDB).

   See "Setting RU Sizes and Pacing" on page 31 about how to review your VTAM network.

6. Create entries in the DB2 for MVS/ESA CDB to identify which Application Requesters are allowed to connect to the DB2 for MVS/ESA application server. Two basic approaches to define the CDB entries for the Application Requesters in the network are:

   a. You can insert a row in SYSIBM.SYSLUNAMES that provides default values to use for any LU not specifically described in the CDB (the default row contains blanks in the LUNAME column). This approach allows you to define specific attributes for some of the LUs in your network, while establishing defaults for all other LUs.

      For example, you can allow the DALLAS system (another DB2 for MVS/ESA system) to send already-verified distributed database requests (LU 6.2 SECURITY=SAME), while requiring DB2 for OS/2 systems to send passwords. Furthermore, you might not want to record an entry in the CDB for each DB2 for OS/2 system, especially if there is a large number of these systems. Figure 13 on page 39 shows how the CDB can be used to specify SECURITY=SAME for the DALLAS system, while enforcing SECURITY=PGM for all other requesters.

```
INSERT INTO SYSIBM.SYSLUNAMES
    (LUNAME, SYSMODENAME, USERSECURITY, ENCRYPTPSWDS, MODESELECT, USERNAMES)
  VALUES ('LUDALLAS', ' ', 'A', 'N', 'N', ' ');

INSERT INTO SYSIBM.SYSLUNAMES
    (LUNAME, SYSMODENAME, USERSECURITY, ENCRYPTPSWDS, MODESELECT, USERNAMES)
  VALUES (' ', ' ', 'C', 'N', 'N', ' ');
```

Figure 13. Establishing Defaults for Application Requester Connections

> b. You can use the CDB to individually authorize each Application Requester in the network, by setting the CDB in one of these ways:
>
> - Do not record a default row in SYSIBM.SYSLUNAMES. When the default row (the row containing a blank LU name) is not present, DB2 for MVS/ESA requires a row in SYSIBM.SYSLUNAMES containing the LU name for each application requester that attempts to connect. If the matching row is not found in the CDB, the Application Requester is denied access.
>
> - Record a default row in SYSIBM.SYSLUNAMES that specifies come-from checking is required (USERNAMES column set to 'I' or 'B'). This causes DB2 for MVS/ESA to limit access to Application Requesters and end users identified in the SYSIBM.SYSUSERNAMES table, as described in "Come-From Checking" on page 43. You might want to use this approach if your name translation rules require a row with a blank LU name in SYSIBM.SYSLUNAMES, but you do not want DB2 for MVS/ESA to use this row to allow unrestricted access to the DB2 for MVS/ESA application server.
>
> In Figure 14, no row contains blanks in the LUNAME column, so DB2 for MVS/ESA denies access to any LU other than LUDALLAS or LUNYC.

```
INSERT INTO SYSIBM.SYSLUNAMES
    (LUNAME, SYSMODENAME, USERSECURITY, ENCRYPTPSWDS, MODESELECT, USERNAMES)
  VALUES ('LUDALLAS', ' ', 'A', 'N', 'N', ' ');


INSERT INTO SYSIBM.SYSLUNAMES
    (LUNAME, SYSMODENAME, USERSECURITY, ENCRYPTPSWDS, MODESELECT, USERNAMES)
  VALUES ('LUNYC', ' ', 'A', 'N', 'N', ' ');
```

Figure 14. Identifying Individual Application Requester Connections

Defining Secondary Servers

DB2 for MVS/ESA does not implement a database server as defined in DRDA. Instead, DB2 for MVS/ESA provides secondary servers that provide access to multiple DB2 for MVS/ESA systems in a single unit of work using system-directed access.

SQL differences: The SQL supported by system-directed access differs significantly from DRDA remote unit of work:

- The SQL CONNECT statement is not used to establish a connection to a secondary server. Instead, the server is accessed by specifying three-part SQL object names. For example, the following SQL statement is routed to the CHICAGO system-directed access server:

  `SELECT * FROM CHICAGO.USER.TABLE;`

- SQL DDL statements (for example, CREATE) are not allowed.

- System-directed access does not support remote bind (for example, BIND PACKAGE), so you do not have to bind your application at the system-directed access server before attempting to execute the application.

- The SQL statements sent to a secondary server can be static or dynamic, but all the statements are issued dynamically. This occurs because the secondary server does not have a plan or package containing the application's SQL statements, so it is not possible for the server to choose database access paths in advance.

- A single SQL application can access multiple secondary servers simultaneously.

- More than one DB2 for MVS/ESA system can be the target of SQL updates for any given commit scope.

- An application can use multiple LU 6.2 conversations to a secondary server in a single commit scope. The DB2 for MVS/ESA application server usually creates one LU 6.2 conversation for each read-only SQL query. This allows the secondary server to anticipate the SQL application's FETCH requests, and send the answer set before it is actually requested by the application.

SQL object names: When the DB2 for MVS/ESA application server receives an SQL request, it examines the SQL object name to determine where the object resides in the network. DB2 for MVS/ESA accepts either one-, two-, or three-part SQL object names, where the name takes one of the following forms:

objectname specifies the name of a DB2 for MVS/ESA table, view, synonym, or alias.

authid.objectname specifies the owner of the object and the object name.

location.authid.objectname specifies the owning system, the owning user, and the name of the object.

If the location name (the first part of the three-part object name) matches the local DB2 for MVS/ESA system's RDB_NAME, the request identifies a local DB2 for MVS/ESA object.

If the location name does not match the local DB2 for MVS/ESA system's RDB_NAME, the DB2 for MVS/ESA application server reroutes the request to the system identified by the location name using system-directed access. The target system must be another DB2 for MVS/ESA system, because system-directed access is only supported between DB2 for MVS/ESA systems. System-directed access does not support any remote bind functions, so the application does not have to be bound at the server before executing the application. Figure 15 summarizes the process used by DB2 for MVS/ESA to resolve SQL object names.

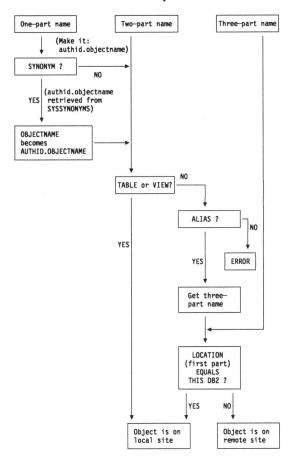

Figure 15. DB2 for MVS/ESA SQL Object Name Resolution

Server definition: If the DB2 for MVS/ESA application server is to reroute SQL requests, you must define each secondary server in the CDB and VTAM. Most of the definition process is similar to the process described in "Defining the Remote Systems" on page 27. To connect secondary servers, do the following:

1. Record the RDB_NAME and LU name values for each server in the CDB and VTAM. The TPN value used by system-directed access is different than the DRDA default value. However, this difference is not important because DB2 for MVS/ESA automatically chooses the correct value.

2. Define the security requirements in SYSIBM.SYSLUNAMES for each secondary server. This process is described in "Provide Security" on page 31.

3. Define the mode name (or names) used between the DB2 for MVS/ESA application server and the secondary servers, and place these mode names in the VTAM mode table. The default mode name is IBMDB2LM.

4. Define the session limits for each secondary server. The process used to establish the session limits is the same as the process described in "Defining the Local System" on page 21. However, system-directed access can establish multiple conversations for each SQL application. You might need to establish higher session limits for the system-directed access connections than you establish for DRDA connections. See "Connecting Distributed Database Systems" in the *DB2 Administration Guide* for specific details on how to calculate the number of LU 6.2 sessions required by system-directed access applications.

As the owner of the database resources, the secondary server controls database security for SQL objects residing at the server. However, this responsibility is shared with the DB2 for MVS/ESA application server making the request. The server controls access to SQL objects as follows:

- The secondary server does not have a copy of the DB2 for MVS/ESA plan, so it depends on the requesting DB2 for MVS/ESA application server to verify that the end user is allowed to execute the package at the requesting system (the application server).

- Static SQL statements are executed dynamically at the secondary server using the privileges granted to the person owning the DB2 for MVS/ESA package at the requesting DB2 for MVS/ESA application server.

- Dynamic SQL statements are executed using the privileges granted to the end user at the Application Requester.

Provide Security

When an Application Requester routes a distributed database request to the DB2 for MVS/ESA application server, the following security considerations can be involved:

Come-from checking
Selection of end user names
Network security parameters
Database manager security
Security enforced by an external security subsystem

Come-From Checking

When the DB2 for MVS/ESA application server receives an end user name from the Application Requester, the application server can restrict the end user names received from a given Application Requester. This is accomplished through the use of *come-from* checking. Come-from checking allows the application server to specify that a given user ID is only allowed to be used by particular partners. For example, the application server can restrict JONES to "come from" DALLAS. If another Application Requester (other than DALLAS) attempts to send the name JONES to the application server, the application server can reject the request because the name did not come from the correct network location.

DB2 for MVS/ESA implements come-from checking as part of inbound end user name translation, which is described in the next section.

Selecting End User Names

As stated earlier in "Provide Security" on page 10, the user ID passed by the Application Requester might not be unique throughout the entire SNA network. The DB2 for MVS/ESA application server might need to perform inbound name translation to create unique end user names throughout the SNA network. Similarly, the DB2 for MVS/ESA application server might need to perform outbound name translation to provide a unique end user name to the secondary servers involved in the application (see "Provide Security" on page 31 for information concerning outbound end user name translation).

Inbound name translation is enabled by setting the USERNAMES column of the SYSIBM.SYSLUNAMES table to 'I' (inbound translation) or 'B' (both inbound and outbound translation). When inbound name translation is in effect, DB2 for MVS/ESA translates the user ID sent by the Application Requester and the DB2 for MVS/ESA plan owner's name (if the Application Requester is another DB2 for MVS/ESA system).

If the Application Requester sends both a user ID and a password on the APPC ALLOCATE verb, the user ID and password are validated before the user ID is translated. The PASSWORD column in SYSIBM.SYSUSERNAMES is not used for password validation. Instead, the user ID and password are presented to the external security system (RACF or a RACF-equivalent product) for validation.

When the incoming user ID on the ALLOCATE verb is verified, DB2 for MVS/ESA has authorization exits you can use to provide a list of secondary AUTHIDs and perform additional security checks. See the *DB2 Administration Guide*, for details.

The inbound name translation process searches for a row in the SYSIBM.SYSUSERNAMES table, which must fit one of the patterns shown in the following precedence list (TYPE.AUTHID.LUNAME):

1. I.AUTHID.LUNAME—A specific end user from a specific Application Requester
2. I.AUTHID.blank—A specific end user from any Application Requester
3. I.blank.LUNAME—Any end user from a specific Application Requester

If no row is found, remote access is denied. If a row is found, remote access is allowed and the end user's name is changed to the value provided in the NEWAUTHID column, with a blank NEWAUTHID value indicating that the name is unchanged. Any DB2 for MVS/ESA resource authorization checks (for example, SQL table privileges) made by DB2 for MVS/ESA are performed on the translated end user names, rather than on the original user names.

When the DB2 for MVS/ESA application server receives an end user name from the Application Requester, several objectives can be accomplished by using the DB2 for MVS/ESA inbound name translation capability:

- You can change an end user's name to make it unique. For example, the following SQL statements translate the end user name JONES from the NEWYORK application requester (LUNAME LUNYC) to a different name (NYJONES).

```
INSERT INTO SYSIBM.SYSLUNAMES
      (LUNAME, SYSMODENAME, USERSECURITY, ENCRYPTPSWDS,
              MODESELECT, USERNAMES)
   VALUES ('LUNYC', ' ', 'A', 'N', 'N', 'I');

INSERT INTO SYSIBM.SYSUSERNAMES
      (TYPE, AUTHID, LUNAME, NEWAUTHID, PASSWORD)
   VALUES ('I', 'JONES', 'LUNYC', 'NYJONES', ' ');
```

- You can change the end user's name so that a group of end users are all represented by a single name. For example, you might want to represent all users from the NEWYORK Application Requester (LUNAME LUNYC) with the user name NYUSER. This allows you to grant SQL privileges to the name NYUSER and to control the SQL access given to users from NEWYORK.

```
INSERT INTO SYSIBM.SYSLUNAMES
      (LUNAME, SYSMODENAME, USERSECURITY, ENCRYPTPSWDS,
              MODESELECT, USERNAMES)
   VALUES ('LUNYC', ' ', 'A', 'N', 'N', 'I');

INSERT INTO SYSIBM.SYSUSERNAMES
      (TYPE, AUTHID, LUNAME, NEWAUTHID, PASSWORD)
   VALUES ('I', ' ', 'LUNYC', 'NYUSER', ' ');
```

- You can restrict the end user names transmitted by a particular Application Requester. This use of end user name translation accomplishes the come-from check described in "Come-From Checking" on page 43. For example, the SQL statements that follow allow only SMITH and JONES as end user names from the NEWYORK Application Requester. Any other name is denied access, because it is not listed in the SYSIBM.SYSUSERNAMES table.

```
INSERT INTO SYSIBM.SYSLUNAMES
    (LUNAME, SYSMODENAME, USERSECURITY, ENCRYPTPSWDS,
            MODESELECT, USERNAMES)
  VALUES ('LUNYC', ' ', 'A', 'N', 'N', 'I');

INSERT INTO SYSIBM.SYSUSERNAMES
    (TYPE, AUTHID, LUNAME, NEWAUTHID, PASSWORD)
  VALUES ('I', 'SMITH', 'LUNYC', ' ', ' ');

INSERT INTO SYSIBM.SYSUSERNAMES
    (TYPE, AUTHID, LUNAME, NEWAUTHID, PASSWORD)
  VALUES ('I', 'JONES', 'LUNYC', ' ', ' ');
```

- You can restrict the Application Requesters allowed to connect to the DB2 for MVS/ESA application server. This is yet another feature of come-from checking. The following example accepts any end user name sent by the NEWYORK Application Requester (LUNYC) or the CHICAGO Application Requester (LUCHI). Other Application Requesters are denied access, because the default SYSIBM.SYSLUNAMES row specifies inbound name translation for all inbound requests.

```
INSERT INTO SYSIBM.SYSLUNAMES
    (LUNAME, SYSMODENAME, USERSECURITY, ENCRYPTPSWDS,
            MODESELECT, USERNAMES)
  VALUES (' ', ' ', 'A', 'N', 'N', 'I');

INSERT INTO SYSIBM.SYSUSERNAMES
    (TYPE, AUTHID, LUNAME, NEWAUTHID, PASSWORD)
  VALUES ('I', ' ', 'LUNYC', ' ', ' ');

INSERT INTO SYSIBM.SYSUSERNAMES
    (TYPE, AUTHID, LUNAME, NEWAUTHID, PASSWORD)
  VALUES ('I', ' ', 'LUCHI', ' ', ' ');
```

Provide Network Security

LU 6.2 provides three major network security features:

Session-level security
Conversation-level security
Encryption

"Network Security" on page 33 discusses how to specify session-level security and encryption with DB2 for MVS/ESA. The DB2 for MVS/ESA application server uses session-level security and encryption in exactly the same manner as the DB2 for MVS/ESA Application Requester.

The only remaining network security consideration is SNA conversation-level security. Some aspects of conversation-level security are unique for a DB2 for MVS/ESA application server. The DB2 for MVS/ESA application server plays two distinct roles in network security:

- As a requester to secondary servers, the DB2 for MVS/ESA application server is responsible for issuing APPC requests that contain the SNA conversation-level security parameters required by the secondary servers. The DB2 for MVS/ESA application server uses the USERNAMES column of the SYSIBM.SYSLUNAMES table and the SYSIBM.SYSUSERNAMES table to define the SNA conversation level security requirements for each secondary server. The details of these definitions are identical to those in "Network Security" on page 33.

- As the server for the Application Requester, the DB2 for MVS/ESA application server dictates the SNA conversation level security requirements for the Application Requester. DB2 for MVS/ESA uses the USERSECURITY column of the SYSIBM.SYSLUNAMES table to determine the conversation security required from each Application Requester in the network. The following values are used in the USERSECURITY column:

  C

    This indicates that DB2 for MVS/ESA requires the Application Requester to send a user ID and password (LU 6.2 SECURITY=PGM) with each distributed database request. If the ENCRYPTPSWDS column in SYSIBM.SYSLUNAMES contains 'Y', DB2 for MVS/ESA assumes the password is already in RACF encrypted format (this is only possible for a DB2 for MVS/ESA Application Requester). If the ENCRYPTPSWDS column does not contain 'Y', DB2 for MVS/ESA expects the password in the standard LU 6.2 format (EBCDIC character representation). In either case, DB2 for MVS/ESA passes the user ID and password values to the security subsystem for validation. You must have a security subsystem that provides APPC user ID and password verification; for example, RACF has the capability to verify APPC user IDs and passwords. If the security subsystem rejects the user ID-password pair, distributed database access is denied.

  Any other value

    This indicates the Application Requester is allowed to send either an already-verified user ID (LU 6.2 SECURITY=SAME) or a user ID and password (LU 6.2 SECURITY=PGM). If a user ID and password are sent, DB2 for MVS/ESA processes them as described for 'C' above. If the request contains only a user ID, the security subsystem is called to authenticate the user unless the SYSUSERNAMES table is used to manage inbound user IDs.

If a security violation is discovered, LU 6.2 requires the DB2 for MVS/ESA application server to return the SNA security failure sense code ('080F6051'X) to the Application Requester. Because this sense code does not describe the cause of the failure, DB2 for MVS/ESA provides two methods for recording the cause of distributed security violations:

- A DSNL030I message is produced, which provides the requester's LUWID and a DB2 reason code describing the failure. DSNL030I also includes the AUTHID, if known, that was sent from the application request that was rejected.

- An alert is recorded in the NETVIEW hardware monitor database, which contains the same information provided in the DSNL030I message.

Database Manager Security

As the owner of database resources, the DB2 for MVS/ESA application server controls the database security functions for SQL objects residing at the DB2 for MVS/ESA application server. Access to DB2 for MVS/ESA-managed objects is controlled by privileges, which are granted to users by the DB2 for MVS/ESA administrator or the owners of individual objects. The two basic classes of objects that the DB2 for MVS/ESA application server controls are:

- **Packages**— Individual end users are authorized to create, replace, and run packages with the DB2 for MVS/ESA GRANT statement. When an end user owns a package, that user can automatically run or replace the package. Other end users must be specifically authorized to run a package at the DB2 for MVS/ESA application server with the GRANT USE statement. USE can be granted to individual end users or to PUBLIC, which allows all end users to run the package.

  When an application is bound to DB2 for MVS/ESA, the package contains the SQL statements contained in the application program. These SQL statements are classified as:

  Static SQL

  Static SQL means that the SQL statement and the SQL objects referenced by the statement are known at the time the application is bound to DB2 for MVS/ESA. The person creating the package must have authority to execute each of the static SQL statements contained in the package.

  When end users are granted authority to execute a package, they automatically have authority to execute each of the static SQL statements contained in the package. Thus, end users do not need any DB2 for MVS/ESA table privileges if the package they execute contains only static SQL statements.

  Dynamic SQL

  Dynamic SQL describes an SQL statement that is not known until the program executes. In other words, the SQL statement is built by the program and dynamically bound to DB2 for MVS/ESA with the SQL PREPARE statement. When an end user executes a dynamic SQL statement, the user must have the table privileges required to execute the SQL statement. Because the SQL statement is not known at the time the plan or package is created, the end user is not automatically given the required authority by the package owner.

- **SQL objects**— These are tables, views, synonyms, or aliases. DB2 for MVS/ESA users can be granted various levels of authority to create, delete, change, or read individual SQL objects. This authority is required to bind static SQL statements or to execute dynamic SQL statements.

When you create a package, the DISABLE/ENABLE option allows you to control which DB2 for MVS/ESA connection types can run the package. You can use RACF and DB2 for MVS/ESA security exit routines to selectively allow end users to use DDF. You can use RLF to specify limits on processor time for remote binds and dynamic SQL executions.

Consider a DB2 for MVS/ESA package named MYPKG, which is owned by JOE. JOE can allow SAL to execute the package by issuing the DB2 for MVS/ESA GRANT USE statement. When SAL executes the package, the following occurs:

- DB2 for MVS/ESA verifies that SAL was given USE authority for the package.

- SAL can issue every static SQL statement in the package because JOE had the required SQL object privileges to create the package.

- If the package has dynamic SQL statements, SAL must have SQL table privileges of her own. For example, SAL cannot issue SELECT * FROM JOE.TABLE5 unless she is granted read access to JOE.TABLE5.

Security Subsystem

The DB2 for MVS/ESA application server use of the security subsystem (RACF or a RACF-equivalent product) is dependent on how you define the inbound name translation function in the SYSIBM.SYSLUNAMES table:

- If you specify 'I' or 'B' for the USERNAMES column, inbound name translation is active, and DB2 for MVS/ESA assumes that the DB2 for MVS/ESA administrator is using inbound name translation to perform part of the system security enforcement. The external security subsystem is called only if the Application Requester sends a request containing both user ID and password (SECURITY=PGM). You must have a security subsystem that provides APPC user ID and password verification; for example, RACF has the capability to verify APPC user IDs and passwords.

  If the request from the Application Requester contains only a user ID (SECURITY=SAME), the external security system is not called at all, because the inbound name translation rules define which users are allowed to connect to the DB2 for MVS/ESA application server.

- If you specify something other than 'I' or 'B' for the USERNAMES column, the following security subsystem checks are performed:

  - When a distributed database request is received from the Application Requester, DB2 for MVS/ESA calls the external security system to validate the end user's user ID (and password if it is provided).

  - The external security system is called to verify that the end user is authorized to connect to the DB2 for MVS/ESA subsystem.

- In either case, an authorization exit is driven to provide a list of secondary authorization IDs. For more information, see the *DB2 Administration Guide*.

Represent Data

You must ensure that your DB2 for MVS/ESA subsystem has the ability to convert from each application requester's CCSID to your DB2 for MVS/ESA subsystem's installation CCSID. Refer to "Represent Data" on page 36 for more information.

Chapter 3. Connecting DB2 for VM and VSE in a DRDA Network

SQL/DS (DB2 for VM) Version 3 Release 3 is the first DB2 for VM release to provide both DRDA application server and application requester support in the VM systems. SQL/DS (DB2 for VSE) Version 3 Release 4 is the first DB2 for VSE release to provide application server support for the VSE/ESA systems. DB2 for VM does not support DRDA for VM/XA* systems.

The information in this chapter is in the same format as the information described in Chapter 1, "Introducing DRDA Connectivity" on page 2. The emphasis in this chapter is mainly on connecting a DB2 for VM and VSE system to unlike remote DRDA systems. For information on connecting two DB2 for VM and VSE systems, refer to *Connectivity Planning, Administration, and Operation* manuals for VM/SP and VM/ESA and *SQL/DS System Administration* manuals for VM/SP, VM/ESA, or VSE.

Use Table 3 on page 50 to find other information in this manual to help you with the specific type of connection you are interested in.

---

* Trademark of IBM Corporation

Table 3. Where to Find Additional Information on DB2 for VM and VSE Connections

Type of Connection	Also Read
DB2 for VM and VSE and DB2 for MVS/ESA	Chapter 2, "Connecting DB2 for MVS/ESA in a DRDA Network" on page 15
	Chapter 6, "DB2 for MVS/ESA and DB2 for VM via CTC" on page 129
	Chapter 7, "DB2 for MVS/ESA and DB2 for VM via Channel-Attached NCP" on page 138
	Chapter 8, "DB2 for MVS/ESA and DB2 for VM via Link-Attached NCP" on page 148
DB2 for VM and VSE and DB2 for OS/400	Chapter 4, "Connecting DB2 for OS/400 in a DRDA Network" on page 88
	Chapter 10, "DB2 for OS/400 and DB2 for VM via Token Ring and NCP" on page 165
DB2 for VM and VSE and DB2 for AIX	Chapter 11, "DB2 for AIX and DB2 for MVS/ESA, DB2 for VM and VSE, or DB2 for OS/400 via Token Ring" on page 173
	Chapter 20, "Configuring DDCS for AIX" on page 330
DB2 for VM and VSE and DB2 for OS/2	Chapter 15, "DB2 for OS/2 and DB2 for VM and VSE via Token Ring" on page 235
	Chapter 16, "DB2 for OS/2 and DB2 for MVS/ESA or DB2 for VM via SDLC" on page 264
	Chapter 18, "DB2 for OS/2 and DB2 for MVS/ESA or DB2 for VM and VSE via 3174 Controller" on page 288
	Chapter 19, "DB2 for OS/2 and Other DRDA Servers" on page 304

DB2 for VM

Each DB2 for VM database management system can manage one or more databases (one at a time) and is typically referred to by the name of the database it manages currently. This relational database name is unique within a set of interconnected SNA networks.

The various DRDA and VM components involved in distributed database processing are described below. These components enable the DB2 for VM database management system to access local relational databases and to communicate with remote DRDA systems in the SNA network.

AVS APPC/VTAM support (AVS) is a VM component that enables VM applications to access the SNA network. It provides the logical unit (LU) function as defined by SNA. An LU is referred to as a *gateway* in the VM environment. AVS runs in a group control system as a VTAM application. It converts APPC/VM macro calls into APPC/VTAM macro calls and vice versa. APPC/VM uses AVS to route and translate data streams. AVS allows DB2 for VM requests to be routed between the local VM system and remote SNA locations. AVS must be used whenever DB2 for VM applications or databases are communicating with non-DB2 for VM databases or applications.

On the application requester side, a user must be authorized to connect through an AVS gateway before the requests can be sent. On the application server side, the receiving AVS gateway must also be authorized to connect to the DB2 for VM server machine before AVS can pass on the user's requests. The authorization is done by providing the appropriate IUCV directory control statements in the user machine, database machine, and the sending and receiving AVS machines. For details on how to do this, see VM/SP or VM/ESA *Connectivity Planning, Administration, and Operation* manuals.

APPC/VM APPC/VM is the VM assembler-level API that provides a subset of the LU 6.2 function set as defined by SNA. In practical terms, it provides the LU 6.2 verbs that enable DB2 for VM applications to connect to and process in local and remote database management systems. The LU 6.2 verbs supported by APPC/VM are listed in *VM/SP Programming Guide and Reference* and *VM/ESA CP Programming Services*.

Communications Directory

The Communications Directory is a CMS NAMES file that serves a specific role in the establishment of APPC conversations between an Application Requester and an application server. The directory provides the necessary information for routing and establishing an APPC conversation with the target server. This information includes such items as LU name, TPN, security, mode name, user ID, password, and database name.

DB2 for VM uses the COMDIR tag :dbname to resolve the RDB_NAME to its corresponding routing data.

This special file and its communication function are described in VM/SP or VM/ESA *Connectivity Planning, Administration, and Operation*.

GCS Group control system is a VM component that consists of:

- A shared segment that runs in a virtual machine

- A virtual machine supervisor that bands many virtual machines together in a group and supervises their operations

- An interface between the following program products:

  - Virtual Telecommunications Access Method (VTAM)
  - APPC/VTAM Support (AVS)
  - Remote Spooling Communications Subsystem (RSCS)
  - Control Program (CP)

GCS supervises the execution of VTAM applications such as AVS in a VM environment. Virtual machines running under the supervision of GCS do not use CMS.

Resource adapter

The resource adapter is the portion of DB2 for VM logic that resides in your virtual machine and enables your application to request access to an DB2 for VM server. The DRDA Application Requester function is integrated into the resource adapter.

TSAF

Transparent Services Access Facility is a VM component that provides communications support between interconnected VM systems. Up to eight VM systems can participate in a TSAF collection, which can be considered analogous to a VM local area network (or wide area network). Each participating VM system must have a TSAF virtual machine in operation. Within a TSAF collection, all user IDs and resource IDs are unique.

DB2 for VM uses TSAF to route distributed database requests to other DB2 for VM machines within the TSAF collection. If the local VM system does not have an AVS virtual machine, DB2 for VM uses TSAF to route DRDA requests to a VM system that does have an AVS virtual machine. AVS allows the request to be forwarded to other TSAF collections and non-DB2 for VM systems.

A TSAF collection is viewed as one or more logical units in the SNA network. Resources defined as global within a TSAF collection can be accessed by remote APPC programs residing anywhere in the collection.

Typically, a TSAF collection operates in stand-alone fashion, independent of VTAM and the SNA network. However, it can cooperate with AVS and VTAM to make its global resources accessible by remote APPC programs residing anywhere in the SNA network. This requires that an AVS machine and a VTAM machine are operating on one or more of the TSAF members. TSAF is described in VM/SP or VM/ESA *Connectivity Planning, Administration, and Operation*.

VTAM

Virtual Telecommunications Access Method provides the network communications support for connectivity. DB2 for VM uses VTAM services through AVS to route connections and requests to remote DRDA systems. VTAM is used *only* for remote requests that access the SNA network.

*IDENT

AVS and TSAF use the transaction program name (TPN) to route requests between VM systems that are connected via TSAF and AVS. The TPN can be an SNA-registered TPN or a valid alphanumeric name. VM refers to the TPN value as a resource ID. For an DB2 for VM server to be accessible to remote DRDA systems, the DB2 for VM server uses the VM IDENTIFY (*IDENT) system service to define itself as the manager of a global resource

ID (TPN). After the server is identified as a global resource, TSAF and AVS can route DRDA requests to the DB2 for VM server, if the received TPN matches the resource ID. *IDENT is described in *VM/SP Connectivity Programming Guide and Reference* and *VM/ESA: CP Programming Services*.

DB2 for VM communications flow example: The following example shows how each component plays a role in establishing communications between an Application Requester and an application server.

Although this book is more concerned with connectivity between unlike systems, an example between two DB2 for VM systems shows the various communications components in their sending and receiving capacities. Figure 16 shows how the application requester connects to AVS and uses VTAM to access the SNA network. Access to remote resources are not routed through the local application server.

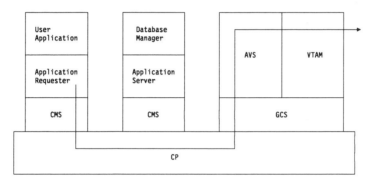

Figure 16. Requesting Access to a Remote Resource

Suppose a DB2 for VM Application Requester that operates in TSAF collection **A** is to access remote data managed by a DB2 for VM application server that operates in TSAF collection **B**. By definition, this implies that TSAF machines are operating on the two hosts where the Application Requester and the application server reside. Also, an AVS component and a VTAM machine are operating on a VM system in TSAF collection **A**, and another pair of AVS and VTAM machines are operating on a VM system in TSAF collection **B**. AVS and VTAM might also reside on the same system as the Application Requester and the application server.

After the VTAM machine starts, it defines the local AVS gateway to the SNA network and activates one or more sessions to use later for establishing conversations.

After the AVS machine starts, it negotiates session limits between the local AVS gateway and the potential partner LUs.

The application server might or might not be active. The operator must start it before it can process requests from a like or unlike Application Requester. After the application server starts, it registers the resource ID that it manages with the host VM system. Each registration creates an entry in an internal resource table maintained by the VM system.

The application requester issues an APPC/VM CONNECT statement to establish an LU 6.2 conversation with the application server. The CONNECT function uses the CMS Communications Directory to resolve the relational database name into its associated LU name and TPN that comprise the address of the application server in the SNA network. The CMS Communications Directory also determines the level of conversation security and security tokens, such as user ID and password, to pass to the remote site for authorization purposes. If SECURITY=PGM is used, the Application Requester must pass a user ID and password to the application server. You can specify the user ID and password in the CMS Communications Directory or in the APPCPASS record defined with the application requester user's CP directory. If SECURITY=SAME is used, then only the VM logon ID of the application requester user is sent to the application server, and no extra password is required.

For example, if you use SECURITY=SAME, the host checks if an AVS machine is operating locally. If it is not, the host establishes a connection between the application requester and the local TSAF machine. The local TSAF machine polls the other TSAF machines in collection **A** for the AVS machine and then establishes a connection to it.

The AVS component in collection **A** converts the APPC/VM connection request to its APPC/VTAM equivalent function call. AVS then uses an existing session or allocates a new session between its gateway (LU) and the remote LU. AVS then establishes a conversation with the remote LU and passes it the LU name, TPN, security level, and user ID. If the remote LU is also a VM system, the session and conversation are handled by the AVS component running on that system.

Figure 17 shows that VTAM routes the inbound connection to the specific AVS gateway and then to the application server.

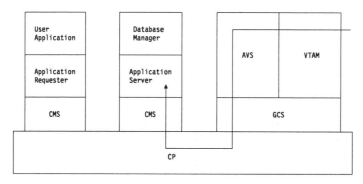

Figure 17. Gaining Access to a Remote Resource

After the remote AVS component establishes the session with its partner (source) AVS, it accepts the conversation and passes the TPN, user ID, and password to the VM host for validation. VM searches for the TPN in its internal resource table. This table contains an entry for each resource ID registered through the *IDENT system service. If the TPN search is successful, VM validates the user ID and password with its directory.[3] If the validation is successful, AVS establishes a connection to the application server and passes it the user ID for database authorization purposes.

If the table search is unsuccessful, AVS rationalizes that the TPN might reside in another VM system in collection **B** and establishes a connection to the local TSAF machine, passing it the user ID, password, and TPN. The TSAF machine polls the other TSAF machines in collection **B**. If one of these machines acknowledges the existence of the TPN in its resource table, the local TSAF machine connects to the remote TSAF machine and passes it the user ID and password to be verified with its VM directory. If the validation is successful, the remote TSAF machine connects to the application server and passes it the user ID for database authorization.

Depending on the routing complexity of the connection, the APPC conversation between the Application Requester and application server can involve additional systems. However, all the intermediate connections are managed by VM and are transparent to the Application Requester or the user application. Figure 18 shows the networking capabilities of DB2 for VM applications.

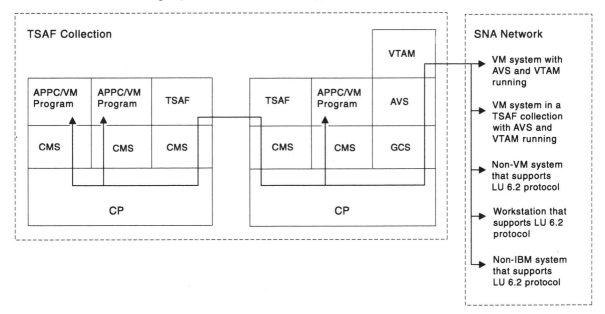

Figure 18. Summary of APPC Communication for DB2 for VM Applications

The APPC/VM interface lets DB2 for VM applications communicate with APPC programs located in:

- Same VM system
- Different VM system
- VM system in an SNA network that has AVS and VTAM running

---

3 Or RACF or equivalent security product.

- VM system in a different TSAF collection that has AVS and VTAM running
- Non-VM system in an SNA network that supports the LU 6.2 protocol
- Non-IBM system in an SNA network that supports the LU 6.2 protocol

DB2 for VM Implementation

As shown in Figure 19, a VM application must go through the DB2 for VM application requester (resource adapter) to access any DB2 for VM or DRDA application server database. A DB2 for VM application server database can receive SQL requests from any DB2 for VM or DRDA Application Requester.

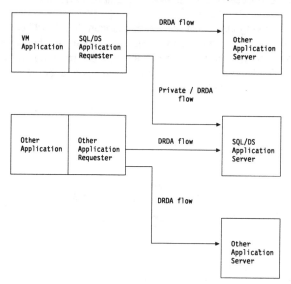

Figure 19. DB2 for VM Application Requester and Application Server

Options for Preprocessing or Running an Application

DB2 for VM supports three processing options on the SQLINIT command that allow the user and the database administrator to enable the distributed database support. The user can specify one of the following SQLINIT options before preprocessing or running the application:

PROTOCOL(SQLDS) Requests the use of the private SQLDS protocol. This is the default option. It can be used between a DB2 for VM application requester and server, in a local or remote environment. The DB2 for VM application server assumes that the requester uses the same CCSIDs as the server. The CCSID defaults[4] set up by the requester via SQLINIT are ignored, and no LU 6.2 LUWID is associated with the conversation. If you use only DB2

---

4 In DB2 for VM, the application requester and the application server specify the default CCSID by specifying a CHARNAME option for SQLINIT and SQLSTART respectively. The CHARNAME is a symbolic name that is mapped internally to the appropriate CCSIDs.

for VM systems, and the same default CCSID everywhere, then this is the most efficient option.

PROTOCOL(AUTO) Requests the DB2 for VM application requester to find out if the application server is a like or unlike system. It then automatically selects the use of the private SQLDS protocol for a like system, or the DRDA protocol for an unlike system. It can be used between like (local and remote) and unlike systems. If the application server is not set with PROTOCOL=SQLDS, then the application requester and server can have different CCSID defaults. The requests and replies are converted appropriately. AUTO is the recommended option for any of the following cases:

- If you need to access both like and unlike systems
- If the CCSID defaults are different at the requester and server (and the PROTOCOL option of the application server is not SQLDS)
- If you need an LU 6.2 LUWID associated with each conversation so that you can easily trace a task back to its originating site. This is useful if you manage a lot of remote DB2 for VM systems in your distributed database network.

PROTOCOL(DRDA) Forces the DB2 for VM application requester to use only the DRDA protocol to communicate with the application server. You can use this option between like (local and remote) and unlike systems. If the application server is a like system, then DRDA protocol is used between the two DB2 for VM systems. If the application server is of SQL/DS (DB2 for VM) release before Version 3 Release 3, then the connection fails because it does not understand DRDA. The application requester and application server can have different CCSID defaults. The requests and replies are converted appropriately. You can use this option between two DB2 for VM systems for testing or for specific applications where the use of the DRDA protocol might provide better throughput due to the use of larger buffer size for sending and receiving data.

Options for Starting the Database Server Machine

The database administrator can specify one of the following options when starting the database server machine. DB2 for VM application requesters that specify SQLINIT PROTOCOL(DRDA) and non-DB2 for VM application requesters use DRDA protocol.

SQLDS The default and recommended option if the application server needs to provide support only for DB2 for VM application requesters that use the private (SQLDS) flow.

The application server is sensitive to the processing option selected by the application requester. If a DB2 for VM requester specifies PROTOCOL(SQLDS) or runs a release before V3R3 of SQL/DS (DB2 for VM), the processing on the DB2 for VM server continues normally with private flows. If the DB2 for VM requester specifies PROTOCOL(AUTO), the DB2 for VM server notifies the requester to switch to private flows. No CCSID information is exchanged between the application requester and the application server. The application server assumes that the application requester CCSIDs are the same as the application server CCSIDs. If the DB2 for VM requester specifies PROTOCOL(DRDA), the conversation is terminated. If a non-DB2 for VM application requester attempts to access the DB2 for VM server, the conversation is terminated.

AUTO   The recommended option if the application server needs to provide support for both the private protocol and the DRDA protocol. The DB2 for VM application requesters that specify PROTOCOL(SQLDS) or PROTOCOL(AUTO) communicate in the private flow. For an application requester that specifies SQLDS, no CCSID information is exchanged, and the application server assumes that the application requester CCSIDs are the same as the application server CCSIDs. For a requester that specifies AUTO, CCSID information is exchanged, and CCSID conversion of requests and replies are done appropriately. The DRDA flow is required by any non-DB2 for VM DRDA requesters, or by any DB2 for VM requesters that specify PROTOCOL(DRDA).

Table 4 on page 59 compares functional characteristics of the DB2 for VM application requester SQLINIT processing options.

Table 4. Comparison of DB2 for VM Application Requester SQLINIT Processing Options

[SQLDS]	[AUTO]	[DRDA]
Both partners must be DB2 for VM systems	Connects to any DRDA system	Connects to any DRDA system
Can communicate with partner locally, through TSAF or AVS/VTAM	Can communicate with a DB2 for VM system locally, or with a remote DB2 for VM system through TSAF or AVS. With an unlike system, must communicate through AVS.	Can communicate with a DB2 for VM system locally, or with a remote DB2 for VM system through TSAF or AVS. With an unlike system, must communicate through AVS.
Supports static, dynamic, and extended dynamic SQL	Supports static, dynamic, and extended dynamic SQL	Supports static, dynamic, and extended dynamic SQL5
CCSIDs defined by SQLINIT for the application requester are ignored by the DB2 for VM application server	CCSIDs defined by SQLINIT for the Application Requester are honored by the DB2 for VM application server and proper conversion is performed (if the application server is set to AUTO as well)	CCSIDs defined by SQLINIT for the Application Requester are honored by the DB2 for VM application server and proper conversion is performed
Fixed 8K blocksize; OPEN call returns no rows; Application Requester must explicitly close cursor	DB2 for VM to DB2 for VM: SQLDS method; all others: DRDA method	Variable 1K to 32K blocksize; more compact data packaging; OPEN call returns one block of rows; application server can implicitly close cursor saving Application Requester from sending a CLOSE call
Can use cursor INSERT and PUTs to insert a block of rows at a time using fixed 8K blocksize	DB2 for VM to DB2 for VM: SQLDS method; all others: DRDA method	PUTs are converted into regular single row inserts and sent out one row at a time
All DB2 for VM-unique commands are supported	DB2 for VM to DB2 for VM: SQLDS method; all others: DRDA method	DB2 for VM operator commands, some DB2 for VM statements, and some ISQL and DBSU commands are not supported (See the *SQL/DS Reference for IBM VM Systems*)
LUWID is not supported	LUWID is supported	LUWID is supported

Setting Up the Application Requester in a VM Environment

DB2 for VM implements the DRDA Application Requester support as an integral part of the resource adapter that resides on the end user virtual machine with the application. You can use the Application Requester support even when the virtual machine of the local database management system is not active. You can activate the DRDA application requester support by running the SQLINIT EXEC with PROTOCOL(AUTO) or PROTOCOL(DRDA) (see "Options for Preprocessing or Running an Application" on page 56).

When DB2 for VM acts as an Application Requester, it can connect to a DB2 for VM application server or any other product server that supports the DRDA architecture. For

---

5 Extended dynamic SQL is supported with DRDA flows by converting into static or dynamic statements. Some restrictions apply.

the DB2 for VM Application Requester to provide distributed database access, you need to know how to do the following:

- "Provide Network Information." The application requester must be able to accept RDB_NAME values and translate them into SNA NETID.LUNAME values. DB2 for VM uses the CMS Communications Directory to catalog RDB_NAMEs and their corresponding network parameters. The Communications Directory enables the application requester to pass the required SNA information to VTAM when issuing distributed database requests.

- "Provide Security" on page 67. For the application server to accept remote database requests, the Application Requester must provide the security information required by the application server. DB2 for VM uses the Communications Directory and CP directory on the application requester side, and the CP directory or RACF optionally on the application server side to provide required network security information when issuing distributed database requests.

- "Represent Data" on page 70. The application requester must have a CCSID that is compatible with the application server.

Provide Network Information

Much of the processing in a distributed database environment requires messages to be exchanged with other locations in your network. To perform this process correctly, take the following steps:

Define the local system
Define the remote systems
Define the communications subsystem
Set RU sizes and pacing

Defining the Local System

The DB2 for VM application requester and the DB2 for VM application server are independent of each other. The DB2 for VM application requester directs connection requests directly to local or remote application servers. It does not, however, define itself as the target of inbound connection requests. Only the DB2 for VM application server can accept (or reject) inbound connection requests. Therefore, the DB2 for VM application requester does not identify an RDB_NAME and TPN for itself, as DB2 for MVS/ESA does.

Define the DB2 for VM application requester to the SNA network as follows:

1. Define gateway names using VTAM APPL definition statements.

   The application requester must have defined gateway names (for example, the LU names) to route its outbound requests into the network. Figure 20 on page 61 shows an example of this. These statements reside on the VTAM virtual machine. When VTAM starts, the gateways are identified to the network but are not activated until the controlling AVS virtual machine starts. Each AVS virtual machine can define multiple gateways on a VM host.

```
        VBUILD TYPE=APPL
****************************************************************
*                                                            *
*      Gateway Definition for Toronto DB2 for VM System      *
*                                                            *
****************************************************************
TORGATE   APPL  APPC=YES,                                     X
                AUTHEXIT=YES,                                 X
                AUTOSES=1,                                    X
                DMINWNL=10,                                   X
                DMINWNR=10,                                   X
                DSESLIM=20,                                   X
                EAS=9999,                                     X
                MAXPVT=100K,                                  X
                MODETAB=RDBMODES,                             X
                PARSESS=YES,                                  X
                SECACPT=ALREADYV,                             X
                VPACING=2
```

Figure 20. Example of an AVS Gateway Definition

The following list describes the VTAM APPL statement keywords that are applicable to topics in this manual. (The VTAM APPL statement supports many more keywords than are shown here.)

TORGATE   VTAM uses the APPL statement label as the gateway (LU) name. In Figure 20, the gateway TORGATE is defined. The VTAM APPL statement does not specify the NETID. The NETID is automatically assigned for all VTAM applications in the VTAM system.

AUTOSES=1   Gateway TORGATE specifies that one SNA contention winner session automatically starts when you issue an APPC Change Number of Sessions (CNOS) command. You must supply a nonzero value with AUTOSES for AVS to be informed in all cases when CNOS processing fails. You do not have to automatically start all the APPC sessions between any two distributed database partners. If the AUTOSES value is less than the contention winner limit (DMINWNL), VTAM delays starting the remaining sessions until they are required by a distributed database application. See Chapter 24, "LU 6.2 and APPC: Concepts" on page 399 for more information on CNOS processing and how it relates to the number of APPC conversations that two database systems can support.

DMINWNL=10   Gateway TORGATE specifies that this DB2 for VM system is the contention winner on at least 10 sessions. CNOS processing uses the DMINWNL parameter for the default, but it can be overridden for any given partner by issuing the AGW CNOS command from the AVS virtual machine.

DMINWNR=10   Gateway TORGATE specifies that this partner system is the contention winner on at least 10 sessions. CNOS processing uses the DMINWNR parameter for the default, but it can be overridden for any given partner by issuing the AGW CNOS command from the AVS virtual machine.

DSESLIM=20   The total number of sessions (both winner and loser) allowed between gateway TORGATE and all partner distributed systems for a specific mode group name is 20. CNOS processing uses the DSESLIM parameter as the default, but it can be overridden for any given partner by issuing the AGW CNOS command from the AVS virtual machine. If the partner cannot support the number of sessions specified by the DSESLIM, DMINWNL, or DMINWNR parameters, the CNOS process negotiates new values for these parameters that are acceptable to the partner.

EAS=9999   An estimate of the total number of sessions that are required by this VTAM LU.

MODETAB=RDBMODES

The name of the VTAM mode table is RDBMODES. This table contains all the mode names this gateway can use to communicate with other distributed database partners. See "Creating a VTAM Mode Table" on page 437 for information on how to create a VTAM mode name table.

SECACPT=ALREADYV

This is the security acceptance parameter that identifies the highest APPC conversation security level this gateway supports when it is presented with a distributed database request from a remote partner. SECACPT=ALREADYV is recommended if you are using VTAM Version 3 Release 3 or later. Earlier versions of VTAM do not support this option. The ALREADYV option supports the following security levels:

SECURITY=NONE, a request containing no security information. DB2 for VM rejects DRDA requests using this security level.

SECURITY=PGM, a request containing the requester's user ID and password. DB2 for VM accepts DRDA requests using this security level.

SECURITY=SAME indicates an already-verified request that contains only the requester's user ID.

For versions of VTAM before Version 3 Release 3, the CONV value indicates this gateway can accept SECURITY=NONE and SECURITY=PGM from other partners that request data from this DB2 for VM system. DB2 for VM rejects DRDA requests using SECURITY=NONE.

VERIFY=NONE   Identifies the level of SNA session security (partner LU verification) required by this DB2 for VM system. The NONE value indicates that partner LU verification is not required.

DB2 for VM does not restrict your choice for the VERIFY keyword, but the VTAM version you are running can influence this choice. In a nontrusted network, DB2 for VM recommends coding VERIFY=REQUIRED. If you choose VERIFY=OPTIONAL, VTAM performs partner LU verification only for those partners that provide the support. VERIFY=REQUIRED causes VTAM to reject partners that cannot perform partner LU verification. "Session-Level Security" on page 441 describes the steps you must take to implement partner LU verification in VTAM and RACF.

For a more detailed description of partner LU verification, see "LU 6.2 Security" on page 409.

VPACING=2   This parameter sets the session pacing count used between the partner LU and this gateway. Session pacing is very important for distributed database systems. For more details on session pacing considerations see "VTAM Pacing" on page 433.

2. Activate the gateway.

Gateway enabling is performed from the AVS virtual machine operating on the same host (or other hosts within the same TSAF collection) as the DB2 for VM Application Requester. Include an AGW ACTIVATE GATEWAY GLOBAL command in the AVS machine's profile or issue this command interactively from the AVS machine console to automatically enable the gateway each time AVS is started.

3. Use the AGW CNOS command to negotiate the number of sessions between the gateway and each of its partner LUs.

Ensure that the MAXCONN value in the CP directory of the AVS gateway machine is large enough to support the total number of sessions required.

Issue the AGW DEACTIVE GATEWAY command from the AVS virtual machine to disable the gateway. The gateway definition remains. The gateway can be enabled again at any time using the AGW ACTIVATE GATEWAY GLOBAL command.

See *VM/SP Connectivity Planning, Administration and Operation* or *VM/ESA Connectivity Planning, Administration and Operation* for AVS command formats.

4. Make sure that the VTAM NETID is defined to the DB2 FOR VM DBMS during installation.

The NETID of the host (or other hosts within the same TSAF collection) where the Application Requester resides is supplied by VTAM as the request enters the network. The NETID is stored in the CMS file SNA NETID and resides in the DB2 for VM production disk accessed by the Application Requester. The Application Requester uses this NETID for the generation of the LUWID that flows with each conversation.

Defining the Remote Systems

You must define the remote systems by registering the LU names that enable VTAM to locate the desired network destination. When AVS starts, it identifies the global gateway names (the LU names) available for routing SQL requests into the network to VTAM. A gateway name must be unique within the set of LU names recognized by the local VTAM system so that both inbound and outbound requests are routed to the proper LU name. This is the best way to ensure gateway name uniqueness throughout the user network. This in turn simplifies the VTAM resource definition process.

When a DB2 for VM application requests data from a remote system, DB2 for VM searches the CMS Communications Directory for the following information relating to the remote system:

- Gateway name (local LU name)
- Remote LU name
- Remote TPN
- Conversation security level required by the application server
- User ID identifying application requester at the application server
- Password authorizing application requester at the application server
- Mode name describing session characteristics to use to communicate with the application server
- RDB_NAME

The CMS Communications Directory is a CMS file with file type NAMES, which is created and managed by a DB2 for VM system administrator. As the administrator, you can use XEDIT to create this file and add the desired entries to identify each potential DRDA partner. Each entry in the directory is a set of tags and their associated values. Figure 21 shows a sample entry. When a search is performed, the search key is compared to the :dbname tag value of each entry in the file until a match is found or the end of the file is reached. In the example in Figure 21, the sales manager in Toronto wants to create a monthly sales report for the Montreal branch by accessing data remotely from the MONTREAL_SALES database.

```
 SCOMDIR  NAMES    A1  V 132  Trunc=132 Size=10 Line=1 Col=1 Alt=8
 ====>
 00001   :nick.MTLSALES
 00002                   :tpn.SALES
 00003                   :luname.TORGATE MTLGATE
 00004                   :modename.BATCH
 00005                   :security.PGM
 00006                   :userid.SALESMGR
 00007                   :password.GREATMTH
 00008                   :dbname.MONTREAL_SALES
 00009
```

Figure 21. A sample entry in a CMS Communications Directory

The :tpn tag identifies the transaction program name that activates the application server. The first part of the :luname tag identifies the AVS gateway (local LU) used to gain access to the SNA network. The second part identifies the remote LU name. The :modename tag identifies the VTAM mode that defines the characteristics of the sessions allocated between the local and remote LUs. Request unit (RU) size, pacing, and class of service (COS) are examples of such characteristics. The :security tag indicates the level of security to use on the conversation connecting the Application Requester to the application server.

The CMS Communications Directory is on a public system disk accessible to all application requesters in a particular VM system. Any program or product that requires remote access through VTAM can use the CMS Communications Directory.

You can access two levels of the CMS Communications Directory: system-level and user-level. For example, you can create a system-level directory on a public system disk accessible to all Application Requesters in a particular VM system. You can also create your own user-level directory to override existing entries or introduce new entries not appearing in the system-level directory. The user-level directory is searched first, and if the search fails, then the system-level directory is searched. The system-level directory is an extension of the user-level directory; it is searched only if the values are not found in the user-level directory.

Each of these directories is identified to the application and activated through the CMS SET COMDIR command. For example, you can use the following command sequence to identify both system and user-level directories (on the S and A minidisks respectively) but choose to activate only the system-level directory for searches:

```
SET COMDIR FILE SYSTEM SCOMDIR NAMES S

SET COMDIR FILE USER UCOMDIR NAMES A

SET COMDIR OFF USER
```

The CMS Communications Directory is described in detail in VM/SP or VM/ESA *Connectivity Planning, Administration and Operation*. The CMS SET COMDIR command is described in VM/SP or VM/ESA *CMS Command Reference*.

Defining the Communications Subsystem

In the VM environment, a combination of components performs communication management. The components involved in the communication among unlike DRDA systems are APPC/VM, CMS Communications Directory, TSAF, AVS, and VTAM.

APPC/VM is the LU 6.2 assembler-level API that the DB2 for VM Application Requester uses to request communications services. The CMS Communications Directory provides the routing and security information of the distributed partner system. AVS activates the gateway and translates outbound APPC/VM flows into APPC/VTAM flows, and inbound APPC/VTAM flows into APPC/VM flows.

APPC/VM, TSAF, and AVS rely on the CMS Communications Directory, VTAM, and *IDENT to route requests to the proper DRDA partner.

For VTAM to communicate with the partner applications identified in the CMS Communications Directory, you must provide the following information:

1. Define the LU name of each Application Requester and application server to VTAM. The placement and syntax of these definitions is dependent on how the

remote system is logically and physically connected to the VTAM system. See "VTAM Remote System Connections" on page 440 for information describing which VTAM statements define remote system connections.

2. Create an entry in the VTAM mode table for each mode name specified in the CMS Communications Directory. These entries describe the request unit (RU) size, pacing window size, and class of service for a particular mode name. See "Creating a VTAM Mode Table" on page 437 for details on how to perform this task.

3. If you intend to use partner LU verification (session-level security), supply VTAM and RACF profiles (or equivalent) for the verification algorithm. See "Session-Level Security" on page 441 for more information.

AVS session limit considerations: When an application requester uses AVS to communicate with a remote application server, a connection is initiated. If this connection causes the established session limit to be exceeded, AVS defers the connection to a pending state until a session becomes available. When a session becomes available, AVS allocates the pended connection on the session, and control is returned to the user application. To avoid this situation, plan for peak usage by increasing session limit to allow for some additional connections. Ensure that the MAXCONN value in the CP directory of the AVS machine is large enough to support peak usage by the APPC/VM connections.

Setting RU Sizes and Pacing

The entries you define in the VTAM mode table specify request unit (RU) sizes and pacing counts. Failure to define these values correctly can have an adverse effect on all VTAM applications. See "VTAM Pacing" on page 433 for information on how to specify this information in your VTAM definition statements.

After choosing request unit (RU) sizes, session limits, and pacing counts, consider the impact these values can have on your existing SNA network. You should review the following items when you install a new distributed database system:

- For VTAM CTC connections, verify that the MAXBFRU parameter is large enough to handle your RU size plus the 29 bytes VTAM adds for the SNA request header and transmission header. MAXBFRU is measured in units of 4K bytes, so MAXBFRU must be at least 2 to accommodate a 4K RU.

- For NCP connections, make sure that MAXDATA is large enough to handle your RU size plus 29 bytes. If you specify a RU size of 4K, MAXDATA must be at least 4125.

  If you specify the NCP MAXBFRU parameter, select a value that can accommodate your RU size plus 29 bytes. For NCP, the MAXBFRU parameter defines the number of VTAM I/O buffers that can hold the PIU. If you choose an IOBUF buffer size of 441, MAXBFRU=10 processes a 4K RU correctly, because 10*441 is greater than 4096+29.

- "VTAM Buffer Pools" on page 428 describes how to assess the impact your distributed database has on the VTAM IOBUF pool. If too much of the IOBUF pool resource is consumed, VTAM performance is degraded for all VTAM applications.

Provide Security

When a remote system performs distributed database processing on behalf of an SQL application, it must be able to satisfy the security requirements of the Application Requester, the application server, and the network connecting them. These requirements fall into one or more of the following categories:

- Selection of end user names
- Network security parameters
- Database manager security
- Security enforced by an external security subsystem

Selecting End User Names

In both SQL and LU 6.2, end users are assigned a 1- to 8-character user ID. This user ID value must be unique within a particular operating system, but is not necessarily unique throughout the SNA network. For example, there can be a user named JONES in the TORONTO system and another user named JONES on the MONTREAL system. If these two users are the same person, no conflict exists. However, if the JONES in TORONTO is not the same person as the JONES in MONTREAL, the SNA network (and consequently the distributed database systems within that network) cannot distinguish between JONES in TORONTO and JONES in MONTREAL. If no steps are taken to prevent this situation, JONES in TORONTO can use the privileges granted to JONES in MONTREAL and vice versa.

To eliminate naming conflicts, DB2 for VM provides support for end user name translation. However, the system does not enforce translation of user IDs. If system-enforced translation is required, you should ensure that proper inbound translation is performed at the application server.

Outbound translation is performed using the CMS Communications Directory. An entry in the CMS Communications Directory must specify :security.PGM. In this case, the corresponding values in the :userid and :password tags flow to the remote site (application server) in the connection request.

By creating the entry shown in Figure 22, the user with ID JONES on the local (TORONTO) system is mapped to user ID JONEST when he connects to the MONTREAL_SALES_DB application server on the MONTREAL system. In this way, the user ID ambiguity is eliminated.

```
 UCOMDIR  NAMES     A1  V 132  Trunc=132 Size=10 Line=1 Col=1 Alt=8
 ====>
 00001  :nick.MTLSALES
 00002              :tpn.SALES
 00003              :luname.TORLU MTLGATE
 00004              :modename.BATCH
 00005              :security.PGM
 00006              :userid.JONEST
 00007              :password.JONESPW
 00008              :dbname.MONTREAL_SALES_DB
 00009
```

Figure 22. Outbound Name Translation

Network Security

Having selected the end user name that represents the application requester at the remote site (application server), the application requester must provide the required LU 6.2 network security information. LU 6.2 provides three major network security mechanisms:

- Session-level security, specified using the VERIFY parameter on the VTAM APPL statement. See the discussion in "Session-Level Security" on page 441 for a description of how to specify session-level security options.

- Conversation-level security, specified in the CMS Communications Directory.

- Encryption (not supported in VTAM Version 3 Release 2 and Version 3 Release 3, supported in VTAM Version 3 Release 4 on MVS.)

For more information on LU 6.2 security, see "LU 6.2 Security" on page 409.

Because the application server is responsible for managing the database resources, the application server dictates which network security mechanisms the application requester must provide. You must record the application server's security requirements in the application requester's communications directory by setting the appropriate value in the :security tag.

The SNA conversation-level security options supported by DRDA are:

SECURITY=SAME

This is also known as already-verified security, because only the end user's ID (logon ID) is sent to the remote system. The password is not sent. This level of conversation security is used when :security.SAME is specified in the application requester's communications directory for that application server. When this option is used, outbound end user name translation is not performed. The user ID sent to the remote DRDA site is the CMS user's logon ID. The :userid tag in the CMS Communications Directory is ignored for :security.SAME.

SECURITY=PGM

This option causes both the end user's ID and password to be sent to the remote system (application server) for validation. This security option is used when :security.PGM is specified in the CMS Communications Directory entry of the application requester. When this option is used, outbound end user name translation is performed.

DB2 for VM does not support password encryption. The password can be specified in the :password tag, or it can be stored in the end user's CP directory entry using an APPCPASS directory statement. The APPCPASS statement is recommended if you want to maximize the security of the password. If the password is not specified in the CMS Communications Directory entry, the user's system (VM) directory entry is searched for an APPCPASS statement.

APPCPASS statement: VM provides the APPCPASS statement to maximize the security of the user ID and password used by the Application Requester to connect to an application server. The APPCPASS is flexible in that it allows you to store security information in one of the following ways:

- **User ID and password:** In this case the :userid and :password tags in the CMS Communications Directory must be set to blanks.

- **User ID only:** In this case the :userid tag in the CMS Communications Directory must be set to blanks, and the :password tag must be set to the user's password.

- **Password only:** In this case the :password tag in the CMS Communications Directory must be set to blanks, and the :userid tag must be set to the user's ID.

Figure 23 illustrates the case where the user ID is stored in the user's communications directory and the password is stored in the user's VM directory entry. In the communications directory entry, the user ID is set to MTLSOU, but the password is not set.

```
 UCOMDIR   NAMES     A1  V 132  Trunc=132 Size=8  Line=1 Col=1 Alt=8
 ====>
 00001  :nick.MTLSALES
 00002                :tpn.SALES
 00003                :luname.TORGATE MTLGATE
 00004                :modename.BATCH
 00005                :security.PGM
 00006                :userid.MTLSOU
 00007                :password.
 00008                :dbname.MONTREAL_SALES_DB
 00009
```

Figure 23. Example of a communications directory entry without a password. The password is stored in the user's VM directory entry.

When APPC/VM initiates the connection between the Application Requester and the application server using conversation SECURITY=PGM, it reads the :userid and :password tag values and passes them to the application server. If one or both of these tags is set to blanks, it searches the user's VM directory entry for the missing information. In this case, you must have an APPCPASS statement in the VM directory entry as follows:

```
APPCPASS TORGATE MTLGATE MTLSOU Q6VBN8XP
```

This statement tells APPC/VM that the user (Application Requester) requesting the connection via the (local) AVS gateway TORGATE, the partner LU named MTLGATE, and the user ID MTLSOU should send the password Q6VBN8XP to the application server. The user is known by these two pieces of identification at the application server.

Placing the APPCPASS statement in the VM directory is not an end user task. The end user must place a request with the VM systems programmer to do this.

For more information on conversation-level security and the APPCPASS statement refer to VM/SP or VM/ESA *Connectivity Planning, Administration, and Operation.*

Database Manager Security

As part of the overall distributed database security framework in DRDA, the Application Requester can play a role in controlling which end users are allowed to make distributed database requests. In DB2 for VM, the Application Requester can participate in distributed database security in three ways:

Outbound user name translation

You can use outbound user name translation to control access to a particular application server, based on the identity of the end user making the request. DB2 for VM attempts to translate the end user's name before sending the request to the remote site. However, the best way is to have the application server perform come-from checking and inbound translation, because VM Application Requester users can potentially override the outbound translation with their CMS User Communications Directory.

Application preprocessing

End users preprocess remote applications to a particular application server by using the DB2 for VM SQLPREP EXEC or the Database Service Utility (DBSU) RELOAD PACKAGE command. DB2 for VM does not restrict the use of these services. When an end user preprocesses an application, that user owns the resulting package.

Application execution

For the DB2 for VM end user to run a remote application, the end user must have authority at the remote site (application server) to run the remote package associated with the particular application. The creator (owner) of the package is automatically authorized to run the package. Other end users can be given authority to run the package with the DB2 for VM GRANT EXECUTE statement. In this way, the owner of a distributed database application can control the use of the application on a user-by-user basis.

Security Subsystem

The external security subsystem on VM systems is provided by either RACF or equivalent products that provide an interface compatible with RACF. The DB2 for VM Application Requester does not interface directly to the external security subsystem. The external security subsystem is not used to provide passwords for conversation-level security. If you choose to use session-level security, the external security subsystem is called by VTAM to validate the identity of the remote LU name during partner LU verification.

Represent Data

The application requester must have the appropriate default CHARNAME and CCSID values. Choosing the correct values ensures the integrity of character data representation and reduces performance overhead associated with CCSID conversion.

For example, if your DB2 for VM application requester is generated with code page 37 and character set 697(CP/CS 37/697) for US ENGLISH characters, then the application requester should set the default CHARNAME to ENGLISH. This is because CP/CS 37/697 corresponds to the CCSID of 37, which corresponds to the CHARNAME of ENGLISH.

The default CHARNAME of a newly installed or migrated system is INTERNATIONAL and the CCSID is 500. This is probably *not* correct for your installation. To display the values of the current default CCSIDs, use the following command:

SQLINIT QUERY

See Appendix C, "CCSID Values" on page 448 and Appendix D, "DB2 for VM Character Conversion Values" on page 453 for the CCSID and other values that you should specify.

The appropriate CCSID value for the application requester might be one that is not supported by conversion tables at the application server. If this is the case, you can establish the connection by doing one of the following:

- Have the application server update its CCSID conversion table to support the conversion between the application requester default CCSID and the application server default CCSID (refer to the application server product manuals for details on how to add CCSID conversion support).

- Change the application requester default CCSID to one that is supported by the application server. This might cause data integrity problems, and you must be aware of the consequences. An example of such a consequence follows:

  An application requester uses a controller defined with CP/CS 37/697. The application server does not support a conversion from CCSID 37, but does support a conversion from CCSID 285 (this is CHARNAME UK-ENGLISH for SQL/DS).

  If the application requester is changed to use a default CHARNAME of UK-ENGLISH (and CCSID of 285) then data integrity will not be maintained. For example, where a British pound sign character (£) is meant by the application server, the application requester displays a dollar sign ($). Other characters might also be different.

  To change the CCSID value of a DB2 for VM application requester, you must specify the CHARNAME parameter of the SQLINIT EXEC. See the *SQL/DS System Administration* manual for more detailed information.

The appropriate CCSID value for the application server might be one that is not supported by conversion tables at the application requester. If this is the case, you can establish the connection by doing one of the following:

- Update the conversion table used by the application requester to support the conversion between the application server default CCSID and the application requester default CCSID. See *SQL/DS System Administration* for details on how to update the SYSTEM.SYSSTRINGS system table. This table is used to create the CMS file ARISSTR MACRO, which is used by the application requester for CCSID conversion support.

- Have the application server change its default CCSID. This should be done only if appropriate, taking into account the goals of choosing the application server default CCSID. The application server default CCSID affects all application requesters that connect to it, the operator terminal used with the application server, and the data stored in tables on the application server.

Setting Up the Application Server in a VM Environment

The application server support in DB2 for VM allows DB2 for VM to act as a server for DRDA application requesters. The application requester connected to an DB2 for VM application server can be one of the following:

- A DB2 for VM requester
- A DB2 for MVS/ESA requester
- A DB2 for OS/400 requester
- A DB2 for AIX requester
- A DB2 for OS/2 requester
- Any other product that supports DRDA Application Requester protocols

For any application requester connected to a DB2 for VM application server, the DB2 for VM application server allows the application requester to access database objects (such as tables) stored locally at the DB2 for VM application server. The application requester must create a package containing the application's SQL statements at the DB2 for VM application server before the connection can be established.

Provide Network Information

For the DB2 for VM application server to process distributed database requests, you must take the following steps:

- Define the application server to the local communication subsystem.
- Provide the necessary security.

Defining the Application Server

For the application server to receive distributed database requests, define the application server to the local communications subsystem and assign a unique RDB_NAME. Follow these steps to define the application server:

1. Select the gateway name and RDB_NAME for the DB2 for VM application server. To define these names to DB2 for VM and VTAM, use the procedures described in "Provide Network Information" on page 60. The RDB_NAME you choose for DB2 for VM must be supplied to all users (Application Requesters) that might require connection to the DB2 for VM application server.

   The NETID is defined to VTAM as a startup parameter, and all distributed requests from the Application Requester are routed to it correctly. The DB2 for VM application server does not set the NETID.

The DB2 for VM application server does not determine which gateway to use to route the inbound distributed requests from the Application Requester. The Application Requester always controls this. In the case of an DB2 for VM Application Requester, the CMS Communications Directory specifies it using the :luname and :tpn tags.

2. Ensure that the CP directory for the application server machine has an IUCV *IDENT statement. This identifies the server as a global resource.

3. Create an entry in the VTAM mode name table for each mode name that an Application Requester requests. These entries describe session characteristics such as RU size, pacing count, and class of service for a particular mode name. See Appendix A, "VTAM Considerations" on page 428 for information on how to perform this task.

4. Define session limits for the Application Requesters that connect to the DB2 for VM application server. The VTAM APPL statement defines default session limits for all partner systems. To establish unique defaults for a particular partner, use the AGW CNOS command from the AVS virtual machine running at the application server site. (Session limits are usually requested by the application requester.)

After choosing RU sizes, session limits, and pacing counts, consider the impact these values have on the VTAM IOBUF pool. See Appendix A, "VTAM Considerations" on page 428 to see how you assess the impact your distributed database has on the VTAM IOBUF pool.

Mapping the server name to a RESID: A resource ID (RESID) is the VM term for transaction program name. In the VM environment, it is commonly defined as an alphanumeric name up to 8 bytes long. You normally define a RESID that is identical to the server name, to keep administration easy. Figure 24 shows a sample RESID names file.

```
 RESID  NAMES     A1  V 132  Trunc=132 Size=4  Line=1 Col=1 Alt=3
 ====>
 00001  :nick.MTLTPN
 00002              :dbname.MONTREAL_SALES_DB
 00003              :resid.SALES
 00004
```

Figure 24. Example of a RESID names file

See Figure 23 on page 69 for the Communications Directory entry that defines this dbname and RESID (as the TPN). If the application server name can't be the same as the RESID, then the DB2 for VM application server uses a RESID NAMES file to provide the mapping. This mapping is needed if you:

- Use a RESID different from the server name
- Use a server name longer than 8 bytes
- Use a RESID with a 4-byte hexadecimal value, such as the default DRDA TPN X'07F6C4C2'

During installation, the default is to use the server name specified on the SQLDBINS EXEC as the RESID. To create a mapping entry in the RESID NAMES file, specify the RESID parameter on SQLDBINS.

When you start up the database using SQLSTART DB(server_name), DB2 for VM looks up the corresponding RESID and informs VM that this is the resource that VM is to control. If an entry is not found in the RESID NAMES file, DB2 for VM assumes the RESID is the same as the server name and tells VM so. For more information, see the *SQL/DS System Administration* manual.

Provide Security

When an Application Requester routes a distributed database request to the DB2 for VM application server, the following security considerations can apply:

- Inbound end user name translation
- Network security parameters
- Database manager security
- Security enforced by an external security subsystem

End User Names

In both SQL and LU 6.2, end users are assigned a 1- to 8-byte user ID. This user ID must be unique within a particular operating system, but does not need to be unique throughout the SNA network. To eliminate naming conflicts, DB2 for VM can optionally use the user ID translation function provided by AVS, but only under the following conditions:

- The DB2 for VM application server must run in a VM/ESA (370 or ESA feature) environment.

- The inbound connection request must be routed through an AVS gateway.

- The partner Application Requester must use conversation SECURITY=SAME (also known as *already verified* in SNA terminology).

If a connection is routed to a server through AVS using the SECURITY=SAME option, then AVS user ID translation is required. The AGW ADD USERID command, issued from the AVS machine, must provide security clearance to the connecting users coming from a specific remote LU or AVS gateway. A mapping must exist for all inbound LUs and user IDs that connect using SECURITY=SAME. The command is flexible; you can accept all user IDs from a particular LU or all remote LUs generically. Or you can accept only a specific set of user IDs from a specific LU.

If you use the AGW ADD USERID command to authorize the inbound (already-verified) user IDs at the local AVS machine, no validation is performed by the host. This means that the authorized ID does not necessarily exist on the host, but the connection is accepted anyway.

Two ways to change the current AVS user ID authorization are:

- Stop AVS, using the AGW STOP command. This nullifies the user ID authorization in its entirety.

- Delete the user ID, using the AGW DELETE USERID command.

As an example, the case of identical user IDs in different cities shows how the AVS translation function can resolve a naming conflict. Suppose a user exists with an ID of JONES in the Toronto system, and another user exists with the same ID in the Montreal system. If JONES in Montreal wants to access data in the Toronto system, the following actions at the Toronto system eliminate the naming conflict and prevent JONES in Montreal from using the privileges granted to JONES at the Toronto system:

1. The AVS operator must use the AGW ADD USERID command to translate the ID of the Montreal user to a local user ID. For example, if the operator issues AGW ADD USERID MTLGATE JONES MONTJON, the Montreal user is known as MONTJON at the Toronto system. If all other Montreal users are allowed to connect (connecting via remote LU MTLGATE) and are known locally by their remote user IDs, then the operator must issue the command AGW ADD USERID MTLGATE * =. These AVS commands can also be added to the AVS profile so that they are executed automatically when AVS is started.

2. The DBA must use the DB2 FOR VM GRANT command to grant a set of privileges specifically for the translated user ID, MONTJON in this particular case.

These actions can also be performed at the Montreal system to ensure JONES in Toronto does not use privileges granted to JONES in Montreal when accessing remote data at the Montreal system.

The AVS commands that support user ID translation are described in *VM/ESA Connectivity Planning, Administration and Operation*.

Network Security
LU 6.2 provides three major network security features:

    Session-level security
    Conversation-level security
    Encryption

See "Network Security" on page 68 for the discussion on how to specify session-level security for DB2 for VM. The DB2 for VM application server uses session-level security the same way the DB2 for VM Application Requester does.

The Application Requester can send either an already-verified user ID (SECURITY=SAME) or a user ID and password (SECURITY=PGM). If a user ID and password are sent, CP, RACF, or an equivalent validates them with the VM directory at the application server host. If validation fails, the connection request is rejected; otherwise it is accepted. If the request contains only a user ID, DB2 for VM accepts the request without validating the user ID.

Note: DB2 for VM does not provide encryption capability because VM/SP Release 6 and VM/ESA Release 1 do not support encryption.

Database Manager Security

The DB2 for VM application server verifies if the user ID given by VM has CONNECT authority to access the database, and then rejects the connection if it does not have authority.

As the owner of database resources, the DB2 for VM application server controls the database security functions for SQL objects residing at the DB2 for VM application server. Access to objects managed by DB2 for VM is controlled through a set of privileges, which are granted to users by the DB2 for VM system administrator or the owner of the particular object. The DB2 for VM application server controls two classes of objects:

- **Packages:** Individual end users are authorized to create, replace, and run packages with the DB2 for VM GRANT statement. When an end user creates a package, that user is automatically authorized to run or replace a package. Other end users must be specifically authorized to run a package at the DB2 for VM application server with the GRANT EXECUTE statement. The RUN privilege can be granted to individual end users or to PUBLIC, which allows all end users to run the package.

   When an application is preprocessed on DB2 for VM, the package contains the SQL statements contained in the application program. These SQL statements are classified as:

   Static SQL: This means the SQL statement and the SQL objects referenced by the statement are known at the time the application is preprocessed. The creator of the package must have authority to execute each of the static SQL statements in the package.

   When an end user is granted the privilege to execute a package, the end user automatically has the authority to execute each of the static SQL statements contained in the package. Thus, end users do not need any DB2 for VM table privileges if the package contains only static SQL statements.

   Dynamic SQL: Describes an SQL statement that is not known until the package is run. The SQL statement is built by the program and dynamically preprocessed to DB2 for VM with the SQL PREPARE statement or the EXECUTE IMMEDIATE statement. When an end user runs a dynamic SQL statement, the user must have the table privileges required to execute the SQL statement. Because the SQL statement is not known when the package is created, the end user is not automatically given the required authority by the package owner.

- **SQL objects:** These can be tables, views, and synonyms. DB2 for VM users can be granted various levels of authority to create, delete, change, or read individual SQL objects. This authority is required to preprocess static SQL statements or execute dynamic SQL statements.

Security Subsystem

The use of this subsystem by the DB2 for VM application server is optional. If the application server needs to check the identity of the application requester LU name,

VTAM calls the security subsystem to perform the partner LU verification exchange. The decision to perform partner LU verification is made depending on the value specified in the VERIFY parameter of the VTAM APPL statement for the gateway that the DB2 for VM application server uses to receive inbound distributed database requests.

The security subsystem can also be called by CP to validate the user ID and password sent from the application requester. If the security subsystem is RACF and you do not have a RACF system profile, the validation is performed by RACF. If you do have a RACF system profile, for example, RACFPROF, use the following instructions to request this validation from RACF. The method used to do this depends on the version of your VM operating system.

If you are using VM/SP Release 6 or VM/ESA Release 1.0—370 Feature, use the following commands:

```
RALTER VMEVENT RACFPROF DELMEM (APPCPWVL/NOCTL

RALTER VMEVENT RACFPROF ADDMEM (APPCPWVL/CTL

SETEVENT REFRESH RACFPROF
```

If you are using VM/ESA Release 1.0—ESA Feature, you do not have to issue any commands to request validation be performed by RACF. It is the default.

If you are using VM/ESA Release 1.1, use the following commands:

```
RALTER VMXEVENT RACFPROF DELMEM (APPCPWVL/NOCTL

RALTER VMXEVENT RACFPROF ADDMEM (APPCPWVL/CTL

SETEVENT REFRESH RACFPROF
```

Represent Data

You must choose the most appropriate default CHARNAME and CCSID for your installation. Using the most appropriate values ensures the integrity of the character data representation and reduces the performance overhead associated with CCSID conversion.

For example, if your DB2 for VM application server is accessed only by local users whose terminal controllers are generated with code page 37 and character set 697 (CP/CS 37/697) for the US ENGLISH characters, then you should set the application server default CHARNAME to ENGLISH. This is because CP/CS 37/697 corresponds to the CCSID of 37, which corresponds to the CHARNAME of ENGLISH.

To eliminate unnecessary CCSID conversion, choose an application server default CCSID to be the same as the CCSID of the application requesters that access your application server most often.

Following is an example of how these two goals can be in conflict:

An application server has less than five application requesters that are local (for VM application requesters, the protocol parameter would be set to SQL/DS) and many (around 100) application requesters that access the application server using the DRDA protocol. The local application requesters have controllers that are defined with CP/CS 37/697. The remote application requesters use CCSID 285.

If the application server default CHARNAME is set to ENGLISH, this keeps the data integrity for the local application requesters, but incurs CCSID conversion overhead for all the remote application requesters.

If the application server default CHARNAME is set to UK-ENGLISH, this avoids the CCSID conversion overhead incurred for all the remote application requesters, but causes data integrity problems for the local application requesters—certain characters are not displayed correctly at the local application requesters; for example, a British pound sign (£) is displayed as a dollar sign ($).

To display the current CCSID of the system, query the SYSTEM.SYSOPTIONS table. The application server default CCSID is usually the value of CCSIDMIXED. If this value is zero, then the system default CCSID is the value of CCSIDSBCS. The CHARNAME, CCSIDSBCS, CCSIDMIXED, and CCSIDGRAPHIC values in this table are updated to the values used as the system defaults every time the database is started. The values in this table might not always be the system defaults. A user with DBA authority might have changed these values, though this is not recommended. To change the application server default CCSID, you must specify the CHARNAME parameter of the SQLSTART EXEC the next time the application server is started. See the *SQL/DS System Administration* manual for more detailed information.

For a newly installed database, the application server default CHARNAME is INTERNATIONAL, and the application server default CCSID is 500. This is probably *not* correct for your system. The default CHARNAME for a migrated system is ENGLISH, and the default CCSID is 37.

See Appendix C, "CCSID Values" on page 448 and Appendix D, "DB2 for VM Character Conversion Values" on page 453 for CCSID and other values you should specify.

DB2 for VSE

In the VSE/ESA operating environment, DB2 for VSE provides the application server function in a DRDA environment. The application requester function is not provided. The various DB2 for VSE and VSE components involved in distributed database processing are described in this section. These components enable the DB2 for VSE database management system operating under VSE/ESA 1.3.0 to communicate with remote DRDA application requesters in an SNA network.

CICS(ISC)   The Customer Information Control System, intersystem communication component provides the SNA LU 6.2 (APPC) functions to the DB2 for VSE application server.

ACF/VTAM CICS(ISC) uses ACF/VTAM to establish, or bind, LU-to-LU sessions with remote systems. DB2 for VSE uses LU 6.2 basic conversations over these sessions to communicate with remote DRDA application requesters.

AXE The APPC-XPCC-Exchange transaction is a CICS transaction activated by the remote DRDA application requester. It routes the DRDA data stream between the remote application requester and the DB2 for VSE application server using the CICS LU 6.2 support and the VSE XPCC functions.

DBNAME Directory

The DBNAME (database name) directory maps an incoming request for conversation allocation to a predetermined application server identified by the incoming TPN. See the *SQL/DS System Administration Guide for VSE* for more details.

XPCC Cross Partition Communication Control is the VSE macro interface that provides data transfer between VSE partitions.

DB2 for VSE Application Server Implementation

Figure 25 shows how each component plays a role in establishing communications between the DB2 for VSE application server and the remote Application Requester.

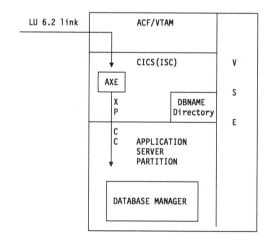

Figure 25. Gaining Access to the Application Server

The application requester issues an APPC ALLOCATE verb with a specific transaction program name (TPN) to establish an LU 6.2 conversation with the application server. Upon receiving the ALLOCATE verb, CICS verifies that an AXE transaction is defined with that TPN, and performs a CICS sign-on. If the conversation security level for the CICS connection is VERIFY, both user ID and password are expected from the application requester, and are used in the sign-on. The CICS sign-on table (DFHSNT) must be updated with this user ID and password so that the connection is accepted. If the security level is set to IDENTIFY, only the user ID is required, and CICS entrusts

the security check to the remote system. If the security check is successful, CICS
starts the AXE transaction to route requests and replies between the application
requester and an application server. The TPN used by the application requester must
be defined in the DB2 for VSE DBNAME directory pointing to an operating DB2 for VSE
server within the VSE system.

Starting the Database Server with the RMTUSERS Parameter

You can specify the RMTUSERS parameter when starting the database server to set
the maximum number of remote application requesters that are allowed to connect to
the server. This is similar to the MAXCONN value in the VM directory of the DB2 for
VM database server machine. This parameter helps to balance the workload between
local and remote processing.

When the RMTUSERS value is greater than the number of available DB2 for VSE
agents (defined by NCUSER), some remote users must wait for a DB2 for VSE agent
to service their request. Normally a DB2 for VSE agent is reassigned to a waiting user
at the end of a logical unit of work (LUW). The DB2 for VSE application server
supports privileged access that allows a remote user to keep a DB2 for VSE agent for
multiple LUWs until the end of the conversation.

Limitations

Unlike its VM counterpart, the DB2 for VSE application server accepts DRDA flows
from remote application requesters. Private protocols are not supported. As a result,
VM application requesters cannot access a VSE server with PROTOCOL=SQLDS.

The DB2 for VSE DRDA server cannot route requests from remote application
requesters to a DB2 for VM server using VSE guest sharing. Such requests should be
sent directly to the DB2 for VM DRDA server.

Setting Up the Application Server in a VSE Environment

The application server support for DB2 for VSE allows DB2 for VSE to act as a server
for DRDA application requesters. The application requester connected to a DB2 for
VSE application server can be one of the following:

- A DB2 for VM requester
- A DB2 for MVS/ESA requester
- A DB2 for OS/400 requester
- A DB2 for AIX requester
- A DB2 for OS/2 requester
- Any other product that supports DRDA Application Requester protocols

Provide Network Information

The following steps are required to establish the network connection to the VSE
application server:

1. Establish CICS LU 6.2 sessions to the remote systems
2. Define the application server

Establishing CICS LU 6.2 sessions

The DB2 for VSE application server communicates with its application requester via CICS LU 6.2 links. The CICS partition used for this purpose must have LU 6.2 links to the remote systems with the application requesters. The *CICS/VSE Intercommunications Guide* contains details on defining and establishing CICS LU 6.2 links with remote systems.

CICS installation and resource definition for LU 6.2 communications

1. Install modules required for ISC.

   You must include the following modules in your system by using SIT or initialization overrides:

   - The EXEC interface programs (specify EXEC=YES or allow it to default).
   - The intersystem communication programs (specify ISC=YES).
   - The terminal control program generated by DFHSG PROGRAM=TCP. A version specifying ACCMETH=VTAM, CHNASSY=YES, and VTAMDEV=LUTYPE6 is required.

2. Define CICS to ACF/VTAM.

   To support LU 6.2 connections, CICS must be defined to ACF/VTAM as a VTAM application major node. The application major node name coded in the VTAM APPL statement is the APPLID for the CICS partition specified in the SIT by the APPLID parameter. It is the LU name used by VTAM (and hence used by the CICS communication partners) to identify the CICS system.

   Figure 26 is an example of a VTAM APPL statement defined for CICS.

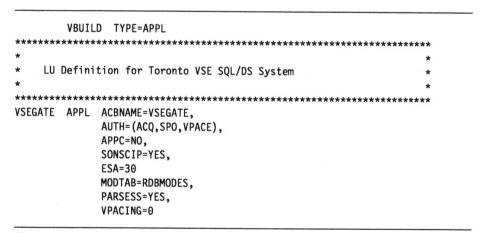

```
        VBUILD  TYPE=APPL
*************************************************************************
*                                                                     *
*    LU Definition for Toronto VSE SQL/DS System                      *
*                                                                     *
*************************************************************************
VSEGATE  APPL  ACBNAME=VSEGATE,
               AUTH=(ACQ,SPO,VPACE),
               APPC=NO,
               SONSCIP=YES,
               ESA=30
               MODTAB=RDBMODES,
               PARSESS=YES,
               VPACING=0
```

Figure 26. Example VTAM APPL Definition for CICS

AUTH=(ACQ,SPO,VPACE)

   ACQ allows CICS to acquire LU 6.2 sessions.

   SPO allows CICS to issue the MODIFY vtamname USERVAR command.

VPACE allows pacing of the intersystem flows.

ESA=30 This option specifies the number of network-addressable units that CICS can establish sessions. The number must include the total number of parallel sessions for this CICS system.

PARSESS=YES Specifies LUTYPE6 parallel session support.

SONSCIP=YES Specifies session outage notification (SON) support. SON enables CICS, in particular cases, to recover a failed session without requiring operator intervention.

APPC=NO For ACF/VTAM Version 3.2 or later, this is necessary to let CICS use VTAM macros. CICS does not issue APPCCMD macro instructions.

3. Define links to remote systems using LU 6.2 protocol.

   a. Define the remote LU 6.2 system

   Use the CEDA DEFINE CONNECTION command on resource definition online (RDO). You can define session level security at this time. The default is no session-level security. You must define conversation-level security at this time. ATTACHSEC=IDENTIFY is the minimum security level required by DRDA. Define all users in the CICS sign-on table (DFHSNT). You can test the validity of a user ID by performing a CESN logon at a CICS terminal. Refer to "Provide Security" on page 83 for details.

   b. Define groups of LU 6.2 sessions with the remote system.

   Use the CEDA DEFINE SESSIONS command to define groups of parallel sessions for each link to a remote system. Unique LOGMODE names, already defined in the VTAM LOGMODE table, identify the groups of sessions.

Issue the CEDA EXPAND GROUP(group-name) instruction at a CICS terminal to review the RDO definitions.

After you've installed the RDO definitions, issue CEMT INQUIRE CONNECTION to see that the connection to the remote systems are inservice and acquired (with the INS ACQ status command). The remote system should be communicating and the DEFINE CONNECTION command include AUTOCONNECT=YES and INSERVICE=YES.

Sample definitions: Refer to "DB2 for OS/2 and DB2 for VSE via Token Ring" on page 253 for sample definitions.

Defining the Application Server

1. Update the SQL/DS DBNAME directory.

   With LU 6.2 sessions established, a remote application requester can start a conversation with the DB2 for VSE application server. It does so by allocating an LU 6.2 conversation with the application server, specifying a TPN (transaction program name). This TPN must be the CICS transaction ID of the AXE transaction responsible for routing requests to or from the DB2 for VSE server. The TPN must be in the DB2 for VSE DBNAME directory mapped to the DB2 for VSE server to be accessed by the application requester. The DB2 for VSE database administrator is responsible for updating the DBNAME directory and informing the remote users of the TPN-to-server mapping.

Both the TPN and its corresponding server name (database name as defined in the DBNAME directory) must be identified to the application requester:

- The application requester uses the TPN to initiate the AXE router transaction. Refer to Figure 123 on page 261 for a TPN definition using CICS RDO.

- The application requester quotes the server name in the initial DRDA flow as the target database name. The DB2 for VSE server uses this server name to verify that the application requester is accessing the right server. A mismatch in server name denies the Application Requester access to the server, and the Application Requester ends the conversation.

2. Use the procedure ARISBDID to build and assemble the DBNAME directory (member ARISDIRD.A).

Preparing and Starting the DB2 for VSE Application Server

1. The AXE transaction maintains an error log that is a CICS temporary storage queue named ARIAXELG. This error log contains useful error messages recording communication problems and abnormal termination of the DRDA sessions. Define this log as "recoverable" using the CICS TST.

2. Run procedure ARIS342D to install the DRDA application server support.

3. Start DB2 for VM with the DBNAME parameter and the RMTUSERS parameter:

   - The DBNAME used must be defined in the DBNAME directory.
   - The RMTUSERS parameter must be nonzero.

4. All remote users must be authorized by the DB2 for VSE server with different levels of authorization. Refer to *SQL/DS Database Administration for VSE* for more details.

Problem determination

- If the application requester succeeded in reaching its partner CICS with a valid TPN (TPN defined in the DBNAME directory), an AXE transaction is started. The use count on program ARICAXED is increased by one (verified by issuing CEMT I PR(ARICAXED)).

- To ensure that a remote user ID is established in the CICS sign-on table, perform a local sign-on using the CESN transaction with the remote user's user ID and password. The local sign-on must be successful.

Provide Security

The DB2 for VSE application server depends on CICS for intersystem communication security. CICS offers several levels of security:

- Bind-time security

The CICS implementation of the SNA LU 6.2 session-level LU-to-LU verification. The implementation of bind-time security is optional in the LU 6.2 architecture. On the application server side, it can be enabled by supplying a BINDPASSWORD in the CEDA DEFINE CONNECTION command when defining the connection to the Application Requester. On the application requester, the partner LU that serves the Application Requester must also support bind-time security and use the same password for partner-LU verification.

You can use bind-time security to stop unauthorized remote systems from establishing (binding) sessions with CICS.

- Link security

  Link security can be used to limit a remote system (and its resident DRDA application requester) to attach a certain set of AXE transactions only.

  For example, you can define two AXE transactions: AXE2 with security key 2, and AXE3 with security key 3. Application requesters from a remote system can be assigned an operator security of 3 (for example, using the OPERSECURITY parameter in the CEDA DEFINE SESSION command), allowing them to attach AXE3 only. AXE3 might not have privileged access to the server while AXE2 has privileged access. Refer to the *System Administration for VSE* for a description of privileged access to the application server by remote application requesters.

  Refer to the *CICS Intercommunication Guide* for how to enable link security.

- User security

  The CICS implementation of the SNA LU 6.2 conversation-level security providing end user verification.

  User security validates the user ID with the CICS sign-on table (DFHSNT) before accepting a request to start a conversation. For example, DRDA application requesters not defined in the CICS sign-on table are not allowed to attach an AXE transaction to start a conversation with the DB2 for VSE server.

  User security level for a remote system can be selected in the CEDA DEFINE CONNECTION command using the ATTACHSEC parameter. The three levels of attach securities are:

  - LOCAL. Not supported by DRDA.
  - IDENTIFY. Equivalent to SECURITY=SAME (or already-verified) in LU 6.2 terminology. With this security level, CICS "trusts" the remote system to verify its users before allowing them to allocate a conversation to the DB2 for VSE server. Only the user ID is required for the CICS sign-on process. However, if the password is also passed, CICS performs the sign-on with the password.
    - VERIFY. Equivalent to SECURITY=PGM in LU 6.2 terminology. With this security level, CICS expects the remote system to send both the user ID and password when allocating the conversation, and rejects the connection if a password is not supplied.

- SNA LU 6.2 session-level mandatory cryptography. Not supported.

Because the application server is responsible for managing the database resources, it dictates which network security mechanisms the application requester must provide. For example, with a DB2 for VM application requester, you must record the application server's conversation-level security requirements in the application requester's communications directory by setting the appropriate value in the :security tag, as in Figure 27:

```
:nick.VSE1      :tpn.TOR3
                :luname.TORGATE VSEGATE
                :modename.IBMRDB
                :security.PGM
                :userid.SALESMGR
                :password.PROFIT
                :dbname.TORONTO3



Where: TOR3     - AXE transaction ID mapped to database TORONTO3.
       TORGATE - VM/APPC gateway.
       VSEGATE - APPLID of the CICS/VSE partition serving as gateway
                 to TORONTO3.
       SALESMGR/PROFIT - USERID/PASSWORD defined in the DFHSNT of
                         VSEGATE, and authorized in TORONTO3
```

Figure 27. Sample CMS Communication Directory entry

Database Manager Security

User ID translation is not supported by the VSE application server. CICS uses the user ID transmitted directly from the requester.

After being started by an application requester, the AXE transaction extracts the user ID from CICS and passes it on to the DB2 for VSE server. To set up the required level of user authority on database resources, you must update the user ID into the DB2 for VSE catalog SYSTEM.SYSUSERAUTH.

The DB2 for VSE application server verifies if the user ID given by CICS has CONNECT authority to access the database, and rejects the connection if it does not have authority.

As the owner of database resources, the DB2 for VSE application server controls the database security functions for SQL objects residing at the DB2 for VSE application server. Access to objects managed by DB2 for VSE is controlled through a set of privileges, which are granted to users by the DB2 for VSE system administrator or the owner of the particular object. The DB2 for VSE application server controls two classes of objects:

- **Packages:** Individual end users are authorized to create, replace, and run packages with the DB2 for VSE GRANT statement. When an end user creates a package, that user is automatically authorized to run or replace a package. Other end users must be specifically authorized to run a package at the DB2 for VSE application server with the GRANT EXECUTE statement: The RUN privilege can be granted to individual end users or to PUBLIC, which allows all end users to run the package.

When an application is preprocessed on DB2 for VSE, the package contains the SQL statements contained in the application program. These SQL statements are classified as:

Static SQL: This means the SQL statement and the SQL objects referenced by the statement are known at the time the application is preprocessed. The creator of the package must have authority to execute each of the static SQL statements in the package.

When an end user is granted the privilege to execute a package, that user automatically has the authority to execute each of the static SQL statements contained in the package. Thus, end users do not need any DB2 for VSE table privileges if the package contains only static SQL statements.

Dynamic SQL: Describes an SQL statement that is not known until the package is run. The SQL statement is built by the program and dynamically preprocessed to DB2 for VSE with the SQL PREPARE statement or the EXECUTE IMMEDIATE statement. When an end user runs a dynamic SQL statement, the user must have the table privileges required to execute the SQL statement. Because the SQL statement is not known when the package is created, the end user is not automatically given the required authority by the package owner.

- **SQL objects:** These can be tables, views, and synonyms. DB2 for VSE users can be granted various levels of authority to create, delete, change, or read individual SQL objects. This authority is required to preprocess static SQL statements or execute dynamic SQL statements.

Represent Data

See "Represent Data" on page 77.

Checklist for Enabling a DB2 for VSE DRDA Application Server

The following checklist summarizes the steps needed to enable a DRDA application server, starting with the assumption that your VSE system is installed with ACF/VTAM as its teleprocessing access method, and that VTAM definitions needed to communicate with the remote systems, such as NCP definitions are completed.

1. Define CICS to ACF/VTAM.

2. Assemble the VTAM LOGMODE table with the IBMRDB entry.

3. Assemble the CICS sign-on table with all remote user IDs and passwords defined.

4. Start CICS with the right SIT information:

   - ISC=YES

   - TST=YES, ARIAXELG defined as RECOVERABLE in the DFHTST and assembled

   - APPLID=LU name (as defined in the VTAM APPL statement)

5. Define the remote systems to CICS (RDO can be used):

   - CEDA DEF CONNECTION
   - CEDA DEF SESSION

     These statements should have all definitions under one group, for example, named IBMG. Install the group with: CEDA INSTALL GROUP(IBMG).

6. Update the DBNAME directory (ARISDIRD.A):

   - Define all TPNs listed in the directory to CICS. TPNs not defined to CICS are not usable.
   - Define each DB2 for VSE DRDA application server in the directory with a valid TPN.

7. Run procedure ARISBDID to assemble the updated DBNAME directory.

8. Prepare the DB2 for VSE server:

   - Run procedure ARIS342D to install the DRDA support.
   - If online DB2 for VSE applications (for example, ISQL) are run from the CICS partition, grant schedule authority to the CICS APPLID specified in the CICS SIT table.
   - Grant authority to all remote users.

9. Start DB2 for VSE with the correct RMTUSERS parameter and, optionally, the DBNAME parameter.

10. Prepare applications on the VSE DRDA application server.

Chapter 4. Connecting DB2 for OS/400 in a DRDA Network

OS/400 contains the IBM relational database management system for AS/400[*] systems. OS/400 Version 2 Release 1 Modification 1 is the first release of OS/400 to share distributed relational data with other database management systems supporting the DRDA protocols.

The following sections explain how to connect an AS/400 system to a distributed relational database. The emphasis in this chapter is on connecting an AS/400 system to unlike DRDA systems. For information on connecting two AS/400 systems, see *AS/400 Distributed Database Programming*.

Use Table 5 to find other information in this manual to help you with the specific type of connection you are interested in.

Table 5. Where to Find Additional Information on OS/400 Connections

Type of Connection	Also Read
DB2 for OS/400 and DB2 for MVS/ESA	Chapter 2, "Connecting DB2 for MVS/ESA in a DRDA Network" on page 15
	Chapter 9, "DB2 for OS/400 and DB2 for MVS/ESA via SDLC" on page 160
DB2 for OS/400 and DB2 for VM and VSE	Chapter 3, "Connecting DB2 for VM and VSE in a DRDA Network" on page 49
	Chapter 10, "DB2 for OS/400 and DB2 for VM via Token Ring and NCP" on page 165
DB2 for OS/400 and DB2 for OS/2	Chapter 13, "DB2 for OS/2 and DB2 for OS/400 via Token Ring" on page 194
	Chapter 17, "DB2 for OS/2 and Multiple Hosts" on page 272
	Chapter 19, "DB2 for OS/2 and Other DRDA Servers" on page 304
DB2 for OS/400 and DB2 for AIX	Chapter 11, "DB2 for AIX and DB2 for MVS/ESA, DB2 for VM and VSE, or DB2 for OS/400 via Token Ring" on page 173
	Chapter 20, "Configuring DDCS for AIX" on page 330
DB2 for OS/400 and DB2 for OS/2	Chapter 13, "DB2 for OS/2 and DB2 for OS/400 via Token Ring" on page 194
	Chapter 17, "DB2 for OS/2 and Multiple Hosts" on page 272
	Chapter 19, "DB2 for OS/2 and Other DRDA Servers" on page 304

---

[*] Trademark of IBM Corporation

DB2 for OS/400 Implementation

This chapter describes how the AS/400 system provides support for distributed database systems. The OS/400 Version 2 Release 1 Modification 1 licensed program supports DRDA remote unit of work. This support is part of the OS/400 operating system. This means you do not need the SQL/400[*] licensed program to use the DRDA support or to run programs with imbedded SQL/400 statements.

Setting Up the Application Requester

The AS/400 system implements the DRDA application requester support as an integral part of the OS/400 operating system. Because application requester support is part of the OS/400 operating system, it is active whenever the operating system is active. This is also true of the AS/400 database manager.

When the AS/400 system acts as an application requester, it can connect to any application server that supports DRDA. For the AS/400 application requester to provide distributed database access, you need to consider the following:

> Providing network information
> Providing security
> Representing Data

Provide Network Information

The Application Requester must be able to accept a relational database name and translate it into an SNA NETID.LUNAME value. The AS/400 system uses the relational database directory to register relational database names and their corresponding network parameters. This directory allows the AS/400 application requester to pass the required SNA information to establish communications in a distributed database network.

Much of the processing in a distributed database environment requires messages to be exchanged with other locations in the network. For this processing to be performed correctly, you need to do the following:

> Define the local system
> Define the remote system
> Define communications
> Set request and response unit size and pacing

Defining the Local System

In a distributed database environment, the OS/400 program uses the relational database directory to register relational database names on the network and associate them with their corresponding network parameters. The relational database directory allows an application requester to accept a relational database name from the

---

[*] Trademark of IBM Corporation

application and translate this name into the appropriate SNA NETID.LUNAME values for communications processing.

Each application requester in the distributed database network must have an entry in its Relational Database Directory for its local relational database and one for each remote relational database the application requester accesses. Any AS/400 system in the distributed database network that acts only as an application server must have an entry in its relational database directory for the local relational database only. For more information about the relational database directory, see *AS/400 Distributed Database Programming*.

The two steps to defining an application requester to the network are:

1. Create the appropriate line, controller, device, and mode descriptions so the AS/400 system can identify itself and the remote systems in the network. This is discussed in "Defining Communications" on page 91.

2. Name the local database by adding an entry with a remote location name of *LOCAL to the relational database directory. To do this, use the Add Relational Database Directory Entry (ADDRDBDIRE) command. The following example shows the ADDRDBDIRE command, where the name of the application requester's database is ROCHESTERDB:

```
ADDRDBDIRE RDB(ROCHESTERDB) RMTLOCNAME(*LOCAL)
```

For more detail on relational database directory commands, see the *AS/400 Distributed Database Programming* book.

Defining the Remote System

The two steps to defining the remote system are:

1. Create the appropriate line, controller, device, and mode descriptions so the AS/400 system can identify the remote systems and itself in the network. This is discussed in "Defining Communications" on page 91.

2. Define the remote databases to the local database by adding an entry for each remote database in the relational database directory. The information you can specify with the ADDRDBDIRE and CHGRDBDIRE commands includes:

   - Remote database name
   - Remote location name of the database
   - Local location name
   - Mode name used to establish the communications
   - Remote network identifier
   - Name of the device used for the communications
   - Transaction program name of the remote database

   For most cases, the only information needed is the remote database name and the remote location name[6] of the database. When only the remote location name is

---

6 "Location name" in OS/400 is synonymous with "LU name" in DB2 for MVS/ESA. "Remote location name" means "partner or remote LU name."

specified, default values are used for the remaining parameters. The system selects a device description using the remote location name.

If more than one device description contains the same remote location name and a specific device description is required, then the values for local location name and remote network identifier in the relational database directory entry should match the values in the device description. The selection of device descriptions can be complicated if the same remote location name is used in more than one device description. Use unique remote location names in each device description to avoid confusion. The transaction program name of the remote database defaults to the DRDA default transaction program name of X'07F6C4C2'.

The communications information in the relational database is used to establish a conversation with the remote system.

Defining Communications

This section describes configuring communications on the AS/400 system using Advanced Program-to-Program Networking* (APPN*). The AS/400 system also allows advanced program-to-program communications (APPC) configurations, which do not provide network routing support. An AS/400 distributed database works with either configuration. For more information about APPC configurations, see *OS/400 Communications Configuration*.

AnyNet Support on the AS/400 allows APPC applications to run over Transmission Control Protocol/Internet Protocol (TCP/IP) networks. Examples in the sections that follow include DDM, Systems Network Architecture Distribution Services, Alerts, and 5250 Display Station Pass-Through. These applications, along with DRDA, can run unchanged over TCP/IP networks with some additional configuration. To specify AnyNet support, you specify *ANYNW on the LINKTYPE parameter of the CRTCTLAPPC command.

For more information on APPC over TCP/IP, refer to *OS/400 Communications Configuration* and *OS/400 TCP/IP Configuration and Reference*.

APPN provides networking support that allows the AS/400 system to participate in and control a network of systems without requiring the networking support traditionally provided by a mainframe system. The following steps tell how to configure an AS/400 system for APPN support.

1. Define the network attributes using the Change Network Attributes (CHGNETA) command.

   The network attributes contain:

   - The local system name
   - The name of the system in the APPN network
   - The local network identifier
   - The network node type

---

* Trademark of IBM Corporation

- The names of the network servers used by the AS/400 system, if the machine is an end node
- The network control points, if the AS/400 is an end node

2. Create the line description.

   The line description describes the physical line connection and the data link protocol to be used between the AS/400 system and the network. Use the following commands to create line descriptions:

   - Create line description (Ethernet) (CRTLINETH)
   - Create line description (SDLC) (CRTLINSDLC)
   - Create line description (token ring) (CRTLINTRN)
   - Create line description (X.25) (CRTLINX25)

3. Create controller descriptions.

   The controller description describes the adjacent systems in the network. Indicate the use of APPN support by specifying APPN(*YES) when creating the controller description. Use the following commands to create controller descriptions:

   - Create controller description (APPC) (CRTCTLAPPC)
   - Create controller description (SNA HOST) (CRTCTLHOST)

   If the AUTOCRTCTL parameter on a token-ring or Ethernet line description is set to *YES, then a controller description is automatically created when the system receives a session start request over the token-ring or Ethernet line.

4. Create a class-of-service description.

   Use class-of-service description to select the communication routes (transmission groups) and give transmission priority. Five class-of-service descriptions are supplied by the system:

#CONNECT	The default class of service.
#BATCH	A class of service for batch jobs.
#BATCHSC	The same as #BATCH except a data link security of at least a packet-switched network is required. In packet-switched networks, data does not always follow the same path through the network.
#INTER	A class of service tailored for interactive communications.
#INTERSC	The same as #INTER except a data link security of at least a packet-switched network is required.

   Create other class-of-service descriptions using the Create Class-of-Service (CRTCOSD) command.

5. Create a mode description.

   The mode description gives the session characteristics and number of sessions that can be used to negotiate the allowed values between the local and remote location. The mode description also points to the class of service that is used for the conversation. Five predefined modes are shipped with the system:

BLANK	The default mode name specified in the network attributes when the system is shipped.
#BATCH	A mode tailored for batch jobs.
#BATCHSC	The same as #BATCH except the associated class-of-service description requires a data link security of at least a packet-switched network.
#INTER	A mode tailored for interactive communications.
#INTERSC	The same as #INTER except the associated class-of-service description requires a data link security of at least a packet-switched network.

Other mode descriptions can be created using the Create Mode Description (CRTMODD) command.

6. Create device descriptions.

   The device description provides the characteristics of the logical connection between the local and remote systems. You do not have to manually create device descriptions if the AS/400 system is running to a host system with APPN and as an independent logical unit (LU). The AS/400 system automatically creates the device description and attaches it to the appropriate controller description when the session is established. If the AS/400 system is a dependent LU, then you must manually create the device descriptions using the Create Device Description (CRTDEVAPPC) command. In the device description, specify APPN(*YES) to indicate that the APPN is being used.

7. Create APPN location lists.

   If additional local locations (called *LUs* on other systems) or special characteristics of remote locations for APPN are required, then you need to create APPN location lists. The local location name is the control point name specified in the network attributes. If you need additional locations for the AS/400 system, an APPN local location list is required. An example of a special characteristic of a remote location is if the remote location is in a network other than the one the local location is in. If the conditions exist, an APPN remote location list is required. Create APPN location lists by using the Create Configuration List (CRTCFGL) command.

8. Activate (vary on) communications.

   You can activate the communication descriptions by using the Vary Configuration (VRYCFG) command or the Work With Configuration Status (WRKCFGSTS) command. If the line descriptions are activated, then the appropriate controllers and devices attached to that line are also activated. The WRKCFGSTS command is also useful for viewing the status of each connection.

Notes:

1. The controller description is equivalent to the IBM Network Control Program and Virtual Telecommunications Access Method (NCP/VTAM) physical unit (PU) macros.

2. The device description is equivalent to the NCP/VTAM logical unit (LU) macro. The device description contains information similar to that stored in the Communications Manager/2 1.1 partner LU profile.

3. The mode description is equivalent to the NCP/VTAM mode tables and the Communications Manager Transmission Service Mode profile.

For more information about configuring for networking support and working with location lists, see the *OS/400 Communications Configuration* and *APPN Support*. For examples showing use of CL commands to define system configurations, see *AS/400 Distributed Database Programming*.

Setting RU Size and Pacing

RU sizes and pacing are controlled by values specified in the mode description. When you create the mode description, defaults are provided for both RU size and pacing. The default values are an AS/400 estimate for most environments including a distributed database. If the default is taken for RU size, the AS/400 system estimates the best value to use. When the AS/400 system is communicating with another system that supports adaptive pacing, the pacing values specified are only a starting point. The pacing is adjusted by each system depending on the system's ability to handle the data sent to it. For systems that do not support adaptive pacing, the pacing values are negotiated at session start, and remain the same for the life of the session. For more information, see *OS/400 Communications Configuration*.

Provide Security

When a remote system performs distributed database processing on behalf of an SQL application, it must be able to satisfy the security requirements of the application requester, the application server, and the network connecting them. These requirements fall into one or more of the categories that follow:

Selection of end user names
Network security parameters
Database manager security
Security enforced by AS/400 security

Selecting End User Names

On AS/400 systems, end users are assigned a 1- to 10-character user ID that is unique to that system, but not necessarily unique within the network. This user ID is the one passed to the remote system when the connection is being established between two databases. To avoid conflicts between user IDs on systems in the network, outbound name translation is often used to change the user ID to resolve the conflict before it is sent over the network. However, the AS/400 system does not provide any outbound name translation to resolve potential conflicts at the server. These conflicts must be resolved at the application server, unless you use the additional USER or USING clauses

on the AS/400 SQL CONNECT statement. USER is a valid ID on the application
server, and USING is the corresponding password for the user.

Network Security
After the application requester selects the end user names to represent the remote
application, it must provide the required LU 6.2 network security information. LU 6.2
provides three major network security features:

- Session-level security, controlled by the LOCPWD keyword on the CRTDEVAPPC
  command
- Conversation-level security, controlled by the OS/400 operating system
- Encryption, not supported by the OS/400 operating system

Session-level security is provided through LU-to-LU verification. Each LU has a key
that must match the key at the remote LU. You specify the key on the LOCPWD
keyword on the CRTDEVAPPC command.

Because the application server is responsible for managing the database resources, the
application server dictates which network security features are required of the
application requester. The AS/400 security administrator must verify the security
requirements of each application server so they require no more than the AS/400
application requester supports.

The following are possible SNA conversation security options:

SECURITY=SAME
> Also known as already-verified security. Only the user ID of an application
> user is sent to the remote system. No password is sent. Before the
> AS/400 Version 2 Release 2 Modification 0, this level of conversation
> security was the only level supported by an AS/400 application requester.

SECURITY=PGM
> Causes both the user ID and the password of the application user to be
> sent to the remote system for validation. Before the AS/400 Version 2
> Release 2 Modification 0, this security option was not supported by an
> AS/400 application requester.

SECURITY=NONE
> Not supported when AS/400 is an application requester.

Database Manager Security
The AS/400 system does not have an external security subsystem. All security is
handled through the OS/400 operating system as discussed in the following section,
"System Security."

System Security
The OS/400 operating system controls authorization to all objects on the system,
including programs, packages, tables, views, and collections.

The application requester controls authorization to objects that reside on the application requester. The security for objects on the application server is controlled at the application server, on the basis of which user ID is sent from the application requester. The user ID sent to the application server is associated with the user of the AS/400 application requester or the user ID given in the USER clause of the AS/400 SQL CONNECT statement. For example, CONNECT TO rdbname USER userid USING password.

Security of objects can be managed using the object authority CL commands or with the SQL statements GRANT and REVOKE. The object CL authority commands include Grant Object Authority (GRTOBJAUT) and Revoke Object Authority (RVKOBJAUT). These commands work on any object on the system. The statements GRANT and REVOKE only work on SQL objects: tables, views, and packages. If you need to change authorization for other objects such as programs or collections, use the GRTOBJAUT and RVKOBJAUT commands.

Granting and Revoking Authority: Enter the following command on an AS/400 system to grant *USE authority to user USER1 to program PGMA:

```
GRTOBJAUT OBJ(PGMA) OBJTYPE(*PGM) USER(USER1) AUT(*USE)
```

The command to revoke the same authority:

```
RVKOBJAUT OBJ(PGMA) OBJTYPE(*PGM) USER(USER1) AUT(*USE)
```

*PGM identifies the object type in this example as a program. *SQLPKG is used to operate on a package, *LIB is used for a collection, and *FILE is used for a table.

GRTOBJAUT and RVKOBJAUT can also be used to prevent users from creating programs and packages. When authority is revoked from any of the CRTSQLxxx commands (where xxx = RPG, C, CBL, FTN, or PLI) used to create programs, a user is not able to create programs. If authority is revoked to the CRTSQLPKG command, the user is not able to create packages from the application requester or on the application server.

For example, enter the following command on an AS/400 system to grant *USE authority to user USER1 to the CRTSQLPKG command:

```
GRTOBJAUT OBJ(CRTSQLPKG) OBJTYPE(*CMD) USER(USER1) AUT(*USE)
```

This affects the execution of crtsqlpkg on the application requester. On the application server, this command allows the creation of packages.

The command to revoke the same authority is:

```
RVKOBJAUT OBJ(CRTSQLPKG) OBJTYPE(*CMD) USER(USER1) AUT(*USE)
```

Applying Default Authorization: When objects are created, they are given a default authorization. By default, the creator of a table, view, or program is given all authority on those objects. Also by default, the public is given the same authority on those objects as they (the public) have on the objects' library or collection.

For more information on system security see *AS/400 Security - Reference*.

Represent Data

Products supporting DRDA automatically perform any necessary conversions at the receiving system. For this to happen the application requester CCSID value must be a supported value for conversion by the receiving system.

The tables in Appendix C, "CCSID Values" on page 448 describe the CCSIDs and conversions provided by the IBM database products. The shipped default CCSID value for the OS/400 is 65535, also referred to X'FFFF'. This default value is not compatible with the other IBM products. The *AS/400 National Language Support* book explains the OS/400 system CCSID support in detail.

On an application requester, you should be concerned with the CCSID associated with:

- Requesting Job

  OS/400 work management support initializes the job CCSID to the CCSID on the user profile. If a CCSID does not exist on the user profile, work management support gets the CCSID (QCCSID) from the system value. The system value QCCSID is initially set to CCSID 65535.

  The job CCSID can be changed by using the Change Job (CHGJOB) command. Or for subsequent jobs use the Change User Profile (CHGUSRPRF) command to change the CCSID value of the user profile. In a CL program, use the Retrieve Job Attributes (RTVJOBA) command to get the current job CCSID. Interactively, use the Work with Job (WRKJOB) command and select option 2, Display Job Definition Attributes on the Work with Job display.

- Database Source Files

  Database source files default to the job CCSID at file creation if a CCSID is not explicitly specified on the Create Physical File (CRTPF) or Create Source Physical File (CRTSRCPF) command.

  You can use the Display File Description (DSPFD) command to view the CCSID of a file or the Display File Field Description (DSPFFD) command to view the CCSID of the fields of a file.

  Use the Change Physical File (CHGPF) command to change the CCSID of a physical file. A physical file cannot always be changed if one or more of the following conditions exist:

  - Logical files are defined over the physical file. In this case you must do the following:

    1. Save the logical and physical files along with their access paths.
    2. Print a list of authorities for logical files (DSPOBJAUT).
    3. Delete the logical files.
    4. Change the physical files.
    5. Restore the physical and logical files and their access paths over the changed physical files.
    6. Grant private authority to the logical files (see the list that you printed).

  - Files or fields are explicitly assigned a CCSID value. To change a physical file with the CCSID assigned at the field level, recreate the physical file and copy

the data to the new file using the FMTOPT(*MAP) parameter on the Copy File
(CPYF) command.

– Record formats are being shared.

Setting Up the Application Server

The application server support on the AS/400 system allows it to act as a server for
DRDA application requesters. The application requester connected to an AS/400
application server can be one of the following:

- A DB2 for OS/400 requester
- A DB2 for MVS/ESA requester
- A DB2 for VM and VSE requester
- A DB2 for AIX requester
- A DB2 for OS/2 requester
- Any other product that supports the DRDA application requester protocols

The application requester is permitted to access tables stored locally at the AS/400
application server. The application requester must create a package at the AS/400
application server before any SQL statements can be run. The AS/400 application
server uses the package containing the application's SQL statements at program run
time.

Provide Network Information

To process distributed database requests on the AS/400 application server, you need
to:

> Define the application server system
> Name the application server database
> Set request and response unit sizes and pacing

Defining the Application Server

Defining the application server to the network is identical to defining the application
requester to the network. You need to create line, controller, device, and mode
descriptions to define both the application server and the application requester that
sends the requests. For information on how to define the application server to the
network, see "Defining the Local System" on page 89 and "Defining the Remote
System" on page 90. See also *AS/400 Distributed Database Programming*.

The transaction program name used to start an AS/400 application server database is
the DRDA default X'07F6C4C2'. This transaction program name is defined within the
AS/400 system to start the application server.

Naming the Application Server Database

You name the application server database (at the application server location) in the
same way that you identify the application requester database (at the application
requester location). Use the Add Relational Database Directory Entry (ADDRDBDIRE)
command, and specify *LOCAL as the remote location.

Setting RU Sizes and Pacing

Network definitions must be reviewed to determine if the distributed database network impacts the existing network. These considerations are the same for the application server and the application requester. See "Setting RU Size and Pacing" on page 94 for more information.

Provide Security

When an application requester routes a distributed database request to the AS/400 application server, the following security considerations can be involved:

Selection of end user names
Network security parameters
Database manager security
AS/400 security

Selecting End User Names

The application requester sends a user ID to the application server for security processing. The job running on the AS/400 application server uses this user ID.

The AS/400 application server does not provide inbound user ID translation to resolve conflicts among user IDs that are not unique or group multiple users under a single user ID. Each user ID sent from an Application Requester must exist on the application server. A method to group incoming requests into a single user ID, with loss of some security, is to specify a default user ID in a communications entry in the subsystem that is handling the remote job start requests. See the descriptions of addcmne and chgcmne in the *AS/400 CL Reference*.

Network Security

LU 6.2 provides three major network security features:

- Session-level security
- Conversation-level security
- Encryption (not supported by the AS/400 system)

The AS/400 application server uses session-level security in exactly the same manner as the AS/400 application requester.

The application server controls the SNA conversation levels used for the conversation. The SECURELOC parameter on the APPC device description or the secure location value on the APPN remote location list determines what is accepted from the application requester for the conversation.

The possible SNA conversation security options are:

SECURITY=SAME
Also known as already-verified security. Only the user ID of the application user is required by the application server. No password is sent. Use this level of conversation security at the application server by setting the

SECURELOC parameter on the APPC device description to *YES or by setting the secure location value on the APPN remote location list to *YES.

SECURITY=PGM

Causes both the user ID and password to be required by the application server for validation. Use this level of conversation security at the application server by setting the default user ID in the AS/400 subsystem communications entry to *NONE (no default user ID) and by setting the SECURELOC parameter or the secure location value to *NO.

SECURITY=NONE

An application server does not expect a user ID or password. The conversation is allowed using a default user profile on the application server. To use this option, specify a default user profile in the subsystem communications directory and specify *NO for the SECURELOC parameter or the secure location value.

SNADS requires a default user ID, so SNADS should have its own subsystem for the normal case where you don't want a default user id for DRDA applications.

A method for grouping incoming start job requests into a single user ID was mentioned in "Selecting End User Names" on page 99. This method does not verify the user ID sent from the Application Requester. The application server job is started under a default user ID, and the user who initiated the connection from the application server has access at the application server even if the user ID sent has restricted authorization. This is done by defining the application server as a nonsecure location, specifying a default user ID in the AS/400 subsystem communications entry, and configuring the application requester to send a user ID only during connection processing. If a password is sent, the user ID that accompanies it is used instead of the default user ID.

The AS/400 subsystem communications entries are distinguished by the device and mode name used to start the conversation. By assigning different default user IDs to different device/mode pairs, users can be grouped by how they are communicating with the application server.

The AS/400 system also offers a network security feature that is used only for distributed database and distributed file management. A network attribute for these types of system access exists that either rejects all attempts to access or allows the security to be controlled by the system on an object-by-object basis.

Database Manager Security

All security is handled through the OS/400 security function.

System Security

The AS/400 system does not have an external security subsystem. All security is handled by the OS/400 security function that is an integral part of the operating system. The operating system controls authorization to all objects on the system, including programs, packages, tables, views, and collections.

The application server controls authorizations to the objects that reside on the application server. The security control for those objects is based on which user ID starts the application server job. This user ID is determined as described in "Selecting End User Names" on page 99.

Security of objects can be managed through the use of the object authority CL commands or through the SQL statements GRANT and REVOKE. The object authority CL commands include Grant Object Authority (GRTOBJAUT) and Revoke Object Authority (RVKOBJAUT). Use these CL commands for any object on the system. Use the statements GRANT and REVOKE only for SQL objects: tables, views, and packages. If authorization needs to be changed to other objects, such as programs or collections, use the GRTOBJAUT and RVKOBJAUT commands.

When objects are created on the system, they are given a default authorization. The user ID that creates tables, views, and packages is given all authority. All other user IDs (the public) are given the same authority they have to the collection or library in which the object is created.

Authority to objects referenced by static or dynamic statements within the package are checked at package run time. If the creator of the package does not have authority to the referenced objects, warning messages are returned when the package is created. At execution time, the user executing the package adopts the authority of the creator of the package. If the creator of the package is authorized to a table, but the user running the package is not authorized, the user adopts the authority of the package creator and is allowed to use the table.

For more information on system security see *AS/400 Security - Reference*.

Represent Data

Products supporting DRDA automatically perform any necessary conversions at the application server. For this to happen the application server CCSID value must be a supported value for conversion by the application requester.

The tables in Appendix C, "CCSID Values" on page 448 describe the CCSIDs and conversions provided by the IBM database products. The shipped default CCSID value for the OS/400 is 65535, also referred to as X'FFFF'. This default value is not compatible with the other IBM products. The system CCSID can be displayed by the CL command DSPSYSVAL QCCSID. It can be changed by the CHGSYSVAL command. For example, CHGSYSVAL QCCSID VALUE(37). The system CCSID can also be overridden by the CCSID associated with the DRDA server job. This CCSID can be set by use of the CHGUSRPRF CL command. For example, CHGUSRPRF MYUSERID CCSID(37). *AS/400 National Language Support* explains the OS/400 system CCSID support in detail.

On an application server you should be concerned with the CCSID associated with:

- Servicing job in the communication subsystem

  The CCSID of your servicing job must be compatible with the application requester. This CCSID is established by the user profile of the user ID requesting the connection. OS/400 work management support initializes the job CCSID to the CCSID on the user profile. If a CCSID does not exist on the user profile, work management support gets the CCSID (QCCSID) from the system value. The system value QCCSID is initially set to CCSID 65535.

Before initiating a request to the OS/400, you should sign on and use the Change User Profile (CHGUSRPRF) to assign an acceptable CCSID value.

- SQL collections

   An SQL collection consists of an OS/400 library object, a journal, a journal receiver, and optionally, an IDDU data dictionary if the WITH DATA DICTIONARY clause is specified on the CREATE COLLECTION statement. The physical and logical files used for some of these objects default to the job CCSID at the time of creation. If you query the data dictionary or the catalog from an application requester that does not support the CCSID value of these files, you might see non displayable or distorted data. Or the application requester might issue a message saying the CCSID value is not supported. To correct this you need to create a new SQL collection with a job CCSID value that is acceptable to the other system.

   The job CCSID can be changed by using the Change Job (CHGJOB) command. Or for subsequent jobs, use the Change User Profile (CHGUSRPRF) command to change the CCSID value of the user profile. In a CL program, use the Retrieve Job Attributes (RTVJOBA) command to get the current job CCSID. Interactively, use the Work with Job (WRKJOB) command and select option 2, Display Job Definition Attributes on the Work with Job display.

- SQL tables and other OS/400 files accessed via DRDA

   An SQL table corresponds to an OS/400 physical file within a library of the same name as your collection. The columns of a table also correspond to the field definitions of a physical file. The CCSID values for the table or columns of the table might not be compatible with the application requester. To change this value refer to "Represent Data" on page 97, which describes changing database source files. A major source of CCSID incompatibility in versions of OS/400 prior to Version 3 Release 1 was that many files or SQL tables were tagged with the CCSID 65535 by default. In Version 3 Release 1, the CCSID of these files will be changed automatically to some other more appropriate value.

Chapter 5. Connecting DB2 for OS/2 or AIX in a DRDA Network

This chapter describes how the IBM DB2 products for OS/2, AIX, and other UNIX-based systems implement DRDA.

Table 6. Where to Find Additional Information on DB2 for AIX Connections

Type of Connection	Also Read
DB2 for OS/2 or AIX and DB2 for MVS	Chapter 2, "Connecting DB2 for MVS/ESA in a DRDA Network" on page 15
DB2 for OS/2 or AIX and DB2 for VSE or VM (SQL/DS)	Chapter 3, "Connecting DB2 for VM and VSE in a DRDA Network" on page 49
DB2 for OS/2 or AIX and DB2 for OS/400	Chapter 4, "Connecting DB2 for OS/400 in a DRDA Network" on page 88

Product Family Overview

IBM relational database management system products are available on many different operating systems, including MVS, VM, VSE, OS/400, OS/2, AIX, HP-UX, Solaris, and others. All of these products are called DATABASE 2 (DB2), collectively known as the DB2 family.

This section describes all the DB2 and related products available for the Intel[**] (OS/2, DOS, and Windows) and UNIX-based platforms (AIX, HP-UX, and Solaris). These products are collectively known as *the common server versions of DB2*. This is to distinguish that these products run on similar platforms and share the same code-base. Each of these platforms consists of a set of products and components that includes the following:

- DB2 (the relational database engine)
- Distributed Database Connection Services (for use in accessing DRDA application servers)
- Administrator's Kits (for use at the client or server workstation to administer databases)
- Client Application Enablers (for use at the client workstation)
- Software Developer's Kits (for use at the client or server workstation to create applications).

The following diagram shows the conceptual relationship between these products. Information on the valid configurations and environments is discussed later in this document. For availability or to order any of the common server products contact an

---

[**] Trademark of Intel Corporation

[**] Trademark of Microsoft Corporation

[**] Trademark of Novell, Inc.

IBM representative at a local branch office; or, contact any authorized IBM software remarketer; or, contact IBM directly by phoning one of the following numbers:

- 1-800-IBM-CALL or 1-800-3IBM-OS2 in the United States.
- 1-800-465-7999 extension 850 in Canada.

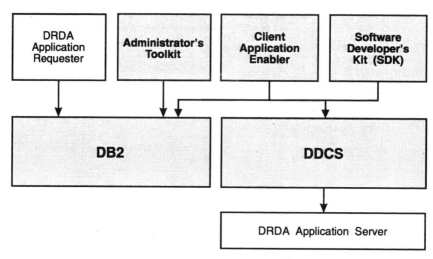

Figure 28. DB2 Product Components

Each of these components is described below.

Component	Features
DB2 (base functions)	The following are the basic functions of DB2:

- Provides a full-function relational database management system
- Provides a cost-based optimizer which supports extremely complex queries
- Ensures data integrity through declarative referential integrity, forward recovery, and multi-level concurrency control
- Provides a command line processor for interactive entry of commands and SQL statements
- Provides flexible management of very large databases
- Supports the creation of multi-media, object oriented, and bill-of-material applications through the support of user-defined functions (UDFs), user-defined types (UDTs), triggers, constraints, large objects (LOBs) and recursive SQL
- Installs on a wide range of computers, from small desktop systems to high-end servers
- Includes a base set of graphical user interface tools to manage databases, including configuration, backup and recovery, directory management, and media management
- Acts as a client to other remote RDBMSs as described in the Client Application Enabler section
- Provides the capability for an application to read or update tables in more than one database from within a single unit of work with full data integrity. This capability is provided through Distributed Unit of Work (DUOW) functionality, also known as 2-phase commit.

Component	Features
DB2 Single-User	The single-user version of DB2 contains all of the base functions described above, plus the following additions: • Provides an application development environment as described in the DB2 SDK section • Provides a database administrator's environment as described in the DB2 Administrator's Toolkit section (excluding DB2 Visual Explain) • Provides DB2 Visual Explain to graphically view and navigate complex access plans.
DB2 Server	The server version of the product contains all of the base functions described above, plus the following additions: • Allows the RDBMS to accept requests from DB2 clients on local and wide area networks. Supports remote clients using DRDA, Client Application Enabler or any other product that supports DRDA application requester function • Provides support for popular communication protocols • Provides a client/server database that supports clients that do not require knowledge of the physical location of the database. These clients may be DOS, Windows, OS/2, and UNIX-based, as well as DRDA application requesters such as MVS, VM, and OS/400. • Supports stored procedures that reduce network traffic between clients and servers • Exploits Distributed Computing Environment (DCE) Directory Services for simplified management of network addressing information
Client Application Enabler	• Provides run-time support to allow applications to access remote database servers. Available for popular platforms such as OS/2, DOS, Windows, and several UNIX-based operating systems • Provides support for popular communication protocols • Allows applications to access any supported database server, including DRDA application servers such as DB2 for MVS, DB2 for VSE and VM, and DB2 for OS/400, through the DDCS products • Provides a command line processor for interactive entry of a subset of DB2 commands • Allows commercially available applications that support DB2 programming interfaces to access DB2 databases. In addition, a Windows client provides a Microsoft[**] Open Database Connectivity (ODBC) driver that allows applications that support the ODBC specification to access IBM DB2 family databases • Administration of multiple remote DB2 clients is simplified through the support of DCE Directory Services.

Software Developer's Kit (SDK)	• Designed to meet the needs of database application developers
	• A collection of tools that help create database applications, including:
	  – Precompilers, programming libraries, header files, code samples, and a complete set of documentation for developing applications with embedded SQL
	  – Programming libraries, header files, code samples, and a complete set of documentation for developing applications using the DB2 Call Level Interface (DB2 CLI)
	  – APIs to administer databases on supported servers
	  – Support for application development in several programming languages
	  – An API for implementing precompiler support for compilers not specifically supported by the DB2 SDK products
	  – Command line processor for interactive entry of SQL statements
	  – Command line processor for interactive and batch entry of DB2 commands
	  – Client Application Enabler to provide client function.

Component	Features

Administrator's Kit	• Designed to meet the needs of database administrators (DBAs)
	• A collection of tools that helps manage and administer the database, including:
	  – A graphical DBA Utility for configuration, backup and recovery, directory management, and media management
	  – Client Application Enabler to provide client function
	  – Command line processor for interactive entry of commands and SQL statements
	  – DB2 Visual Explain to graphically view and navigate complex access plans
	  – DB2 Visual Explain to monitor the performance of your DB2 system for tuning purposes.

Distributed Database Connection Services (DDCS) Single-User	• Provides local applications transparent read and update access to enterprise data stored in DRDA application servers, such as
	  – DATABASE 2 for MVS (DB2 for MVS)
	  – DATABASE 2 for VSE and VM (DB2 for VSE and VM formerly SQL/DS)
	  – DATABASE 2 for OS/400 (DB2 for OS/400).
	• Supports DRDA stored procedures that reduce network traffic between clients and servers.

DDCS Multi-User Gateway	The multi-user gateway version of DDCS provides the following functions in addition to those listed above: • Provides OS/2, DOS, Windows, and UNIX-based clients with transparent read and update access to enterprise data stored in DRDA application servers • Provides support for popular communication protocols • Exploits DCE Directory Services for simplified management of network addressing information

Application Server in DB2 for Common Servers

The DB2 Common Server products can act as DRDA application servers. If you want the application server function, you must configure the workstation containing the database for APPC.

Note: DRDA AS is currently on DB2 for AIX and on DB2 for OS/2.

DRDA Application Server Feature

The DATABASE 2 (DB2) Distributed Relational Database Architecture (DRDA) Application Server (AS) feature enables DB2 to function as a database server for Application Requesters using the DRDA protocol in addition to other clients that use DB2 private protocols; it provides support for DRDA level 1. With the AS feature installed, applications using DRDA Application Requesters (DRDA AR) can create packages at the DB2 server and subsequently execute them subject to the SQL supported at the server.

DRDA Application Requesters Supported

The following IBM Application Requesters are supported,

• DB2 for MVS Version 2.3 AR (PTF UN54600 and PTF UN75958 applied).

• DB2 for MVS Version 3.1 AR (PTF UN75959 applied).

- DDCS Version 2.3

- DB2 for VM (DB2 for VM and VSE) Version 3.3 AR (with PTF UN47865 applied).

- DB2 for VM (DB2 for VM and VSE) Version 3.4 AR.

For information about other ARs, contact your supplier.

For information on configurating as a DRDA Application Server, see Chapter 21, "Configuring DB2 for OS/2 as a DRDA Application Server" on page 349 or Chapter 22, "Configuring DB2 for AIX as a DRDA Application Server (DRDA AS)" on page 359.

Application Requester Support in DB2 for Common Servers

These days, many organizations use personal computers and UNIX-based workstations, but keep their most important data on mainframes or minicomputers. Connecting PC and UNIX-based applications to enterprise data has long been a problem.

IBM DDCS products are designed to address this problem. They enable DOS, Windows, OS/2, and UNIX-based applications to access data stored in relational databases on MVS, VSE, VM, and OS/400. Data stored in certain non-relational databases such as IMS can also be accessed when DDCS is used in conjunction with data replication products such as IBM Data Propagator Non-Relational.

The DB2 Common Server products do not, by themselves, act as DRDA application requesters. Instead, if you want the application requester function, you must install and configure a Distributed Database Connection Services (DDCS) product. You install the DDCS product on an OS/2 or UNIX-based workstation, called the DDCS workstation. If you install the remote client support component of DDCS, remote clients (such as DOS, Windows, OS/2, AIX, HP-UX, and Solaris) are also supported.

For information about how to configure DDCS, refer to Chapter 19, "DB2 for OS/2 and Other DRDA Servers" on page 304 and Chapter 20, "Configuring DDCS for AIX" on page 330.

You could also use DDCS to access DB2 common servers; however, this is not recommended. The Client Application Enablers provided with OS/2 and UNIX-based DB2 products are a more effective and less expensive solution.

Figure 29 on page 108 and Figure 30 on page 109 illustrate how DDCS connects to other systems.

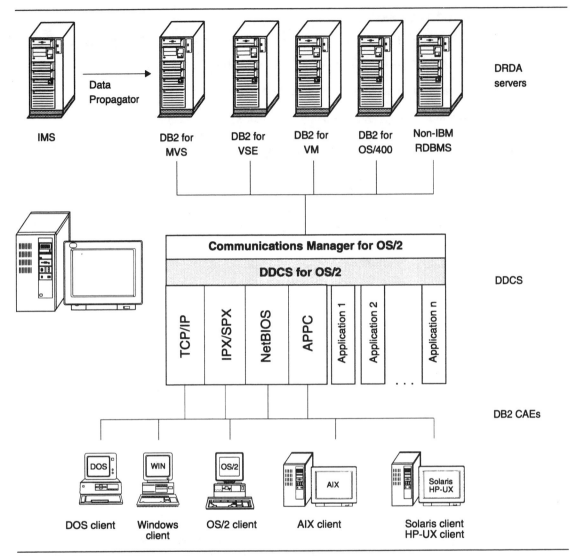

Figure 29. DDCS for OS/2 Connections

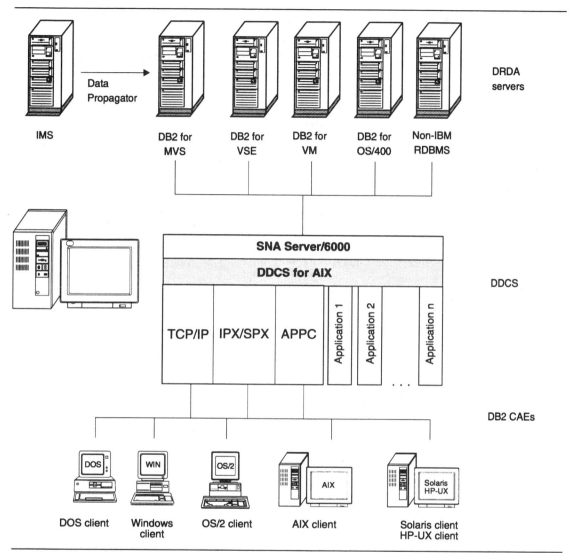

Figure 30. DDCS for AIX Connections

Notes:

1. These figures include remote clients. If you do not want remote clients, you do not need to install remote client support. In some environments, IBM may offer a single-user DDCS system which supports applications running on the DDCS workstation.

2. These figures show DOS, Windows, OS/2, AIX, Solaris, and HP-UX clients. To see if any additional clients are supported, check the announcement literature.

3. The communications protocols that are supported depend on the operating system, release of the DDCS workstation and the remote client. For more information, see "Supported Protocols."

4. You do not need to have DB2 installed on the DDCS workstation. If you want a complete relational database management system on the DDCS workstation, order DB2.

5. DDCS does not provide application development tools; however, IBM does provide DB2 Software Developer's Kits (SDKs) for DOS, Windows, OS/2 and UNIX-based platforms. You can use these SDKs to develop applications that work with DDCS. The SDKs provide programming tools, utilities, documentation, and code samples.

6. C programmers developing Windows applications that use the Microsoft ODBC interface should use the *Microsoft Open Database Connectivity Software Development Kit*. Programmers who want to develop applications using the COBOL programming language can use Micro Focus COBOL and other development tools offered by Micro Focus, Inc. and IBM. In addition, there are a variety of 4GL development environments, application generators, CASE and other tools available from a number of vendors that can be used to develop applications that use DDCS.

Supported Protocols

The following table summarizes all the possible client/server configurations.

Table 7 (Page 1 of 2). Clients, Servers, and Protocols Supported

Client Type	DB2 for OS/2 1.0	DB2 for OS/2 1.2	DB2 for OS/2 2.1	DB2 for AIX 1.1, 1.2	DB2 for AIX 2.1	DB2 for HP-UX 1.1, 1.2	DB2 for Solaris 1.2	DB2 Parallel Edition 1.1
DB2/2 OS/2 Client 1.0	APPC, NetBIOS	APPC, NetBIOS	APPC, NetBIOS	APPC	APPC	N/A	N/A	APPC
DB2/2 DOS Client 1.0	NetBIOS	NetBIOS	NetBIOS	N/A	N/A	N/A	N/A	N/A
CAE for AIX 1.1, 2.1	N/A	N/A	APPC, TCP/IP	APPC, TCP/IP	APPC, TCP/IP	TCP/IP	TCP/IP	APPC, TCP/IP
CAE for OS/2 1.1	APPC	APPC	APPC, TCP/IP	APPC, TCP/IP	APPC, TCP/IP	TCP/IP	TCP/IP	APPC, TCP/IP

Table 7 (Page 2 of 2). Clients, Servers, and Protocols Supported

Client Type	DB2 for OS/2 1.0	DB2 for OS/2 1.2	DB2 for OS/2 2.1	DB2 for AIX 1.1, 1.2	DB2 for AIX 2.1	DB2 for HP-UX 1.1, 1.2	DB2 for Solaris 1.2	DB2 Parallel Edition 1.1
CAE for OS/2 1.2, 2.1	APPC, NetBIOS	APPC, NetBIOS, IPX/SPX	APPC, NetBIOS, IPX/SPX, TCP/IP	APPC, TCP/IP	APPC, TCP/IP, IPX/SPX	TCP/IP	TCP/IP	APPC, TCP/IP
CAE for DOS 1.1	N/A	N/A	TCP/IP	TCP/IP	TCP/IP	TCP/IP	TCP/IP	TCP/IP
CAE for DOS 1.2	NetBIOS	NetBIOS, IPX/SPX	NetBIOS, IPX/SPX, TCP/IP	TCP/IP, IPX/SPX	TCP/IP, IPX/SPX	TCP/IP, IPX/SPX	TCP/IP, IPX/SPX	TCP/IP, IPX/SPX
CAE for Windows 2.1	NetBIOS	NetBIOS, IPX/SPX	NetBIOS, IPX/SPX, TCP/IP	TCP/IP, IPX/SPX	TCP/IP, IPX/SPX	TCP/IP, IPX/SPX	TCP/IP, IPX/SPX	TCP/IP, IPX/SPX
CAE for HP-UX 1.1, 1.2	N/A	N/A	APPC, TCP/IP	APPC, TCP/IP	APPC, TCP/IP	TCP/IP	TCP/IP	APPC, TCP/IP
CAE for Solaris 1.1, 1.2	N/A	N/A	TCP/IP, APPC	TCP/IP, APPC	TCP/IP, APPC	TCP/IP	TCP/IP	TCP/IP, APPC

Legend and notes:

DB2 for OS/2 Clients

DB2 for OS/2 1.0 Distributed Client Features for DOS and OS/2 were replaced by Client Application Enabler for DOS and Client Application Enabler for OS/2 respectively. Existing DOS Distributed Client Features can connect to all DB2 for OS/2 servers using the NetBIOS protocol. Existing OS/2 Distributed Client Features can connect to all DB2 for OS/2 servers using either NetBIOS or APPC, and DB2 for AIX servers using APPC.

CAE DB2 Client Application Enabler

N/A This option is not available.

NetBIOS, APPC, TCP/IP, or IPX/SPX

The protocol that is required for this case.

NOVIX is not installed on a DB2 client or server. It is installed on a Novell[**] fileserver. Clients would need IPX/SPX installed and the fileserver and DB2 server would need TCP/IP installed.

APPC If your communications environment is configured with APPN instead of APPC, the client will support it.

DDCS Security

As DDCS administrator, you can determine where user names and passwords are validated. There are four possibilities:

- Validation at the client
- Validation at the DDCS workstation
- Validation at the DRDA server
- Validation at the both the DDCS workstation and the DRDA server.

You determine where validation occurs by setting the Authentication type parameter in the system database directory and the Security type parameter in the node directory. For more information about updating these directories, see "Updating Database Directories" on page 115.

Note: If you use DCE Directory Services, authentication works differently. For more information, see "Security with DCE Directory Services" on page 123.

The following authentication types are allowed:

CLIENT   The user name and password are validated at the client.
SERVER   The user name and password are validated at the DDCS workstation.
DCS   The user name and password are validated at the DRDA server.

The following security types are allowed:

SAME   Only the user name is passed to the DRDA server.
PROGRAM   The user name and password are passed to the DRDA server.

Table 8 shows the possible combinations of these values on the DDCS workstation, and where validation is performed for each combination. Only the combinations shown in this table are supported by DDCS.

Table 8. Valid Security Scenarios		
Authentication	**Security**	**Validation**
CLIENT	SAME	Remote client or DDCS workstation
SERVER	SAME	DDCS workstation
SERVER	PROGRAM	DDCS workstation and DRDA server
DCS	PROGRAM	DRDA server

Each combination is described in more detail below:

- If authentication is CLIENT and security is SAME, the user name and password are validated only at the remote client (for a local client, the user name and password are validated only at the DDCS workstation).

  The user is expected to be authenticated at the location he or she first signs on to. The user ID is sent across the network, but not the password. Use this type of security only if all client workstations have adequate security facilities.

- If authentication is SERVER and security is SAME, the user name and password are validated at the DDCS workstation only. The password is sent across the network from the remote client to the DDCS workstation but not to the DRDA server.

- If authentication is SERVER and security is PROGRAM, the user name and password are validated at both the DDCS workstation and the DRDA server. The password is sent across the network from the remote client to the DDCS workstation and from the DDCS workstation to the DRDA server.

  Because validation is performed in two places, the same set of user names and passwords must be maintained at both the DDCS workstation and the DRDA server.

- If authentication is DCS and security is PROGRAM, the user name and password are validated at the DRDA server only. The password is sent across the network from the remote client to the DDCS workstation and from the DDCS workstation to the DRDA server.

If remote clients are connected to the DDCS workstation, specify the following:

- If a remote client is connected to the DDCS workstation via APPC, specify an APPC security type of NONE at the remote client. (Security type NONE is supported at remote clients but not supported at the DDCS workstation).

- If the authentication type at the DDCS workstation is CLIENT, specify CLIENT at each remote client. If the authentication type at the DDCS workstation is either SERVER or DCS, specify either SERVER or DCS at each remote client. (Which of these two values you specify at the remote client makes no difference.)

Notes:

1. For UNIX-based systems, all single users using security type SAME must belong to the system group.

2. For UNIX-based systems with remote clients, the instance of the DDCS product running on the DDCS workstation must belong to the system group.

3. For OS/2 based systems, when using security type SAME, the userids must be defined to UPM at the DDCS workstation.

4. Access to a DRDA server is controlled by its own security mechanisms or subsystems; for example, the Virtual Telecommunications Access Method (VTAM) and Resource Access Control Facility (RACF). Access to protected database objects is controlled by the SQL **GRANT** and **REVOKE** statements.

Remote Unit of Work Support

A unit of work is a single logical transaction. It consists of a sequence of SQL statements in which either all of the operations are successfully performed or the sequence as a whole is considered unsuccessful.

Remote unit of work lets a user or application program read or update data at one location per unit of work. It supports access to one database within a unit of work.

While an application program can update several remote databases, it can only access one database within a unit of work.

Remote unit of work has the following characteristics:

- Multiple requests per unit of work are supported.

- Multiple cursors per unit of work are supported.

- Each unit of work can access only one database.

- The application program either commits or rolls back the unit of work. In certain error circumstances, the server may roll back the unit of work.

The precompiler fails if an object referenced in your application program does not exist. There are three possible ways to deal with an application that accesses remote databases:

- You can split the application into several files, each of which accesses only one database. (For example, each unit of work could be a separate source file.) You then prep and bind each file against the one database that it accesses.

- You can ensure that each table exists in the database against which you prep. (Perhaps each database contains the same tables, or you create dummy versions of each table in one database.) You then bind against each database.

- You can use only dynamic SQL for remote databases.

Distributed Unit of Work Support

Distributed unit of work (DUOW) allows an application to access more than one database within a unit of work; that is, the application can switch between databases before committing the data. This gives an application programmer the ability to do work involving multiple databases, local and remote, at the same time.

DDCS lets you read multiple databases within a unit of work. Whether you can update multiple databases depends on the products you are using:

- If the application is executed under CICS for AIX Version 1.2 or the AIX Encina Monitor Version 1.3, you can update multiple databases within a unit of work for the following database products:

  - DB2 for MVS, Version 3.1 or later
  - DB2 for OS/400, Version 3.1 or later
  - OS/2 or UNIX-based DB2 products, Version 2.1 or later.

  With DB2 for VSE, VM and previous versions of the other DB2 products, the OS/2 or UNIX-based DB2 products, Version 2.1 or later, can participate in a two-phase commit transaction as a read-only participant.

- If you are not using DDCS you can update multiple databases within a unit of work, with a two-phase commit, only if *all* of the updated databases are OS/2 or UNIX-based DB2 Version 2 databases.

A transaction manager (also called syncpoint manager) coordinates the commit among multiple databases. If you use a transaction processing (TP) Monitor environment, such as CICS for AIX, the TP Monitor uses its own transaction manager; otherwise, the Transaction Manager supplied with DB2 is used.

For information about running DDCS in a TP monitor environment, see *DDCS for AIX Installation and Configuration Guide.*.

When to Use DUOW

DUOW is most useful when you want to work with two or more databases and maintain data integrity. For example, if each branch of a bank has its own database, a money transfer application could do the following:

- Connect to the sender's database
- Read the sender's account balance and verify that enough money is present.
- Reduce the sender's account balance by the transfer amount.
- Connect to the recipient's database
- Increase the recipient's account balance by the transfer amount.
- Commit the databases.

By doing this within one unit of work, you ensure that either both databases are updated or neither database is updated.

Updating Database Directories

DDCS uses the following directories to manage information about databases that it connects to:

- The node directory, which contains network address and communication protocol information for every DRDA server that DDCS accesses

- The database connection services (DCS) directory, which contains information specific to DRDA server databases

- The system database directory, which contains name and location information for every database that DDCS accesses

For each DRDA AS that you connect to, you must update these directories on each client or store equivalent information in a global DCE directory. For more information about DCE, see "Using DCE Directory Services" on page 118. This section assumes that you are not using DCE Directory Services.

Notes:

1. The node directory and the systems database directories are used at the client workstation for remote client only.

2. Before updating the database directories, you should configure communications on the DRDA server and workstations. This is described in Chapter 19, "DB2 for OS/2 and Other DRDA Servers" on page 304 and Chapter 20, "Configuring DDCS for AIX" on page 330.

Node Directory

You can specify the following information in the node directory:

Note: The following discussion pertains to directories at the DDCS workstation.

Node name

A nickname for the DRDA server system on which the remote database resides. This name is user-defined. Use the same node name in both the node directory and the system database directory.

Format: 1–8 single-byte alphanumeric characters, including the number sign (#), at sign (@), dollar sign ($), and underscore (_). It cannot begin with an underscore or a number.

Symbolic destination name

The symbolic destination name that was specified in the CPI Communications Side Information Table

Security type

The type of security checking that will be done. The valid options are SAME and PROGRAM. For more information, see "DDCS Security" on page 112.

DCS Directory

You can specify the following information in the DCS directory:

Database name

A nickname for the DRDA server database. This name is user-defined. Use the same database name in both the DCS directory and the system database directory.

Format: 1–8 single-byte alphanumeric characters, including the number sign (#), at sign (@), dollar sign ($), and underscore (_). It cannot begin with an underscore or a number.

Target database name

The database on the DRDA server system, as follows:

MVS	The LOCATION value /it.VSE or VM
	The database name
OS/400	The relational database name
other	For OS/2 and UNIX-based systems, the database alias.

The default is the value that you specify for Database name.

Application requester

The name of the application requester library that forwards SQL requests to DRDA application servers. The application requester handles requests on behalf of an application program. The default is the DDCS application requester.

Parameter string

If you want to change the defaults, specify either or all of the following parameters in the following order:

map-file   The name of an SQLCODE mapping file that overrides the default SQLCODE mapping. To turn off SQLCODE mapping, specify **NOMAP**. For more information refer to the DDCS User's Guide.

,D   Specify a comma followed by a **D** to disconnect the application from the DRDA server database when any of the following SQLCODEs are returned:

SQL30000N	SQL30053N	SQL30072N
SQL30040N	SQL30060N	SQL30073N
SQL30050N	SQL30070N	SQL30074N
SQL30051N	SQL30071N	SQL30090N

Whether or not you specify **,D** the following SQLCODEs cause a disconnect:

SQL30020N	SQL30041N	SQL30081N
SQL30021N	SQL30061N	

,,INTERRUPT_ENABLED

If INTERRUPT_ENABLED is configured in the DCS directory, at the DDCS workstation, and a client application issues an interrupt while connected to the DRDA server, DDCS will perform the interrupt by dropping the connection and rolling back the unit of work. The application will receive a sqlcode (-30081) indicating that the connection to the server has been terminated. The application must then establish a new connection with the DRDA server, in order to process additional database requests.

For example, you could specify any of the following:

```
NOMAP
d:\sqllib\map\dcs1new.map                    (OS/2)
/u/username/sqllib/map/dcs1new.map,D         (AIX)
,D
,,INTERRUPT_ENABLED
d:\sqllib\map\dcs1new.map,,INTERRUPT_ENABLED (OS/2)
```

or accept the defaults by not specifying a parameter string.

Note: If DDCS disconnects due to an error, a rollback will occur automatically.

System Database Directory

You can specify the following information in the system database directory:

Database name
The same value that you specified in the DCS directory.

Database alias
An alias for the DRDA server database. This name will be used by any application program that accesses the database. By default, the value that you specify for Database name is used.

Format: 1–8 single-byte alphanumeric characters, including the number sign (#), at sign (@), dollar sign ($), and underscore (_). It cannot begin with an underscore or a number.

Node name
The same value that you specified in the node directory.

Authentication
Specifies where the validation of the user's name and password will be done. The valid options are: SERVER, CLIENT, and DCS. For more information, see "DDCS Security" on page 112.

Defining Multiple Entries for the Same Database

For each database you must define at least one entry in each of the three directories (node directory, DCS directory, and system database directory). In some cases, you might want to define more than one entry for the database.

For example, you might want to turn off SQLCODE mapping for applications that were ported from the DRDA server but accept the default mapping for applications that were developed for the client/server environment. You would do this as follows:

- Define one entry in the node directory.

- Define two entries in the DCS directory, with different database names, for one entry specify NOMAP in the parameter string.

- Define two entries in the system database directory, with different database aliases, and the two database names that you specified in the DCS directory.

Both aliases access the same database, one with SQLCODE mapping and the other without SQLCODE mapping.

Using DCE Directory Services

With DCE Directory Services, you can store information in a global directory rather than having to store information on each client. At present, this is supported for AIX clients only. (The DDCS workstation can be either AIX or OS/2.)

To use a DCE directory you would create the following DCE directory objects

- The database object, which contains information about a database

- The database locator object, which contains information about the connection between remote clients and the DDCS workstation

- The routing information object, which matches database objects to database locator objects

Note: Before creating these objects, you should configure communications on the DRDA server and workstations. This is described in Chapter 19, "DB2 for OS/2 and Other DRDA Servers" on page 304 and Chapter 20, "Configuring DDCS for AIX" on page 330.

Creating a Database Object

For each DRDA server database that you will access, use the DCE command "cdscp create object" to create a database object; for example,

cdscp create object *database_global_name*

Add the following attributes to the object:

DB_Object_Type
D for database

DB_Product_Name
The relational database product (for example, DB2_for_MVS)

DB_Native_Database_Name
The database on the DRDA server system, as follows:

MVS   The LOCATION value
VSE or VM The database name
OS/400   The relational database name

DB_Database_Protocol
DRDA

DB_Authentication
Either SERVER and CLIENT, as described in "Security with DCE Directory Services" on page 123.

DB_Communication_Protocol
The following information about the communication protocol between the DDCS workstation and the DRDA server:

1. The communication protocol (APPC)
2. The network ID of the DRDA server database
3. The LU name for the DRDA server database
4. The transaction program name for connections to the DRDA server. For DB2 for MVS, specify **DB2DRDA**. For any other operating system, specify a valid value that is not in hexadecimal format.
5. The mode name
6. The security type, as described in "Security with DCE Directory Services" on page 123.

For example, you could put the following lines into a file:

```
create object /.../cdscell1/subsys/database/DBMVS01
add     object /.../cdscell1/subsys/database/DBMVS01    DB_Object_Type \
        = D
add     object /.../cdscell1/subsys/database/DBMVS01    DB_Product_Name \
        = DB2_for_MVS
add     object /.../cdscell1/subsys/database/DBMVS01    DB_Database_Protocol \
        = DRDA
add     object /.../cdscell1/subsys/database/DBMVS01    DB_Native_Database_Name \
        = NEW_YORK
add     object /.../cdscell1/subsys/database/DBMVS01    DB_Authentication \
        = SERVER
add     object /.../cdscell1/subsys/database/DBMVS01    DB_Communication_Protocol \
        = APPC;SPIFNET;NYM2DB2;DB2DRDA;IBMRDB;PROGRAM
```

and then enter the command:

```
cdscp < filename
```

Note: In the file, specify a backslash (\) whenever you want a statement to continue to the next line.

Creating a Database Locator Object

For your DDCS workstation, use the DCE command "`cdscp create object`" to create a database locator object. For example:

```
cdscp create object object_global_name
```

Add the following attributes to the object:

DB_Object_Type
> L for locator object

DB_Communication_Protocol
> The following information about each communication protocol between the DDCS workstation and remote clients.

> For APPC:

> 1. The communication protocol (APPC)
> 2. The network ID of the DDCS workstation
> 3. The local LU name for the DDCS workstation
> 4. The transaction program name for connections from remote clients.
> 5. The mode name
> 6. The security type, as described in "Security with DCE Directory Services" on page 123.

> For TCP/IP:

> 1. The communication protocol (TCPIP, no slash)
> 2. The host name of the DDCS workstation
> 3. The connection port used by the DDCS workstation to accept connections from remote clients

For example, you could put the following lines into a file:

```
create object /.../cdscell1/subsys/database/DBAIX01
add    object /.../cdscell1/subsys/database/DBAIX01
          DB_Object_Type \
          = L
add    object /.../cdscell1/subsys/database/DBAIX01
          DB_Communication_Protocol \
          = TCPIP;AIX001;3700
add    object /.../cdscell1/subsys/database/DBAIX01
          DB_Communication_Protocol \
          = APPC;SPIFNET;NYX1GW01;NYSERVER;IBMRDB;PROGRAM
```

and then enter the command:

```
cdscp < filename
```

Creating a Routing Information Object

Use the DCE command "`cdscp create object`" to create a routing information object. For example:

```
cdscp create object object_global_name
```

Add a DB_Object_Type attribute of R.

For each database object, add one DB_Target_Database_Info attribute. Each DB_Target_Database_Info attribute consists of the following parameters:

Database

The name of a database object, including the full path. Specify *OTHERDBS to indicate all other databases that are not specified explicitly.

Outbound protocol

The database protocol for DRDA server connections (DRDA)

Inbound protocol

The database protocol for remote client connections (DB2RA),

Authenticate at Gateway

0 (for No) or 1 (for Yes), as described in "Security with DCE Directory Services" on page 123.

SQLMAP file

A parameter string to be used by the gateway. The content and format of this string are specific to the gateway product.

If the gateway is a DDCS instance then refer to "DCS Directory" on page 116 for the content of the parameter string.

Database Locator

The name of a database locator object representing the DDCS workstation

For example, you could put the following lines into a file:

```
create object /.../cdscell1/subsys/database/route1
add     object /.../cdscell1/subsys/database/route1
          DB_Object_Type \
          = R
add     object /.../cdscell1/subsys/database/route1
          DB_Target_Database_Info \
          = /.../cdscell1/subsys/database/DBMVS01;DRDA;DB2RA;0;;\
/.../cdscell1/subsys/database/DBAIX01
add     object /.../cdscell1/subsys/database/route1
          DB_Target_Database_Info \
          = *OTHERDBS;DRDA;DB2RA;0;;\
/.../cdscell1/subsys/database/DBAIX02
```

and then enter the command:

```
cdscp < filename
```

Setting Configuration Parameters

Update the Database Manager configuration of the client as follows:

```
db2 UPDATE DATABASE MANAGER CONFIGURATION USING
  [DIR_PATH_NAME path]
  [DIR_OBJ_NAME loc_obj]
  DIR_TYPE DCE
  [ROUTE_OBJ_NAME route_obj]
  [DFT_CLIENT_COMM protocol]
```

where:

- *path* is the default path used to form the complete name of target databases (default /.:/subsys/database/)
- *loc_obj* is used to identify the client in the DCE name space
- DIR_TYPE DCE specifies that DCE directories are used by the client application
- *route_obj* is the name of the routing information object
- *protocol* is the communication protocol between the client and the DDCS workstation. You can specify either APPC, TCPIP, or both.

Note: The following parameters can be temporarily overwritten by the corresponding environment variable

DB2PATHNAME	DIR_PATH_	DB2ROUTE	ROUTE_OBJ_NAME
DB2CLIENTCOMM	DFT_CLIENT_COMM		

Cataloging the Database

If a database is in a different path than the default, or if you want to use an alias that is different than the database name, you can catalog the database. You can use the command line processor CATALOG GLOBAL DATABASE command as follows:

```
db2 CATALOG GLOBAL DATABASE database_global_name
  AS alias
  USING DIRECTORY DCE
```

The alias will be used by any application program that accesses the database.

For example:

```
db2 CATALOG GLOBAL DATABASE /.../cdscell2/subsys/database/dbmvs12 AS NYC3
    USING DIRECTORY DCE
```

Security with DCE Directory Services

As DDCS administrator, you can determine where user names and passwords are validated. With DCE directories, you do this by setting the following:

- The security type of the communication protocol in the database locator object representing the DDCS workstation
- The authentication type in the database object
- The security type of the communication protocol in the database object
- The authenticate at gateway parameter in the routing information object

Table 9 shows the possible combinations of these values and where validation is performed for each combination. Only the combinations shown in this table are supported by DDCS with DCE Directory Services.

Table 9. Valid Security Scenarios with DCE				
Locator obj.	Database object		Routing obj.	Validation
Security	Authent.	Security	Authent. at Gateway	
SAME or NONE	CLIENT	SAME	0	Remote client (or DDCS workstation)
PROGRAM	CLIENT	SAME	1	DDCS workstation
PROGRAM	SERVER	PROGRAM	0	DRDA server
PROGRAM	SERVER	PROGRAM	1	DDCS workstation and DRDA server

Each combination is described in more detail below:

- In the first case, the user name and password are validated only at the remote client. (For a local client, running on the DDCS workstation, the user name and password are validated only at the DDCS workstation.)

  The user is expected to be authenticated at the location he or she first signs on to. The user ID is sent across the network, but not the password. Use this type of security only if all client workstations have adequate security facilities.

- In the second case, the user name and password are validated at the DDCS workstation only. The password is sent across the network from the remote client to the DDCS workstation but not to the DRDA server.

- In the third case, the user name and password are validated at the DRDA server only. The password is sent across the network from the remote client to the DDCS workstation and from the DDCS workstation to the DRDA server.

- In the fourth case, the user name and password are validated at both the DDCS workstation and the DRDA server. The password is sent across the network from the remote client to the DDCS workstation and from the DDCS workstation to the DRDA server.

Because validation is performed in two places, the same set of user names and passwords must be maintained at both the DDCS workstation and the DRDA server.

Notes:

1. For UNIX-based systems, all users using security type SAME must belong to the system group.

2. For UNIX-based systems with remote clients, the instance of the DDCS product running on the DDCS workstation must belong to the system group.

3. For OS/2 based systems, when using security type SAME, the userids must be defined to UPM at the DDCS workstation.

4. Access to a DRDA server is controlled by its own security mechanisms or subsystems; for example, the Virtual Telecommunications Access Method (VTAM) and Resource Access Control Facility (RACF). Access to protected database objects is controlled by the SQL **GRANT** and **REVOKE** statements.

Part 2. Spiffy Network Scenarios

This part describes a hypothetical business called "Spiffy." Spiffy's network implements several combinations of IBM products supporting DRDA, as shown in Figure 31 on page 127. The scenarios in the following chapters show how to interconnect IBM relational database products:

Chapter 6, "DB2 for MVS/ESA and DB2 for VM via CTC" shows how an MVS mainframe and a VM mainframe at the Spiffy New York Headquarters use a channel-to-channel connection to allow their DB2 for MVS/ESA and DB2 for VM systems to exchange data.

Chapter 7, "DB2 for MVS/ESA and DB2 for VM via Channel-Attached NCP" shows how an MVS mainframe and a VM mainframe at Spiffy Headquarters share an NCP (Network Control Program), allowing their respective DB2 for MVS/ESA and DB2 for VM systems to exchange data.

Chapter 8, "DB2 for MVS/ESA and DB2 for VM via Link-Attached NCP" shows how Spiffy uses two NCPs to allow the Spiffy New York Headquarters DB2 for MVS/ESA system to connect to the Spiffy Regional DB2 for VM system in Los Angeles.

Chapter 9, "DB2 for OS/400 and DB2 for MVS/ESA via SDLC" shows how an NCP and an SDLC (Synchronous Data Link Control) connection can interconnect DB2 for OS/400 and DB2 for MVS/ESA. This configuration also works for DB2 for VM and VSE connecting to DB2 for OS/400.

Chapter 10, "DB2 for OS/400 and DB2 for VM via Token Ring and NCP" shows how Spiffy's mainframe NCP connects with an AS/400 token-ring LAN to give the company's executives access to the Spiffy corporate database systems.

Chapter 11, "DB2 for AIX and DB2 for MVS/ESA, DB2 for VM and VSE, or DB2 for OS/400 via Token Ring" shows how DB2 for AIX workstations connect to host systems using a token-ring LAN.

Chapter 12, "DB2 for AIX and DB2 for MVS/ESA via SDLC" shows how a DB2 for AIX with DDCS for AIX workstation connects with DB2 for MVS/ESA via SDLC.

Chapter 13, "DB2 for OS/2 and DB2 for OS/400 via Token Ring" shows how an OS/400 system connects with DB2 for OS/2 workstations using a token-ring LAN.

Chapter 14, "DB2 for OS/2 and DB2 for MVS/ESA via Token Ring" shows how DB2 for OS/2 workstations at Spiffy Headquarters use a token-ring LAN and NCP to connect to DB2 for MVS/ESA.

Chapter 15, "DB2 for OS/2 and DB2 for VM and VSE via Token Ring" shows how token ring and NCP can interconnect DB2 for OS/2 workstations and DB2 for VM.

Chapter 16, "DB2 for OS/2 and DB2 for MVS/ESA or DB2 for VM via SDLC" shows how NCP and SDLC can connect a DB2 for OS/2 workstation at a remote site to DB2 for VM. This configuration also works for DB2 for MVS/ESA connecting to a workstation.

Chapter 17, "DB2 for OS/2 and Multiple Hosts" shows how to connect DB2 for OS/2 token ring to two different host systems: AS/400 and DB2 for MVS/ESA

Chapter 18, "DB2 for OS/2 and DB2 for MVS/ESA or DB2 for VM and VSE via 3174 Controller" shows how several DB2 for OS/2 workstations can connect to a DB2 for MVS/ESA host using a 3174 control unit.

Chapter 19, "DB2 for OS/2 and Other DRDA Servers" shows how you configure the DDCS for OS/2 workstation and DRDA servers.

Chapter 20, "Configuring DDCS for AIX" shows how you configure the DDCS for AIX workstation and DRDA servers.

Chapter 21, "Configuring DB2 for OS/2 as a DRDA Application Server" shows how you configure DB2 for OS/2 as a DRDA Application Server.

Chapter 22, "Configuring DB2 for AIX as a DRDA Application Server (DRDA AS)" shows how you configure DB2 for AIX as a DRDA Application Server.

Note: All parameters given in the following scenarios are intended as starting points only. They might not represent the best possible configurations for your systems.

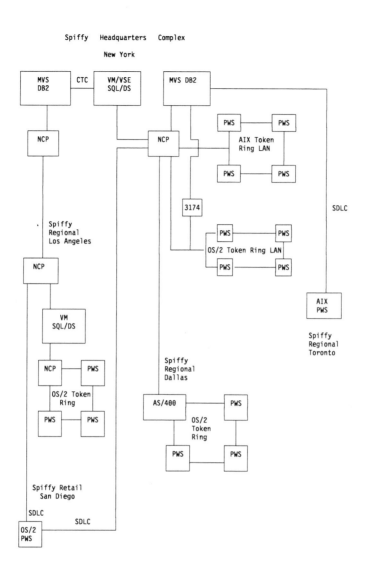

Figure 31. Spiffy Network

Cross-System Terminology

Table 10 and Table 11, respectively, show the host terminology for key SNA and DRDA connectivity parameters. When possible, the real parameter names are used. Because in OS/2 there are no commands to define resources, the names of the parameters are the ones used in the Communications Manager/2 windows. Likewise, the parameters are the ones used in the system management interface tool (SMIT).

Table 10. Key SNA Connectivity Parameters Cross Reference

Parameter	MVS/VM/VSE	OS/400	AIX/6000	OS/2
Token-ring address	LOCADDR (NCP)	ADPTADR	Link address	Network adapter address
IDBLK	IDBLK	EXCHID	Xid node ID (first 3 digits, hex)	Local node ID
IDNUM	IDNUM	EXCHID	Xid node ID (last 5 digits, hex)	Local node ID
MAXDATA	MAXDATA	MAXDATA	Max I-field size	Max I-field size
Partner token-ring address	DIALNO	ADPTADR	Remote link address	LAN destination address (hex)
Network name	NETID	LCLNETID	Network name	Network ID
Control point name	SSCPNAME	LCLCPNAME	Control point name	Local node name
Logical unit name	APPL	LCLLOCNAME	Logical unit name	Logical unit name
Partner logical unit name	APPL	RMTLOCNAME	Remote logical unit name	Partner logical unit
Mode name	MODEENT	MODE	Mode name	Transmission service mode
RU size	RUSIZES	MAXLENRU	Maximum RU size	Maximum RU size
Pacing	PACING, VPACING	INPACING	Receive pacing	Receive window count

Table 11. Key DRDA Connectivity Parameters Cross Reference

Parameter	MVS	VM/VSE	AS/400	AIX/6000, OS/2
RDB name	LOCATION NAME	DBNAME	RDB	See note
Partner RDB name	LOCATION NAME	DBNAME	RDB	See note
Transaction program prefix				See note
Transaction program name	LINKATTR	RESID	TNSPGM	See note

Note: Because DB2 for OS/2 and DB2 for AIX cannot act as DRDA servers, the DRDA parameters are not applicable.

Chapter 6. DB2 for MVS/ESA and DB2 for VM via CTC

The Spiffy New York Headquarters has three mainframe systems. Two of those systems (NYMVS1 and NYVM) are connected using a channel-to-channel (CTC) adapter. Figure 32 shows how the two VTAM systems are connected.

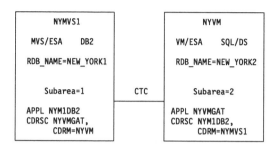

Figure 32. VTAM Channel-to-Channel Attachment

The figure shows some of the definitions that must be in place in each VTAM system for the applications on each system to communicate:

- VTAM assigns each system a *Cross Domain Resource Manager (CDRM)* name. In the figure, there are two CDRM names: NYMVS1 and NYVM.

- Each system is assigned a subarea number, which allows VTAM to route requests to the correct CDRM.

- A VTAM APPL statement is created on each system, defining the LU name associated with the database system residing on that VTAM system. In the example, NYM1DB2 resides on NYMVS1, and NYVMGAT resides on NYVM.

- A VTAM CDRSC statement is coded on each VTAM system. The CDRSC statement gives the name of a remote VTAM application and the CDRM that should receive requests directed to the remote application. In the example, NYMVS1 has a CDRSC statement defining NYVMGAT at NYVM. Similarly, NYVM has a CDRSC statement defining NYM1DB2 at NYMVS1.

You must specify several parameters to allow the DB2 for MVS/ESA and DB2 for VM users to use a distributed database connection. These parameters are summarized in Table 12 on page 130.

Table 12. Overview of Values Required to Connect DB2 for MVS/ESA and DB2 for VM via CTC

Parameter	Definitions for MVS system	Definitions for VM system
DB2 for MVS/ESA LUNAME	1. VTAM APPL statement 2. DB2 BSDS	1. VTAM CDRSC statement 2. NY1DB2 entry in CMS Communications Directory7
DB2 for MVS/ESA TPN	n/a	NY1DB2 entry in CMS Communications Directory7
DB2 for MVS/ESA Application Requester can send SNA SECURITY=SAME on requests to DB2 for VM	USERNAMES column in SYSIBM.SYSLUNAMES	VTAM APPL SECACPT=ALREADYV
USERID for requests sent to DB2 for VM application server	Current DB2 AUTHID	Validated by RACF or CP
DB2 for VM LUNAME	1. VTAM CDRSC statement 2. LUNAME column in SYSIBM.SYSLUNAMES	1. VTAM APPL statement 2. NYSQLDS entry in CMS Communications Directory7
DB2 for VM TPN	n/a	RESID NAMES file
DB2 for VM Application Requester can send SNA SECURITY=SAME on requests to DB2 for MVS/ESA	1. USERSECURITY column of SYSIBM.SYSLUNAMES table 2. VTAM APPL SECACPT=ALREADYV	NY1DB2 entry in CMS Communications Directory7
USERID for requests sent to DB2 for MVS/ESA application server	Validated by RACF	Current CMS ID
MODENAME	VTAM MODEENT macro	1. VTAM MODEENT macro 2. NYSQLDS entry in CMS Communications Directory7
Support RU size 4096	1. MAXBFRU on VTAM LINE macro 2. RUSIZES on VTAM MODEENT macro	1. MAXBFRU on VTAM LINE macro 2. RUSIZES on VTAM MODEENT macro
Set PACING to 2	1. VPACING on VTAM APPL statement 2. Nonzero SSNDPAC on VTAM MODEENT	1. VPACING on VTAM APPL statement 2. Nonzero SSNDPAC on VTAM MODEENT

The following items are required to implement the example shown in Figure 32 on page 129:

1. Define VTAM buffer pool parameters for both VTAM systems as follows:

   ```
   IOBUF=(320,441,20,F,64,48,768)
   ```

2. The definition for the channel-to-channel adapter on NYMVS1 is shown in Figure 33 on page 131. The following two items are important:

---

7 When DB2 for VM is the server, the CMS Communications Directory does not apply.

a. The DELAY keyword influences how long VTAM should wait before transmitting its CTC writer buffers of low-priority data (PIU TP0 and TP1 priorities). DELAY=0 minimizes the delay on the CTC adapter when the traffic is light. If an installation does not want to use DELAY=0, an alternative is to use TP2 priority for distributed data requests, which causes immediate transmission of the data (regardless of the DELAY setting).

b. The MAXBFRU keyword defines how many CTC 4K write buffers (for the VTAM that services NYMVS1) to reserve for transmitting PIUs to NYVM. Remember, a PIU is 29 bytes longer than an RU. If you specify 4K for your RU size (which is the recommended value), you must specify a MAXBFRU of at least 2 to accommodate a complete PIU. If you specify MAXBFRU=1 (the VTAM default), you get a X'800A0000' SNA sense code from VTAM, indicating that the PIU was truncated during transmission.

In this case, MAXBFRU=8 was selected. This allows VTAM to send multiple PIUs to NYVM with a single I/O operation, when several PIUs are ready for transmission.

The sum of the number of MAXBFRU buffers from each VTAM CTC connection side is allocated in each participating VTAM. Because MAXBFRU=8 was selected for both NYMVS1 and NYVM, sixteen 4K buffers are allocated in both VTAMs to support the VTAM CTC read/write activity.

```
*************************************************************************
**         CTC DEFINITIONS  FOR NYMVS1                               **
*************************************************************************
MV1CTC    VBUILD TYPE=CA          CTC MAJOR NODE DEFINITION
MV1GRPB   GROUP LNCTL=CTCA,       CTCA LINE TYPE                    X
                MIH=YES,REPLYTO=10.0
MV1CTCL   LINE  ADDRESS=(500),    CTC ADDRESS FOR THIS LINE         X
                DELAY=0,          CTC DELAY                         X
                MAXBFRU=8,        MAX BUFFER USED                   X
                ISTATUS=ACTIVE    INITIAL STATUS IS ACTIVE
MV1CTCP   PU    ISTATUS=ACTIVE
```

Figure 33. VTAM CTC Definitions for NYMVS1

3. The VTAM PATH statement tells NYMVS1 how to route requests to the subarea reserved for NYVM (subarea 2). Figure 34 on page 132 shows the VTAM PATH statement for NYMVS1. There is a direct connection between NYMVS1 and NYVM. If the two systems were not directly connected, the PATH statement would define the subarea number of the first VTAM or NCP system in the route between subarea 1 and subarea 2.

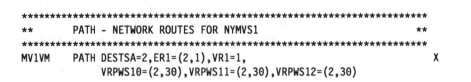

```
**********************************************************************
**          PATH - NETWORK ROUTES FOR NYMVS1                      **
**********************************************************************
MV1VM       PATH DESTSA=2,ER1=(2,1),VR1=1,                          X
               VRPWS10=(2,30),VRPWS11=(2,30),VRPWS12=(2,30)
```

Figure 34. VTAM CTC PATH Statement for NYMVS1

4. The VTAM CDRSC statement describes a network application that can be found on another VTAM network node. In Figure 35, the CDRSC defines the AVS gateway on the NYVM system, which uses the LU name NYVMGAT. AVS is the VM product that provides the SNA communication capabilities for DB2 for VM.

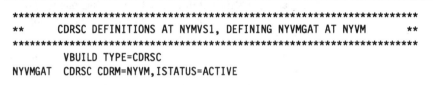

```
**********************************************************************
**       CDRSC DEFINITIONS AT NYMVS1, DEFINING NYVMGAT AT NYVM     **
**********************************************************************
            VBUILD TYPE=CDRSC
NYVMGAT     CDRSC CDRM=NYVM,ISTATUS=ACTIVE
```

Figure 35. CDRSC for NYVMGAT at NYVM

5. The CDRM definitions define the VTAM systems in the network and the subarea numbers assigned to each VTAM. Both the local and remote VTAMs must be defined as CDRMs, as shown in Figure 36.

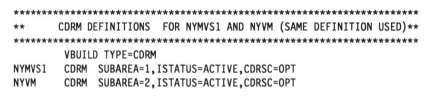

```
**********************************************************************
**       CDRM DEFINITIONS  FOR NYMVS1 AND NYVM (SAME DEFINITION USED)**
**********************************************************************
            VBUILD TYPE=CDRM
NYMVS1      CDRM  SUBAREA=1,ISTATUS=ACTIVE,CDRSC=OPT
NYVM        CDRM  SUBAREA=2,ISTATUS=ACTIVE,CDRSC=OPT
```

Figure 36. VTAM CDRM Definitions for NYMVS1

6. After the VTAM definitions for NYMVS1 are complete, you need to create similar definitions for the NYVM system. The CTC definition shown in Figure 37 on page 133 defines the CTC for the NYVM system:

```
**********************************************************************
**         CTC DEFINITIONS   FOR  NYVM                             **
**********************************************************************
VM1CTC    VBUILD TYPE=CA          CTC MAJOR NODE DEFINITION
VM1GRPB   GROUP LNCTL=CTCA,       CTCA LINE TYPE                    X
                MIH=YES,REPLYTO=10.0
VM1CTCL   LINE  ADDRESS=(500),    CTC ADDRESS FOR THIS LINE         X
                DELAY=0,          CTC DELAY                         X
                MAXBFRU=8,        MAX BUFFER USED                   X
                ISTATUS=ACTIVE    INITIAL STATUS IS ACTIVE
VM1CTCP   PU    ISTATUS=ACTIVE
```

Figure 37. VTAM CTC for NYVM

7. The VTAM PATH statement tells NYVM how to route requests to the subarea
   reserved for NYMVS1 (subarea 1). The direct connection between NYMVS1 and
   NYVM is defined by the PATH statement, as shown in Figure 38.

```
**********************************************************************
**         PATH - NETWORK ROUTES FOR NYVM                          **
**********************************************************************
SYSVM1    PATH DESTSA=1,ER1=(1,1),VR1=1,                            X
                VRPWS10=(2,30),VRPWS11=(2,30),VRPWS12=(2,30)
```

Figure 38. VTAM PATH Statement at NYVM

8. The CDRSC definition shown in Figure 39 allows NYVM to find the distributed
   database system with LU name NYM1DB2 and to locate the network node that
   owns the LU (NYMVS1).

```
**********************************************************************
**       CDRSC DEFINITIONS AT NYVM,  DEFINING NYM1DB2 AT NYMVS1    **
**********************************************************************
          VBUILD TYPE=CDRSC
NYM1DB2   CDRSC CDRM=NYMVS1,ISTATUS=ACTIVE
```

Figure 39. CDRSC for NYM1DB2 at NYMVS1

9. The CDRM definitions shown in Figure 40 on page 134 tell VTAM at NYVM which
   subarea numbers are assigned to NYMVS1 and NYVM.

```
**********************************************************************
**      CDRM DEFINITIONS  FOR NYMVS1 AND NYVM (SAME DEFINITION USED)**
**********************************************************************
        VBUILD TYPE=CDRM
NYMVS1  CDRM  SUBAREA=1,ISTATUS=ACTIVE,CDRSC=OPT
NYVM    CDRM  SUBAREA=2,ISTATUS=ACTIVE,CDRSC=OPT
```

Figure 40. VTAM CDRM Definitions for NYVM

10. The following information is used at the NYMVS1 system to initialize the DDF record in the DB2 for MVS/ESA BSDS.

    ```
    DDF    LOCATION=NEW_YORK1,LUNAME=NYM1DB2,PASSWORD=NYM1PSWD
    ```

11. The VTAM APPL statement for the DB2 for MVS/ESA system at NYMVS1 is shown in Figure 41.

```
DB2APPLS VBUILD TYPE=APPL
NYM1DB2  APPL  APPC=YES,                                            X
               AUTH=(ACQ),                                          X
               AUTOSES=1,                                           X
               DMINWNL=10,                                          X
               DMINWNR=10,                                          X
               DSESLIM=20,                                          X
               EAS=9999,                                            X
               MODETAB=RDBMODES,                                    X
               PRTCT=NYM1PSWD,                                      X
               SECACPT=ALREADYV,                                    X
               SRBEXIT=YES,                                         X
               VERIFY=NONE,                                         X
               VPACING=2,                                           X
               SYNCLVL=SYNCPT,                                      X
               ATNLOSS=ALL
```

Figure 41. DB2 for MVS/ESA APPL Definition for NYMVS1

Note: The VTAM mode table definition is in Figure 180 on page 439.

12. A special file, RESID NAMES, is required to allow the DB2 for VM application server to associate a TPN with the selected RDB_NAME, if at least one of the following conditions is true:

    - RDB_NAME is longer than 8 bytes
    - A registered SNA service TPN is selected
    - RDB_NAME and TPN are not identical

    The terms RESID (resource ID) and TPN are used interchangeably in the VM environment. Figure 42 on page 135 shows a sample RESID NAMES file that can be used at NYVM to associate the TPN NYVMDB to the RDB_NAME NEW_YORK2.

```
:nick.NYDBDS
          :resid.NEW_YORK2
          :dbname.NYVMDB
```

Figure 42. RESID NAMES File at NYVM DB2 for VM Server

To complete the association, database files residing on the DB2 for VM production disk, usually accessed as the Q disk, must be renamed as follows:

```
RENAME current SQLDBM    Q NEW_YORK2 SQLDBM    Q
RENAME current SQLDBGEN Q NEW_YORK2 SQLDBGEN Q
RENAME current SQLFDEF   Q NEW_YORK2 SQLFDEF   Q
```

where current is the current filename.

When the DB2 for VM application server is started with the RDB_NAME NYVMDB, it is associated with the TPN NEW_YORK2.

13. The SQL statements that populate the DB2 for MVS/ESA CDB at NYMVS1 are shown in Figure 43.

```
INSERT INTO SYSIBM.SYSLOCATIONS
    (LOCATION, LOCTYPE, LINKNAME, LINKATTR)
  VALUES ('NEW_YORK2', ' ', 'NYVMGAT', 'NYVMDB');


INSERT INTO SYSIBM.SYSLUNAMES
    (LUNAME, SYSMODENAME, USERSECURITY, ENCRYPTPSWDS, MODESELECT, USERNAMES)
  VALUES ('NYVMGAT', ' ', 'A', 'N', 'N', ' ');
```

Figure 43. SQL for DB2 for MVS/ESA CDB at NEW_YORK1

The statements tell DB2 for MVS/ESA the following:

- The NEW_YORK2 database (RDB_NAME) is at LU NYVMGAT.

- The TPN for the NEW_YORK2 database is NYVMDB (this is the VM resource ID value).

- The NEW_YORK2 database accepts already-verified requests (SNA SECURITY=SAME) and does not require any end user name translation.

- The NEW_YORK1 DB2 for MVS/ESA system should accept already-verified requests from the NEW_YORK2 DB2 for VM system.

14. Figure 44 on page 136 shows the VTAM APPL statement for AVS. DB2 for VM uses AVS to communicate with the NEW_YORK1 system.

```
              VBUILD TYPE=APPL
NYVMGAT   APPL  APPC=YES,                                                      X
               AUTHEXIT=YES,                                                   X
               AUTOSES=1,                                                      X
               DSESLIM=20,                                                     X
               DMINWNL=10,                                                     X
               DMINWNR=10,                                                     X
               EAS=9999,                                                       X
               MAXPVT=100K,                                                    X
               MODETAB=RDBMODES,                                               X
               PARSESS=YES,                                                    X
               SECACPT=ALREADYV,              ALLOW SNA SECURITY=SAME          X
               VERIFY=NONE,                                                    X
               VPACING=2
```

Figure 44. VTAM APPL Definition for AVS at NYVM

Note: The VTAM mode table definition is shown in Figure 180 on page 439.

15. Figure 45 shows the CMS Communications Directory entry on NYVM used to define the DB2 for MVS/ESA system at NYMVS1. This Communications Directory entry is used by CMS users when they use the DB2 for VM Application Requester to request data from DB2 for MVS/ESA at NYMVS1.

    If the CMS Communications Directory in Figure 45 is stored in a file called UCOMDIR NAMES A, this file can be activated as a user-level communication directory by issuing the following command:

    ```
    SET COMDIR FILE USER UCOMDIR NAMES A
    ```

```
:nick.NY1DB2
              :tpn."6DB
              :luname.NYVMGAT NYM1DB2
              :modename.IBMRDB
              :security.SAME
              :dbname.NEW_YORK1
```

Figure 45. CMS Communications Directory Entry at NYVM for DB2 for MVS/ESA

Note: The TPN for DB2 for MVS/ESA is X'07F6C4C2', resulting in an unprintable character in the CMS Communications Directory.

The directory entry in Figure 45 specifies SNA already-verified security (SNA SECURITY=SAME). VM/SP 6 systems cannot support already-verified conversations. If you don't want to use already-verified conversations, you need to use SNA conversations that transmit passwords between DB2 for VM and DB2 for MVS/ESA (SNA SECURITY=PGM). Chapter 8, "DB2 for MVS/ESA and DB2 for VM via Link-Attached NCP" on page 148 describes how to define connections using SECURITY=PGM.

16. The DB2 for VM logical unit is referred to as an AVS gateway in the VM
    environment. Activate the AVS gateway with the following commands:

```
AGW ACTIVATE GATEWAY NYVMGAT GLOBAL
AGW CNOS NYVMGAT NYM1DB2 IBMRDB 20 10 10
AGW ADD USERID NYVMGAT * =
```

The AVS machine's profile can be set to automatically activate the gateway, or the
operator can explicitly perform the activation from the AVS console.

The first command activates the NYVMGAT gateway in the network. The second
command establishes 20 APPC sessions between gateway NYVMGAT and DB2
LU NYM1DB2. The third command maps user IDs on inbound (to DB2 for VM)
already-verified requests to user IDs recognized at the DB2 for VM application
server. This third command is required; the last two operands allow for more
specific mappings. For more information, see *VM/SP Connectivity, Planning,
Administration and Operation.*

Ensure that the CCSIDs are appropriately assigned for each system.

Chapter 7. DB2 for MVS/ESA and DB2 for VM via Channel-Attached NCP

Figure 46 shows the connection between the Spiffy Headquarters VM system and the second MVS system at Spiffy Headquarters. The VTAM and NCP definitions required to establish this connection are described in this chapter. Both of these machines are connected to other systems in the Spiffy network. The VTAM or NCP definitions required to connect to the other Spiffy systems are not shown.

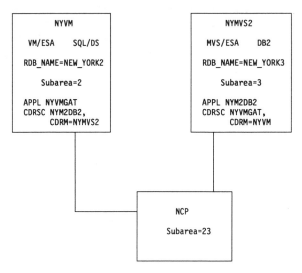

Figure 46. NCP Connecting Two VTAM Systems

In the figure, both NYVM and NYMVS2 are channel-attached to a single NCP. (Figure 49 on page 143 shows the NCP definitions required to connect NYVM and NYMVS2.)

To install a connection of this type, you must code NCP definitions in addition to your normal VTAM definitions. The macros contained in the NCP definitions are processed by both NCP and VTAM. Some of the NCP definition macros are used by VTAM, some are used by both VTAM and NCP, and the remaining macros are used only by NCP. For example:

- VTAM is the only user of the PCCU macro information.
- The BUILD and HOST macros are used by both VTAM and NCP. These macros allow VTAM and NCP to determine the subarea numbers of the systems connected to the NCP, including the subarea number of the NCP itself.

If you are routing distributed database traffic through an existing NCP, you may have to adjust some of your NCP parameters to accommodate the distributed database traffic:

- The MAXDATA value must be large enough to handle the largest PIU (the largest RU plus the 29-byte SNA header). In the example, MAXDATA is 4302, which is sufficient for the 4096 byte RUs that are being transmitted.

- If you specify the MAXBFRU parameter, the value for MAXBFRU must be able to process the largest PIU. MAXBFRU specifies the maximum number of VTAM IOBUF entries allowed for a single PIU. In the example, the value for MAXBFRU must be at least 10 to process 4K RUs, because the VTAM buffer size is 441 bytes.

- Specifying DELAY=0 on the LINE macro associated with the host channel adapter helps eliminate delays when the data traffic through the NCP is light.

- Specify DELAY=0 for the PCCU macro associated with the host.

Table 13 on page 140 provides an overview of the parameters you must define on the VM and MVS systems and on the NCP that connects them.

Table 13. Overview of Values Required to Connect DB2 for VM and DB2 for MVS/ESA via Channel-Attached NCP

Parameter	Definitions for MVS System	Definitions for VM System
DB2 for MVS/ESA LUNAME	1. VTAM APPL statement 2. DB2 BSDS	1. VTAM CDRSC statement 2. NY1DB2 entry in CMS Communications Directory[8]
DB2 for MVS/ESA TPN	n/a	NY1DB2 entry in CMS Communications Directory[8]
DB2 for MVS/ESA Application Requester can send SNA SECURITY=SAME on requests to DB2 for VM	USERNAMES column in SYSIBM.SYSLUNAMES	VTAM APPL SECACPT=ALREADYV
USERID for requests sent to DB2 for VM application server	Current DB2 AUTHID	Validated by RACF or CP
DB2 for VM LUNAME	1. VTAM CDRSC statement 2. LUNAME column in SYSIBM.SYSLUNAMES	1. VTAM APPL statement 2. NYSQLDS entry in CMS Communications Directory[8]
DB2 for VM TPN	n/a	RESID NAMES file
DB2 for VM Application Requester can send SNA SECURITY=SAME on requests to DB2 for MVS/ESA	1. USERSECURITY column of SYSIBM.SYSLUNAMES table 2. VTAM APPL SECACPT=ALREADYV	NY1DB2 entry in CMS Communications Directory[8]
USERID for requests sent to DB2 for MVS/ESA application server	Validated by RACF	Current CMS ID
MODENAME	VTAM MODEENT macro	1. VTAM MODEENT macro 2. NYSQLDS entry in CMS Communications Directory[8]
Support RU size 4096	1. MAXBFRU on NCP HOST macro 2. MAXDATA on the NCP PCCU macro 3. RUSIZES on VTAM MODEENT macro	1. MAXBFRU on NCP HOST macro 2. MAXDATA on the NCP PCCU macro 3. RUSIZES on VTAM MODEENT macro
Set PACING to 2	1. VPACING on VTAM APPL statement 2. Nonzero SSNDPAC on VTAM MODEENT	1. VPACING on VTAM APPL statement 2. Nonzero SSNDPAC on VTAM MODEENT

The VTAM and NCP definitions required to connect NYVM and NYMVS2 are shown in Figure 47, Figure 48 on page 142, and Figure 49 on page 143.

---

8 When VM is the server, the CMS Communications Directory does not apply.

```
**********************************************************************
**      CDRSC DEFINITIONS AT NYVM, DEFINING NYM2DB2 AT NYMVS2      **
**********************************************************************
         VBUILD TYPE=CDRSC
NYM2DB2  CDRSC CDRM=NYMVS2,ISTATUS=ACTIVE


            o
            o
            o


**********************************************************************
**       PATH - NETWORK ROUTES FOR NYVM                           **
**********************************************************************
PATH3     PATH DESTSA=3,ER1=(23,1),VR1=1,                           X
             VRPWS10=(2,30),VRPWS11=(2,30),VRPWS12=(2,30)
PATH23    PATH DESTSA=23,ER1=(23,1),VR1=1,                          X
             VRPWS10=(2,30),VRPWS11=(2,30),VRPWS12=(2,30)


            o
            o
            o


**********************************************************************
**     CDRM DEFINITIONS FOR NYVM AND NYMVS2 (SAME DEFINITION USED)**
**********************************************************************
         VBUILD TYPE=CDRM
NYVM      CDRM  SUBAREA=2,ISTATUS=ACTIVE,CDRSC=OPT
NYMVS2    CDRM  SUBAREA=3,ISTATUS=ACTIVE,CDRSC=OPT
```

Figure 47. VTAM Definitions at NYVM

```
**********************************************************************
**      CDRSC DEFINITIONS AT NYMVS2,  DEFINING NYVMGAT AT NYVM      **
**********************************************************************
        VBUILD TYPE=CDRSC
NYVMGAT CDRSC CDRM=NYVM,ISTATUS=ACTIVE


        o
        o
        o


**********************************************************************
**      PATH - NETWORK ROUTES FOR NYMVS2                            **
**********************************************************************
PATH2   PATH DESTSA=2,ER1=(23,1),VR1=1,                              X
             VRPWS10=(2,30),VRPWS11=(2,30),VRPWS12=(2,30)
PATH23  PATH DESTSA=23,ER1=(23,1),VR1=1,                             X
             VRPWS10=(2,30),VRPWS11=(2,30),VRPWS12=(2,30)


        o
        o
        o


**********************************************************************
**      CDRM DEFINITIONS FOR NYVM AND NYMVS2 (SAME DEFINITION USED) **
**********************************************************************
        VBUILD TYPE=CDRM
NYVM    CDRM  SUBAREA=2,ISTATUS=ACTIVE,CDRSC=OPT
NYMVS2  CDRM  SUBAREA=3,ISTATUS=ACTIVE,CDRSC=OPT
```

Figure 48. VTAM Definitions at NYMVS2

```
***************************************************************************
*                                                                         *
*       ACFNCPBD: NCPGEN FOR SUBAREA 23 FOR 3745-210          4/23/91    *
*                USING NCP VERSION 5.4                                   *
*                HOST SUBAREA 2 3                                        *
*                                                                         *
*                                                                         *
***************************************************************************
NCPOPT    OPTIONS USERGEN=FNMNDFGN,NEWDEFN=(YES,ECHO)
*
PCCU2     PCCU  AUTODMP=NO,        DEFAULT                              C
                AUTOIPL=NO,        DEFAULT                              C
                AUTOSYN=YES,       DEFAULT                              C
                BACKUP=YES,        RESOURCES TO BACKUP HOST ON FAIL     C
                CHANCON=UNCOND,    UNCOND CHANNEL CONTACT REQUEST       C
                CUADDR=C02,        CHANNEL-ATTACHMENT ADDRESS           C
                DELAY=0,           FORCE DELAY TO ZERO                  C
                NETID=SPIFNET,     HOST NETID                           C
                DUMPDS=DUMPDS,     3745 DUMP DATA SET                   C
                MAXDATA=4302,      MAXIMUM PIU SIZE                     C
                OWNER=HOST2,       RESOURCE OWNING HOST                 C
                SUBAREA=2,         PCCU2 HOST SUBAREA ADDRESS           C
                VFYLM=YES          VERIFY NCP LOAD MODULE NAME          C
*
PCCU3     PCCU  AUTODMP=NO,        DEFAULT                              C
                AUTOIPL=NO,        DEFAULT                              C
                AUTOSYN=YES,       DEFAULT                              C
                BACKUP=YES,        RESOURCES TO BACKUP HOST ON FAIL     C
                CHANCON=UNCOND,    UNCOND CHANNEL CONTACT REQUEST       C
                CUADDR=C02,        CHANNEL-ATTACHMENT ADDRESS           C
                DELAY=0,           FORCE DELAY TO ZERO                  C
                NETID=SPIFNET,     HOST NETID                           C
                DUMPDS=DUMPDS,     3745 DUMP DATA SET                   C
                MAXDATA=4302,      MAXIMUM PIU SIZE                     C
                OWNER=HOST3,       RESOURCE OWNING HOST                 C
                SUBAREA=3,         PCCU2 HOST SUBAREA ADDRESS           C
                VFYLM=YES          VERIFY NCP LOAD MODULE NAME
*
```

Figure 49 (Part 1 of 3). Channel-Attached NCP Definitions for Subarea 23

```
*                                                                      *
***********************************************************************
*
ACFNCPBD BUILD BFRS=240,              NCP BUFFER SIZE                    C
               CATRACE=(YES,20),      NCP INCLUDES CA TRACE/20 ENTRIES   C
               LOADLIB=NCPLOAD,       LIBRARY FOR NCP LOAD MODULE        C
               MAXSSCP=8,             NUMBER OF SSCPS IN SESSION         C
               MODEL=3745,            MACHINE TYPE                       C
               MEMSIZE=4M,            MAX AMOUNT OF STORAGE NCP USES     C
               NETID=SPIFNET,         NETWORK NAME                       C
               NEWNAME=DDBLC0,        NCP LOAD MODULE NAME               C
               NPA=YES,               NETWORK PERFORMANCE ANALYZER       C
               NUMHSAS=8,             SUBAREAS WITH VR ENDING THIS NCP   C
               OLT=NO,                ONLINE TERMINAL/LINE TEST FACILITY C
               QUALIFY=NCM5725,       LOADLIB NAME QUALIFIER             C
               SUBAREA=23,            NCP SUBAREA                        C
               TRACE=YES,             ADDRESS TRACE OPTION               C
               TRANSFER=18,           =(4096+51)--ROUNDED UP             C
               TYPGEN=NCP,            THIS IS AN NCP GEN                 C
               TYPSYS=MVS,            MVS OPERATING SYSTEM               C
               USGTIER=5,             NCP USER TIER 3 OR HIGHER FOR 3745 C
               VERSION=V5R4           LEVEL OF THIS NCP
*
         SYSCNTRL OPTIONS=(BHSASSC,ENDCALL,MODE,RCNTRL,RCOND,RECMD,      C
              RIMM,NAKLIM,SESSION,SSPAUSE,XMTLMT,BACKUP,DVSINIT,         C
              LNSTAT,SESINIT,STORDSP,DLRID,RDEVQ)
*
*
HOST2    HOST BFRPAD=0,               REQUIRED VALUE FOR VTAM            C
              INBFRS=18,              RECEIVE HOST DATA XFER ALLOCATION  C
              MAXBFRU=10,             HOST BUFFER ALLOCATION             C
              SUBAREA=2,              HOST2 SUBAREA                      C
              UNITSZ=441              VTAM IOBUFF SIZE
*
HOST3    HOST BFRPAD=0,               REQUIRED VALUE FOR VTAM            C
              INBFRS=18,              RECEIVE HOST DATA XFER ALLOCATION  C
              MAXBFRU=10,             HOST BUFFER ALLOCATION             C
              SUBAREA=3,              HOST3 SUBAREA                      C
              UNITSZ=441              VTAM IOBUFF SIZE
*
```

Figure 49 (Part 2 of 3). Channel-Attached NCP Definitions for Subarea 23

```
*************************************************************************
*         PATH DEFINITIONS                                              *
*************************************************************************
*
          PATH  DESTSA=2,             SUBAREA ADDRESS                    C
                ER0=(2,1),            ADJACENT SUBAREA/TRANSMIT GROUP    C
                VR0=0                 VIRTUAL ROUTE
          PATH  DESTSA=3,             SUBAREA ADDRESS                    C
                ER0=(3,1),            ADJACENT SUBAREA/TRANSMIT GROUP    C
                VR0=0                 VIRTUAL ROUTE
*
*************************************************************
* NETWORK PERFORMANCE ANALYZER LINE  GROUP              *
*************************************************************
*
GRNPAS7 GROUP LNCTL=SDLC,NPARSC=YES,VIRTUAL=YES
LNNPAS7 LINE
PUNPAS7 PU
LUNPAS7 LU    MAXCOLL=64,LOCADDR=1,VPACING=0
*
*************************************************************
CHANGRP GROUP LNCTL=CA,              CHANNEL ADAPTER LINE CONTROL       C
              CA=TYPE6,              CHANNEL ADAPTER TYPE               C
              DELAY=0,               CHANNEL ATTENTION DELAY            C
              TIMEOUT=500.0,         INTERVAL BEFORE CHANNEL DISCONTACT C
              NCPCA=ACTIVE           VTAM STATUS OF CHANNEL ADAPTERS
CA0     LINE  ADDRESS=00,            CA PHYSICAL POSITION 1             C
              INBFRS=18,             #BUF FOR EACH TRANSFER TO HOST     C
              CA=TYPE6               CHANNEL ADAPTER TYPE
PUCHAN0 PU    PUTYPE=5,              SUBAREA CHANNEL ATTACHMENT         C
              TGN=1                  TRANSMISSION GROUP 1
CA1     LINE  ADDRESS=01,            CA PHYSICAL POSITION 2             C
              INBFRS=18,             #BUF FOR EACH TRANSFER TO HOST     C
              CA=TYPE6               CHANNEL ADAPTER TYPE
PUCHAN1 PU    PUTYPE=5,              SUBAREA CHANNEL ATTACHMENT         C
              TGN=1                  TRANSMISSION GROUP 1
*
          GENEND
          END
```

Figure 49 (Part 3 of 3). Channel-Attached NCP Definitions for Subarea 23

The following information is used at the NYMVS2 system to initialize the DDF record in the DB2 for MVS/ESA bootstrap data set.

```
DDF    LOCATION=NEW_YORK3,LUNAME=NYM2DB2,PASSWORD=NYM2PSWD
```

The VTAM APPL statement for the DB2 for MVS/ESA system at NYMVS2 is shown in Figure 50 on page 146.

```
DB2APPLS VBUILD TYPE=APPL
NYM2DB2  APPL  APPC=YES,                                        X
              AUTH=(ACQ),                                       X
              AUTOSES=1,                                        X
              DMINWNL=10,                                       X
              DMINWNR=10,                                       X
              DSESLIM=20,                                       X
              EAS=9999,                                         X
              MODETAB=RDBMODES,                                 X
              PRTCT=NYM2PSWD,                                   X
              SECACPT=ALREADYV,                                 X
              SRBEXIT=YES,                                      X
              VERIFY=NONE,                                      X
              VPACING=2,                                        X
              SYNCLVL=SYNCPT,                                   X
              ATNLOSS=ALL
```

Figure 50. DB2 for MVS/ESA APPL Definition for NYMVS2

The VTAM mode table definition is shown in Figure 180 on page 439.

The SQL statements used to populate the DB2 for MVS/ESA CDB at NYMVS2 are identical to those given in Figure 43 on page 135.

The VTAM APPL statement used to define the AVS gateway is described in Figure 44 on page 136.

Figure 51 shows the RESID NAMES file entry.

```
:nick.NEWYORK2
               :tpn.NYVMDB
               :dbname.NEW_YORK2
```

Figure 51. RESID NAMES file at NYVM for DB2 for MVS/ESA

The following command is used to start the DB2 for VM system:
```
SQLSTART DB(NEW_YORK2) PROTOCOL(AUTO) ...
```

Figure 52 shows the CMS Communications Directory entry on NYVM used to define the DB2 for MVS/ESA system at NYMVS2. If the CMS Communications Directory entry in Figure 52 is stored in a file called UCOMDIR NAMES A, this file can be activated as a user-level communications directory by issuing the following command:
```
SET COMDIR FILE USER UCOMDIR NAMES A
```

```
:nick.NY2DB2
               :tpn."6DB
               :luname.NYVMGAT NYM2DB2
               :modename.IBMRDB
               :security.SAME
               :dbname.NEW_YORK3
```

Figure 52. CMS Communications Directory File at NYMVS2 for DB2 for MVS/ESA

Note: The TPN for DB2 for MVS/ESA is X'07F6C4C2', resulting in an unprintable character in the CMS Communications Directory file.

Ensure that the CCSIDs are appropriately assigned for each system.

Chapter 8. DB2 for MVS/ESA and DB2 for VM via Link-Attached NCP

Spiffy uses a pair of 3745 control units and a T1 communication link to connect the New York DB2 for MVS/ESA system to the DB2 for VM system in Los Angeles. In the NCP manuals, this type of connection is referred to as a "nonswitched SDLC subarea connection."

As before, the material in this chapter does not include any VTAM or NCP definitions required to connect the machines to other parts of Spiffy's network.

The link-attached NCP configuration requires the following network information:

1. VTAM definitions on the NYMVS1 system.

2. NCP definitions on the NYMVS1 system, defining the NCP parameters for the 3745 attached to the NYMVS1 system.

3. NCP definitions on the LAVM system, defining the NCP parameters for the 3745 attached to the LAVM system.

4. VTAM definitions on the LAVM system.

Note: This scenario applies to VTAM 3.2.

Figure 53 shows how the two sites are connected.

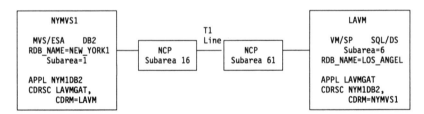

Figure 53. VTAM Systems Connected with Link-Attached NCPs

Table 14 gives an overview of the values required to connect DB2 for VM and DB2 for MVS/ESA.

Table 14. Overview of Values Required to Connect DB2 for VM and DB2 for MVS/ESA

Parameter	Definitions for MVS System	Definitions for VM System
DB2 for MVS/ESA LUNAME	1. VTAM APPL statement 2. DB2 BSDS	1. VTAM CDRSC statement 2. NY1DB2 entry in CMS Communications Directory[9]
DB2 for MVS/ESA TPN	N/A	NY1DB2 entry in CMS Communications Directory[9]
DB2 for MVS/ESA Application Requester must send SNA SECURITY=PGM on requests to DB2 for VM	USERNAMES column in SYSIBM.SYSLUNAMES	VTAM APPL SECACPT=ALREADYV
USERID and PASSWORD used for requests sent to DB2 for VM application server	DB2 SYSIBM.SYSUSERNAMES table	Validated by RACF or CP
DB2 for VM LUNAME	1. VTAM CDRSC statement 2. LINKNAME column in SYSIBM.SYSLOCATIONS 3. LUNAME column in SYSIBM.SYSLUNAMES	1. VTAM APPL statement 2. NYSQLDS entry in CMS Communications Directory[9]
DB2 for VM TPN	LINKATTR column in SYSIBM.SYSLOCATIONS	RESID NAMES file
DB2 for VM Application Requester must send SNA SECURITY=PGM on requests to DB2 for MVS/ESA	1. USERSECURITY column of SYSIBM.SYSLUNAMES table 2. VTAM APPL SECACPT=ALREADYV	NY1DB2 entry in CMS Communications Directory[9]
USERID and PASSWORD for requests sent to DB2 for MVS/ESA application server	Validated by RACF	VM directory APPCPASS statement
MODENAME	VTAM MODEENT macro	1. VTAM MODEENT macro 2. NYSQLDS entry in CMS Communications Directory[9]
Support RU size 4096	1. MAXBFRU on NCP HOST macro 2. MAXDATA on the NCP PCCU macro 3. RUSIZES on VTAM MODEENT macro	1. MAXBFRU on NCP HOST macro 2. MAXDATA on the NCP PCCU macro 3. RUSIZES on VTAM MODEENT macro
Set PACING to 2	1. VPACING on VTAM APPL statement 2. Nonzero SSNDPAC on VTAM MODEENT	1. VPACING on VTAM APPL statement 2. Nonzero SSNDPAC on VTAM MODEENT

---

9 When VM is the server, the CMS Communications Directory does not apply.

Both VTAM systems use the VTAM buffer pool parameters shown as follows:

```
IOBUF=(320,441,20,F,64,48,768)
```

The VTAM definitions for the NYMVS1 system are given in Figure 54.

```
*********************************************************************
**     CDRSC DEFINITIONS AT NYMVS1, DEFINING LAVMGAT AT LAVM     **
*********************************************************************
          VBUILD TYPE=CDRSC
LAVMGAT   CDRSC CDRM=LAVM,ISTATUS=ACTIVE


              o
              o
              o


*********************************************************************
**         PATH - NETWORK ROUTES FOR LAVM                        **
*********************************************************************
PATH6     PATH DESTSA=6,ER1=(16,1),VR1=1,                        X
               VRPWS10=(2,30),VRPWS11=(2,30),VRPWS12=(2,30)
PATH16    PATH DESTSA=16,ER1=(16,1),VR1=1,                       X
               VRPWS10=(2,30),VRPWS11=(2,30),VRPWS12=(2,30)


              o
              o
              o


*********************************************************************
**     CDRM DEFINITIONS FOR LAVM AND NYMVS1 (SAME DEFINITION USED)**
*********************************************************************
          VBUILD TYPE=CDRM
NYMVS1    CDRM  SUBAREA=1,ISTATUS=ACTIVE,CDRSC=OPT
LAVM      CDRM  SUBAREA=6,ISTATUS=ACTIVE,CDRSC=OPT
```

Figure 54. VTAM Definitions at NYMVS1

The NCP definitions for the New York 3745 controller are given in Figure 55 on
page 151. As stated earlier, you should review your NCP definitions to make sure the
following parameters are specified correctly:

- The MAXDATA value must be large enough to handle the largest PIU (the largest
  RU plus the 29-byte SNA header). In the example, MAXDATA is 4302, which is
  sufficient for the 4096 byte RUs that are being transmitted.

- The value for MAXBFRU must be able to process the largest PIU. In our example,
  the value for MAXBFRU must be at least 10 to process 4K RUs, because our
  VTAM buffer size is 441 bytes.

- Specifying DELAY=0 on the LINE macro associated with the host channel adapter
  helps eliminate delays when the data traffic through the NCP is light.

- Specify DELAY=0 for the PCCU macro associated with the host.

```
NCPOPT    OPTIONS   NEWDEFN=YES
************************************************************************
VTAMG     PCCU  CUADDR=CBF,                                         C
                AUTODMP=NO,                                         C
                AUTOIPL=NO,                                         C
                AUTOSYN=YES,                                        C
                BACKUP=YES,                                         C
                DELAY=0                                             C
                VFYLM=YES,                                          C
                CHANCON=UNCOND,                                     C
                MAXDATA=4302,                                       C
                NETID=SPIFNET,              HOST NETID              C
                DUMPDS=NCPDUMP,                                     C
                OWNER=HOSTG,                                        C
                SUBAREA=1
*
NCPT1G    BUILD TYPGEN=NCP,                                         C
                LTRACE=3,                                           C
                BFRS=240,                                           C
                CATRACE=(YES,20),                                   C
                NUMHSAS=8,                                          C
                SUBAREA=16,                                         C
                MAXSSCP=8,                                          C
                MODEL=3745,                                         C
                USGTIER=5,                                          C
                OLT=NO,                                             C
                NPA=NO,                                             C
                TRACE=(YES,20),                                     C
                TYPSYS=OS,                                          C
                QUALIFY=NCM5725,                                    C
                LOADLIB=LOADLIB,                                    C
                NEWNAME=NCPT1G,                                     C
                VERSION=V5R4,                                       C
                NETID=SPIFNET,                                      C
                BACKUP=1200
*
          SYSCNTRL OPTIONS=(BHSASSC,ENDCALL,MODE,RCNTRL,RCOND,RECMD, C
                RIMM,NAKLIM,SESSION,SSPAUSE,XMTLMT,BACKUP,DVSINIT,    C
                LNSTAT,SESINIT,STORDSP,DLRID,RDEVQ)
*
HOSTG     HOST  BFRPAD=0,                                          C
                INBFRS=18,                                          C
                MAXBFRU=10,                                         C
                STATMOD=YES,                                        C
                SUBAREA=1,                                          C
                UNITSZ=441              *** SAME AS VTAM IOBUF  **
*
```

Figure 55 (Part 1 of 3). NCP Definitions for Subarea 16

```
***********************************************************************
*    PATH DEFINITIONS                                               *
***********************************************************************
*
        PATH  DESTSA=1,ER0=(1,1),                                  C
              VR0=0
        PATH  DESTSA=61,ER0=(61,1),          THE OTHER NCP         C
              VR0=0
        PATH  DESTSA=6,ER0=(61,1),           THE LAVM SYSTEM       C
              VR0=0
*
***********************************************************************
*  DEFINITION OF SDLCST FOR THE PRIMARY END GROUP        *
***********************************************************************
*
G2APRI   SDLCST GROUP=G2APRI0,                                     C
                MAXOUT=7,                                          C
                MODE=PRI,                                          C
                PASSLIM=254,                                       C
                RETRIES=(7,4,6),                                   C
                SERVLIM=254
*
***********************************************************************
*  DEFINITION OF SDLCST FOR THE SECONDARY END GROUP      *
***********************************************************************
*
G2ASEC   SDLCST GROUP=G2ASEC0,                                     C
                MAXOUT=7,                                          C
                MODE=SEC,                                          C
                PASSLIM=254,                                       C
                RETRIES=(15,0,0),                                  C
                TADDR=C1
*
***********************************************************************
*  DEFINITION FOR THE STAND ALONE GROUP  (PRIMARY)           *
***********************************************************************
*
G2APRI0  GROUP AVGPB=420,                                          C
               DIAL=NO,                                            C
               DUPLEX=FULL,                                        C
               LNCTL=SDLC,                                         C
               MODE=PRI,                                           C
               MONLINK=YES,                                        C
               REPLYTO=3,                                          C
               TEXTTO=1.0,                                         C
               TYPE=NCP
*
```

Figure 55 (Part 2 of 3). NCP Definitions for Subarea 16

```
*****************************************************************
*  DEFINITION FOR THE STAND ALONE GROUP  (SECONDARY)          *
*****************************************************************
*
G2ASEC0  GROUP ACTIVTO=90,                                         C
               AVGPB=420,                                          C
               DIAL=NO,                                            C
               DUPLEX=FULL,                                        C
               LNCTL=SDLC,                                         C
               MODE=SEC,                                           C
               MONLINK=YES,                                        C
               REPLYTO=3,                                          C
               TEXTTO=1.0,                                         C
               TYPE=NCP
*
*****************************************************************
*  DEFINITION FOR THE REGULAR GROUP MACRO FOR LINES           *
*****************************************************************
*
G2ACOM   GROUP DIAL=NO,                                            C
               DUPLEX=FULL,                                        C
               LNCTL=SDLC,                                         C
               CLOCKNG=EXT,                                        C
               REPLYTO=3,                                          C
               TEXTTO=1.0,                                         C
               TYPE=NCP
*
*****************************************************************
*  LINK FROM NCP SUBAREA 16 TO NCP SUBAREA 61                 *
*****************************************************************
*
LK2B2A1  LINE  ADDRESS=(1028,FULL),                               C
               AVGPB=420,                                          C
               SDLCST=(G2APRI,G2ASEC),                             C
               SPEED=1544000,                                      C
               TADDR=C1
LS2B2A1  PU    ANS=CONT,                                           C
               ISTATUS=ACTIVE,                                     C
               MAXOUT=127,                                         C
               MODULO=128,                                         C
               PUTYPE=4,                                           C
               BLOCK=(8192,16),                                    C
               SRT=(32768,256),                                    C
               TGN=1
*****************************************************************
LNCTLS   GROUP LNCTL=CA,CA=TYPE6,DELAY=0.0,TIMEOUT=500.0
CA0      LINE ADDRESS=00
PUCHAN0  PU PUTYPE=5,TGN=1
*
         GENEND
         END
```

Figure 55 (Part 3 of 3). NCP Definitions for Subarea 16

Figure 56 on page 154 gives the NCP definitions for the NCP in Los Angeles.

```
NCPOPT   OPTIONS   NEWDEFN=YES
**************************************************************************
VTAMF    PCCU   CUADDR=BAF,                                          C
                AUTODMP=NO,                                          C
                AUTOIPL=NO,                                          C
                AUTOSYN=YES,                                         C
                BACKUP=YES,                                          C
                DELAY=0                                              C
                VFYLM=YES,                                           C
                CHANCON=UNCOND,                                      C
                MAXDATA=4302,                                        C
                NETID=SPIFNET,                      HOST NETID       C
                DUMPDS=NCPDUMP,                                      C
                OWNER=HOSTF,                                         C
                SUBAREA=6
*
NCPT1F   BUILD  TYPGEN=NCP,                                          C
                LTRACE=3,                                            C
                BFRS=240,                                            C
                CATRACE=(YES,20),                                    C
                NUMHSAS=8,                                           C
                SUBAREA=61,                                          C
                MAXSSCP=8,                                           C
                MODEL=3745,                                          C
                USGTIER=5,                                           C
                OLT=NO,                                              C
                NPA=NO,                                              C
                TRACE=(YES,20),                                      C
                TYPSYS=OS,                                           C
                QUALIFY=NCM5725,                                     C
                LOADLIB=LOADLIB,                                     C
                NEWNAME=NCPT1F,                                      C
                VERSION=V5R4,                                        C
                NETID=SPIFNET,                                       C
                BACKUP=1200
*
         SYSCNTRL OPTIONS=(BHSASSC,ENDCALL,MODE,RCNTRL,RCOND,RECMD,  C
                RIMM,NAKLIM,SESSION,SSPAUSE,XMTLMT,BACKUP,DVSINIT,   C
                LNSTAT,SESINIT,STORDSP,DLRID,RDEVQ)
*
HOSTF    HOST   BFRPAD=0,                                            C
                INBFRS=18,                                           C
                MAXBFRU=10,                                          C
                STATMOD=YES,                                         C
                SUBAREA=6,                                           C
                UNITSZ=441                 *** SAME AS VTAM IOBUF  **
*
```

Figure 56 (Part 1 of 3). NCP Definitions for Subarea 61

```
*************************************************************************
*    PATH DEFINITIONS                                                  *
*************************************************************************
*
         PATH  DESTSA=6,ER0=(6,1),           THE LAVM SYSTEM      C
               VR0=0
         PATH  DESTSA=16,ER0=(16,1),         THE OTHER NCP        C
               VR0=0
         PATH  DESTSA=1,ER0=(16,1),          THE NYMVS1 SYSTEM    C
               VR0=0
*
***********************************************************************
*  DEFINITION OF SDLCST FOR THE PRIMARY END GROUP         *
***********************************************************************
*
G2APRI   SDLCST GROUP=G2APRI0,                                   C
                MAXOUT=7,                                        C
                MODE=PRI,                                        C
                PASSLIM=254,                                     C
                RETRIES=(7,4,6),                                 C
                SERVLIM=254
*
***********************************************************************
*  DEFINITION OF SDLCST FOR THE SECONDARY END GROUP       *
***********************************************************************
*
G2ASEC   SDLCST GROUP=G2ASEC0,                                   C
                MAXOUT=7,                                        C
                MODE=SEC,                                        C
                PASSLIM=254,                                     C
                RETRIES=(15,0,0),                                C
                TADDR=C1
*
***********************************************************************
*  DEFINITION FOR THE STAND ALONE GROUP   (PRIMARY)            *
***********************************************************************
*
G2APRI0  GROUP AVGPB=420,                                        C
                DIAL=NO,                                         C
                DUPLEX=FULL,                                     C
                LNCTL=SDLC,                                      C
                MODE=PRI,                                        C
                MONLINK=YES,                                     C
                REPLYTO=3,                                       C
                TEXTTO=1.0,                                      C
                TYPE=NCP
*
```

Figure 56 (Part 2 of 3). NCP Definitions for Subarea 61

```
****************************************************************
*   DEFINITION FOR THE STAND ALONE GROUP   (SECONDARY)         *
****************************************************************
*
G2ASEC0   GROUP ACTIVTO=90,                                        C
                AVGPB=420,                                         C
                DIAL=NO,                                           C
                DUPLEX=FULL,                                       C
                LNCTL=SDLC,                                        C
                MODE=SEC,                                          C
                MONLINK=YES,                                       C
                REPLYTO=3,                                         C
                TEXTTO=1.0,                                        C
                TYPE=NCP
*
****************************************************************
*   DEFINITION FOR THE REGULAR GROUP MACRO FOR LINES           *
****************************************************************
*
G2ACOM    GROUP DIAL=NO,                                           C
                DUPLEX=FULL,                                       C
                LNCTL=SDLC,                                        C
                CLOCKNG=EXT,                                       C
                REPLYTO=3,                                         C
                TEXTTO=1.0,                                        C
                TYPE=NCP
*
****************************************************************
*   LINK FROM NCP SUBAREA 61 TO NCP SUBAREA 16                 *
****************************************************************
*
LK2A2B1   LINE  ADDRESS=(1028,FULL),                               C
                AVGPB=420,                                         C
                SDLCST=(G2APRI,G2ASEC),                            C
                SPEED=1544000,                                     C
                TADDR=C1
LS2A2B1   PU    ANS=CONT,                                          C
                ISTATUS=ACTIVE,                                    C
                MAXOUT=127,                                        C
                MODULO=128,                                        C
                PUTYPE=4,                                          C
                BLOCK=(8192,16),                                   C
                SRT=(32768,256),                                   C
                TGN=1
****************************************************************
LNCTLS    GROUP LNCTL=CA,CA=TYPE6,DELAY=0.0,TIMEOUT=500.0
CA0       LINE ADDRESS=00
PUCHAN0   PU PUTYPE=5,TGN=1
*
          GENEND
          END
```

Figure 56 (Part 3 of 3). NCP Definitions for Subarea 61

Figure 57 on page 157 shows the VTAM definitions required at the LAVM system.

```
**********************************************************************
**      CDRSC DEFINITIONS AT LAVM, DEFINING NYM1DB2 AT NYMVS1      **
**********************************************************************
        VBUILD TYPE=CDRSC
NYM1DB2 CDRSC CDRM=NYMVS1,ISTATUS=ACTIVE


        o
        o
        o


**********************************************************************
**      PATH - NETWORK ROUTES FOR LAVM                            **
**********************************************************************
PATH1   PATH DESTSA=1,ER1=(61,1),VR1=1,                           X
             VRPWS10=(2,30),VRPWS11=(2,30),VRPWS12=(2,30)
PATH61  PATH DESTSA=61,ER1=(61,1),VR1=1,                          X
             VRPWS10=(2,30),VRPWS11=(2,30),VRPWS12=(2,30)


        o
        o
        o


**********************************************************************
**      CDRM DEFINITIONS FOR LAVM AND NYMVS1 (SAME DEFINITION USED)**
**********************************************************************
        VBUILD TYPE=CDRM
NYMVS1  CDRM  SUBAREA=1,ISTATUS=ACTIVE,CDRSC=OPT
LAVM    CDRM  SUBAREA=6,ISTATUS=ACTIVE,CDRSC=OPT
```

Figure 57. VTAM Definitions at LAVM

The following information is used at the NYMVS1 system to initialize the DDF record in the DB2 for MVS/ESA BSDS.

```
DDF    LOCATION=NEW_YORK1,LUNAME=NYM1DB2,PASSWORD=NYM1PSWD
```

(Figure 41 on page 134 gave the VTAM APPL statement for the DB2 for MVS/ESA system at NYMVS1.)

Figure 58 on page 158 shows the SQL statements used to populate the DB2 for MVS/ESA CDB at NYMVS1. The statements tell DB2 for MVS/ESA the following:

- The LOS_ANGEL database (RDB_NAME) is at LU LAVMGAT.

- The TPN for the LOS_ANGEL database is LAVMDB (this is the VM resource ID value).

- The LOS_ANGEL database requires a user ID and password (SNA SECURITY=PGM) on distributed database requests.

- The NEW_YORK1 DB2 for MVS/ESA system requires a user ID and password (SNA SECURITY=PGM) on distributed database requests sent from the LAVM system.

- The MVS user JONES can send distributed database requests to the LAVM system. Those requests use JONES for the VM user ID and JONESPWD for the VM password.

```
INSERT INTO SYSIBM.SYSLOCATIONS
    (LOCATION, LOCTYPE, LINKNAME, LINKATTR)
  VALUES ('LOS_ANGEL', ' ', 'LAVMGAT', 'LAVMDB');


INSERT INTO SYSIBM.SYSLUNAMES
    (LUNAME, SYSMODENAME, USERSECURITY, ENCRYPTPSWDS, MODESELECT, USERNAMES)
  VALUES ('LAVMGAT', ' ', 'C', 'N', 'N', 'O');


INSERT INTO SYSIBM.SYSUSERNAMES
    (TYPE, AUTHID, LUNAME, NEWAUTHID, PASSWORD)
  VALUES ('O', 'JONES', 'LAVMGAT', ' ', 'JONESPWD');
```

Figure 58. SQL for DB2 for MVS/ESA CDB at CDRM NYMVS1

Figure 59 shows the VTAM APPL statement for AVS at LAVM. AVS provides the SNA communication capability for DB2 for VM, allowing DB2 for VM to communicate with DB2 for MVS/ESA.

```
        VBUILD TYPE=APPL
LAVMGAT  APPL  APPC=YES,                                              X
               AUTHEXIT=YES,                                         X
               AUTOSES=1,                                            X
               DSESLIM=20,                                           X
               DMINWNL=10,                                           X
               DMINWNR=10,                                           X
               EAS=9999,                                             X
               MAXPVT=100K,                                          X
               MODETAB=RDBMODES,                                     X
               PARSESS=YES,                                          X
               SECACPT=ALREADYV,       REQUIRE SNA SECURITY=PGM      X
               VPACING=2
```

Figure 59. VTAM APPL Definition for AVS at LAVM

Figure 60 shows the CMS RESID NAMES file at LAVM that allows DB2 for VM to associate a TPN value with its RDB_NAME. The values in this entry allow DB2 for VM to determine its TPN and RDB_NAME values.

```
:nick.LASQLDS
            :tpn.LAVMDB
            :dbname.LOS_ANGEL
```

Figure 60. RESID NAMES File at LAVM for DB2 for VM

The following command is used to start the DB2 for VM system:

```
SQLSTART DB(LOS_ANGEL) PROTOCOL(AUTO) ...
```

Figure 61 on page 159 shows the CMS Communications Directory entry at LAVM used to define the DB2 for MVS/ESA system at NYMVS1. This Communications Directory entry allows CMS users running the DB2 for VM Application Requester to request data from DB2 for MVS/ESA at NYMVS1.

```
:nick.NY1DB2
            :tpn."6DB
            :luname.LAVMGAT NYM1DB2
            :modename.IBMRDB
            :security.PGM
            :dbname.NEW_YORK1
```

Figure 61. CMS Communications Directory Entry at NYMVS1 for DB2 for MVS/ESA

Note: The TPN for DB2 for MVS/ESA is X'07F6C4C2', resulting in an unprintable character (which appears as " in the example) in the CMS Communications Directory.

If the CMS Communications Directory entry in Figure 61 is stored in a file called UCOMDIR NAMES A, this file can be activated as a user-level communications directory by issuing the following command:

```
SET COMDIR FILE USER UCOMDIR NAMES A
```

The NEW_YORK1 database requires passwords from each VM user. Because the Communications Directory entry for the NEW_YORK1 system does not contain MVS user ID and password values, all VM users must have an APPCPASS statement in their CP directory entry. The APPCPASS statement is used to supply the MVS user ID and password for the NEW_YORK1 system. The example shown in Figure 62 allows a VM user to use the MVS user ID SMITH and the password SMITHPWD at the NEW_YORK1 database (LU name NYM1DB2).

```
APPCPASS LAVMGAT  NYM1DB2  SMITH SMITHPWD
```

Figure 62. APPCPASS Definition for LAVM Users

Ensure that the CCSIDs are appropriately assigned on each system.

Chapter 9. DB2 for OS/400 and DB2 for MVS/ESA via SDLC

Figure 63 shows a phone line connection (synchronous data link control, SDLC) between the Spiffy Headquarters system (DB2 for MVS/ESA) and the Spiffy Regional site at Dallas (a DB2 for OS/400 system). The Dallas OS/400 is a PU 2.1 system.

Note: The VTAM and NCP information presented in this chapter is also applicable to DB2 for VM and VSE.

The material presented in this chapter does not include any VTAM or NCP definitions required to connect the machines to other parts of Spiffy's network.

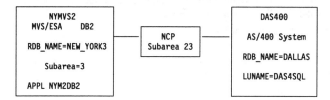

Figure 63. AS/400 Using SDLC to Connect to DB2 for MVS/ESA

Table 15 gives an overview of the definitions you need to connect DB2 for MVS/ESA and DB2 for OS/400 systems.

Table 15 (Page 1 of 3). Overview of Values Required to Connect DB2 for MVS/ESA and DB2 for OS/400

Parameter	Definitions for MVS System	Definitions for OS/400
DB2 LU name	1. VTAM APPL statement 2. DB2 BSDS	Remote location name* in OS/400 configuration list
DB2 for MVS/ESA TP name	N/A	Relational Database Directory entry
DB2 for MVS/ESA can send SNA SECURITY=SAME on requests to OS/400	USERNAMES column in SYSIBM.SYSLUNAMES	SECURELOC(*YES) specified in OS/400 configuration list entry
User ID used for requests sent to OS/400 application server	Current DB2 AUTHID	Validated by OS/400
OS/400 LU name	1. NCP LU statement 2. LINKNAME column in SYSIBM.SYSLOCATIONS 3. LUNAME column in SYSIBM.SYSLUNAMES	Local location name* in OS/400 configuration list
OS/400 TPN	LINKATTR column in SYSIBM.SYSLOCATIONS	N/A

*"Location name" in OS/400 is synonymous with "LU name" in DB2 for MVS/ESA. "Remote location name" means "partner or remote LU name" and "local location name" means "local LU name."

Table 15 (Page 2 of 3). Overview of Values Required to Connect DB2 for MVS/ESA and DB2 for OS/400

Parameter	Definitions for MVS System	Definitions for OS/400
OS/400 is a PU 2.1	1. XID=YES on NCP PU statement 2. LOCADDR=0 on NCP LU statement	1. OS/400 controller description 2. Entry for this location existing in configuration list

*"Location name" in OS/400 is synonymous with "LU name" in DB2 for MVS/ESA. "Remote location name" means "partner or remote LU name" and "local location name" means "local LU name."

Table 15 (Page 3 of 3). Overview of Values Required to Connect DB2 for MVS/ESA and DB2 for OS/400

Parameter	**Definitions for MVS System**	**Definitions for OS/400**
OS/400 must send SNA SECURITY=SAME on requests to DB2 for MVS/ESA application server if the OS/400 is older than V2R2M0	1. USERSECURITY column of SYSIBM.SYSLUNAMES table 2. VTAM APPL SECACPT=ALREADYV	OS/400 application requester can send SNA SECURITY=PGM in V2R2M0
USERID for requests sent to DB2 for MVS/ESA	Validated by RACF	User profile of user running application
Mode name	VTAM MODEENT macro	Mode description exists on OS/400
Support RU size 4096	1. MAXBFRU on NCP HOST macro 2. MAXDATA on the NCP PCCU macro 3. RUSIZES on VTAM MODEENT macro	OS/400 mode description
Set PACING to 2	1. VPACING on VTAM APPL statement 2. Nonzero SSNDPAC on VTAM MODEENT 3. VPACING on NCP PU statement	OS/400 mode description

*"Location name" in OS/400 is synonymous with "LU name" in DB2 for MVS/ESA. "Remote location name" means "partner or remote LU name" and "local location name" means "local LU name."

Chapter 7, "DB2 for MVS/ESA and DB2 for VM via Channel-Attached NCP" on page 138 gave the NCP and VTAM definitions required to define an NCP connected to the NYMVS2 system. To connect the OS/400 in Dallas to the NYMVS2 system, you need to add the NCP parameters shown in Figure 64 to the NCP definitions given earlier in Figure 49 on page 143. The XID=YES and LOCADDR=0 keywords indicate that the OS/400 is a PU 2.1 system.

```
DAS4LINE LINE  ADDRESS=055,NRZI=YES,ANS=CONTINUE,MAXDATA=521
DAS4PU   PU    PUTYPE=2,ADDR=C1,MAXDATA=2057,XID=YES,VPACING=2
DAS4SQL  LU    LOCADDR=0,RESSCB=4,MODETAB=RDBMODES
```

Figure 64. NCP Parameters for DAS400

You also need to update the CDB of the NEW_YORK3 DB2 for MVS/ESA system to allow DB2 for OS/400 and DB2 for MVS/ESA systems to communicate. The SQL statements shown in Figure 65 on page 163 must be issued to add the DB2 for OS/400 to the CDB for NEW_YORK3.

```
INSERT INTO SYSIBM.SYSLOCATIONS
    (LOCATION, LOCTYPE, LINKNAME, LINKATTR)
  VALUES ('DALLAS', ' ', 'DAS4SQL', ' ');


INSERT INTO SYSIBM.SYSLUNAMES
    (LUNAME, SYSMODENAME, USERSECURITY, ENCRYPTPSWDS, MODESELECT, USERNAMES)
  VALUES ('DAS4SQL', ' ', 'A', 'N', 'N', ' ');
```

Figure 65. SQL for DB2 for MVS/ESA CDB at NEW_YORK3

The statements tell DB2 for MVS/ESA the following:

- The DALLAS database (RDB_NAME) is at LU DAS4SQL.

- The DALLAS database accepts already-verified requests, and does not require any end-user name translation.

- The NEW_YORK3 DB2 for MVS/ESA system accepts already-verified requests from AS/400, and does not require any end-user name translation from the Dallas AS/400 system.

The network attributes define the AS/400 system:

```
CHGNETA SYSNAME(DAS4SQL) LCLNETID(SPIFNET) LCLCPNAME(DAS4SQL)
        LCLLOCNAME(DAS4SQL)
```

The line description defines the AS/400 system to the network:

```
CRTLINSDLC LIND(DB2SDLC) RSRCNAME(LIN031) MAXFRAME(521)
```

The value for the RSRCNAME parameter is system dependent an   d identifies which physical line is being used for this configuration. The resource names can be found using the Work with Hardware Resources (WRKHDWRSC) command.

The controller description describes the MVS machine:

```
CRTCTLAPPC CTLD(DB2SDLCC) LINKTYPE(*SDLC) LINE(DB2SDLCL)
           RMTCPNAME(NYMVS2) NETID(RMNETID)
           STNADR(C1) MAXFRAME(521)
```

The configuration list entries define the remote LU names:

```
ADDCFGLE TYPE(*APPNRMT) APPNRMTE((NYM2DB2 *NETATR DAS4SQL NYMVS2
                                  SPIFNET *NONE *YES))
```

Add one remote entry for each remote LU name in the network. The entries are shown as lists. Use the OS/400 command prompt facility to see the meaning of each item in the list. In the example, the first item is the remote LU name (remote location name), and the fifth item in the list is the remote network ID.

Create a mode description:

```
CRTMODD MODD(IBMRDB)
```

Make the configuration available for use:

```
VFYCFG CFGOBJ(DB2SDLCL) CFGTYPE(*LIN) STATUS(*ON)
```

Add an entry to the Relational Database Directory for the remote database:

```
ADDRDBDIRE RDB(NEW_YORK3) RMTLOCNAME(NYM2DB2)
```

Ensure that the CCSIDs are appropriately assigned at each system.

Chapter 10. DB2 for OS/400 and DB2 for VM via Token Ring and NCP

Figure 66 shows DB2 for OS/400 systems connected to DB2 for VM, using a 3745 control unit and a token-ring LAN. The regional office in Dallas uses this configuration for access to the Spiffy corporate database systems.

The material in this chapter does not include any VTAM or NCP statements required to connect the machines in question to other parts of the Spiffy network.

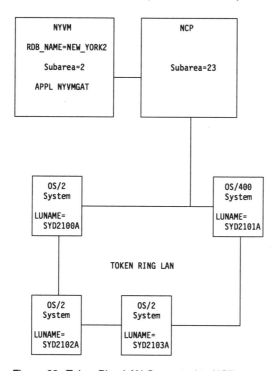

Figure 66. Token Ring LAN Connected to NCP

A device on a token-ring LAN can be defined to NCP as either a switched or nonswitched device. In Figure 67 on page 168, the DB2 for OS/400 systems are defined as PU 2.1 switched devices.

Switched devices are defined to VTAM as *switched major nodes*. For each token-ring device, the following items are recorded in the VTAM switched major node definition:

- The PU name of the device.

- The IDBLK value, which must be 056 for a DB2 for OS/400 system. IDBLK is used during the SNA exchange ID process (XID). The IDBLK value is the first three digits of the EXCHID in the line and controller descriptions for DB2 for OS/400.

- The IDNUM value, which is also used in the SNA XID process. The IDNUM value is the last five digits of the EXCHID in the line and controller descriptions for DB2 for OS/400. In Figure 67 on page 168, the IDNUM value is D2100 for the first LAN station.

- The DIALNO value defines the token-ring LAN address of the device. VTAM and NCP use the DIALNO value to relate PU and LU names to the token-ring LAN station address. For example, the DB2 for OS/400 system at LAN address X'400050132101' has PU name SYD2101 and LU name SYD2101A.

- The LU name associated with the DB2 for OS/400 system is also defined in the VTAM switched major node definitions. Each LU in the example specifies LOCADDR=000, which indicates the LU is a PU 2.1 device.

Table 16 gives an overview of the definitions needed to connect a DB2 for OS/400 system to a DB2 for VM system.

Table 16. Overview of Values Required to Connect DB2 for OS/400 to DB2 for VM and VSE

Parameter	Definitions for VM System	Definitions for AS/400 System
DB2 for VM LU name	VTAM APPL statement	Remote location name[*] in OS/400 configuration list
DB2 for VM TP name	N/A	Relational database directory entry
DB2 for VM application requester must send SNA SECURITY=SAME on requests to OS/400	VTAM APPL SECAPT=ALREADYV	SECURELOC(*YES) specified in OS/400 device description or remote configuration list
OS/400 LU name	VTAM LU statement	Local location name[*] in OS/400 configuration list
OS/400 is a PU 2.1	LOCADDR=0 on VTAM LU statement	1. OS/400 controller description 2. Entry for this location existing in configuration list
OS/400 Application Requester must send SNA SECURITY=SAME on requests to DB2 for VM if OS/400 is older than V2R2M0	VTAM APPL SECACPT=ALREADYV	OS/400 application requester can send SNA SECURITY=PGM in V2R2M0
USERID and PASSWORD for requests sent to DB2 for VM application server	Validated by RACF	User profile of user running application
MODENAME	VTAM MODEENT macro	Mode description exists on OS/400
LAN address of NCP	LOCADD on NCP LINE macro	OS/400 controller description
LAN address of OS/400	DIALNO on VTAM PATH macro	OS/400 line description
Exchange ID for OS/400	IDNUM on VTAM PU macro	OS/400 line description
OS/400 LU address	LOCADDR on VTAM LU macro	OS/400 device description
Support RU size 1024	1. MAXBFRU on NCP HOST macro 2. MAXDATA on NCP PCCU macro 3. RCVBUFC on NCP LINE macro	OS/400 mode description
Set PACING to 2	1. VPACING on VTAM APPL statement 2. Nonzero SSNDPAC on VTAM MODEENT 3. VPACING on VTAM PU macro	OS/400 mode description

[*]"Location name" in OS/400 is synonymous with "LU name" in DB2 for MVS/ESA. "Remote location name" means "partner or remote LU name" and "local location name" means "local LU name."

Figure 67 gives the definitions for VTAM switched major nodes.

```
SWA0099   VBUILD  TYPE=SWNET,MAXGRP=1,MAXNO=40
*
SYD2100   PU      ADDR=01,IDBLK=05D,IDNUM=D2100,ANS=CONT,DISCNT=NO,         +
                  IRETRY=YES,ISTATUS=ACTIVE,MAXDATA=4302,MAXOUT=7,          +
                  MAXPATH=1,PUTYPE=2,SECNET=NO,MODETAB=RDBMODES,            +
                  SSCPFM=USSSCS,PACING=0,VPACING=2
PD2100    PATH    DIALNO=0004400050132100,                                  +
                  GRPNM=SY45PG0,GID=1,PID=1,REDIAL=2
SYD2100A  LU      LOCADDR=000
*
SYD2101   PU      ADDR=01,IDBLK=056,IDNUM=D2101,ANS=CONT,DISCNT=NO,         +
                  IRETRY=YES,ISTATUS=ACTIVE,MAXDATA=4302,MAXOUT=7,          +
                  MAXPATH=1,PUTYPE=2,SECNET=NO,MODETAB=RDBMODES,            +
                  SSCPFM=USSSCS,PACING=0,VPACING=2
PD2101    PATH    DIALNO=0004400050132101,                                  +
                  GRPNM=SY45PG0,GID=1,PID=1,REDIAL=2
SYD2101A  LU      LOCADDR=000
*
SYD2102   PU      ADDR=01,IDBLK=05D,IDNUM=D2102,ANS=CONT,DISCNT=NO,         +
                  IRETRY=YES,ISTATUS=ACTIVE,MAXDATA=4302,MAXOUT=7,          +
                  MAXPATH=1,PUTYPE=2,SECNET=NO,MODETAB=RDBMODES,            +
                  SSCPFM=USSSCS,PACING=0,VPACING=2
PD2102    PATH    DIALNO=0004400050132102,                                  +
                  GRPNM=SY45PG0,GID=1,PID=1,REDIAL=2
SYD2102A  LU      LOCADDR=000
*
SYD2103   PU      ADDR=01,IDBLK=05D,IDNUM=D2103,ANS=CONT,DISCNT=NO,         +
                  IRETRY=YES,ISTATUS=ACTIVE,MAXDATA=4302,MAXOUT=7,          +
                  MAXPATH=1,PUTYPE=2,SECNET=NO,MODETAB=RDBMODES,            +
                  SSCPFM=USSSCS,PACING=0,VPACING=2
PD2103    PATH    DIALNO=0004400050132103,                                  +
                  GRPNM=SY45PG0,GID=1,PID=1,REDIAL=2
SYD2103A  LU      LOCADDR=000
```

Figure 67. VTAM Switched Major Node Definitions

The NCP definitions contain several pieces of information critical to connecting token-ring LANs to VTAM:

- The MAXSESS, AUXADDR, and ADDSESS keywords on the BUILD macro define the NCP resources that can support parallel sessions and peripheral primary LUs. This capability is required to support PU 2.1 systems connected to NCP.

- The LUDRPOOL macro defines dynamic buffer pools used to create control blocks for VTAM switched major nodes.

- The LOCADD keyword on the LINE macro defines the token-ring address of the NCP. In Figure 68 on page 169, two token-ring LANs are attached to the NCP. The NCP acts as address X'400009451901' on one LAN and X'400009451902' on the other LAN. When a DB2 for OS/400 system wants to communicate with DB2 for VM, it must use one of these addresses as the LAN destination address.

```
NCPOPT    OPTIONS    NEWDEFN=YES
************************************************************************
VTAM3     PCCU  CUADDR=C02,                                        *** C
                AUTODMP=NO,                                            C
                AUTOIPL=NO,                                            C
                AUTOSYN=YES,                                           C
                BACKUP=YES,                                            C
                DELAY=0,                                               C
                VFYLM=YES,                                             C
                CHANCON=UNCOND,                                        C
                MAXDATA=4302,                                          C
                DUMPDS=DUMPDS,                                         C
                NETID=SPIFNET,                                         C
                OWNER=HOST3,                                           C
                SUBAREA=3                  HOST SUBAREA NUMBER
*
SY23NCP   BUILD TYPGEN=NCP,                                           C
                ADDSESS=800,              ALLOW 800 SPARE SESSIONS     C
                AUXADDR=1000,             ALLOW 1000 DYNAMIC NAU ADDRS C
                LTRACE=3,                                              C
                BFRS=240,                                              C
                CATRACE=(YES,20),                                      C
                NUMHSAS=8,                                             C
                SUBAREA=23,                                            C
                MAXSSCP=8,                                             C
                MAXSESS=15,               ALLOW UP TO 15 SESSION PER LU C
                MODEL=3745,                                            C
                NAMTAB=2000,              ALLOW 2000 DYNAMIC NAMES      C
                USGTIER=5,                                             C
                OLT=NO,                                                C
                NPA=NO,                                                C
                TRACE=(YES,20),                                        C
                TYPSYS=OS,                                             C
                QUALIFY=NCP,                                           C
                LOADLIB=LOADLIB,                                       C
                NEWNAME=SY23NCP,                                       C
                VERSION=V5R4,                                          C
                NETID=SPIFNET,                                         C
                BACKUP=1200
*
          SYSCNTRL OPTIONS=(BHSASSC,ENDCALL,MODE,RCNTRL,RCOND,RECMD,   C
                RIMM,NAKLIM,SESSION,SSPAUSE,XMTLMT,BACKUP,DVSINIT,      C
                LNSTAT,SESINIT,STORDSP,DLRID,RDEVQ)
*
HOST3     HOST  BFRPAD=0,                                             C
                INBFRS=18,                                             C
                MAXBFRU=10,                                            C
                SUBAREA=3,                                             C
                UNITSZ=441                *** SAME AS VTAM IOBUF  **
*
```

Figure 68 (Part 1 of 3). Token-Ring NCP Definitions

```
********************************************************************
*** DYNAMIC RECONFIGURATION POOL SPACE                        ***
********************************************************************
*
DRPOOLLU LUDRPOOL NUMTYP2=90,           RESERVE 90 DEPENDENT LUS       X
              NUMILU=90                  RESERVE 90 INDEPENDENT LUS
*
*
********************************************************************
*    PATH DEFINITIONS                                               *
********************************************************************
*
        PATH  DESTSA=3,ER1=(3,1),VR1=1
*
****
*  ******************************************************************
*     PHYSICAL GROUP FOR NTRI TIC #1 - CCUB                         *
*  ******************************************************************
****
SY70PG0  GROUP ECLTYPE=(PHYSICAL,PERIPHERAL),LNCTL=SDLC
*
SY70PL0  LINE  ADDRESS=(1088,FULL),  TIC ADDRESS IN 3745            C
               ADAPTER=TIC1,          ADAPTER TYPE                  C
               LOCADD=400009451901,   LAN ADAPTER ADDRESS           C
               MAXTSL=2044,           NTRI TRANSMIT FRAME SIZE      C
               PORTADD=0,             PHYSICAL PORT ADDRESS         C
               TRANSFR=18,            MAX BUFFERS ON A TRANSFER     C
               TRSPEED=4,             TRANSMIT SPEED                C
               RCVBUFC=4095           RECEIVE MAX DATA
********
SY1088PU PU
*
SY1088LU LU    ISTATUS=INACTIVE,LOCADDR=0
****
*  ******************************************************************
*     PHYSICAL GROUP FOR NTRI TIC #2 - CCUB                         *
*  ******************************************************************
****
SY70PG1  GROUP ECLTYPE=(PHYSICAL,PERIPHERAL),LNCTL=SDLC
*
SY70PL1  LINE  ADDRESS=(1089,FULL),  TIC ADDRESS IN 3745            C
               ADAPTER=TIC1,          ADAPTER TYPE                  C
               LOCADD=400009451902,   LAN ADAPTER ADDRESS           C
               MAXTSL=2044,           NTRI TRANSMIT FRAME SIZE      C
               PORTADD=1,             PHYSICAL PORT ADDRESS         C
               TRANSFR=18,            MAX BUFFERS ON A TRANSFER     C
               TRSPEED=4,             TRANSMIT SPEED                C
               RCVBUFC=4095           RECEIVE MAX DATA
SY1089PU PU
*
SY1089LU LU    ISTATUS=INACTIVE,LOCADDR=0
****
```

Figure 68 (Part 2 of 3). Token-Ring NCP Definitions

```
* ********************************************************************
*     LOGICAL  GROUP FOR NTRI TIC #1 - CCUB                          *
* ********************************************************************
****
SY70L00  GROUP ECLTYPE=(LOGICAL,PERIPHERAL),LNCTL=SDLC,              C
               PHYPORT=0,                                            C
               AUTOGEN=30,                                           C
               CALL=INOUT
****
* ********************************************************************
*     LOGICAL  GROUP FOR NTRI TIC #2 - CCU                           *
* ********************************************************************
****
SY70L01  GROUP ECLTYPE=(LOGICAL,PERIPHERAL),LNCTL=SDLC,              C
               PHYPORT=1,                                            C
               AUTOGEN=30,                                           C
               CALL=INOUT
*
***********************************
LNCTLS   GROUP LNCTL=CA,CA=TYPE6,DELAY=0.0,TIMEOUT=500.0
CA0      LINE ADDRESS=00
PUCHAN0  PU PUTYPE=5,TGN=1
               GENEND
               END
```

Figure 68 (Part 3 of 3). Token-Ring NCP Definitions

The VTAM APPL definition for the DB2 for VM system at NEW_YORK2 was given in Figure 44 on page 136 in Chapter 6, "DB2 for MVS/ESA and DB2 for VM via CTC."

The OS/400 commands required to define the connection between DB2 for OS/400 and DB2 for VM follow. The commands define an OS/400 system that has the following identifiers:

- SNA LU name: SYD2101A
- NCP IDNUM: D2101
- OS/400's LAN adapter address: X'400050132101'
- LAN destination address (NCP's token-ring address): X'400009451902'

The network attributes define the AS/400 system:

```
CHGNETA SYSNAME(SYD2101A) LCLNETID(SPIFNET) LCLCPNAME(SYD2101A)
        LCLLOCNAME(SYD2101A)
```

The line description defines the AS/400 system to the network:

```
CRTLINTRN LIND(SQLDSLAN) RSRCNAME(LIN031) MAXFRAME(4302)
          ADPTADR(400050132101) EXCHID(056D2101)
```

The value for the RSRCNAME parameter is system dependent and identifies which physical line is being used for this configuration. The resource names can be found using the Work with Hardware Resources (WRKHDWRSC) command.

The controller description describes the virtual machine:

```
CRTCTLAPPC CTLD(SQLDSCTL) LINKTYPE(*LAN) LINE(SQLDSLAN)
           RMTCPNAME(NYVM) NETID(RMNETID)
           STNADR(01) ADPTADR(400009451902)
```

The configuration list entries define the remote LU names:

```
ADDCFGLE TYPE(*APPNRMT) APPNRMTE((NYVMGAT *NETATR SYD2101A NYVM
                                   SPIFNET *NONE *YES))
```

Add one remote entry for each remote LU name in the network. The entries are shown as lists. Use the OS/400 command prompt facility to see the meaning of each item in the list. In the example, the first item is the remote LU (remote location name), and the fifth item in the list is the remote network ID.

Create a mode description:

```
CRTMODD MODD(IBMRDB)
```

Make the configuration available for use:

```
VFYCFG CFGOBJ(SQLDSLAN) CFGTYPE(*LIN) STATUS(*ON)
```

Add an entry to the Relational Database Directory for the remote database:

```
ADDRDBDIRE RDB(NEW_YORK2) RMTLOCNAME(NYVMGAT) TNSPGMNAME(NYVMDB)
```

Ensure that the CCSIDs are appropriately assigned at each system.

Chapter 11. DB2 for AIX and DB2 for MVS/ESA, DB2 for VM and VSE, or DB2 for OS/400 via Token Ring

Figure 69 shows a DB2 for AIX system connected to DB2 for MVS/ESA, DB2 for VM and VSE and DB2 for OS/400. The Spiffy New York City sales office uses this configuration to access pricing, inventory, and employee information from the corporate database. In this scenario, three DB2 for AIX clients are attached to a DDCS for AIX workstation, which acts as a gateway to the host.

The material in this chapter does not include any VTAM or NCP statements required to connect the machines in question to the other parts of the Spiffy network. You should read Chapter 5, "Connecting DB2 for OS/2 or AIX in a DRDA Network" on page 103 to become familiar with the concepts before you study the examples in this chapter.

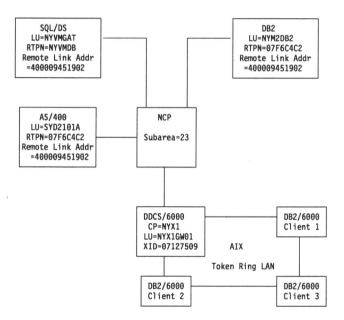

Figure 69. AIX Token Ring Connection to Hosts

Connecting DB2 for AIX to a host application server requires three steps:

- Configuring SNA Services for AIX
- Cataloging the database connection in DB2 for AIX
- Configuring the host server.

Configuring SNA Services for AIX

To connect the DDCS for AIX gateway to the host, you need DDCS for AIX and SNA Services/6000 installed on your RISC System/6000. This section shows how to configure SNA Services for AIX to support SNA LU 6.2 (APPC) connections.

The following information is intended primarily for people who are unfamiliar with SNA LU 6.2 profiles and AIX. It explains how to prepare a minimal SNA configuration for use with DDCS for AIX on a machine on which SNA has not been configured.

Methods of Entering the Configuration Values

Four methods for entering the information shown in the scenario are:

msmit The Motif, GUI-based version of the system management interface tool (SMIT). This is the default when smit is entered on the command line from a bit-mapped display (HFT or X-Terminal).

smitty The ASCII character based version of SMIT. This is the default when smit is entered on the command line from an ASCII terminal.

SNA profiles ASCII text files containing the SNA profiles. You can edit these files by using either the Import SNA Configuration Profiles menu through SMIT or the importsna -l <filename> command.

DDCS for AIX provides template SNA profile files that you can alter and import. They are found in the directory /INSTHOME/sqllib/samples/ddcs.

mksnaobj The AIX command used to make individual profiles.

This scenario uses the ASCII version of SMIT (smitty). All the entry fields and labels are the same if you use the MOTIF version.

Values You Need for the Configuration

You need the following information before you start the configurations:

CP name Specifies the local control point name and describes the characteristics of the physical unit (PU) associated with the local system. The same control point profile can be used with many attachment profiles.

XID node ID The node ID of the physical unit. This 8-character hex ID is exchanged with the remote physical unit when a connection is first established. This verifies that the correct physical units are being connected. The sources for this ID are:

- AS/400 — EXCHID (optional)
- VM, MVS — first 3 characters are IDBLK, last 5 characters are IDNUM (also known as NCP address).

Network name The name of the network to which this LU is attached

Remote LU name The name of the remote LU or adjacent CP name that forms the other half of the connection. The name must match the name that is defined for the local LU on the remote system:

- DB2 for MVS/ESA — DB2 for MVS/ESA APPL LU in VTAM
- DB2 for VM and VSE — Name of the AVS gateway. Each AVS virtual machine may define multiple AVS gateways.

- AS/400 — Local Control Point from the DSPNETA command

Remote link address

The network address of the remote station. Get this 12-digit hexadecimal number from the owner of the remote station.

- DB2 for MVS/ESA, DB2 for VM and VSE — NCP address
- AS/400 — ADPTADR field of the DSPLIND command.

Remote transaction program name

Get information about the remote transaction program from the remote site. If the remote transaction program is the same as one of your local transaction programs, look in the TPN profile for that local program to determine the values to enter in the remote transaction name profile for the remote program. Service transaction programs are specified in hexadecimal EBCDIC format.

Getting to the SNA Profiles

You must perform the SNA configuration for DDCS for AIX while you are logged on as a root user.

All configurations in this scenario start from the Advanced SNA Configuration menu.

Select the screens in the following order to get to the Advanced SNA Configuration screen:

1. Communications Applications and Services
2. SNA Services
3. Configure SNA Profiles
4. Advanced SNA Configuration

You must complete the following profiles to establish an APPC connection from DDCS for AIX to the host server. This sets up the SNA profiles for the host server. The order in which they are completed is arbitrary.

- Attachment Profile (see section on page 177)
- Logical Link Profile (see section on page 178)
- Physical Link Profile (see section on page 179)
- Local LU Profile (see section on page 180)
- Logical Connection Profile (see section on page 180)
- Mode Profile (see section on page 181)
- Mode List (see section on page 182)
- CPI Communications Side Information Profile (see section on page 183)
- Control Point Profile (see section on page 183)

Verify Profiles Are Correct

You should verify your profiles after you finish modifying them. You can also use verification while you are creating a new profile database or when making extensive changes to existing profiles. If you change only a connection profile, you should make sure references to other profiles exist. Select the following menu choice or use the verifysna command.

Your profile database is checked for inconsistencies across different profiles. All profiles are checked for existing references on the database and to ensure values do not conflict.

Verification can take several minutes. For each error message received, note the necessary information, make the necessary changes, and then run the verification again to ensure that problems are corrected.

Using the verifysna command, you can check a list of profiles to determine if they are correct. The verifysna command does not guarantee that all network parameters are accurate. Only parameters that can be checked within the local system are verified.

Stopping and Starting SNA

After setting up the profiles you must stop and then start SNA using the following commands:

```
stopsrc -c -s sna
startsrc -s sna
```

Sample SNA Profiles

It is helpful to use naming conventions in assigning the SNA profile names. In the following scenario all profile names are suffixed with an indication of the type of the profile. These are the suffixes used in the sample profiles:

AP — Attachment Profile
CONN — Logical Connection
CP — Control Point
cpic — CPI Communications Side Information
LL — Logical Link
LU — Logical Unit
ML — Mode List
PL — Physical Link

Usually, the prefix for many of the names in the example is the CP name of the node used, in this scenario, NYX1. Table 17 on page 177 shows parameters and sample values.

Table 17. Sample Host Values

Parameter Name	DB2 for MVS/ESA	DB2 for VM and VSE	OS/400
CP name	NYX1	NYX1	NYX1
Remote link address	400009451902	400009451902	400009451902
XID node ID	07127509	07127509	07127509
Network name	SPIFNET	SPIFNET	SPIFNET
Local LU name	NYX1GW01	NYX1GW01	NYX1GW01
Remote LU name	NYM2DB2	NYVMGAT	SYD2101A
Remote transaction program	07F6C4C2	NYVMDB	07F6C4C2

The procedure used to define each of the profiles for the connection of the DDCS for AIX gateway is the same for connections to DB2 for MVS/ESA, DB2 for VM and VSE, and DB2 for OS/400. The only difference in the example is that the DB2 for VM and VSE connection uses an EBCDIC Remote Transaction Program Name, whereas the other connections specify the name using the hexadecimal representation.

There is one set of static profiles for each AIX machine. The Control Point, Physical Link, and Logical Link profiles are static. After they are set, they do not change, unless you decide to use other devices (different token-ring adapter, ethernet, and so on). These profiles do not change with the addition of new DDCS for AIX gateways.

Attachment Profile

Select the screens in the following order to configure the attachment profile:

1. Physical Units
2. Token Ring
3. Token-Ring Attachment
4. Add a Profile

Table 18 on page 178 shows the parameters and sample values. Figure 70 on page 178 shows the resulting profile.

Table 18. Sample Attachment Profile Values

Parameter Name	DB2 for MVS/ESA	DB2 for VM and VSE	AS/400
Profile name	DB2AP	SQLDSAP	AS400AP
Control point profile name	NYX1CP	NYX1CP	NYX1CP
Logical link profile name	NYX1LL	NYX1LL	NYX1LL
Physical link profile name	NYX1PL	NYX1PL	NYX1PL
Call type	Call	Call	Call
Access routing	Link-address	Link-address	Link-address
Remote link address	400009451902	400009451902	400009451902

```
Change / Show SNA Token Ring Attachment Profile

CURRENT profile name                                     DB2AP
CONTROL POINT profile name                               [NYX1CP]
LOGICAL LINK profile name                                [NYX1LL]
PHYSICAL LINK profile name                               [NYX1PL]
STOP ATTACHMENT on inactivity?                           [no]
   If yes, inactivity TIMEOUT (0-10 minutes)             [0]
RESTART on deactivation?                                 no
LU address REGISTRATION?                                 no
   If yes, LU address REGISTRATION PROFILE name          [LDEFAULT]
CALL type                                                call
   If listen,
      AUTO-LISTEN?                                       no
      MINIMUM SAP address (hex 04-ec)                    [04]
      MAXIMUM SAP address (hex 04-ec)                    [EC]
   If call, ACCESS ROUTING                               link_address
      If link-name, REMOTE LINK name                     []
      If link-address,
         Remote LINK address                             [400009451902]
         Remote SAP address (hex 04-ec)                  [04]
```

Figure 70. Sample Attachment Profile

Logical Link Profile

Select the screens in the following order to configure the Logical Link Profile:

1. Physical Units
2. Token Ring
3. Token-Ring Data Link Control
4. Token-Ring Logical Link
5. Add a Profile

The only parameter that needs to change in this profile is the profile name. The value of the profile name is NYX1LL.

Figure 71 on page 179 shows the resulting profile:

```
Change / Show SNA Token-Ring Logical Link Profile

CURRENT profile name                                  NYX1LL
TRANSMIT window count (1-127)                         [10]
DYNAMIC window increment (1-127)                      [1]
RETRANSMIT count (1-30)                               [8]
RECEIVE window count (1-127)                          [127]
RING ACCESS priority                                  0
RETRY limit                                           [20]
DROP LINK on inactivity?                              yes
INACTIVITY timeout (1-120 seconds)                    [48]
RESPONSE timeout (1-40, 500 msec intervals)          [2]
ACKNOWLEDGE timeout (1-40, 500 msec intervals)       [1]
FORCE DISCONNECT timeout (1-600 seconds)             [120]
DEFINITION of maximum I-FIELD size                    system_defined
   If user-defined, max. I-FIELD SIZE (265-30729)    [30729]
TRACE link?                                            no
   If yes, TRACE SIZE                                 short
```

Figure 71. Sample Logical Link Profile

Physical Link Profile

Select the screens in the following order to configure the token ring physical link profile:

1. Physical Units
2. Token Ring
3. Token-Ring Data Link Control
4. Token-Ring Physical Link
5. Add a Profile

Table 19 shows the parameters and sample values. Figure 72 shows the resulting profile.

Table 19. Sample Physical Link Profile Values

Parameter Name	DB2 for MVS/ESA	DB2 for VM and VSE	AS/400
Profile name	NYX1PL	NYX1PL	NYX1PL
Local link name	NYX1	NYX1	NYX1

```
Change / Show SNA Token-Ring Physical Link Profile

CURRENT profile name                                  NYX1PL
DATALINK device name                                  [tok0]
LOCAL LINK name                                       [NYX1]
Maximum number of LOGICAL LINKS (1-255)               [32]
Local SAP address (hex 04-ec)                         [04]
```

Figure 72. Sample Physical Link Profile

Local LU Profile

Your LAN or host administrator must define the logical unit created in this profile to the NCP. Any client (OS/2 or AIX) that connects to this instance of DB2 for AIX uses the LU name defined here in its own SNA configuration to establish a one-to-one conversation.

Select the screens in the following order to configure the local logical link profile:

1. Logical Units
2. LU6.2
3. LU6.2 Local Logical Unit
4. Add a Profile

Table 20 shows the parameters and sample values. Figure 73 shows the resulting profile.

Table 20. Sample Local LU Profile Values

Parameter Name	DB2 for MVS/ESA	DB2 for VM and VSE	AS/400
Profile name	NYX1GW01	NYX1GW01	NYX1GW01
Network name	SPIFNET	SPIFNET	SPIFNET
Local LU name	NYX1GW01	NYX1GW01	NYX1GW01

```
Change / Show SNA LU6.2 Local LU Profile

CURRENT profile name                    NYX1GW01
TPN LIST profile name                   [TDEFAULT]
NETWORK name                            [SPIFNET]
Local LU NAME                           [NYX1GW01]
INDEPENDENT LU?                         yes
  If no,
    Local LU ADDRESS (1-255)            [1]
    SSCP ID                             []
```

Figure 73. Sample Local LU Profile

Logical Connection Profile

Every incoming conversation with a distinct LU must have an associated logical connection profile.

Select the screens in the following order to configure the logical connection profile:

1. Logical Units
2. LU6.2
3. LU6.2 Logical Connection
4. Add a Profile

Table 21 on page 181 shows the parameters and sample values. Figure 74 on page 181 shows the resulting profile.

Table 21. Sample Logical Connection Values

Parameter Name	DB2 for MVS/ESA	DB2 for VM and VSE	AS/400
Profile name	DB2CONN	SQLDSCONN	AS400CONN
Attachment profile name	DB2AP	SQLDSAP	AS400AP
Local LU profile name	NYX1GW01	NYX1GW01	NYX1GW01
Network name	SPIFNET	SPIFNET	USIBM2P
Remote LU name	NYM2DB2	NYVMGAT	SYD2101A
Mode list profile name	IBMRDBML	IBMRDBML	IBMRDBML
Session concurrency	Parallel	Parallel	Parallel

```
Change / Show SNA LU6.2 Logical Connection Profile

CURRENT profile name                              DB2CONN
ATTACHMENT profile name                           [DB2AP]
LOCAL LU profile name                             [NYX1GW01]
NETWORK name                                      [SPIFNET]
STOP CONNECTION on inactivity?                    no
   If yes, TIMEOUT (0-10 minutes)                 [0]
REMOTE LU name                                    [NYM2DB2]
SECURITY Accepted                                 none
   If conversation or already_verified,
   CONVERSATION SECURITY ACCESS LIST profile      [CONVDEFAULT]
      (If no name entered, /etc/passwd used)
REMOTE TPN LIST profile name                      [DEFAULT]
MODE LIST profile name                            [IBMRDBML]
INTERFACE type                                    extended
   If extended, SESSION CONCURRENCY               parallel
Node VERIFICATION?                                no
```

Figure 74. Sample Logical Connection Profile

Mode Profile

The values entered in the mode profile must match the values in the IBMRDB mode on the OS/2 and AIX clients and on the host databases for the session to be successfully established.

Select the screens in the following order to configure the mode profile:

1. Logical Units
2. LU6.2
3. LU6.2 Mode
4. Add a Profile

Table 22 shows the parameters and sample values. Figure 75 shows the resulting profile.

Table 22. Sample Mode Profile Values

Parameter Name	Value
Profile name	IBMRDB
Mode name	IBMRDB
Maximum number of sessions	30
Minimum contention winners	15
Minimum contention losers	15
RECEIVE pacing	3
SEND pacing	3
Maximum RU size	2048

```
Change / Show SNA LU6.2 Mode Profile

CURRENT profile name                      IBMRDB
MODE name                                 [IBMRDB]
Maximum number of SESSIONS (1-999)        [30]
Minimum contention WINNERS (0-499)        [15]
Minimum contention LOSERS (0-500)         [15]
RECEIVE pacing (0-63)                     [3]
SEND pacing (0-63)                        [3]
Maximum RU SIZE (256,288,...,3840)        [2048]
RECOVERY level                            no_reconnect
```

Figure 75. Sample Mode Profile

Mode List

Select the screens in the following order to configure the mode list profile:

1. Logical Units
2. LU6.2
3. LU6.2 Mode List
4. Add a Profile

Table 23 shows the parameters and sample values.

Table 23. Sample Mode List Values

Parameter Name	Value
Profile name	IBMRDBML
Name 1	IBMRDB

When the profile is displayed, the NAME 1 value above should be in the list.

CPI Communications Side Information

Select the screens in the following order to configure the CPI communications side information profile:

1. Logical Units
2. LU6.2
3. LU6.2 CPI Communications Side Information
4. Add a Profile

Table 24 shows the parameters and sample values. Figure 76 shows the resulting DB2 for MVS/ESA profile.

Table 24. Sample CPI Communications Side Information Values

Parameter Name	DB2 for MVS/ESA	DB2 for VM and VSE	AS/400
Profile name	db2cpic	sqlcpic	as4cpic
Partner LU name	DB2CONN	SQLDSCONN	AS400CONN
Remote transaction program name	07F6C4C2	NYVMDB	07F6C4C2
Service transaction program name	Yes	No	Yes
Mode name	IBMRDB	IBMRDB	IBMRDB

```
Change / Show LU6.2 CPI Communications Side Information Profile

CURRENT profile name                          db2cpic

PARTNER LU name                               [DB2CONN]
   Enter the name of the LU6.2 Connection
   profile which contains the destination
   remote LU name

REMOTE TRANSACTION PROGRAM name (RTPN)        [07F6C4C2]
   SERVICE transaction program?               yes

MODE name                                     [IBMRDB]
```

Figure 76. Sample CPI Communications Side Information Profile

Control Point

Select the screens in the following order to configure the control point profile:

1. Nodes
2. Control Point
3. Add a Profile

Table 25 on page 184 shows the parameters and sample values. Figure 77 on page 184 shows the resulting profile.

Table 25. Sample Control Point Profile Values

Parameter Name	Value
Profile name	NYX1CP
XID Node ID	07127509
Network name	SPIFNET
Control point name	NYX1

```
    Change / Show SNA Control Point Profile

    PROFILE name                                  [NYX1CP]
    XID node ID                                   [07127509]
    NETWORK name                                  [SPIFNET]
    CONTROL POINT name                            [NYX1]
```

Figure 77. Sample Control Point Profile

Resulting SNA Configuration Database Profile

Figure 78 shows the configuration for the DB2 for MVS/ESA connection only. The other connections are analogous.

```
DB2CONN_CONNECTION:
     type = CONNECTION
     profile_name = DB2CONN
     attachment_profile_name = DB2AP
     local_lu_profile_name = NYX1GW01
     network_name = SPIFNET
     remote_lu_name = NYM2DB2
     stop_connection_on_inactivity = no
     lu_type = lu6.2
     interface_type = extended
     remote_tpn_list_name = RDEFAULT
     mode_list_name = IBMRDBML
     node_verification = no
     inactivity_timeout_value = 0
     notify = no
     parallel_sessions = parallel
     negotiate_session_limits = yes
     security_accepted = none
     conversation_security_access_list_name = CONVDEFAULT
```

Figure 78 (Part 1 of 4). Sample SNA Configuration Database Profile

```
NYX1GW01_LOCALLU:
     type = LOCALLU
     profile_name = NYX1GW01
     local_lu_name = NYX1GW01
     network_name = SPIFNET
     lu_type = lu6.2
     independent_lu = yes
     tpn_list_name = TDEFAULT
     local_lu_address = 1
     sscp_id =
     number_of_rows = 24
     number_of_columns = 80

DB2AP_ATTACHMENT:
     type = ATTACHMENT
     profile_name = DB2AP
     control_point_profile_name = NYX1CP
     logical_link_profile_name = NYX1LL
     physical_link_profile_name = NYX1PL
     logical_link_type = token_ring
     restart_on_deactivation = no
     stop_attachment_on_inactivity = no
     station_type = secondary
     physical_link_type = token_ring
     remote_secondary_station_address = 1
     smart_modem_command_sequence =
     length_of_command_sequence = 0
     call_type = call
     x25_level = 1984
     listen_name = IBMQLLC
     autolisten = no
     timeout_value = 0
     remote_link_name_ethernet =
     remote_link_name_token_ring =
     remote_link_address = 400009451902
     selection_sequence =
     length_of_selection_sequence = 0
     network_type = switched
     access_routing = link_address
     remote_sap_address = 04
     remote_sap_address_range_lower = 04
     remote_sap_address_range_upper = EC
     virtual_circuit_type = switched
     remote_station_X.25_address =
     optional_X.25_facilities = no
     logical_channel_number_of_PVC = 1
     reverse_charging = no
     rpoa = no
```

Figure 78 (Part 2 of 4). Sample SNA Configuration Database Profile

```
            default_packet_size = no
            default_window_size = no
            default_throughput_class = no
            closed_user_group = no
            closed_user_group_outgoing = no
            network_user_id = no
            network_user_id_name =
            data_network_identification_code =
            packet_size_for_received_data = 128
            packet_size_for_transmit_data = 128
            window_size_for_received_data = 2
            window_size_for_transmit_data = 2
            throughput_class_for_received_data = 9600
            throughput_class_for_transmit_data = 9600
            index_to_selected_closed_user_group = 0
            lu_address_registration = no
            lu_address_registration_name = LDEFAULT

sna_SNA:
        type = SNA
        profile_name = sna
        total_active_open_connections = 200
        total_sessions = 200
        total_conversations = 200
        server_synonym_name = sna
        nmvt_action_when_no_nmvt_process = reject
        restart_action = once
        stdin = /dev/null
        stdout = /dev/console
        stderr = /dev/console
        sna_error_log = no


NYX1CP_CONTROLPOINT:
        type = CONTROLPOINT
        profile_name = NYX1CP
        xid_node_id = 05D27509
        network_name = SPIFNET
        cp_name = NYX1


IBMRDB_MODE:
        type = MODE
        profile_name = IBMRDB
        mode_name = IBMRDB
        maximum_number_of_sessions = 30
        minimum_contention_winners = 15
        minimum_contention_losers = 15
        receive_pacing = 3
        send_pacing = 3
        maximum_ru_size = 2048
        recovery_level = no_reconnect
```

Figure 78 (Part 3 of 4). Sample SNA Configuration Database Profile

```
IBMRDBML_MODELIST:
     type = MODELIST
     Listname = IBMRDBML
     list_members = IBMRDB


NYX1LL_TOKENRINGLOGICAL:
     type = TOKENRINGLOGICAL
     profile_name = NYX1LL
     retry_limit = 20
     transmit_window_count = 7
     dynamic_window_increment = 1
     retransmit_count = 8
     receive_window_count = 7
     ring_access_priority = 0
     inactivity_timeout = 48
     drop_link_on_inactivity = yes
     response_timeout = 2
     acknowledgement_timeout = 1
     force_disconnect_timeout = 120
     link_trace = yes
     trace_entry_size = long
     logical_link_type = token_ring
     maximum_i_field = system_defined
     maximum_i_field_size = 30729
     physical_link_type = token_ring


NYX1PL_TOKENRINGPHYSICAL:
     type = TOKENRINGPHYSICAL
     profile_name = NYX1PL
     device_name = tok0
     local_link_name = NYX1
     local_sap_address = 04
     physical_link_type = token_ring
     maximum_number_of_logical_links = 32


db2cpic_CPICSIDE:
     type = CPICSIDE
     profile_name = db2cpic
     partner_lu_name = DB2CONN
     remote_TP_name =
     rtpn_name_hex = 07F6C4C2
     service_TP = yes
     mode_name = IBMRDB
```

Figure 78 (Part 4 of 4). Sample SNA Configuration Database Profile

Cataloging the Database Connection in DB2 for AIX

This section shows the database commands required to connect DDCS for AIX with the DB2 for MVS/ESA database as an example.

Cataloging the CPIC Node

Cataloging the CPIC node identifies which node will be used to access the CPIC profile information to the database. It also specifies how passwords are specified to the remote system. The following is the command syntax to catalog the CPIC node:

```
db2 CATALOG CPIC NODE nodename REMOTE symbolic_destination_name SECURITY security_type
```

nodename is an arbitrary name you assign.   symbolic_destination_name is the CPIC
node profile name from SNA Services/6000. This field is case-sensitive.
security_type is the APPC security: same or program.

Example:

```
db2 CATALOG CPIC NODE DB2NODE REMOTE db2cpic SECURITY program
```

Cataloging the Remote Database

The following command specifies which CPIC node to use in connecting to a database
and the method to verify authority to connect with that database:

```
db2 CATALOG DATABASE database-name AT NODE nodename AUTHENTICATION authentication_type
```

database-name is an arbitrary name you assign.   nodename is the name used in
CATALOG CPIC NODE.   authentication_type can be: server, client, or DCS.

Example:

```
db2 CATALOG DATABASE DB2DB AT NODE DB2NODE AUTHENTICATION DCS
```

Cataloging the DCS Database

The following command associates the local database name with the name of the
database on the remote system:

```
CATALOG DCS DATABASE database-name AS target-database-name
```

database-name is the name used in CATALOG DATABASE.   target-database-name is
the actual name of the remote database.

Example:

```
db2 CATALOG DCS DATABASE DB2DB AS NEW_YORK1
```

Configuring the Host

The steps necessary to configure a host connection with DDCS for AIX are similar to
those with DDCS for OS/2. Refer to:

- "Configuring the Host" on page 227 for a DB2 for MVS/ESA host connection
- "Configuring the Host" on page 251 for a DB2 for VM connection
- "DB2 for OS/2 and DB2 for VSE via Token Ring" on page 253 for a DB2 for VSE
  connection
- "Configuring the AS/400" on page 209 for an AS/400 connection

Chapter 12. DB2 for AIX and DB2 for MVS/ESA via SDLC

Figure 79 shows a DB2 for AIX with DDCS for AIX workstation connected to DB2 for MVS/ESA via SDLC. This machine has the following hardware features installed to enable SDLC:

- F/C 2700 — 4-port Multiprotocol Adapter
- F/C 2705 — 4-port MPA Interface Cable
- F/C 2706 — MPA Attachment Cable

The material in this chapter does not include any VTAM or NCP statements required to connect the machines in question to the other parts of the Spiffy network. You should read Chapter 5, "Connecting DB2 for OS/2 or AIX in a DRDA Network" on page 103 to become familiar with the concepts before you study the examples in this chapter.

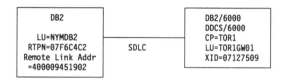

Figure 79. SDLC Connection

Configuring SDLC on SNA Services for AIX

This section assumes that SNA is already set up on the RISC System/6000. Refer to Chapter 11, "DB2 for AIX and DB2 for MVS/ESA, DB2 for VM and VSE, or DB2 for OS/400 via Token Ring" on page 173. The SNA profiles discussed in that chapter must be configured.

To enable the SDLC connection, three additional profiles must be configured:

- SDLC Attachment Profile
- SDLC Negotiable Logical Link Profile
- SDLC Physical Link Profile

If a workstation has only an SDLC connection, replace the Attachment Profile, Logical Link Profile, and Physical Link Profile with the three SDLC profiles.

SDLC Attachment Profile

Select the screens in the following order to configure the SDLC attachment profile:

1. Physical Units
2. SDLC
3. SDLC Attachment
4. Add a Profile

189

Table 26 on page 190 shows the parameters and values that were configured.

Table 26. Sample SDLC Attachment Profile Values

Parameter Name	Value
Current profile name	DB2AP
Control point profile name	NYX1CP
Logical link profile name	NYX1LL
Physical link profile name	NYX1PL
Station Type	negotiable

Figure 80 shows the resulting profile.

```
              Change / Show SNA SDLC Attachment Profile

    PROFILE name                                         [NYX1AP]
    CONTROL POINT profile name                           [NYX1CP]
    LOGICAL LINK profile name                            [NYX1LL]
    PHYSICAL LINK profile name                           [NYX1PL]
    STOP ATTACHMENT on inactivity?                       no
       If yes, inactivity TIMEOUT (0-10 minutes)         [0]
    RESTART on deactivation?                             no
    LU address REGISTRATION?                             no
       If yes, LU address REGISTRATION PROFILE name      [LDEFAULT]
    STATION type                                         negotiable
       If primary,
          REMOTE SECONDARY station address (1-255)       [1]
    PHYSICAL LINK type                                   EIA232D
       If Smart Modem or V.25 bis,
          Modem COMMAND SEQUENCE                         []
       If X.21, NETWORK type                             switched
          If switched, CALL type                         listen
             If call, SELECTION sequence                 []
```

Figure 80. Sample SDLC Attachment Profile

SDLC Negotiable Logical Link Profile

Select the screens in the following order to configure the SDLC Negotiable Logical Link Profile:

1. Physical Units
2. SDLC
3. SDLC Data Link Control
4. SDLC Logical Link
5. SDLC Negotiable Logical Link

6. Add a Profile

The only value that needs to be updated is the profile name. In this scenario, the profile name is NYX1LL.

Figure 81 shows the resulting profile.

```
Change / Show SNA SDLC Negotiable Logical Link Profile

PROFILE name                                        [NYX1LL]
PHYSICAL LINK type                                  EIA232D
TRANSMIT window count                               7
RETRANSMIT count (1-50)                             [10]
Retransmit THRESHOLD (0-100)                        [10]
RETRY limit                                         [20]
DROP LINK on inactivity?                            yes
FORCE DISCONNECT timeout (1-600 seconds)            [120]
DEFINITION of maximum I-FIELD size                  system_defined
   If user-defined, max. I-FIELD SIZE (265-30729)   [265]
TRACE link?                                         no
   If yes, TRACE SIZE                               short
Secondary INACTIVITY timeout (1-120 seconds)        [30]
Local SECONDARY STATION address                     [1]
Primary repoll TIMEOUT (1-250, .1 sec)              [30]
Primary repoll COUNT (3-50 repolls)                 [15]
Primary repoll THRESHOLD (1-100%)                   [10]
```

Figure 81. Sample SDLC Negotiable Logical Link Profile

SDLC Physical Link Profile

Select the screens in the following order to configure the SDLC Negotiable Logical Link Profile:

1. Physical Units
2. SDLC
3. SDLC Data Link Control
4. SDLC Physical Link
5. EIA232D Physical Link
6. Add a Profile

Table 27 shows the parameters and values that were configured.

Table 27. Sample SNA EIA232D Physical Link Profile Values

Parameter name	Value
Profile Name	NYX1PL
Datalink device name	mpq0
Serial encoding	NRZ (NCP Line Definition NRZI=NO on host otherwise use NRZI if NRZI=YES)
Request to send (RTS)	continuous

Figure 82 on page 193 shows the resulting profile.

```
Change / Show SNA EIA232D Physical Link Profile

PROFILE name                                          [NYX1PL]
DATALINK device name                                  [mpq0]
Serial ENCODING                                       NRZ
Request to send (RTS)                                 continuous
DTR control                                           DTR
Bit CLOCKING                                          external
   If internal, TRANSMIT rate (600-38400)             [1200]
NETWORK type                                          switched
   If switched, CALL type                             listen
      If listen,
         AUTO-LISTEN?                                 no
         CALL-OVERRIDE?                               no
         ANSWER MODE                                  automatic
```

Figure 82. Sample SDLC Physical Link Profile

Chapter 13. DB2 for OS/2 and DB2 for OS/400 via Token Ring

Figure 83 shows DB2 for OS/2 systems connected to DB2 for OS/400 using a token-ring LAN. Spiffy Headquarters uses this configuration to give executives access to the Spiffy corporate database systems. In this example, one DB2 for OS/2 system (System 1 in the figure) is installed with a Multi-User Gateway version of the DDCS for OS/2 product. As such, it can provide access to the host for the DB2 for OS/2 client workstations, as well as applications running locally on that workstation. The remaining DB2 for OS/2 systems are configured with the Single-User version of the DDCS for OS/2 product, and provide support access to host data only for applications locally.

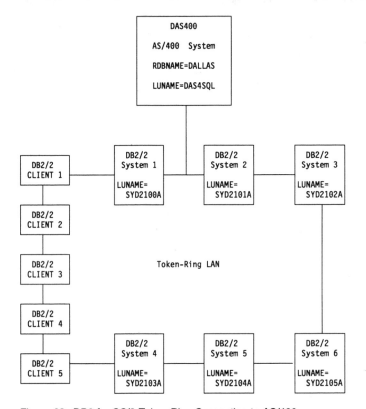

Figure 83. DB2 for OS/2 Token-Ring Connection to AS/400

You should read Chapter 1, "Introducing DRDA Connectivity" on page 2 to become familiar with the concepts before you study the examples in this chapter.

Configuring Communications Manager for OS/2 V1.1

To connect DB2 for OS/2 to the host, you should have DB2 for OS/2 and Communications Manager for OS/2 V1.1 installed on your OS/2 workstation. Communications Manager for OS/2 V1.1 must be configured for APPC. The example

194

below shows you how to configure APPC. This example also assumes you have installed the DDCS for OS/2 product.

If you have not configured a DLC profile for the connection to the host, you must configure the appropriate DLC profile before configuring the SNA network definitions. For more information on configuring DLC profiles, see *Communications Manager/2 Configuration Guide*.

Getting to the Communications Manager Profile List Sheet

Starting from the Communications Manager/2 icon:

1. Click on the **Communications Manager Setup** icon and then the **Setup** pushbutton.

2. Choose a configuration file name and then select **OK**. The Communications Manager Configuration Definition window appears.

3. Select the **Token-ring or other LAN types** from the Workstation Connection Type list.

4. Select **APPC APIs** from the Feature or Application list.

5. Click on the **Configure...** pushbutton. The Communications Manager Profile List Sheet window appears.

Specifying Local Node Characteristics

At the Communications Manager Profile List Sheet window, select **SNA local node characteristics**, then click on the **Configure...** pushbutton at the bottom of the menu. The Local Node Characteristics window appears (Figure 84 on page 196).

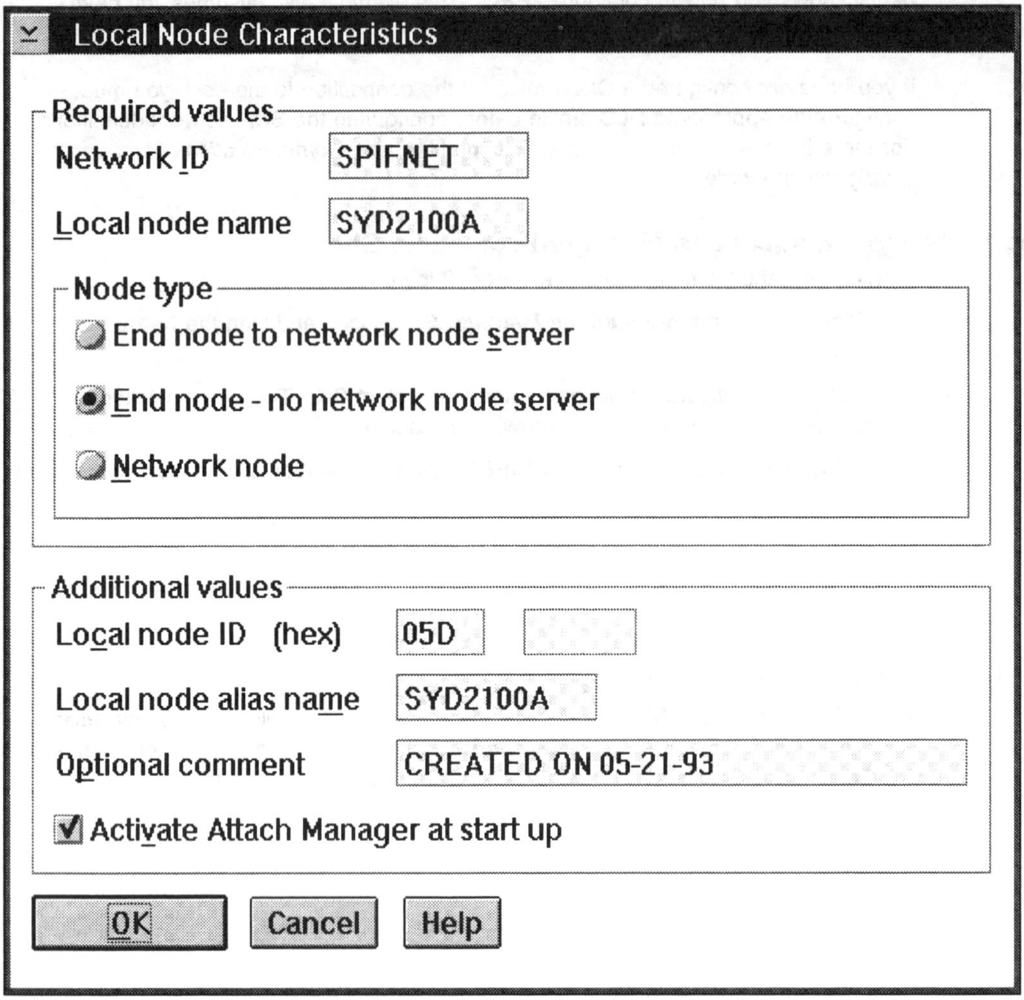

Local Node Characteristics

Required values

Network ID   `SPIFNET`

Local node name   `SYD2100A`

Node type

◯ End node to network node server

● End node - no network node server

◯ Network node

Additional values

Local node ID   (hex)   `05D`   `[        ]`

Local node alias name   `SYD2100A`

Optional comment   `CREATED ON 05-21-93`

☑ Activate Attach Manager at start up

[OK] [Cancel] [Help]

Figure 84. Local Node Characteristics Window

Specify the network ID, the local node name (also known as the PU/CP name), and the local node alias name. When you are finished, click on **OK**. This returns you to the Communications Manager for OS/2 V1.1 Profiles List Sheet window. Table 28 on page 197 gives the sample parameters used for this example and provides a blank column that you can use to fill in the values for your own configuration.

Table 28. Parameters for Local Node Characteristics

Parameter	Example Value	Your Value
Network ID	SPIFNET	
Local node name	SYD2100A	
Local node ID		
Local node alias name	SYD2100A	

Specifying Connections and Partner LUs

Starting at the Communications Manager for OS/2 V1.1 Profile List Sheet:

1. Select **SNA connections**, then click on the **Configure...** pushbutton. A Connections List window appears.

2. Select **To host** from the **Partner type** group.

3. To create a new definition, click on the **Create...** pushbutton.

   To change an existing definition, select a link from the **Link Name** list and click on the **Change...** pushbutton. The Adapter List appears.

4. Select **Token-ring or other LAN types** from the Adapter List.

   The **Configured** field changes to show whether the adapter is configured, and the selections available in the **Adapter number** field change to match the adapter type you selected.

5. Select an adapter number from the **Adapter number** list and click on the **Continue...** pushbutton. The Create a Connection to a Host window appears (Figure 85 on page 198).

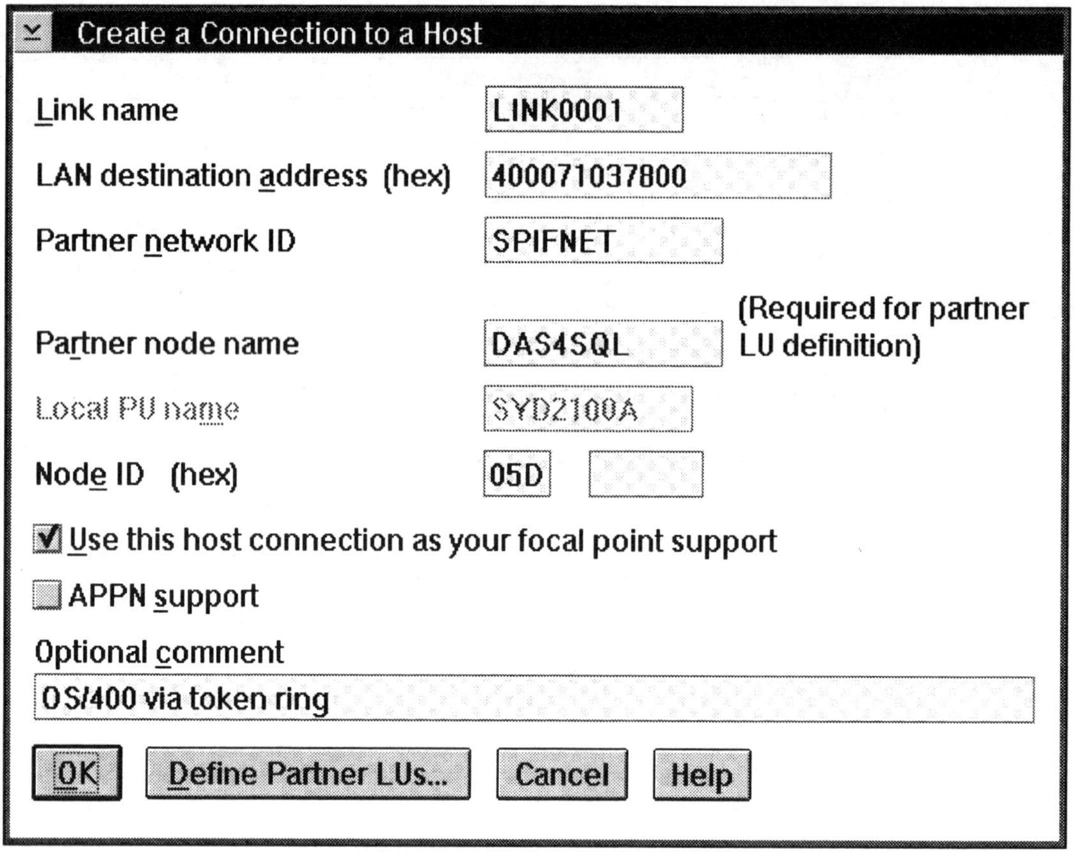

```
┌──────────────────────────────────────────────────────────────────┐
│ ⌄   Create a Connection to a Host                                  │
├──────────────────────────────────────────────────────────────────┤
│                                                                    │
│  Link name                     [LINK0001        ]                  │
│                                                                    │
│  LAN destination address (hex) [400071037800        ]             │
│                                                                    │
│  Partner network ID            [SPIFNET      ]                     │
│                                                                    │
│                                              (Required for partner  │
│  Partner node name             [DAS4SQL      ]  LU definition)     │
│                                                                    │
│  Local PU name                 [SYD2100A     ]                     │
│                                                                    │
│  Node ID  (hex)                [05D ]  [       ]                   │
│                                                                    │
│  ☑ Use this host connection as your focal point support           │
│                                                                    │
│  ☐ APPN support                                                    │
│                                                                    │
│  Optional comment                                                  │
│  [O S/400 via token ring                                        ]  │
│                                                                    │
│  [ OK ]  [ Define Partner LUs... ]  [ Cancel ]  [ Help ]          │
│                                                                    │
└──────────────────────────────────────────────────────────────────┘
```

Figure 85. Create a Connection to a Host Window

6. Enter a link name and the LAN destination address.

7. Enter the network ID and node name for the partner node. The **Define Partner LUs...** pushbutton is enabled.

Note the following correspondences for OS/400:

Partner network ID is the local network ID from the OS/400 display network attributes (DSPNETA) command

Partner node name is the local control point (CP name) from the DSPNETA command

LAN destination address is the local adapter address from the OS/400 Display Line Description (DSPLIND) command or the Work With Line Description (WRKLIND) command when you display the token-ring line description.

Table 29 gives the sample parameters used for this example and provides a blank column that you can use to fill in the values for your own configuration.

Table 29. Parameters for Create Connection to a Host

Parameter	Example Value	Your Value
Link name	LINK0001	
Partner network ID	SPIFNET	
Partner node name	DAS4SQL	
LAN destination address	400071037800	
Comment	OS/400 via token ring	

8. Click on the **Define Partner LUs...** pushbutton. The Create Partner LUs window appears (Figure 86 on page 200).

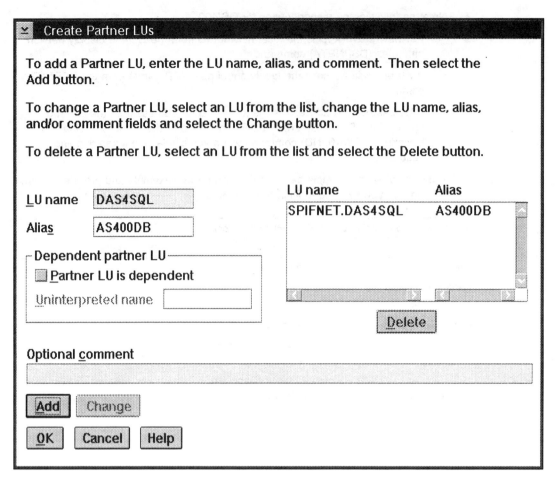

To add a Partner LU, enter the LU name, alias, and comment. Then select the Add button.

To change a Partner LU, select an LU from the list, change the LU name, alias, and/or comment fields and select the Change button.

To delete a Partner LU, select an LU from the list and select the Delete button.

LU name   DAS4SQL

Alias   AS400DB

Dependent partner LU
☐ Partner LU is dependent
Uninterpreted name [   ]

LU name	Alias
SPIFNET.DAS4SQL	AS400DB

Delete

Optional comment
[   ]

Add   Change

OK   Cancel   Help

Create Partner LUs

Figure 86. Create Partner LUs Window

9. Enter an LU name and an alias.

Table 30 gives the sample parameters used for this example and provides a blank column that you can use to fill in the values for your own configuration. The LU name corresponds to the local location name from the OS/400 DSPNETA command.

Table 30. Parameters for Create Partner LUs

Parameter	Example Value	Your Value
LU name	DAS4SQL	
Alias	AS400DB	

10. Click on the **Add** pushbutton.

11. When the partner LU definition is complete, click on the **OK** pushbutton. The Create a Connection to a Host window reappears.

12. Select the **Cancel** pushbutton.

13. Select **Close** from the Connections List.

Specifying the Local LU

You do not need to define a local LU for the workstation when the host is an AS/400. The Communications Manager for OS/2 V1.1 and OS/400 both use APPN for connection identification. The OS/400 takes the OS/2's local node (CP) name as its local LU name.

Specifying the Mode

At the Communications Manager for OS/2 V1.1 Profile List Sheet window, select **SNA Feature**, then click on **Configure....** The SNA Features List appears. Select **Modes** and then click on the **Create...** pushbutton. The Create a Mode Definition window appears (Figure 87).

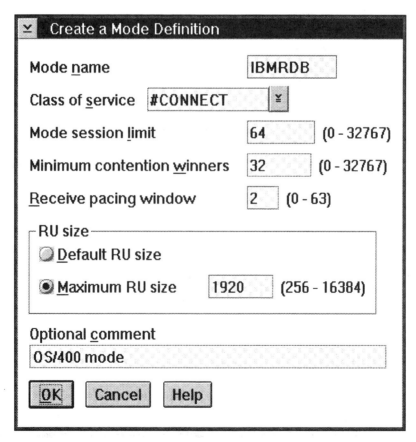

Figure 87. Create a Mode Definition Window

On this window:

1. Specify the **Mode name**. (The mode must be defined on the host).

2. The mode session limit, minimum contention winners, and receive pacing window values are negotiated at the start of the conversation session.[10]

3. Select **Maximum RU size** and specify the value.

When you are finished, select **OK**. This returns you to the SNA Features List window.

Table 31 gives the sample parameters used for this example and provides a blank column that you can use to fill in the values for your own configuration.

Table 31. Parameters for Create a Mode Definition

Parameter	Example Value	Your Value
Mode name	IBMRDB	
Mode session limit	64	
Minimum contention winners	32	
Receive pacing window	2	
Maximum RU size	1920	
Comment	OS/400 mode	

Completing the Configuration

After you complete the steps in the previous sections, you are ready to verify and save your updated configuration file. To do this:

1. Return to the Communications Manager for OS/2 V1.1 Configuration Definition window.
2. Select **Verify configuration** from the **Options** action bar.
3. Select **On**

---

[10] The OS/400 Work With Mode Descriptions (WRKMODD) command shows the current mode descriptions for the AS/400 system. OS/2's mode session limit corresponds to the maximum sessions value; the OS/2 receive pacing value corresponds to OS/400's outbound/inbound pacing values. You can start with the defaults used for the create mode description (CRTMODD) command, or consult with your communications administrator.

Resulting Network Definition File (.NDF)

Figure 88 shows the resulting network definition file.

```
DEFINE_LOCAL_CP  FQ_CP_NAME(SPIFNET.SYD2100A )
                 DESCRIPTION(Created on 04-03-92 at 12:53p)
                 CP_ALIAS(SYD2100A)
                 NAU_ADDRESS(INDEPENDENT_LU)
                 NODE_TYPE(EN)
                 NODE_ID(X'00000')
                 HOST_FP_SUPPORT(YES)
                 HOST_FP_LINK_NAME(LINK0001);

DEFINE_LOGICAL_LINK  LINK_NAME(LINK0001)
                 DESCRIPTION(OS/400 via token ring)
                 FQ_ADJACENT_CP_NAME(SPIFNET.DAS4SQL )
                 ADJACENT_NODE_TYPE(LEN)
                 DLC_NAME(IBMTRNET)
                 ADAPTER_NUMBER(0)
                 DESTINATION_ADDRESS(X'400071037800')
                 CP_CP_SESSION_SUPPORT(NO)
                 ACTIVATE_AT_STARTUP(YES)
                 LIMITED_RESOURCE(USE_ADAPTER_DEFINITION)
                 LINK_STATION_ROLE(USE_ADAPTER_DEFINITION)
                 SOLICIT_SSCP_SESSION(YES)
                 EFFECTIVE_CAPACITY(USE_ADAPTER_DEFINITION)
                 COST_PER_CONNECT_TIME(USE_ADAPTER_DEFINITION)
                 COST_PER_BYTE(USE_ADAPTER_DEFINITION)
                 SECURITY(USE_ADAPTER_DEFINITION)
                 PROPAGATION_DELAY(USE_ADAPTER_DEFINITION)
                 USER_DEFINED_1(USE_ADAPTER_DEFINITION)
                 USER_DEFINED_2(USE_ADAPTER_DEFINITION)
                 USER_DEFINED_3(USE_ADAPTER_DEFINITION);

DEFINE_PARTNER_LU  FQ_PARTNER_LU_NAME(SPIFNET.DAS4SQL )
                 PARTNER_LU_ALIAS(AS400DB)
                 PARTNER_LU_UNINTERPRETED_NAME(DAS4SQL )
                 MAX_MC_LL_SEND_SIZE(32767)
                 CONV_SECURITY_VERIFICATION(NO)
                 PARALLEL_SESSION_SUPPORT(YES);

DEFINE_PARTNER_LU_LOCATION  FQ_PARTNER_LU_NAME(SPIFNET.DAS4SQL)
                 WILDCARD_ENTRY(NO)
                 FQ_OWNING_CP_NAME(SPIFNET.DAS4SQL)
                 LOCAL_NODE_NN_SERVER(NO);
```

Figure 88 (Part 1 of 2). Network Definition File for OS/400

```
DEFINE_MODE    MODE_NAME(MODE0001)
               DESCRIPTION(Created on 04-03-92 at 12:53p)
               COS_NAME(#CONNECT)
               DEFAULT_RU_SIZE(NO)
               MAX_RU_SIZE_UPPER_BOUND(1920)
               RECEIVE_PACING_WINDOW(2)
               MAX_NEGOTIABLE_SESSION_LIMIT(32767)
               PLU_MODE_SESSION_LIMIT(253)
               MIN_CONWINNERS_SOURCE(126);

DEFINE_MODE    MODE_NAME(IBMRDB  )
               DESCRIPTION(OS/400 mode)
               COS_NAME(#CONNECT)
               DEFAULT_RU_SIZE(NO)
               MAX_RU_SIZE_UPPER_BOUND(1920)
               RECEIVE_PACING_WINDOW(2)
               MAX_NEGOTIABLE_SESSION_LIMIT(32767)
               PLU_MODE_SESSION_LIMIT(64)
               MIN_CONWINNERS_SOURCE(32);

DEFINE_DEFAULTS  IMPLICIT_INBOUND_PLU_SUPPORT(YES)
                 DESCRIPTION(Created on 04-03-92 at 12:53p)
                 DEFAULT_MODE_NAME(MODE0001)
                 MAX_MC_LL_SEND_SIZE(32767)
                 DIRECTORY_FOR_INBOUND_ATTACHES(*)
                 DEFAULT_TP_OPERATION(NONQUEUED_AM_STARTED)
                 DEFAULT_TP_PROGRAM_TYPE(BACKGROUND)
                 DEFAULT_TP_CONV_SECURITY_RQD(NO)
                 MAX_HELD_ALERTS(10);

DEFINE_TP      SNA_SERVICE_TP_NAME(X'07',6DB)
               DESCRIPTION(Created on 04-03-92 at 12:53p)
               FILESPEC(C:\SQLLIB\SQLCIAA.EXE)
               CONVERSATION_TYPE(BASIC)
               CONV_SECURITY_RQD(YES)
               SYNC_LEVEL(NONE)
               TP_OPERATION(NONQUEUED_AM_STARTED)
               PROGRAM_TYPE(BACKGROUND)
               RECEIVE_ALLOCATE_TIMEOUT(INFINITE);

DEFINE_TP      SNA_SERVICE_TP_NAME(X'07',6SN)
               DESCRIPTION(Created on 04-03-92 at 12:53p)
               FILESPEC(C:\SQLLIB\SQLCNSM.EXE)
               CONVERSATION_TYPE(BASIC)
               CONV_SECURITY_RQD(YES)
               SYNC_LEVEL(NONE)
               TP_OPERATION(NONQUEUED_AM_STARTED)
               PROGRAM_TYPE(BACKGROUND)
               RECEIVE_ALLOCATE_TIMEOUT(INFINITE);

START_ATTACH_MANAGER;
```

Figure 88 (Part 2 of 2). Network Definition File for OS/400

Cataloging DB2 for OS/2 Directory Entries

You now need to catalog the database, the workstation (node), and the DCS directory.

Select the **Directory Tool** from the **Database 2 for OS/2** folder. The Directory Tool window appears.

Cataloging the Workstation

1. At the Directory Tool window, select **Directory**, and then select **Workstation** from the pull-down menu. The Workstation Directory window appears. If the directory is already displayed, make it the active directory by clicking on it with the mouse.

2. Select **Workstation** and then **Catalog...** from the action bar. The Catalog Workstation window appears (Figure 89).

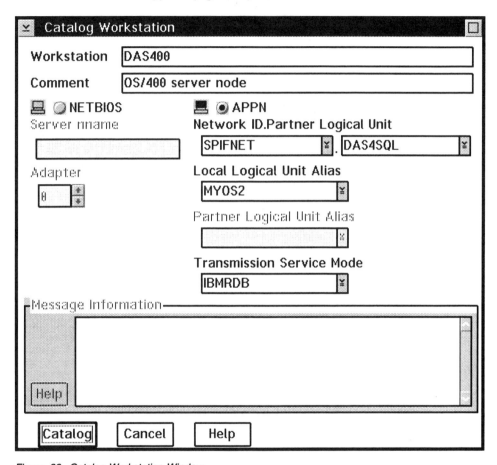

Figure 89. Catalog Workstation Window

On the Catalog Workstation window, do the following:

1. Specify **Workstation**
2. Fill in a **Comment** (optional)
3. Select **APPN**
4. Specify **Network ID**
5. Specify **Partner Logical Unit**
6. Specify **Local Logical Unit Alias**
7. Specify **Transmission Service Mode**

When you are finished, select **Catalog**. If you have not logged on, you will see the logon popup window. Enter your **User ID** and **Password** (your ID must have Administrator or Local Administrator authority) and press Enter. When you see "The operation was successful," select **Cancel**. The workstation you just cataloged should appear in the Workstation Directory window.

Table 32 gives the sample parameters used for this example and provides a blank column that you can use to fill in the values for your own configuration.

Table 32. Parameters for Cataloging the Workstation

Parameter	Example Value	Your Value	Comments
Workstation	DAS400		OS/400 server node
Network ID	SPIFNET		Must match the partner network ID specified in the Create a Connection to a Host window. You can click on the arrow to the right of this box to get a list of network IDs already defined.
Partner logical unit	DAS4SQL		Must match the LU name specified in the Create Partner LUs window. You can click on the arrow to the right of this box to get a list of LU names already defined.
Transmission Service Mode	IBMRDB		Must match the mode name specified in the Creating a Mode Definition menu. You can click on the arrow to the right of this box to get a list of modes already defined.

Cataloging the Database

1. Select **Directory** and **System Database** from the action bar. The System Database Directory window appears. If the directory is already displayed, make it the active directory by clicking on it with the mouse.

2. Select **Database** and then **Catalog...** from the action bar. The Catalog Database window appears (Figure 90 on page 207).

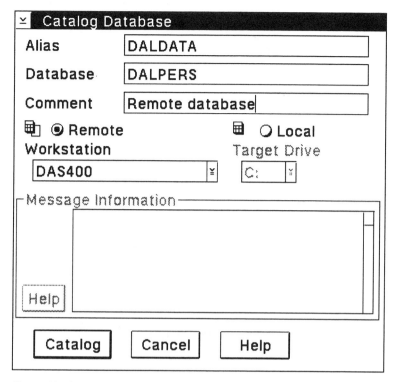

Figure 90. Catalog Database Window

On the Catalog Database window, do the following:

1. Specify **Alias**
2. Specify **Database**
3. Fill in a **Comment** (optional)
4. Select **Remote**
5. Specify **Workstation**

When you are finished, select **Catalog**. When you see "The operation was successful," select **Cancel**. The database you just cataloged should appear in the System Database Directory window.

Table 33 on page 208 gives the sample parameters used for this example and provides a blank column that you can use to fill in the values for your own configuration.

Table 33. Parameters for Cataloging the Database

Parameter	Example Value	Your Value	Comments
Alias	DALDATA		
Database	DALPERS		
Workstation	DAS400		Must match the workstation name specified in the Catalog Workstation menu. You can click on the arrow to the right of this box to get a list of workstations already defined.

Cataloging the DCS Directory

1. Select **Directory** from the menu bar, and then select **Database Connection Services** from the pull-down menu. The Database Connection Services window appears. If the directory is already displayed, make it the active directory by clicking on it with the mouse.

2. Select **Database**, and then select **Catalog...** from the pull-down menu. The Catalog Database window appears (Figure 91).

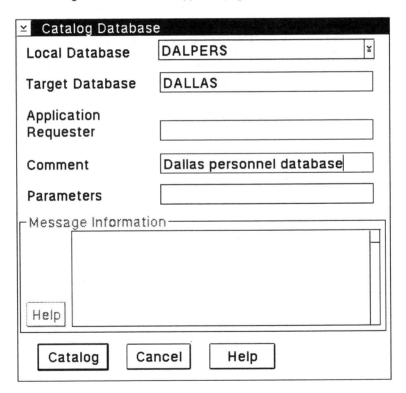

Figure 91. Catalog DCS Database Window

On the Catalog Database window, do the following:

1. Specify **Local Database**
2. Specify **Target Database**
3. Fill in a **Comment** (optional)

When you are finished, click on **Catalog**. When you see "The operation was successful," click on **Cancel**. The database you just cataloged should appear in the Database Connection Services window.

Table 34 gives the sample parameters used for this example and provides a blank column that you can use to fill in the values for your own configuration.

Table 34. Parameters for Cataloging the DCS Directory

Parameter	Example Value	Your Value	Comments
Local database	DALPERS		Must match the Database name specified in the Catalog Database menu (System Database Directory). You can click on the arrow to the right of this box to get a list of databases already defined.
Target DB name	DALLAS		Dallas personnel database. Must match the RDB_NAME on the AS/400. Use the OS/400 WRKRDBDIRE command to view the entry defined as *LOCAL.

Configuring the AS/400

The OS/400 commands required to define the connection between OS/400 and OS/2 via token-ring follow. The commands define an OS/400 system that has the following identifiers:

- SNA LU name: DAS4SQL
- OS/400's LAN adapter address: X'400071037800'

The network attributes define the AS/400 system:

```
CHGNETA SYSNAME(DAS4SQL) LCLNETID(SPIFNET) LCLCPNAME(DAS4SQL)
        LCLLOCNAME(DAS4SQL) DFTMODE(IBMRDB)
```

The line description defines the AS/400 system to the network:

```
CRTLINTRN LIND(OS2LAN) RSRCNAME(LIN061) ADPTADR(400071037800)
        AUTOCRTCTL(*YES)
```

The value for the RSRCNAME parameter is system dependent and identifies which physical line is being used for the configuration. You can find the resource name by using the Work with Hardware Resources (WRKHDWRSC) command.

The AUTOCRTCTL parameter is set to *YES so that the system automatically configures controller and device descriptions to match the OS/2 system trying to connect to the OS/400 system.

To create a mode description:

```
CRTMODD MODD(IBMRDB)
```

Make the configuration available for use:

```
VRYCFG CFGOBJ(OS2LAN) CFGTYPE(*LIN) STATUS(*ON)
```

No entry is added to the Relational Database Directory for the remote database because OS/2 does not support being an application server. An entry for the local relational database must be added:

```
ADDRDBDIRE RDB(DALLAS) RMTLOCNAME(*LOCAL)
```

Additional OS/400 setup is needed for executing SQL statements from the DB2 for OS/2 command line interface. See the Appendix B, "Setting Up the Interactive SQL Utility to Access Unlike Application Servers" on page 442.

Ensure that the CCSID is appropriately assigned. See "Represent Data" on page 101.

Chapter 14. DB2 for OS/2 and DB2 for MVS/ESA via Token Ring

Figure 92 shows DB2 for OS/2 systems connected to DB2 for MVS/ESA, using a 3745 control unit and a token-ring LAN. Spiffy Headquarters uses this configuration to give executives access to the Spiffy corporate database systems. In this example, five DB2 for OS/2 clients are attached to a single DDCS for OS/2 Multi-User Gateway workstation (DB2 for OS/2 system 1), which acts as a gateway to the host. The remaining workstations (DB2 for OS/2 system 2 through DB2 for OS/2 system 6) have the Single-User version of DDCS for OS/2 installed, and communicate directly with the host. This example shows the configuration necessary to connect the DDCS for OS/2 Multi-User Gateway to the host.

The material in this chapter does not include any VTAM or NCP statements required to connect the machines in question to other parts of the Spiffy network. You should read Chapter 1, "Introducing DRDA Connectivity" on page 2 to become familiar with the concepts before you study the examples in this chapter.

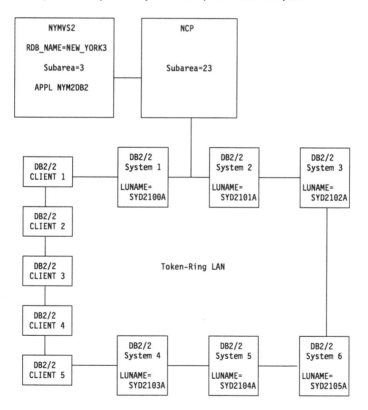

Figure 92. Token-Ring LAN Connected to NCP

Configuring Communications Manager for OS/2 V1.1

To connect DB2 for OS/2 to the host, you should have DB2 for OS/2 and Communications Manager for OS/2 V1.1 installed on your OS/2 workstation. Communications Manager for OS/2 V1.1 must be configured for APPC. The following example shows how to configure APPC. This example also assumes you have installed the DDCS for OS/2 Multi-User Gateway product.

If you have not configured a DLC profile for the connection to the host, you must configure the appropriate DLC profile before configuring the SNA network definitions. For more information on configuring DLC profiles, see *Communications Manager/2 Configuration Guide*.

Getting to the Communications Manager for OS/2 V1.1 Profile List Sheet

Starting from the Communications Manager for OS/2 V1.1 icon:

1. Click on the **Communications Manager for OS/2 V1.1 Setup** icon and then the **Setup** pushbutton.

2. Choose a configuration file name and then click on **OK**. The Communications Manager for OS/2 V1.1 Configuration Definition window appears.

3. Select the **Token-ring or other LAN types** from the Workstation Connection Type list.

4. Select **APPC APIs** from the Feature or Application list.

5. Click on the **Configure...** pushbutton. The Communications Manager for OS/2 V1.1 Profile List Sheet window appears.

Specifying Local Node Characteristics

At the Communications Manager for OS/2 V1.1 Profile List Sheet window, select **SNA local node characteristics**, then click on the **Configure...** (pushbutton at the bottom of the menu). The Local Node Characteristics window appears (Figure 93 on page 213).

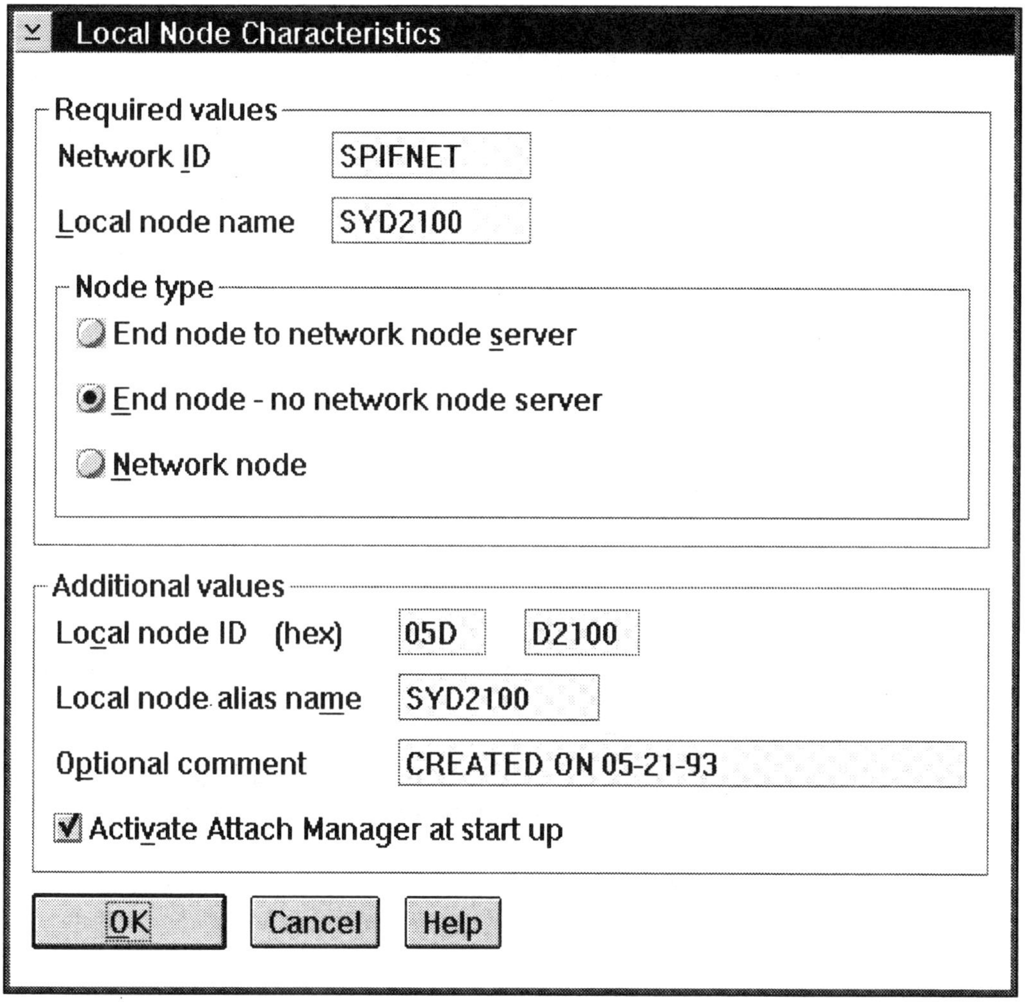

Figure 93. Local Node Characteristics Window

On this panel, specify the network ID, the local node name (also known as the PU/CP name), the local node ID, and the local node alias name. When you are finished, click on **OK**. This returns you to the Communications Manager for OS/2 V1.1 Profile List Sheet window.

Table 35 on page 214 gives the sample parameters used for the example given here and provides a blank column that you can use to fill in the values for your own configuration. These values need to be coordinated with your host administrator.

Table 35. Parameters for Local Node Characteristics

Parameter	Example Value	Your Value	Comments
Network ID	SPIFNET		
Local Node Name	SYD2100		See. Chapter 19, "DB2 for OS/2 and Other DRDA Servers" on page 304.
Local Node ID	D2100		See Chapter 19, "DB2 for OS/2 and Other DRDA Servers" on page 304.
Local Node Alias Name	SYD2100		

Specifying Connections and Partner LUs

1. At the Communications Manager for OS/2 V1.1 Profile List Sheet, select **SNA connections**, then click on the **Configure...** pushbutton. A Connections List window appears.

2. Select **To host** from the **Partner type** group.

3. To create a new definition, click on the **Create...** pushbutton. To change an existing definition, select a link from the **Link Name** list and click on the **Change...** pushbutton. The Adapter List appears.

4. Select **Token-ring or other LAN types** from the Adapter List.

   The **Configured** field changes to show whether the adapter is configured, and the selections available in the **Adapter number** field change to match the adapter type you selected.

5. Select an adapter number from the **Adapter number** list and click on the **Continue...** pushbutton. The Create a Connection to a Host window appears (Figure 94 on page 215).

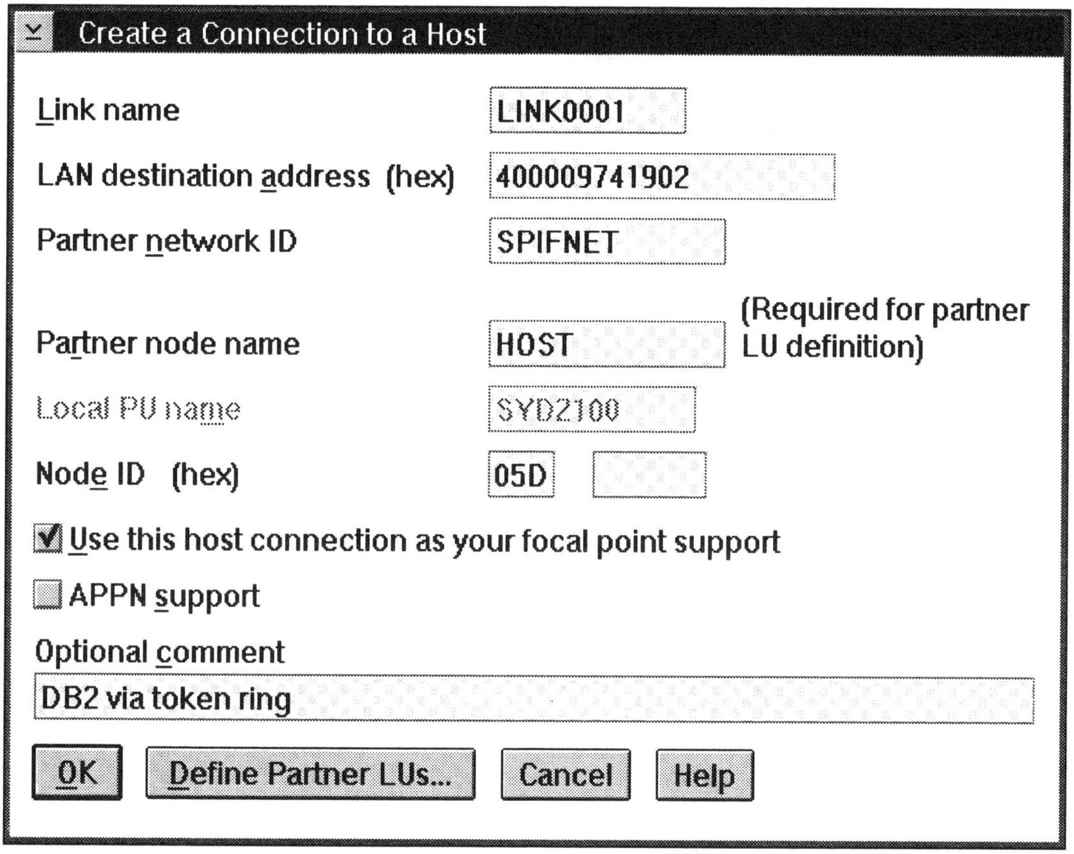

Figure 94. Create a Connection to a Host Window

6. Enter a link name and the LAN destination address.

7. Enter the network ID and node name for the partner node. The **Define Partner LUs...** pushbutton is enabled.

   Table 36 gives the sample parameters used for this example and provides a blank column that you can use for your own configuration. These values need to be checked with your host administrator.

Table 36. Parameters for Host Connection

Parameter	Example value	Your value
Link Name	LINK0001	LINK0001
Partner Network ID	SPIFNET	
Partner Node Name	HOST	
LAN Destination Address	400009451902	
Comment	DB2 via token ring	

8. Click on the **Define Partner LUs...** pushbutton. The Create Partner LUs window appears (Figure 95 on page 216).

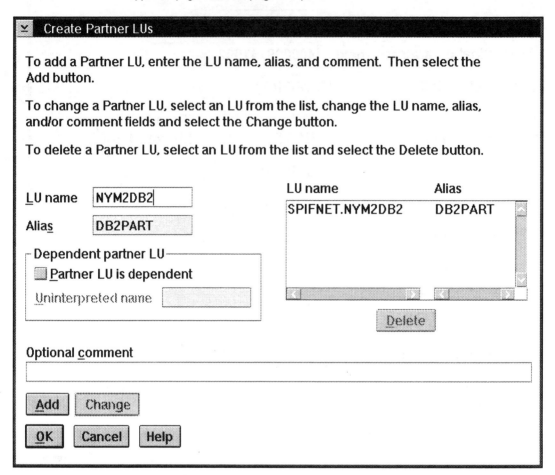

Figure 95. Create Partner LUs Window

9. Enter an LU name and an alias.

Table 37 gives the sample parameters used for this example and provides a blank column that you can use to fill in the values for your own configuration. You need to coordinate with your host administrator for the LU name.

Table 37. Parameters for Create Partner LUs

Parameter	Example Value	Your Value
LU name	NYM2DB2	
Alias	DB2PART	

10. Click on the **Add** pushbutton.

11. When the partner LU definition is complete, click on the **OK** pushbutton. The Create a Connection to a Host window reappears.

12. Click on the **Cancel** pushbutton.

13. Click on **Close** from the Connections List.

Specifying the Local LU

At the Communications Manager for OS/2 V1.1 Profile List Sheet window, select **SNA Features**, then click on **Configure...**. The SNA Features List window appears. From this window select **Local LUs**. Then click on the **Create...** pushbutton. The Create a Local LU window appears (Figure 96).

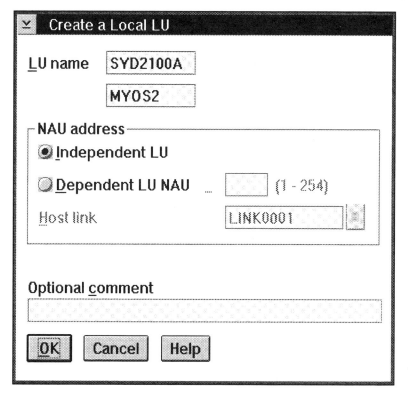

Figure 96. Create a Local LU Window

In this window, specify the local LU name and the local alias and then click on **OK**. This returns you to the SNA Features List window.

Check with your network administrator to verify that this workstation is defined in VTAM as an independent LU. If it is a dependent LU, click on the Dependent LU pushbutton and enter the NAU address that is supplied by your network administrator (the LOCADDR=value from the LU macro in VTAM).

Note: The LU alias is case sensitive.

Table 38 on page 218 gives the sample parameters used for this example and provides a blank column that you can use to fill in the values for your own configuration. You need to ask your host administrator for the LU name.

Table 38. Parameters for Creating a Local LU

Parameter	Example Value	Your Value
LU Name	SYD2100A	
Alias	MYOS2	

Specifying the Mode

At the SNA Features List window, select **Modes**. Then click on the **Create...** pushbutton. The Create a Mode Definition window appears (Figure 97).

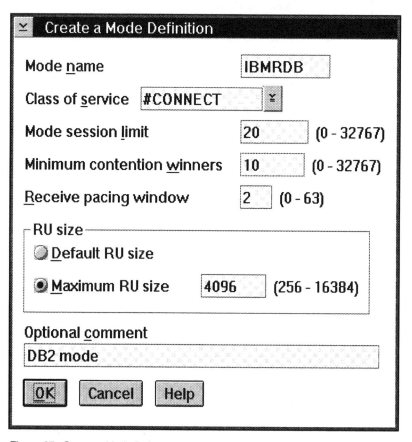

Figure 97. Create a Mode Definition Window

On this window:

1. Specify the **Mode name**.

2. The default values for the **Mode session limit, Minimum contention winners**, and **Receive pacing window** will work in many cases. However, you should coordinate these with your host administrator.

3. Select **Maximum RU size** and specify the **value**.

When you are finished, click on **OK**. This returns you to the SNA Features List window.

Table 39 gives the sample parameters used for this example and provides a blank column that you can use to fill in the values for your own configuration. You need to coordinate these values with your host administrator.

Table 39. Parameters for Creating a Mode Definition

Parameter	Example Value	Your Value
Mode Name	IBMRDB	
Mode Session Limit	20	
Minimum Contention Winners	10	
Receive Pacing Window	2	
Maximum RU Size	4096	
Comment	DB2 mode	

Completing the Configuration

After you complete the steps in the previous sections, you are ready to verify and save your updated configuration file. To do this:

1. Return to the Communications Manager for OS/2 V1.1 Configuration Definition window.
2. Select **Verify configuration** from the **Options** action bar.
3. Select **On**.

Resulting Network Definition File (.NDF)

Figure 98 on page 220 shows the resulting network definition file.

```
DEFINE_LOCAL_CP    FQ_CP_NAME(SPIFNET.SYD2100)
                   DESCRIPTION(Created on 04-03-92 at 12:53p)
                   CP_ALIAS(SYD2100 )
                   NAU_ADDRESS(INDEPENDENT_LU)
                   NODE_TYPE(EN)
                   NODE_ID(X'D2100')
                   HOST_FP_SUPPORT(YES)
                   HOST_FP_LINK_NAME(LINK0001);


DEFINE_LOGICAL_LINK    LINK_NAME(LINK0001)
                       DESCRIPTION(DB2 via token ring)
                       FQ_ADJACENT_CP_NAME(SPIFNET.HOST)
                       ADJACENT_NODE_TYPE(LEN)
                       DLC_NAME(IBMTRNET)
                       ADAPTER_NUMBER(0)
                       DESTINATION_ADDRESS(X'400009451902')
                       CP_CP_SESSION_SUPPORT(NO)
                       ACTIVATE_AT_STARTUP(YES)
                       LIMITED_RESOURCE(USE_ADAPTER_DEFINITION)
                       LINK_STATION_ROLE(USE_ADAPTER_DEFINITION)
                       SOLICIT_SSCP_SESSION(YES)
                       EFFECTIVE_CAPACITY(USE_ADAPTER_DEFINITION)
                       COST_PER_CONNECT_TIME(USE_ADAPTER_DEFINITION)
                       COST_PER_BYTE(USE_ADAPTER_DEFINITION)
                       SECURITY(USE_ADAPTER_DEFINITION)
                       PROPAGATION_DELAY(USE_ADAPTER_DEFINITION)
                       USER_DEFINED_1(USE_ADAPTER_DEFINITION)
                       USER_DEFINED_2(USE_ADAPTER_DEFINITION)
                       USER_DEFINED_3(USE_ADAPTER_DEFINITION);
```

Figure 98 (Part 1 of 3). Network Definition File for DB2 for MVS/ESA

```
DEFINE_LOCAL_LU   LU_NAME(SYD2100A)
                  LU_ALIAS(MYOS2)
                  NAU_ADDRESS(INDEPENDENT_LU);

DEFINE_PARTNER_LU   FQ_PARTNER_LU_NAME(SPFINET.NYM2DB2  )
                    PARTNER_LU_ALIAS(DB2PART)
                    PARTNER_LU_UNINTERPRETED_NAME(NYM2DB2 )
                    MAX_MC_LL_SEND_SIZE(32767)
                    CONV_SECURITY_VERIFICATION(NO)
                    PARALLEL_SESSION_SUPPORT(YES);

DEFINE_PARTNER_LU_LOCATION   FQ_PARTNER_LU_NAME(SPFINET.NYM2DB2)
                             WILDCARD_ENTRY(NO)
                             FQ_OWNING_CP_NAME(SPFINET.HOST)
                             LOCAL_NODE_NN_SERVER(NO);

DEFINE_MODE   MODE_NAME(MODE0001)
              DESCRIPTION(Created on 04-03-92 at 12:53p)
              COS_NAME(#CONNECT)
              DEFAULT_RU_SIZE(NO)
              MAX_RU_SIZE_UPPER_BOUND(1920)
              RECEIVE_PACING_WINDOW(2)
              MAX_NEGOTIABLE_SESSION_LIMIT(32767)
              PLU_MODE_SESSION_LIMIT(253)
              MIN_CONWINNERS_SOURCE(126);

DEFINE_MODE   MODE_NAME(IBMRDB  )
              DESCRIPTION(DB2 mode)
              COS_NAME(#CONNECT)
              DEFAULT_RU_SIZE(NO)
              MAX_RU_SIZE_UPPER_BOUND(4096)
              RECEIVE_PACING_WINDOW(4)
              MAX_NEGOTIABLE_SESSION_LIMIT(32767)
              PLU_MODE_SESSION_LIMIT(20)
              MIN_CONWINNERS_SOURCE(10);

DEFINE_DEFAULTS   IMPLICIT_INBOUND_PLU_SUPPORT(YES)
                  DESCRIPTION(Created on 04-03-92 at 12:53p)
                  DEFAULT_MODE_NAME(MODE0001)
                  MAX_MC_LL_SEND_SIZE(32767)
                  DIRECTORY_FOR_INBOUND_ATTACHES(*)
                  DEFAULT_TP_OPERATION(NONQUEUED_AM_STARTED)
                  DEFAULT_TP_PROGRAM_TYPE(BACKGROUND)
                  DEFAULT_TP_CONV_SECURITY_RQD(NO)
                  MAX_HELD_ALERTS(10);
```

Figure 98 (Part 2 of 3). Network Definition File for DB2 for MVS/ESA

```
DEFINE_TP  SNA_SERVICE_TP_NAME(X'07',6DB)
           DESCRIPTION(Created on 04-03-92 at 12:53p)
           FILESPEC(C:\SQLLIB\SQLCIAA.EXE)
           CONVERSATION_TYPE(BASIC)
           CONV_SECURITY_RQD(YES)
           SYNC_LEVEL(NONE)
           TP_OPERATION(NONQUEUED_AM_STARTED)
           PROGRAM_TYPE(BACKGROUND)
           RECEIVE_ALLOCATE_TIMEOUT(INFINITE);

DEFINE_TP  SNA_SERVICE_TP_NAME(X'07',6SN)
           DESCRIPTION(Created on 04-03-92 at 12:53p)
           FILESPEC(C:\SQLLIB\SQLCNSM.EXE)
           CONVERSATION_TYPE(BASIC)
           CONV_SECURITY_RQD(YES)
           SYNC_LEVEL(NONE)
           TP_OPERATION(NONQUEUED_AM_STARTED)
           PROGRAM_TYPE(BACKGROUND)
           RECEIVE_ALLOCATE_TIMEOUT(INFINITE);

START_ATTACH_MANAGER;
```

Figure 98 (Part 3 of 3). Network Definition File for DB2 for MVS/ESA

Cataloging DB2 for OS/2 Directory Entries

Now you need to catalog the database, the workstation (node), and the DCS database.

Select the **Directory Tool** from the **Database 2 for OS/2** or folder. The Directory Tool window appears.

Cataloging the Workstation

1. At the Directory Tool window, select **Directory** and **Workstation** from the action bar. The Workstation Directory window appears. If the directory is already displayed, make it the active directory by clicking on it with the mouse.

2. Select **Workstation** and then **Catalog...** from the action bar. The Catalog Workstation window appears (Figure 99 on page 223).

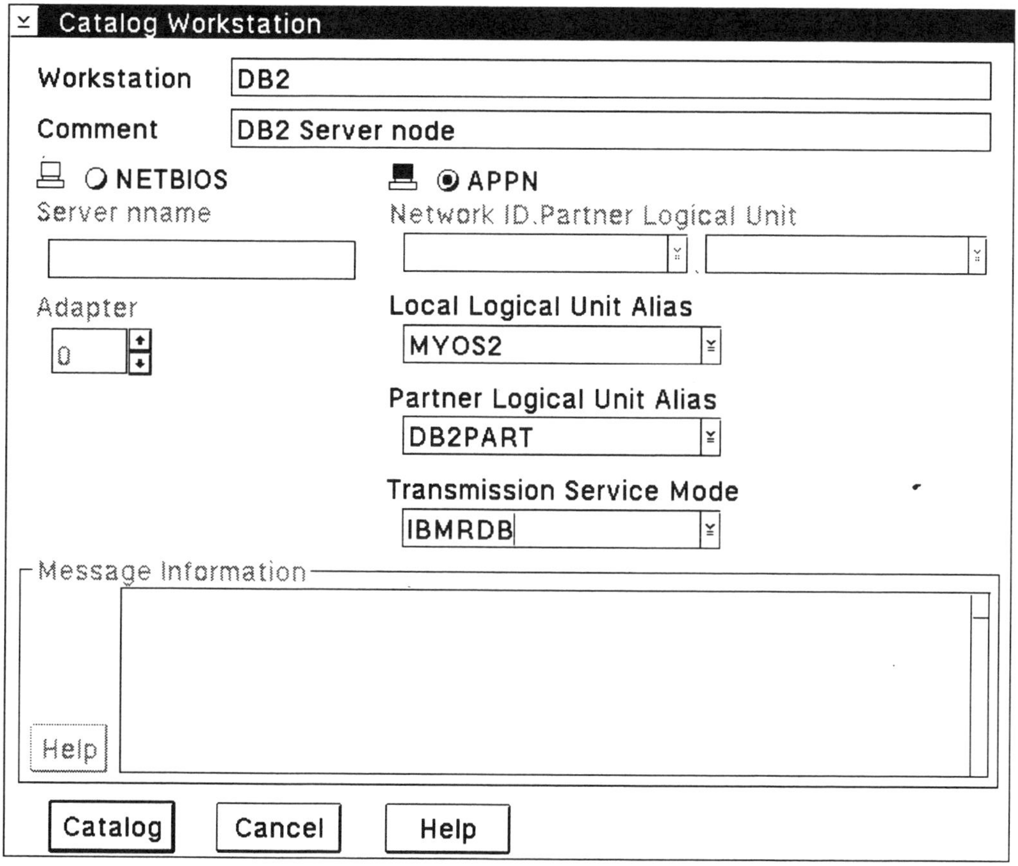

Catalog Workstation

Workstation   `DB2`

Comment   `DB2 Server node`

   ○ NETBIOS   ◉ APPN

Server nname   Network ID.Partner Logical Unit

Adapter   Local Logical Unit Alias

`0`   `MYOS2`

Partner Logical Unit Alias

`DB2PART`

Transmission Service Mode

`IBMRDB`

Message Information

Help

Catalog   Cancel   Help

Figure 99. Catalog Workstation Window

On the Catalog Workstation window, do the following:

1. Specify **Workstation**
2. Enter a **Comment** (optional)
3. Select **APPN**
4. Specify **Local Logical Unit Alias**
5. Specify **Partner Logical Unit Alias**
6. Specify **Transmission Service Mode**

When you are finished, select **Catalog**. If you have not previously logged on, the logon popup window appears. Enter your **User ID** and **Password** and press Enter. When you see "The operation was successful," click on **Cancel**. The workstation you just cataloged should now appear in the Workstation Directory window.

Table 40 on page 224 gives the sample parameters used for this example and provides a blank column that you can use to fill in the values for your own configuration. You need to coordinate with your host administrator for these values.

Table 40. Parameters for Cataloging the Workstation

Parameter	Example Value	Your Value	Comments
Workstation	DB2		
Comment	DB2 server node		
Local logical unit alias	MYOS2		Must match the alias specified in the Creating a Local LU menu. You can click on the arrow to the right of this box to get a list of local LUs already defined.
Partner logical unit alias	DB2PART		Must match the alias specified in the Creating Partner LUs menu. You can click on the arrow to the right of this box to get a list of partner LU aliases already defined.
Transmission service mode	IBMRDB		Must match the mode name specified in the Creating a Mode Definition menu. You can click on the arrow to the right of this box to get a list of modes already defined.

Cataloging the Database

1. Select **Directory** and **System Database** from the action bar. The System Database Directory window appears. If the directory is already displayed, make it the active directory by clicking on it with the mouse.

2. Select **Database** and then **Catalog...** from the action bar. The Catalog Database window appears (Figure 100 on page 225).

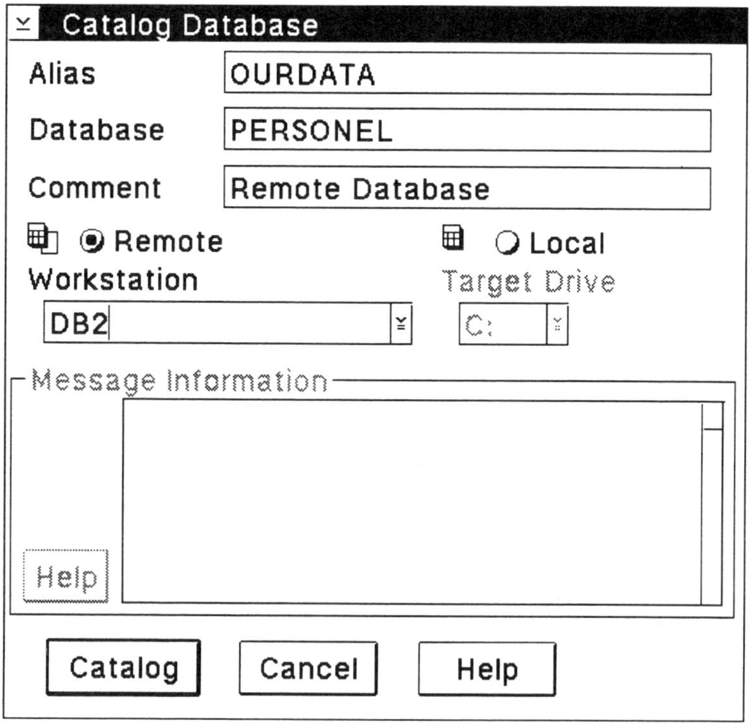

Figure 100. Catalog Database Window

In the Catalog Database window, do the following:

1. Specify **Alias**
2. Specify **Database**
3. Enter a **Comment** (optional)
4. Select **Remote**
5. Specify **Workstation**

When you are finished, select **Catalog**. When you see "The operation was successful," select **Cancel**. The database you just cataloged should now appear in the System Database Directory window.

Table 41 gives the sample parameters used for this example and provides a blank column that you can use to fill in the values for your own configuration. You need to coordinate with your host administrator for these values.

Table 41 (Page 1 of 2). Parameters for Cataloging the Database

Parameter	Example Value	Your Value	Comments
Alias	OURDATA		
Database	PERSONEL		

Table 41 (Page 2 of 2). Parameters for Cataloging the Database

Parameter	Example Value	Your Value	Comments
Comment	Remote database		
Workstation	DB2		Must match the workstation name specified in the Catalog Workstation menu. You can click on the arrow to the right of this box to get a list of workstations already defined.

Cataloging the DCS Database

1. Select **Directory** and **Database Connection Services** from the action bar. The Database Connection Services window appears. If the directory is already displayed, make it the active directory by clicking on it with the mouse.

2. Select **Database** and then **Catalog...** from the action bar. The Catalog Database window appears (Figure 101).

Figure 101. Catalog (DCS) Database Window

In the Catalog Database window, specify the following:

1. **Local Database**

2. **Target Database**
3. **Comment** (optional)

When you are finished, select **Catalog**. When you see "The operation was successful," select **Cancel**. The database you just cataloged should now appear in the Database Connection Services window.

Table 42 gives the sample parameters used for this example and provides a blank column that you can use to fill in the values for your own configuration. You need to coordinate with your host administrator for these values.

Table 42. Parameters for Cataloging the DCS Database

Parameter	Example Value	Your Value	Comments
Local Database	PERSONEL		Must match the Database name specified in the Catalog Database menu (System Database Directory). You can click on the arrow to the right of this box to get a list of databases already defined.
Target database	NEW_YORK3		Must match the RDB_NAME on the host.
Comment	NY personnel database		

Configuring the Host

A device on a token-ring LAN can be defined to NCP as either a switched or nonswitched device. In Figure 102 on page 230, the DB2 for OS/2 systems are defined as PU 2.1 switched devices.

Switched devices are defined to VTAM as *switched major nodes*. For each token-ring device, the following items are recorded in the VTAM switched major node definition:

- The PU name of the device

- The IDBLK value, which must be X'05D' for a Communications Manager for OS/2 V1.1 system. IDBLK is used during the SNA exchange ID process (XID).

- The IDNUM value, which is also used in the SNA XID process. The IDNUM value is also known as the *node ID* or the *PUID*. The node ID in the Communications Manager for OS/2 V1.1 SNA Base Profile must match the IDNUM value in the VTAM switched major node definition. In Figure 102 on page 230, the node ID value is X'D2100' for the first LAN station.

- The DIALNO value defines the token-ring LAN address of the device. VTAM and NCP use the DIALNO value to relate PU and LU names to the token-ring LAN station address. For example, the system at LAN address X'400050132100' has PU name SYD2100 and LU name SYD2100A.

You can determine the LAN address by browsing the C:\IBMCOM\LANTRAN.LOG file. Look for a line that defines the adapter address being used:

```
⋮
Adapter 0 was initialized and opened successfully.
Adapter 0 is using node address 400050132100.
⋮
```

- The LU name associated with the OS/2 system is also defined in the VTAM switched major node definitions. Each LU in our example specifies LOCADDR=000, which indicates the LU is a PU 2.1 device.

Table 43 gives the values needed to make the connection between DB2 for OS/2 systems and the DB2 for MVS/ESA system at Spiffy Headquarters.

Table 43 (Page 1 of 2). Overview of Values Required to Connect DB2 for OS/2 to DB2 for MVS/ESA

Parameter	Definitions for MVS System	Definitions for DB2 for OS/2 System
DB2 for MVS/ESA LUNAME	1. VTAM APPL statement 2. DB2 BSDS	Communications Manager for OS/2 V1.1 Create Partner LUs window
DB2 for MVS/ESA TPN	N/A	Default is .6DB (entered as ASCII, translated to hexadecimal)
Communications Manager for OS/2 V1.1 LUNAME	1. VTAM LU statement 2. LUNAME column in SYSIBM.SYSLUNAMES	Communications Manager for OS/2 V1.1 Create a Local LU window
Communications Manager for OS/2 V1.1 is a PU 2.1	LOCADDR=0 on VTAM LU statement	Communications Manager for OS/2 V1.1 Create a Local Node Definition window - mode session limit > 1
Communications Manager for OS/2 V1.1 Application Requester must send SNA SECURITY=PGM on requests to DB2 for MVS/ESA	1. USERSECURITY column of SYSIBM.SYSLUNAMES table 2. VTAM APPL SECACPT=ALREADYV	Default sent by Communications Manager for OS/2 V1.1
USERID and PASSWORD for requests sent to DB2 for MVS/ESA application server	Validated by RACF	Communications Manager for OS/2 V1.1 User Profile Management
MODENAME	VTAM MODEENT macro	Communications Manager for OS/2 V1.1 Create a Mode Definition window
LAN address of NCP	LOCADD on NCP LINE macro	Communications Manager for OS/2 V1.1 Create a Connection to a Host (or To Peer Node) window
LAN address of Communications Manager for OS/2 V1.1	DIALNO on VTAM PATH macro	Communications Manager for OS/2 V1.1 LANTRAN.LOG file
Node ID for Communications Manager for OS/2 V1.1	IDNUM on VTAM PU macro	Communications Manager for OS/2 V1.1 Local Node Characteristics window
Communications Manager for OS/2 V1.1 LU address	LOCADDR on VTAM LU macro	Communications Manager for OS/2 V1.1 Create a Local LU window

Parameter	Definitions for MVS System	Definitions for DB2 for OS/2 System
Support RU size 4096	1. MAXBFRU on NCP HOST macro 2. MAXDATA on NCP PCCU macro 3. RCVBUFC on NCP LINE macro	Create a Mode Definition window
Set PACING to 2	1. VPACING on VTAM APPL statement 2. Nonzero SSNDPAC on VTAM MODEENT 3. VPACING on VTAM PU macro	Communications Manager for OS/2 V1.1 Create a Mode Definition window

Figure 102 on page 230 gives the VTAM definitions for the switched devices on the token-ring LAN.

Note: The PATH statements are not required if OS/2 always initiates the session. The host cannot initiate the session to OS/2 for this release.

```
SWA0099   VBUILD  TYPE=SWNET,MAXGRP=1,MAXNO=40
*
SYD2100   PU      ADDR=01,IDBLK=05D,IDNUM=D2100,ANS=CONT,DISCNT=NO,      +
                  IRETRY=YES,ISTATUS=ACTIVE,MAXDATA=4302,MAXOUT=7,       +
                  MAXPATH=1,PUTYPE=2,SECNET=NO,MODETAB=RDBMODES,         +
                  SSCPFM=USSSCS,PACING=0,VPACING=2
PD2100    PATH    DIALNO=0004400050132100,                              +
                  GRPNM=SY45PG0,GID=1,PID=1,REDIAL=2
SYD2100A LU       LOCADDR=000
*
SYD2101   PU      ADDR=01,IDBLK=05D,IDNUM=D2101,ANS=CONT,DISCNT=NO,      +
                  IRETRY=YES,ISTATUS=ACTIVE,MAXDATA=4302,MAXOUT=7,       +
                  MAXPATH=1,PUTYPE=2,SECNET=NO,MODETAB=RDBMODES,         +
                  SSCPFM=USSSCS,PACING=0,VPACING=2
PD2101    PATH    DIALNO=0004400050132101,                              +
                  GRPNM=SY45PG0,GID=1,PID=1,REDIAL=2
SYD2101A LU       LOCADDR=000
*
SYD2102   PU      ADDR=01,IDBLK=05D,IDNUM=D2102,ANS=CONT,DISCNT=NO,      +
                  IRETRY=YES,ISTATUS=ACTIVE,MAXDATA=4302,MAXOUT=7,       +
                  MAXPATH=1,PUTYPE=2,SECNET=NO,MODETAB=RDBMODES,         +
                  SSCPFM=USSSCS,PACING=0,VPACING=2
PD2102    PATH    DIALNO=0004400050132102,                              +
                  GRPNM=SY45PG0,GID=1,PID=1,REDIAL=2
SYD2102A LU       LOCADDR=000
*
SYD2103   PU      ADDR=01,IDBLK=05D,IDNUM=D2103,ANS=CONT,DISCNT=NO,      +
                  IRETRY=YES,ISTATUS=ACTIVE,MAXDATA=4302,MAXOUT=7,       +
                  MAXPATH=1,PUTYPE=2,SECNET=NO,MODETAB=RDBMODES,         +
                  SSCPFM=USSSCS,PACING=0,VPACING=2
PD2103    PATH    DIALNO=0004400050132103,                              +
                  GRPNM=SY45PG0,GID=1,PID=1,REDIAL=2
SYD2103A LU       LOCADDR=000
*
SYD2104   PU      ADDR=01,IDBLK=05D,IDNUM=D2104,ANS=CONT,DISCNT=NO,      +
                  IRETRY=YES,ISTATUS=ACTIVE,MAXDATA=4302,MAXOUT=7,       +
                  MAXPATH=1,PUTYPE=2,SECNET=NO,MODETAB=RDBMODES,         +
                  SSCPFM=USSSCS,PACING=0,VPACING=2
PD2104    PATH    DIALNO=0004400050132104,                              +
                  GRPNM=SY45PG0,GID=1,PID=1,REDIAL=2
SYD2104A LU       LOCADDR=000
*
SYD2105   PU      ADDR=01,IDBLK=05D,IDNUM=D2105,ANS=CONT,DISCNT=NO,      +
                  IRETRY=YES,ISTATUS=ACTIVE,MAXDATA=4302,MAXOUT=7,       +
                  MAXPATH=1,PUTYPE=2,SECNET=NO,MODETAB=RDBMODES,         +
                  SSCPFM=USSSCS,PACING=0,VPACING=2
PD2105    PATH    DIALNO=0004400050132105,                              +
                  GRPNM=SY45PG0,GID=1,PID=1,REDIAL=2
SYD2105A LU       LOCADDR=000
```

Figure 102. VTAM Switched Major Node Definitions

The NCP definitions contain several pieces of information critical to connecting token-ring LANs to VTAM:

- The MAXSESS, AUXADDR, and ADDSESS keywords on the BUILD macro define the NCP resources that can support parallel sessions and peripheral primary LUs. This capability is required to support PU 2.1 systems connected to NCP.

- The LUDRPOOL macro defines dynamic buffer pools used to create control blocks for VTAM switched major nodes.

- The LOCADD keyword on the LINE macro defines the token-ring address of the NCP. In Figure 103, two token-ring LANs are attached to the NCP. The NCP acts as address X'400009451901' on one LAN and X'400009451902' on the other LAN. When a DB2 for OS/2 system communicates with DB2 for MVS/ESA, it must use one of these addresses as the LAN destination address.

```
NCPOPT   OPTIONS   NEWDEFN=YES
************************************************************************
VTAM3    PCCU  CUADDR=C02,                                    *** C
               AUTODMP=NO,                                        C
               AUTOIPL=NO,                                        C
               AUTOSYN=YES,                                       C
               BACKUP=YES,                                        C
               DELAY=0,                                           C
               VFYLM=YES,                                         C
               CHANCON=UNCOND,                                    C
               MAXDATA=4302,                                      C
               DUMPDS=DUMPDS,                                     C
               NETID=SPIFNET,                                     C
               OWNER=HOST3,                                       C
               SUBAREA=3              HOST SUBAREA NUMBER
*
SY23NCP  BUILD TYPGEN=NCP,                                        C
               ADDSESS=800,          ALLOW 800 SPARE SESSIONS     C
               AUXADDR=1000,         ALLOW 1000 DYNAMIC NAU ADDRS  C
               LTRACE=3,                                          C
               BFRS=240,                                          C
               CATRACE=(YES,20),                                  C
               NUMHSAS=8,                                         C
               SUBAREA=23,                                        C
               MAXSSCP=8,                                         C
               MAXSESS=15,           ALLOW UP TO 15 SESSION PER LU C
               MODEL=3745,                                        C
               NAMTAB=2000,          ALLOW 2000 DYNAMIC NAMES      C
               USGTIER=5,                                         C
               OLT=NO,                                            C
               NPA=NO,                                            C
               TRACE=(YES,20),                                    C
               TYPSYS=OS,                                         C
               QUALIFY=NCP,                                       C
               LOADLIB=LOADLIB,                                   C
               NEWNAME=SY23NCP,                                   C
               VERSION=V5R4,                                      C
               NETID=SPIFNET,                                     C
               BACKUP=1200
```

Figure 103 (Part 1 of 3). Token-Ring NCP Definitions

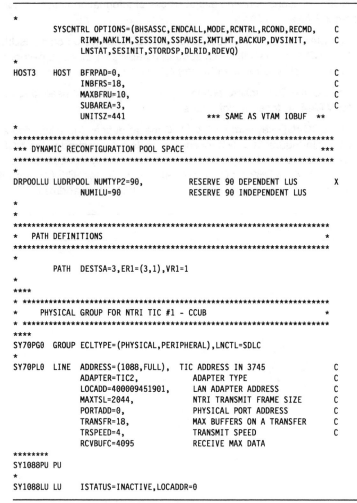

```
*
        SYSCNTRL OPTIONS=(BHSASSC,ENDCALL,MODE,RCNTRL,RCOND,RECMD,        C
                  RIMM,NAKLIM,SESSION,SSPAUSE,XMTLMT,BACKUP,DVSINIT,      C
                  LNSTAT,SESINIT,STORDSP,DLRID,RDEVQ)
*
HOST3   HOST  BFRPAD=0,                                                  C
              INBFRS=18,                                                 C
              MAXBFRU=10,                                                C
              SUBAREA=3,                                                 C
              UNITSZ=441                    *** SAME AS VTAM IOBUF  **
*
*************************************************************************
*** DYNAMIC RECONFIGURATION POOL SPACE                              ***
*************************************************************************
*
DRPOOLLU LUDRPOOL NUMTYP2=90,            RESERVE 90 DEPENDENT LUS        X
                  NUMILU=90              RESERVE 90 INDEPENDENT LUS
*
*
*************************************************************************
*   PATH DEFINITIONS                                                *
*************************************************************************
*
        PATH  DESTSA=3,ER1=(3,1),VR1=1
*
****
* *********************************************************************
*    PHYSICAL GROUP FOR NTRI TIC #1 - CCUB                          *
* *********************************************************************
****
SY70PG0  GROUP ECLTYPE=(PHYSICAL,PERIPHERAL),LNCTL=SDLC
*
SY70PL0  LINE  ADDRESS=(1088,FULL),  TIC ADDRESS IN 3745               C
               ADAPTER=TIC2,         ADAPTER TYPE                      C
               LOCADD=400009451901,  LAN ADAPTER ADDRESS               C
               MAXTSL=2044,          NTRI TRANSMIT FRAME SIZE          C
               PORTADD=0,            PHYSICAL PORT ADDRESS             C
               TRANSFR=18,           MAX BUFFERS ON A TRANSFER         C
               TRSPEED=4,            TRANSMIT SPEED                    C
               RCVBUFC=4095          RECEIVE MAX DATA
********
SY1088PU PU
*
SY1088LU LU    ISTATUS=INACTIVE,LOCADDR=0
```

Figure 103 (Part 2 of 3). Token-Ring NCP Definitions

```
****
* ********************************************************************
*     PHYSICAL GROUP FOR NTRI TIC #2 - CCUB                         *
* ********************************************************************
****
SY70PG1  GROUP ECLTYPE=(PHYSICAL,PERIPHERAL),LNCTL=SDLC
*
SY70PL1  LINE  ADDRESS=(1089,FULL),  TIC ADDRESS IN 3745           C
               ADAPTER=TIC2,          ADAPTER TYPE                  C
               LOCADD=400009451902,   LAN ADAPTER ADDRESS           C
               MAXTSL=2044,           NTRI TRANSMIT FRAME SIZE      C
               PORTADD=1,             PHYSICAL PORT ADDRESS         C
               TRANSFR=18,            MAX BUFFERS ON A TRANSFER     C
               TRSPEED=4,             TRANSMIT SPEED                C
               RCVBUFC=4095           RECEIVE MAX DATA
SY1089PU PU
*
SY1089LU LU    ISTATUS=INACTIVE,LOCADDR=0
****
* ********************************************************************
*     LOGICAL  GROUP FOR NTRI TIC #1 - CCUB                         *
* ********************************************************************
****
SY70L00  GROUP ECLTYPE=(LOGICAL,PERIPHERAL),LNCTL=SDLC,            C
               PHYPORT=0,                                           C
               AUTOGEN=30,                                          C
               CALL=INOUT
****
* ********************************************************************
*     LOGICAL  GROUP FOR NTRI TIC #2 - CCU                          *
* ********************************************************************
****
SY70L01  GROUP ECLTYPE=(LOGICAL,PERIPHERAL),LNCTL=SDLC,            C
               PHYPORT=1,                                           C
               AUTOGEN=30,                                          C
               CALL=INOUT
*
*********************************
LNCTLS   GROUP LNCTL=CA,CA=TYPE6,DELAY=0.0,TIMEOUT=500.0
CA0      LINE ADDRESS=00
PUCHAN0  PU PUTYPE=5,TGN=1
         GENEND
         END
```

Figure 103 (Part 3 of 3). Token-Ring NCP Definitions

(The VTAM APPL definition for the DB2 for MVS/ESA system at NEW_YORK3 was given in Figure 50 on page 146.)

Figure 104 shows the SQL used to define the DB2 for OS/2 systems on the LAN to DB2 for MVS/ESA. The example allows any remote system to connect to DB2 for MVS/ESA, as long as it supplies a valid MVS user ID and password.

```
INSERT INTO SYSIBM.SYSLUNAMES
    (LUNAME, SYSMODENAME, USERSECURITY, ENCRYPTPSWDS, MODESELECT, USERNAMES)
  VALUES (' ', ' ', 'C', 'N', 'N', ' ');
```

Figure 104. SQL for DB2 for MVS/ESA CDB at NEW_YORK3

Chapter 15. DB2 for OS/2 and DB2 for VM and VSE via Token Ring

The Spiffy Headquarters location uses an NCP to connect the DB2 for OS/2 systems to DB2 for VM as shown in Figure 105. Connections to DB2 for VM and VSE from DB2 for OS/2 are similar. For specific information on DB2 for VSE, see "DB2 for OS/2 and DB2 for VSE via Token Ring" on page 253.

In this example, five DB2 for OS/2 clients are attached to a single DDCS for OS/2 Multi-User Gateway workstation (DB2 for OS/2 System 1), which acts as a gateway to the host. The remaining workstations (DB2 for OS/2 System 2 through DB2 for OS/2 System 6) have the Single-User version of DDCS for OS/2 installed, and communicate directly with the host. This example shows the configuration necessary to connect the DDCS for OS/2 Multi-User Gateway to the host.

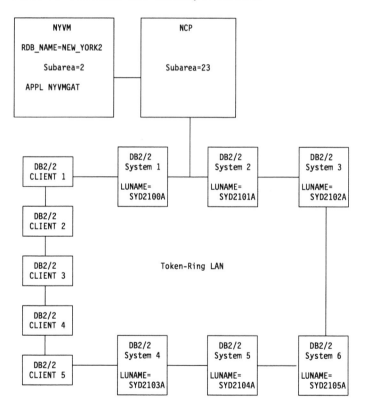

Figure 105. Token-Ring LAN Connected via NCP to DB2 for VM

You should read Chapter 1, "Introducing DRDA Connectivity" on page 2 to become familiar with the concepts before you use the examples in this chapter.

Configuring Communications Manager for OS/2 V1.1

To connect DB2 for OS/2 to the host, you should have DB2 for OS/2 and Communications Manager for OS/2 V1.1 installed on your OS/2 workstation. Communications Manager for OS/2 V1.1 must be configured for APPC. The following example shows you how to configure APPC. This example also assumes you have installed the Multi-User Gateway DDCS for OS/2 product.

If you have not configured a DLC profile for the connection to the host, you must configure the appropriate DLC profile before configuring the SNA network definitions. For more information on configuring DLC profiles, see *Communications Manager/2 Configuration Guide*.

Getting to the Communications Manager for OS/2 V1.1 Profile List Sheet

Starting from the Communications Manager for OS/2 V1.1 icon:

1. Click on the **Communications Manager Setup** icon and then the **Setup** pushbutton.

2. Choose a configuration file name and then click on **OK**. The Communications Manager Configuration Definition window appears.

3. Select **Token-ring or other LAN types** from the Workstation Connection Type list.

4. Select **APPC APIs** from the Feature or Application list.

5. Click on the **Configure...** pushbutton. The Communications Manager Profile List Sheet window appears.

Specifying Local Node Characteristics

At the Communications Manager Profile List Sheet window, select **SNA local node characteristics**, then click on **Configure...**. The Local Node Characteristics window appears (Figure 106 on page 237).

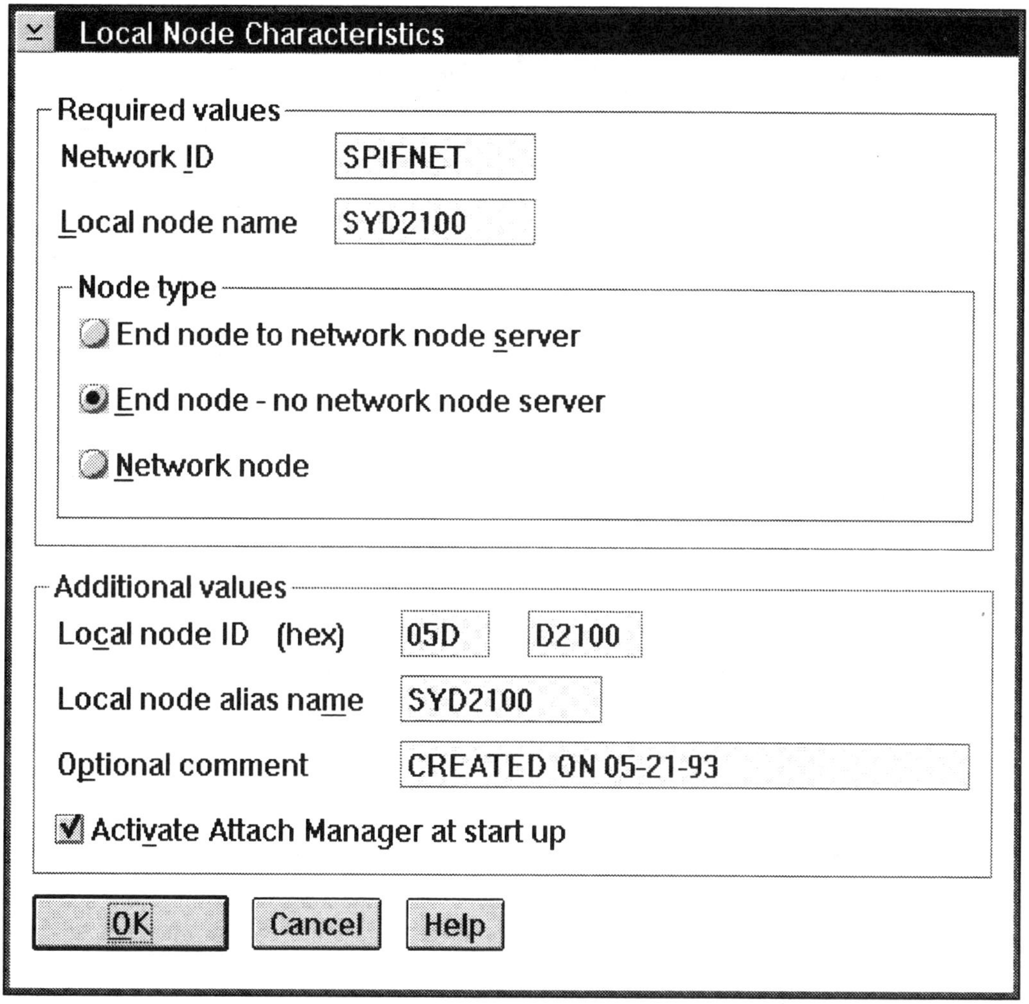

Figure 106. Local Node Characteristics Window

Specify the **Network ID**, the **Local node name** (also known as the PU/CP name), the **Local node ID**, and the **Local node alias name**. When you are finished, click on **OK**. This returns you to the Communications Manager for OS/2 V1.1 Profile List Sheet window.

Table 44 on page 238 gives the sample parameters used for the example given here and provides a blank column that you can use to fill in the values for your own configuration. You need to coordinate these values with your host administrator.

Table 44. Parameters for Local Node Characteristics

Parameter	Example Value	Your Value	Comment
Network ID	SPIFNET		
Local Node Name	SYD2100		See the discussion regarding CPNAME and IDBLK/IDNUM in Chapter 19, "DB2 for OS/2 and Other DRDA Servers" on page 304.
Local Node ID	D2100		See the discussion regarding CPNAME and IDBLK/IDNUM in Chapter 19, "DB2 for OS/2 and Other DRDA Servers" on page 304.
Local Node Alias Name	SYD2100		

Specifying Connections and Partner LUs

1. At the Communications Manager Profile List Sheet, select **SNA connections**, then click on **Configure....** A Connections List window appears.

2. Select **To host** from the **Partner type** group.

3. To create a new definition, click on **Create**. To change an existing definition, select a link from the **Link Name** list and click on **Change....** The Adapter List appears.

4. Select **Token-ring or other LAN types** from the Adapter List.

   The **Configured** field changes to show whether the adapter is configured, and the selections available in the **Adapter number** field change to match the adapter type you selected.

5. Select an adapter number from the **Adapter number** list and click on **Continue....** The Create a Connection to a Host window appears (Figure 107 on page 239).

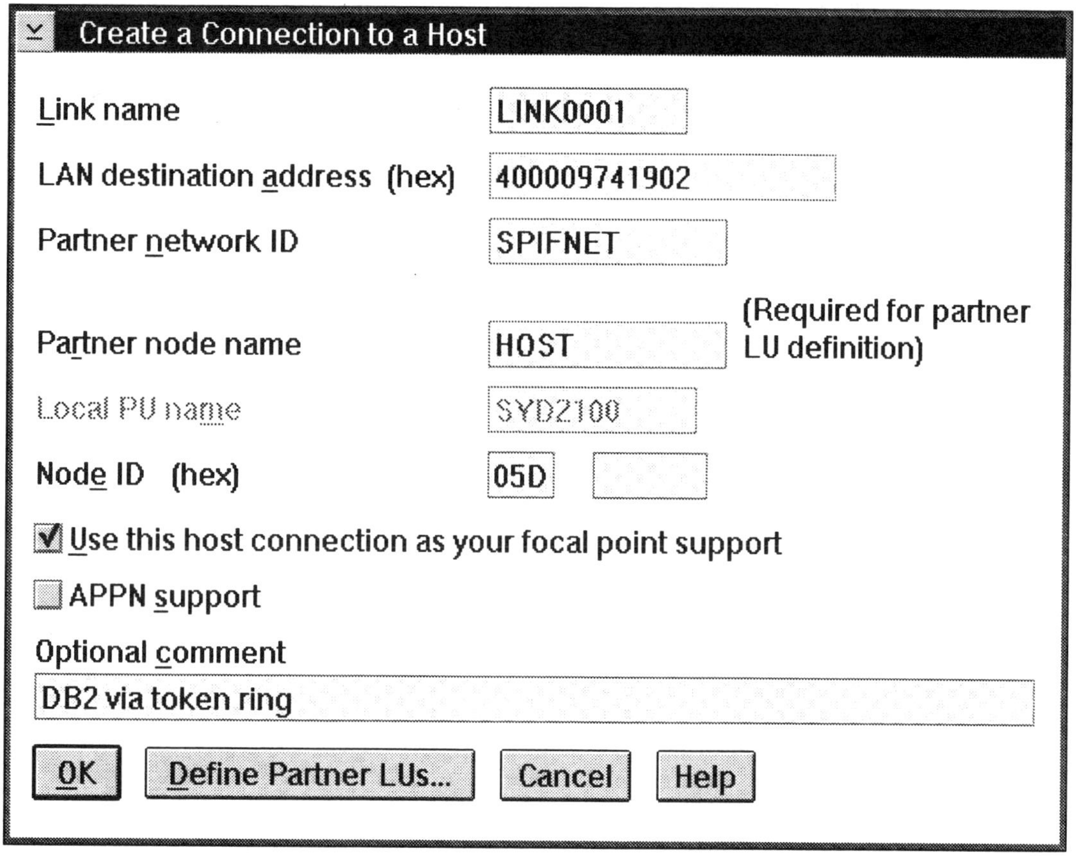

```
┌──────────────────────────────────────────────────────────────────────────┐
│ ⌄  Create a Connection to a Host                                           │
├──────────────────────────────────────────────────────────────────────────┤
│                                                                            │
│  Link name                    LINK0001                                     │
│                                                                            │
│  LAN destination address (hex)  400009741902                               │
│                                                                            │
│  Partner network ID           SPIFNET                                      │
│                                                                            │
│                                                   (Required for partner     │
│  Partner node name            HOST                LU definition)            │
│                                                                            │
│  Local PU name                SYD2100                                       │
│                                                                            │
│  Node ID  (hex)               05D                                          │
│                                                                            │
│  ☑ Use this host connection as your focal point support                    │
│                                                                            │
│  ☐ APPN support                                                            │
│                                                                            │
│  Optional comment                                                          │
│  DB2 via token ring                                                        │
│                                                                            │
│  ┌────┐  ┌─────────────────────┐  ┌────────┐  ┌──────┐                     │
│  │ OK │  │ Define Partner LUs...│  │ Cancel │  │ Help │                     │
│  └────┘  └─────────────────────┘  └────────┘  └──────┘                     │
└──────────────────────────────────────────────────────────────────────────┘
```

Figure 107. Create a Connection to a Host Window

6. Enter a link name and the LAN destination address.

7. Enter the network ID and node name for the partner node. The **Define Partner LUs...** pushbutton is enabled.

   Table 45 gives the sample parameters used for the example given here and provides a blank column that you can use to fill in the values for your own configuration. You need to check with your host administrator for the partner network ID and the LAN destination address.

Table 45. Parameters for Host Connection

Parameter	Example Value	Your Value
Link name	LINK0001	
Partner network ID	SPIFNET	
Partner node name	HOST	
LAN destination address	400009451902	
Comment	DB2 for VM via token ring	

8. Click on the **Define Partner LUs...** pushbutton. The Create Partner LUs window appears (Figure 108 on page 240).

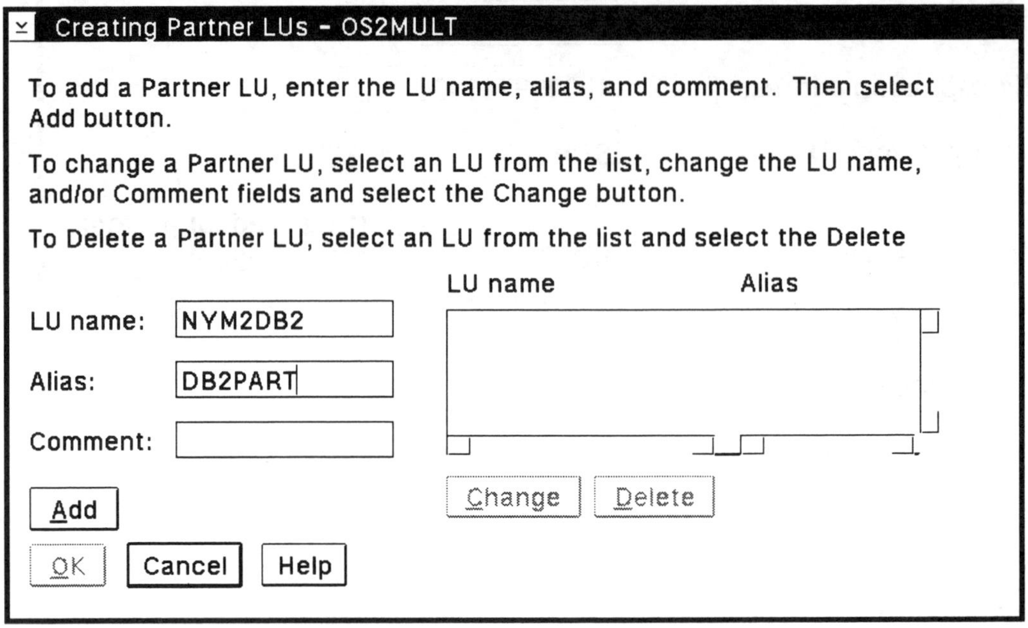

```
┌──────────────────────────────────────────────────────────────────┐
│ ⌄  Creating Partner LUs - OS2MULT                                  │
├──────────────────────────────────────────────────────────────────┤
│                                                                    │
│  To add a Partner LU, enter the LU name, alias, and comment.  Then select │
│  Add button.                                                       │
│                                                                    │
│  To change a Partner LU, select an LU from the list, change the LU name,  │
│  and/or Comment fields and select the Change button.              │
│                                                                    │
│  To Delete a Partner LU, select an LU from the list and select the Delete │
│                                                                    │
│                             LU name              Alias             │
│                          ┌─────────────────────────────────┐       │
│  LU name:  │ NYM2DB2 │   │                                 │       │
│                          │                                 │       │
│  Alias:    │ DB2PART │   │                                 │       │
│                          │                                 │       │
│  Comment:  │         │   └─────────────────────────────────┘       │
│                                                                    │
│  │ Add │                   │ Change │  │ Delete │                  │
│                                                                    │
│  │ OK │  │ Cancel │  │ Help │                                      │
│                                                                    │
└──────────────────────────────────────────────────────────────────┘
```

Figure 108. Create Partner LUs Window

9. Enter an LU name and an alias.

   Table 46 gives the sample parameters used for the example given here and provides a blank column that you can use to fill in the values for your own configuration. You need to check with your host administrator for the LU name value.

Table 46. Parameters for Create Partner LUs

Parameter	Example Value	Your Value
LU name	NYVMGAT	
Alias	SQLDS	

10. Click on the **Add** pushbutton.

11. When the partner LU definition is complete, click on **OK**. The Create a Connection to a Host window reappears.

12. Click on **Cancel**.

13. Click on **Close** from the Connections List.

Specifying the Local LU

At the Communications Manager Profile List Sheet window, select **SNA Features**, then click on **Configure....** The SNA Features List window appears. From this window select **Local LUs**. The Create a Local LU window appears (Figure 109).

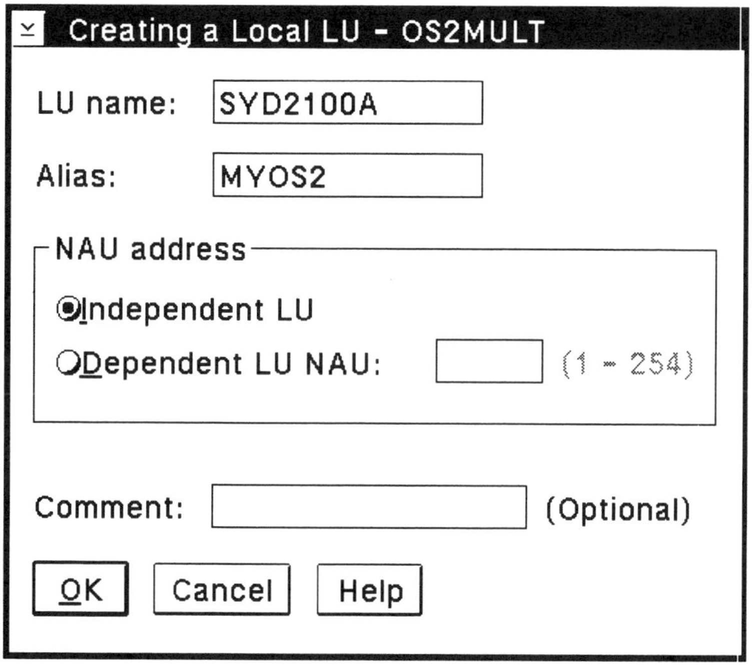

```
┌─────────────────────────────────────────────────────────┐
│ ⌄█ Creating a Local LU - OS2MULT                         │
│                                                          │
│   LU name:   │SYD2100A          │                        │
│                                                          │
│   Alias:     │MYOS2             │                        │
│                                                          │
│   ┌─NAU address──────────────────────────────────────┐  │
│   │                                                   │  │
│   │ ◉Independent LU                                   │  │
│   │                                                   │  │
│   │ ○Dependent LU NAU:    │        │  (1 - 254)       │  │
│   │                                                   │  │
│   └───────────────────────────────────────────────────┘ │
│                                                          │
│                                                          │
│   Comment:   │               │  (Optional)               │
│                                                          │
│   ┌───────┐  ┌─────────┐  ┌───────┐                      │
│   │ OK    │  │ Cancel  │  │ Help  │                      │
│   └───────┘  └─────────┘  └───────┘                      │
└─────────────────────────────────────────────────────────┘
```

Figure 109. Create a Local LU Window

In this window, specify the local **LU name** and the local **Alias** and click on **OK**. This returns you to the SNA Features List window.

Check with your network administrator to verify that this workstation is defined in VTAM as an independent LU. If it is defined as a dependent LU, click on the Dependent LU pushbutton and enter the NAU address supplied by your network administrator (the LOCADDR=value from the LU macro in VTAM).

Note: The LU alias is case sensitive.

Table 47 gives the sample parameters used for the example given here and provides a blank column that you can use to fill in the values for your own configuration. You need to check with your host administrator for the LU name value.

Table 47. Parameters for Create a Local LU

Parameter	Example Value	Your Value
LU name	SYD2100A	
Alias	MYOS2	

Specifying the Mode

At the SNA Features List window, select **Modes**. Then click on the **Create...** pushbutton. The Create a Mode Definition window appears (Figure 110).

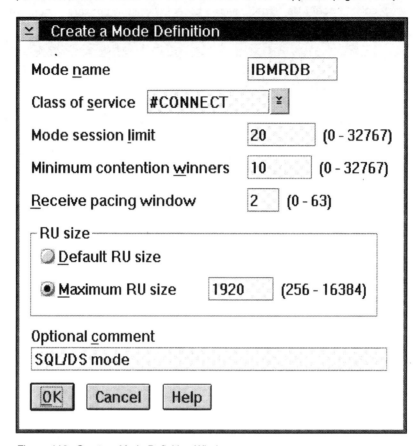

Figure 110. Create a Mode Definition Window

In this window:

1. Specify the **Mode name**.

2. The default values for mode session limit, minimum contention winners, and receive pacing window work in many cases. However, you should coordinate these with your host administrator.

3. Select **Maximum RU size** and specify the value.

When you are finished, select **OK**. This returns you to the SNA Features List window.

Table 48 on page 243 gives the sample parameters used for the example given here and provides a blank column that you can use to fill in the values for your own configuration. You need to check with your host administrator for values for mode name, receive pacing window, and maximum RU size.

Table 48. Parameters for Create a Mode Definition

Parameter	Example Value	Your Value
Mode name	IBMRDB	
Mode session limit	20	
Minimum contention winners	10	
Receive pacing window	2	
Maximum RU size	1920	
Comment	SQL/DS mode	

Completing the Configuration

After you complete the steps in the previous sections, you are ready to verify and save your updated configuration file. To do this:

1. Return to the Communications Manager Configuration Definition window.
2. Select **Verify configuration** from the **Options** action bar.
3. Select **On**.

Resulting Network Definition File (.NDF)

Figure 111 shows the network definition file.

```
DEFINE_LOCAL_CP   FQ_CP_NAME(SPIFNET.SYD2100  )
                  DESCRIPTION(Created on 04-03-92 at 12:53p)
                  CP_ALIAS(SYD2100 )
                  NAU_ADDRESS(INDEPENDENT_LU)
                  NODE_TYPE(EN)
                  NODE_ID(X'D2100')
                  HOST_FP_SUPPORT(YES)
                  HOST_FP_LINK_NAME(LINK0001);

DEFINE_LOGICAL_LINK   LINK_NAME(LINK0001)
                      DESCRIPTION(SQL/DS via token ring)
                      FQ_ADJACENT_CP_NAME(SPIFNET.HOST    )
                      ADJACENT_NODE_TYPE(LEN)
                      DLC_NAME(IBMTRNET)
                      ADAPTER_NUMBER(0)
                      DESTINATION_ADDRESS(X'400009451902')
                      CP_CP_SESSION_SUPPORT(NO)
                      ACTIVATE_AT_STARTUP(YES)
                      LIMITED_RESOURCE(USE_ADAPTER_DEFINITION)
                      LINK_STATION_ROLE(USE_ADAPTER_DEFINITION)
                      SOLICIT_SSCP_SESSION(YES)
                      EFFECTIVE_CAPACITY(USE_ADAPTER_DEFINITION)
                      COST_PER_CONNECT_TIME(USE_ADAPTER_DEFINITION)
                      COST_PER_BYTE(USE_ADAPTER_DEFINITION)
                      SECURITY(USE_ADAPTER_DEFINITION)
                      PROPAGATION_DELAY(USE_ADAPTER_DEFINITION)
                      USER_DEFINED_1(USE_ADAPTER_DEFINITION)
                      USER_DEFINED_2(USE_ADAPTER_DEFINITION)
                      USER_DEFINED_3(USE_ADAPTER_DEFINITION);
```

Figure 111 (Part 1 of 3). Network Definition File for DB2 for VM

```
DEFINE_LOCAL_LU   LU_NAME(SYD2100A)
                  LU_ALIAS(MYOS2)
                  NAU_ADDRESS(INDEPENDENT_LU);

DEFINE_PARTNER_LU   FQ_PARTNER_LU_NAME(SPIFNET.NYVMGAT)
                    PARTNER_LU_ALIAS(SQLDS)
                    PARTNER_LU_UNINTERPRETED_NAME(NYVMGAT )
                    MAX_MC_LL_SEND_SIZE(32767)
                    CONV_SECURITY_VERIFICATION(NO)
                    PARALLEL_SESSION_SUPPORT(YES);

DEFINE_PARTNER_LU_LOCATION   FQ_PARTNER_LU_NAME(SPIFNET.NYVMGAT)
                             WILDCARD_ENTRY(NO)
                             FQ_OWNING_CP_NAME(SPIFNET.HOST)
                             LOCAL_NODE_NN_SERVER(NO);

DEFINE_MODE   MODE_NAME(MODE0001)
              DESCRIPTION(Created on 04-03-92 at 12:53p)
              COS_NAME(#CONNECT)
              DEFAULT_RU_SIZE(NO)
              MAX_RU_SIZE_UPPER_BOUND(1920)
              RECEIVE_PACING_WINDOW(2)
              MAX_NEGOTIABLE_SESSION_LIMIT(32767)
              PLU_MODE_SESSION_LIMIT(253)
              MIN_CONWINNERS_SOURCE(126);


DEFINE_MODE   MODE_NAME(IBMRDB  )
              DESCRIPTION(SQL/DS mode)
              COS_NAME(#CONNECT)
              DEFAULT_RU_SIZE(NO)
              MAX_RU_SIZE_UPPER_BOUND(1920)
              RECEIVE_PACING_WINDOW(4)
              MAX_NEGOTIABLE_SESSION_LIMIT(32767)
              PLU_MODE_SESSION_LIMIT(20)
              MIN_CONWINNERS_SOURCE(10);


DEFINE_DEFAULTS   IMPLICIT_INBOUND_PLU_SUPPORT(YES)
                  DESCRIPTION(Created on 04-03-92 at 12:53p)
                  DEFAULT_MODE_NAME(MODE0001)
                  MAX_MC_LL_SEND_SIZE(32767)
                  DIRECTORY_FOR_INBOUND_ATTACHES(*)
                  DEFAULT_TP_OPERATION(NONQUEUED_AM_STARTED)
                  DEFAULT_TP_PROGRAM_TYPE(BACKGROUND)
                  DEFAULT_TP_CONV_SECURITY_RQD(NO)
                  MAX_HELD_ALERTS(10);
```

Figure 111 (Part 2 of 3). Network Definition File for DB2 for VM

```
DEFINE_TP  SNA_SERVICE_TP_NAME(X'07',6DB)
           DESCRIPTION(Created on 04-03-92 at 12:53p)
           FILESPEC(C:\SQLLIB\SQLCIAA.EXE)
           CONVERSATION_TYPE(BASIC)
           CONV_SECURITY_RQD(YES)
           SYNC_LEVEL(NONE)
           TP_OPERATION(NONQUEUED_AM_STARTED)
           PROGRAM_TYPE(BACKGROUND)
           RECEIVE_ALLOCATE_TIMEOUT(INFINITE);

DEFINE_TP  SNA_SERVICE_TP_NAME(X'07',6SN)
           DESCRIPTION(Created on 04-03-92 at 12:53p)
           FILESPEC(C:\SQLLIB\SQLCNSM.EXE)
           CONVERSATION_TYPE(BASIC)
           CONV_SECURITY_RQD(YES)
           SYNC_LEVEL(NONE)
           TP_OPERATION(NONQUEUED_AM_STARTED)
           PROGRAM_TYPE(BACKGROUND)
           RECEIVE_ALLOCATE_TIMEOUT(INFINITE);

START_ATTACH_MANAGER;
```

Figure 111 (Part 3 of 3). Network Definition File for DB2 for VM

Cataloging DB2 for OS/2 Directory Entries

You now need to catalog the database, the workstation (node), and the DCS database.

Select the **Directory Tool** from the **Database 2 for OS/2** folder. The Directory Tool window appears.

Cataloging the Workstation

1. At the Directory Tool window, select **Directory** and **Workstation** from the action bar. The Workstation Directory window appears. If the directory is already being displayed, make it the active directory by clicking on it with the mouse.

2. Select **Workstation** and then **Catalog...** from the action bar. The Catalog Workstation window appears (Figure 112).

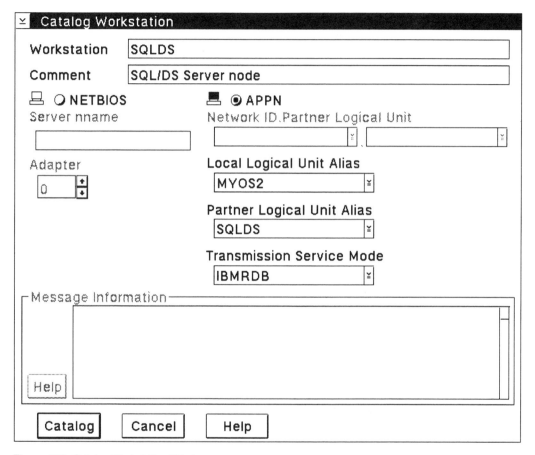

Figure 112. Catalog Workstation Window

On the Catalog Workstation window, do the following:

1. Specify **Workstation**
2. Fill in a **Comment** (optional)
3. Select **APPN**
4. Specify **Local Logical Unit Alias**
5. Specify **Partner Logical Unit Alias**
6. Specify **Transmission Service Mode**

Table 49 on page 248 gives the sample parameters used for the example given here and provides a blank column that you can use to fill in the values for your own configuration.

Table 49. Parameters for Cataloging the Workstation

Parameter	Example Value	Your Value	Comments
Workstation	DB2 for VM		
Comment	DB2 for VM server node		
Local logical unit alias	MYOS2		Must match the alias specified in the Creating a Local LU menu. You can click on the arrow to the right of this box to get a list of local LUs already defined.
Partner logical unit alias	DB2 for VM		Must match the alias specified in the Creating Partner LUs menu. You can click on the arrow to the right of this box to get a list of partner LU aliases already defined.
Transmission service mode	IBMRDB		Must match the mode name specified in the Creating a Mode Definition menu. You can click on the arrow to the right of this box to get a list of modes already defined.

When you are finished, select **Catalog**. If you have not previously logged on, the logon popup window appears. Enter your **User ID** and **Password** (your ID must have Administrator or Local Administrator authority) and press Enter. When you see "The operation was successful," select **Cancel**. The workstation you just cataloged should appear in the Workstation Directory window.

Cataloging the Database

1. Select **Directory** and **System Database** from the action bar. The System Database Directory window appears. If the directory is already being displayed, make it the active directory by clicking on it with the mouse.

2. Select **Database** and then **Catalog...** from the action bar. The Catalog Database window appears (Figure 113 on page 249).

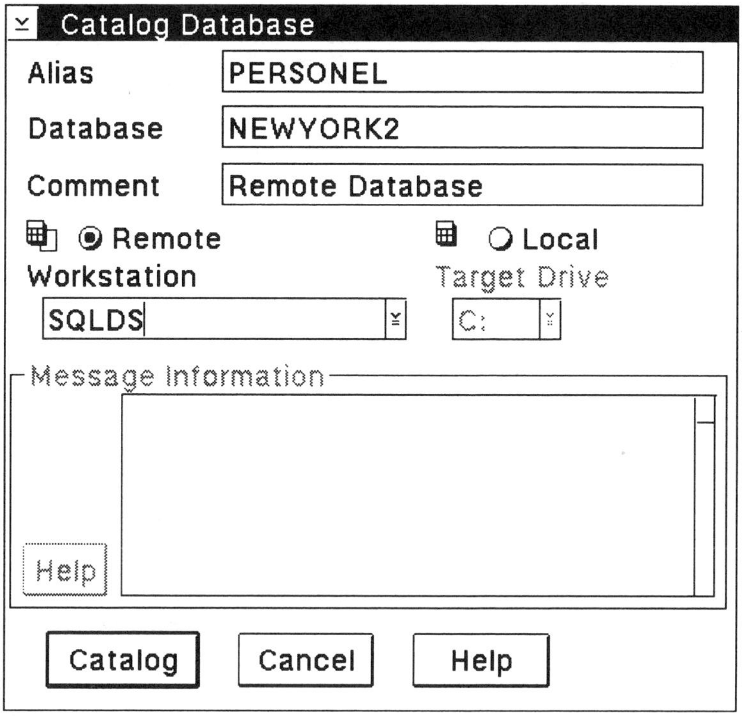

Figure 113. Catalog Database Window

In the Catalog Database window, do the following:

1. Specify **Alias**
2. Specify **Database**
3. Fill in a **Comment** (optional)
4. Select **Remote**
5. Specify **Workstation**

When you are finished, select **Catalog**. When you see "The operation was successful," select **Cancel**. The database you just cataloged should appear in the System Database Directory window.

Table 50 on page 250 gives the sample parameters used for the example given here and provides a blank column that you can use to fill in the values for your own configuration.

Table 50. Parameters for Cataloging the Database

Parameter	Example Value	Your Value
Alias	PERSONEL	
Database	NEWYORK2	.
Comment	Remote database	
Workstation (Must match the workstation name specified in the Catalog Workstation menu. You can click on the arrow to the right of this box to get a list of workstations already defined.)	DB2 for VM	

Cataloging the DCS Database

1. Select **Directory** and **Database Connection Services** from the action bar. The Database Connection Services window appears. If the directory is already displayed, make it the active directory by clicking on it with the mouse.

2. Select **Database** and then **Catalog...** from the action bar. The Catalog Database window appears (Figure 114).

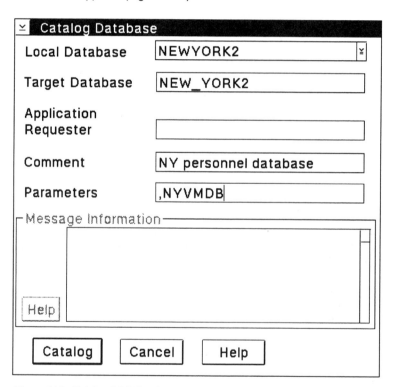

Figure 114. Catalog DCS Database Window

In the Catalog Database window, do the following:

1. Specify **Local Database**

2. Specify **Target Database**
3. Fill in a **Comment** (optional)
4. Specify **Parameters**

Only the Transaction Program Name (TPN) needs to be specified in the PARAMETERS field. This is because DB2 for VM uses the non-Service TPN format. Because DB2 for VM has no Transaction Program Prefix (TPP), remember to include the place holder (,) for the TPP.

When you are finished, select **Catalog**. When you see "The operation was successful," select **Cancel**. The database you just cataloged should appear in the Database Connection Services window.

Table 51 gives the sample parameters used for the example given here and provides a blank column that you can use to fill in the values for your own configuration. You need to coordinate with your host administrator for values for target database and the **Parameters** entry.

Table 51. Parameters for Cataloging the DCS Database

Parameter	Example Value	Your Value	Comment
Local database	NEWYORK2		Must match the Database name specified in the Catalog Database menu (System Database Directory). You can click on the arrow to the right of this box to get a list of databases already defined.
Target database	NEW_YORK2		Must match the RDB_NAME on the host.
Comment	NY personnel database		
Parameters	NYVMDB		

Configuring the Host

To connect the DB2 for OS/2 systems to DB2 for VM, you must update the NCP definitions shown in Figure 103 on page 231 defining the NYVM system. Figure 115 on page 252 shows the statements you must add to the NCP definitions.

```
VTAM2   PCCU  CUADDR=C02,                                        *** C
              AUTODMP=NO,                                            C
              AUTOIPL=NO,                                            C
              AUTOSYN=YES,                                           C
              BACKUP=YES,                                            C
              DELAY=0,                                               C
              VFYLM=YES,                                             C
              CHANCON=UNCOND,                                        C
              MAXDATA=4302,                                          C
              DUMPDS=NCPDUMP,                                        C
              NETID=SPIFNET,                                         C
              OWNER=HOST2,                                           C
              SUBAREA=2                    HOST SUBAREA NUMBER

                 o
                 o
                 o

HOST2   HOST  BFRPAD=0,                                             C
              INBFRS=18,                                            C
              MAXBFRU=10,                                           C
              SUBAREA=2,                                            C
              UNITSZ=441                *** SAME AS VTAM IOBUF  **

                 o
                 o
                 o

        PATH  DESTSA=2,ER1=(2,1),VR1=1

                 o
                 o
                 o

CA1     LINE  ADDRESS=01
PUCHAN1 PU  PUTYPE=5,TGN=1
```

Figure 115. Token-Ring NCP Definitions

The VTAM switched major node definitions for the NYVM system are identical to those shown in The VTAM APPL statement used to define the AVS gateway is shown in Figure 44 on page 136.

Ensure that the appropriate CCSID is assigned. See "Represent Data" on page 77.

DB2 for OS/2 and DB2 for VSE via Token Ring

The Token-Ring LAN and NCP configuration described for DB2 for VM is fully applicable to a DB2 for VSE DRDA application server. With minor modifications, sample definitions for DB2 for VM can be used for the DB2 for VSE application server. Replace the DB2 for VM system in the Spiffy network with a DB2 for VSE system. The VSE system uses subarea 2. The RDB_NAME is changed from NEW_YORK2 to TORONTO3, the APPL (LU_name) changed from NYVMGAT to VSEGATE:

1. Follow the same procedures to configure the Communications Manager for OS/2 V1.1, using TORONTO3 as the RDB_NAME and VSEGATE as the APPL (LU_name). The resulting NDF should be as shown in Figure 116 on page 254.

2. "Cataloging DB2 for OS/2 Directory Entries" on page 246 shows example information needed in the DB2 for OS/2 directories.

3. The VTAM switched Major Node definitions for the DB2 for OS/2 systems remain the same.

4. The Token-Ring NCP definitions remain the same.

5. Use the additional VTAM sample definitions given in "Additional VTAM Definitions" on page 256 to enable the DB2 for VSE server in the Spiffy network.

6. Use the VSE-specific sample definitions given in "Sample DB2 for VSE DBNAME Directory" on page 258 and "Sample CICS Definitions" on page 258 to enable the DB2 for VSE server in the Spiffy network.

Resulting Network Definition File (.NDF)

Figure 116 shows the network definition file.

```
DEFINE_LOCAL_CP   FQ_CP_NAME(SPIFNET.SYD2100  )
                  DESCRIPTION(Created on 12-01-92 at 12:15p)
                  CP_ALIAS(SYD2100 )
                  NAU_ADDRESS(INDEPENDENT_LU)
                  NODE_TYPE(EN)
                  NODE_ID(X'D2100')
                  HOST_FP_SUPPORT(YES)
                  HOST_FP_LINK_NAME(LINK0001);

DEFINE_LOGICAL_LINK   LINK_NAME(LINK0001)
                  DESCRIPTION(SQL/DS on VSE via token ring)
                  FQ_ADJACENT_CP_NAME(SPIFNET.HOST  )
                  ADJACENT_NODE_TYPE(LEN)
                  DLC_NAME(IBMTRNET)
                  ADAPTER_NUMBER(0)
                  DESTINATION_ADDRESS(X'400009451902')
                  CP_CP_SESSION_SUPPORT(NO)
                  ACTIVATE_AT_STARTUP(YES)
                  LIMITED_RESOURCE(USE_ADAPTER_DEFINITION)
                  LINK_STATION_ROLE(USE_ADAPTER_DEFINITION)
                  SOLICIT_SSCP_SESSION(YES)
                  EFFECTIVE_CAPACITY(USE_ADAPTER_DEFINITION)
                  COST_PER_CONNECT_TIME(USE_ADAPTER_DEFINITION)
                  COST_PER_BYTE(USE_ADAPTER_DEFINITION)
                  SECURITY(USE_ADAPTER_DEFINITION)
                  PROPAGATION_DELAY(USE_ADAPTER_DEFINITION)
                  USER_DEFINED_1(USE_ADAPTER_DEFINITION)
                  USER_DEFINED_2(USE_ADAPTER_DEFINITION)
                  USER_DEFINED_3(USE_ADAPTER_DEFINITION);

DEFINE_LOCAL_LU   LU_NAME(SYD2100A)
                  LU_ALIAS(MYOS2   )
                  NAU_ADDRESS(INDEPENDENT_LU);

DEFINE_PARTNER_LU   FQ_PARTNER_LU_NAME(SPIFNET.VSEGATE)
                  PARTNER_LU_ALIAS(SQLVSE)
                  PARTNER_LU_UNINTERPRETED_NAME(VSEGATE)
                  MAX_MC_LL_SEND_SIZE(32767)
                  CONV_SECURITY_VERIFICATION(NO)
                  PARALLEL_SESSION_SUPPORT(YES);

DEFINE_PARTNER_LU_LOCATION   FQ_PARTNER_LU_NAME(SPIFNET.VSEGATE)
                  WILDCARD_ENTRY(NO)
                  FQ_OWNING_CP_NAME(SPIFNET.HOST  )
                  LOCAL_NODE_NN_SERVER(NO);
```

Figure 116 (Part 1 of 2). NDF for DB2 for OS/2 System SYD2100A to Access TORONTO3 via VSEGATE

```
DEFINE_MODE  MODE_NAME(MODE0001)
             DESCRIPTION(Created on 12-01-92 at 12:15p)
             COS_NAME(#CONNECT)
             DEFAULT_RU_SIZE(NO)
             MAX_RU_SIZE_UPPER_BOUND(1920)
             RECEIVE_PACING_WINDOW(2)
             MAX_NEGOTIABLE_SESSION_LIMIT(32767)
             PLU_MODE_SESSION_LIMIT(253)
             MIN_CONWINNERS_SOURCE(126);

DEFINE_MODE  MODE_NAME(IBMRDB )
             DESCRIPTION(SQL/DS VSE mode)
             COS_NAME(#CONNECT)
             DEFAULT_RU_SIZE(NO)
             MAX_RU_SIZE_UPPER_BOUND(1920)
             RECEIVE_PACING_WINDOW(4)
             MAX_NEGOTIABLE_SESSION_LIMIT(32767)
             PLU_MODE_SESSION_LIMIT(20)
             MIN_CONWINNERS_SOURCE(10);

DEFINE_DEFAULTS  IMPLICIT_INBOUND_PLU_SUPPORT(YES)
             DESCRIPTION(Created on 12-01-92 at 12:15p)
             DEFAULT_MODE_NAME(MODE0001)
             MAX_MC_LL_SEND_SIZE(32767)
             DIRECTORY_FOR_INBOUND_ATTACHES(*)
             DEFAULT_TP_OPERATION(NONQUEUED_AM_STARTED)
             DEFAULT_TP_PROGRAM_TYPE(BACKGROUND)
             DEFAULT_TP_CONV_SECURITY_RQD(NO)
             MAX_HELD_ALERTS(10);

DEFINE_TP  SNA_SERVICE_TP_NAME(X'07',6DB)
             DESCRIPTION(Created on 12-01-92 at 12:15p)
             FILESPEC(C:\SQLLIB\SQLCIAA.EXE)
             CONVERSATION_TYPE(BASIC)
             CONV_SECURITY_RQD(YES)
             SYNC_LEVEL(NONE)
             TP_OPERATION(NONQUEUED_AM_STARTED)
             PROGRAM_TYPE(BACKGROUND)
             RECEIVE_ALLOCATE_TIMEOUT(INFINITE);

DEFINE_TP  SNA_SERVICE_TP_NAME(X'07',6SN)
             DESCRIPTION(Created on 12-01-92 at 12:15p)
             FILESPEC(C:\SQLLIB\SQLCNSM.EXE)
             CONVERSATION_TYPE(BASIC)
             CONV_SECURITY_RQD(YES)
             SYNC_LEVEL(NONE)
             TP_OPERATION(NONQUEUED_AM_STARTED)
             PROGRAM_TYPE(BACKGROUND)
             RECEIVE_ALLOCATE_TIMEOUT(INFINITE);

START_ATTACH_MANAGER;
```

Figure 116 (Part 2 of 2). NDF for DB2 for OS/2 System SYD2100A to Access TORONTO3 via VSEGATE

Cataloging DB2 for OS/2 Directory Entries

The following is sample information needed in the DB2 for OS/2 directories.

Cataloging the Workstation

Table 52 gives the sample parameters used in the Spiffy example and provides a blank column that you can use to fill in the values for your own configuration.

Table 52. Parameters for Cataloging the Workstation

Parameter	Example Value	Your Value
Workstation	SQLVSE	
Comment	DB2 for VSE server node	
Local logical unit alias	MYOS2	
Partner logical unit alias	SQLVSE	
Transmission service mode	IBMRDB	

Cataloging the Database

Table 53 gives the sample parameters used in the Spiffy example and provides a blank column that you can use to fill in the values for your own configuration.

Table 53. Parameters for Cataloging the Database

Parameter	Example Value	Your Value
Alias	SALES	
Database	TORONTO_3	
Comment	Remote database	
Workstation	SQLVSE	

Cataloging the DCS Database

Table 54 gives the sample parameters used in the Spiffy example and provides a blank column that you can use to fill in the values for your own configuration. You need to coordinate with your host administrator for values for target database and the parameters entry.

Table 54. Parameters for Cataloging the DCS Database

Parameter	Example Value	Your Value
Local database	TORONTO_3	
Target database	TORONTO3	
Comment	Toronto sales database	
Parameters	TOR3	

Additional VTAM Definitions

This section contains additional VTAM definitions needed for a successful connection.

Figure 117 on page 257 shows a sample VTAM definition for CICS.

```
        VBUILD  TYPE=APPL
***********************************************************************
*                                                                     *
*    LU Definition for Toronto DB2 for VSE System                     *
*                                                                     *
***********************************************************************
VSEGATE APPL  ACBNAME=VSEGATE,        CICS APPLID         *** C
              AUTH=(ACQ,PASS,VPACE),                          C
              APPC=NO,                MUST BE SET TO NO
              SONSCIP=YES,
              EAS=30,
              MODTAB=RDBMODES,
              PARSESS=YES,
              VPACING=0
```

Figure 117. VTAM APPL Definition for CICS

Figure 118 shows a sample VTAM mode table. The DRDA default LOGMODE entry (modename IBMRDB) must be included in the LOGMODE table (RDBMODES in this example).

```
IBMRDB   MODEENT LOGMODE=IBMRDB,      DRDA DEFAULT MODE               *
                 TYPE=0,              NEGOTIABLE BIND                 *
                 PSNDPAC=X'00',       PRIMARY SEND PACING COUNT       *
                 SSNDPAC=X'02',       SECONDARY SEND PACING COUNT     *
                 SRCVPAC=X'00',       SECONDARY RECEIVE PACING COUNT  *
                 RUSIZES=X'8989',     RUSIZES IN-4K    OUT-4K         *
                 FMPROF=X'13',        LU6.2 FM PROFILE                *
                 TSPROF=X'07',        LU6.2 TS PROFILE                *
                 PRIPROT=X'B0',       LU6.2 PRIMARY PROTOCOLS         *
                 SECPROT=X'B0',       LU6.2 SECONDARY PROTOCOLS       *
                 COMPROT=X'50A5',     LU6.2 COMMON PROTOCOLS          *
                 PSERVIC=X'0602000000000000000122F00'  LU6.2 LU TYPE
```

Figure 118. DRDA Default LOGMODE

Sample DB2 for VSE DBNAME Directory

Figure 119 shows a sample DBNAME directory.

```
*TPN     APPLID   *DBNAME              PNM   PRIV       *
*         1    1  22             3     44    5          *
*2..5____0......7_12...............9___45___0_____*
 TOR3    SYSARI03  TORONTO3
 .6DB    SYSARI00  SQLDS
```

Figure 119. Sample DBNAME Directory

Sample CICS Definitions

Figure 120 shows a sample TST definition.

```
        TITLE 'DFHTST WITH THE AXE ERROR LOG'
        PRINT NOGEN
* ******************************************************************* *
TST     DFHTST TYPE=INITIAL
* ******************************************************************* *
*       LOCOL DATAIDS BEGINNING WITH "RECOVER"                        *
* ******************************************************************* *
        DFHTST TYPE=RECOVERY,                                         X
            DATAID=ARIAXELG
* ******************************************************************* *
        DFHTST TYPE=FINAL
        END
```

Figure 120. DFHTST Sample Definition With the AXE Error Log ARIAXELG

Figure 121 shows a sample remote system definition.

```
CEDA DEFine
 Connection    : IBMC
 Group         : IBMG
CONNECTION IDENTIFIERS
 Netname       : SYD2100A
 INDsys        :
REMOTE ATTRIBUTES
 REMOTESystem  :
 REMOTEName    :
CONNECTION PROPERTIES
 ACcessmethod  : Vtam          Vtam | IRc | INdirect | Xm
 Protocol      : Appc          Appc | Lu61
 SInglesess    : No            No | Yes
 Datastream    : User          User | 3270 | SCs | STrfield | Lm
 RECordformat  : U             U | Vb
OPERATIONAL PROPERTIES
 AUtoconnect   : Yes           No | Yes | All
 INService     : Yes           Yes | No
SECURITY
 SEcurityname  :
 ATtachsec     : Verify        Local | Identify | Verify
 Bindpassword  :               PASSWORD NOT SPECIFIED
```

Figure 121. Sample Remote System Definition Using RDO

Figure 122 shows a sample session definition.

```
CEDA  DEFine
 Sessions      : IBMS
 Group         : IBMG
 SESSION IDENTIFIERS
 Connection    : IBMC
 SESSName      :
 NETnameq      :
 MOdename      : IBMRDB
 SESSION PROPERTIES
 Protocol      : Appc              Appc | Lu61
 MAximum       : 00020 , 00010     0-32767
 RECEIVEPfx    :
 RECEIVECount  : No                No | 1-999
 SENDPfx       :
 SENDCount     : No                No | 1-999
 SENDSize      : 04096             1-30720
 RECEIVESize   : 04096             1-30720
 OPERATOR DEFAULTS
 OPERId        :
 OPERPriority  : 000               0-255
 OPERRsl       : 0
 OPERSecurity  : 1
 USERId        :
 SESSION USAGES
 Transaction   :
 SESSPriority  : 000               0-255
 OPERATIONAL PROPERTIES
 Autoconnect   : Yes               No | Yes | All
 INservice     :                   No | Yes
 Buildchain    : Yes               Yes | No
 USERArealen   : 000               0-255
 IOarealen     : 00000 , 00000     0-32767
 RELreq        : No                No | Yes
 Discreq       : No                No | Yes
 NEPclass      : 000               0-255
 RECOVERY
 RECOvoption   : Sysdefault        Sysdefault | None
```

Figure 122. Sample session Definition Using RDO

Figure 123 shows a sample transaction definition. The following example defines two transactions (or TPNs):

- TOR3

- X'07F6C4C2'— the default TPN that must be supported by all DRDA application servers

```
CEDA  DEFine
 TRansaction   : TOR3
 Group         : IBMG
 PROGram       : ARICAXED
 TWasize       : 00000           0-32767
 PROFile       : DFHCICST
 PArtitionset  :
 STatus        : Enabled         Enabled | Disabled
 PRIMedsize    : 00000           0-65520
REMOTE ATTRIBUTES
 DYnamic       : No              No | Yes
 REMOTESystem  :
 REMOTEName    :
 TRProf        :
 Localq        :                 No | Yes
SCHEDULING
 PRIOrity      : 001             0-255
 TClass        : No              No | 1-10
 ALIASES
 TAskreq       :
 Xtranid       : X'07F6C4C2'
RECOVERY
 DTimout       : No              No | 1-7000
 Indoubt       : Backout         Backout | Commit | Wait
 REStart       : No              No | Yes
 SPurge        : No              No | Yes
 TPurge        : No              No | Yes
 DUmp          : Yes             Yes | No
 TRACe         : Yes             Yes | No
SECURITY
 Extsec        : No              No | Yes
 TRANsec       : 01              1-64
 RSL           : 00              0-24 | Public
 RSLC          : No              No | Yes | External
```

Figure 123. Transaction Definition for the Router AXE Using RDO

Figure 124 shows a sample program definition.

```
CEDA DEFine
  PROGram       : ARICAXED
  Group         : IBMG
  Language      : Assembler    CObol | Assembler | C | Pli | Rpg
  RELoad        : No           No | Yes
  RESident      : Yes          No | Yes
  RS1           : 0            0-24 | Public
  Status        : Enabled      Enabled | Disabled
REMOTE ATTRIBUTES
  REMOTESystem  :
  REMOTEName    :
  Transid       :
  Executionset  : Fullapi      Fullapi | Dplsubset
```

Figure 124. Sample Program Definition for the Router AXE Using RDO

Summary of Example Definitions

Figure 125 on page 263 shows related entries in example definitions involving the following components:

- The DDCS for OS/2 workstation: entries in the various database directories
- VTAM definitions:
  - The ACBNAME in the VTAM APPL (application program major node) definition for CICS
  - The NETID specified in the VTAM startup file ATCSTR00
- CICS resource definitions:
  - The Transaction ID in the transaction definition for the AXE router
  - The MODENAME in the session definition for the CICS/VSE-OS/2 link
- The DB2 for VSE DBNAME directory:
  - The DBNAME field
  - The TPN field

DDCS for OS/2 workstation

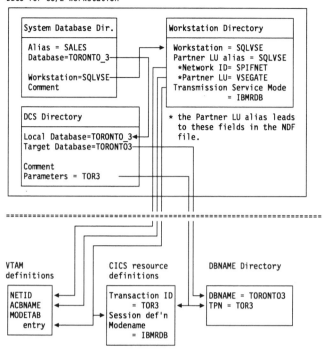

Figure 125. Related Entries in Example Definitions

Chapter 16. DB2 for OS/2 and DB2 for MVS/ESA or DB2 for VM via SDLC

Spiffy uses a phone line (synchronous data link control, SDLC) and a 3724 communications controller to connect the Spiffy retail DB2 for OS/2 system in San Diego to the DB2 for MVS/ESA system at the New York headquarters as shown in Figure 126. The DB2 for OS/2 system is a PU 2.1 device. This scenario also works for DB2 for VM.

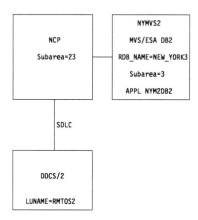

Figure 126. SDLC Connection to NCP

Configuring Communications Manager for OS/2 V1.1 for SDLC

To connect DB2 for OS/2 to the host, you should have DB2 for OS/2 and Communications Manager for OS/2 V1.1 installed on your OS/2 workstation. Communications Manager for OS/2 V1.1 must be configured for APPC. The example below shows you how to configure APPC for SDLC. This example also assumes you have installed the DDCS for OS/2 Multi-User or Single-User product.

Starting from the Communications Manager for OS/2 V1.1 icon:

1. Click on the **Communications Manager Setup** icon and then **Setup**.
2. Choose a configuration file name and then click on **OK**. The Communications Manager Configuration Definition window appears.
3. Select **SDLC** from the **Workstation Connection Type** list.
4. Select **APPC APIs** from the **Feature or Application** list.
5. Click on the **Configure...** pushbutton. The Communications Manager Profile List Sheet window appears.
6. Select **DLC - SDLC** and click on **Configure...**. The SDLC DLC Adapter Parameters window appears (Figure 127 on page 265).

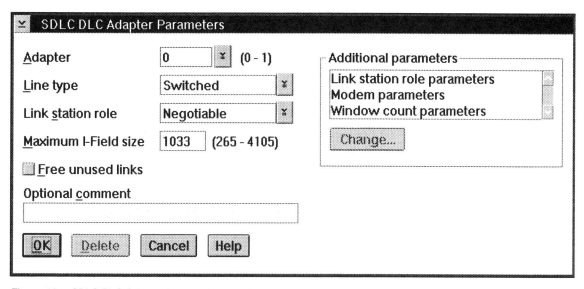

Figure 127. SDLC DLC Adapter Parameters Window

7. Select **0** for the adapter number.
8. Select parameters from the **Additional Parameters** list and click on **Change...** for each selection (Figure 128, Figure 129 on page 266 and Figure 130 on page 266).

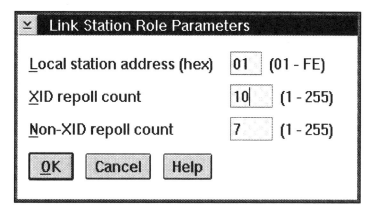

Figure 128. Link Station Role Parameters Window

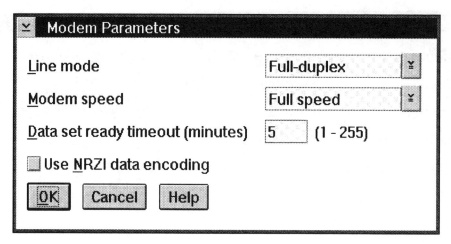

Figure 129. Modem Parameters Window

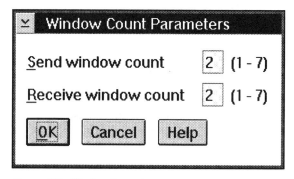

Figure 130. Window Count Parameters Window

In most cases, the default values can be used. However, the **NRZI** (Non-Return to Zero Inverted) parameter setting must match that of your partner's (host) NRZI setting.

Table 55 on page 267 gives the sample parameters used for the example given here and provides a blank column that you can use to fill in the values for your own configuration.

Table 55. Parameters for the SDLC DLC Adapter Profile

Parameter	Example Value	Your Value
Adapter number	0	
Line type	Switched	
Link station role	Negotiable	
Max I-field	1033	
Free unused link	no	
Local station address (in hex)	01	
XID repoll count	10	
Non-XID repoll count	7	
Line mode	Full duplex	
Modem speed	Full speed	
Data set ready timeout	5	
NRZI	no	
Send window count	2	
Receive window count	2	

When the definition is complete, click on **OK**.

To complete the configuration:

1. Return to the Communications Manager Configuration Definition window.
2. Select **Verify configuration** from the **Options** action bar.
3. Select **On**
4. You will be prompted to install the SDLC software.

Continuing Your Communications Manager for OS/2 V1.1 Configuration

Now that you have configured and installed SDLC, you are ready to continue configuring for APPC. This configuration is virtually identical to configuring for token ring. The exceptions are:

- No LAN destination address parameter is in the Create a Connection to a Host window.

- Select **SDLC Adapters 0,1 Regular or User-dialed ISDN** in the Adapter List, as shown in Figure 131.

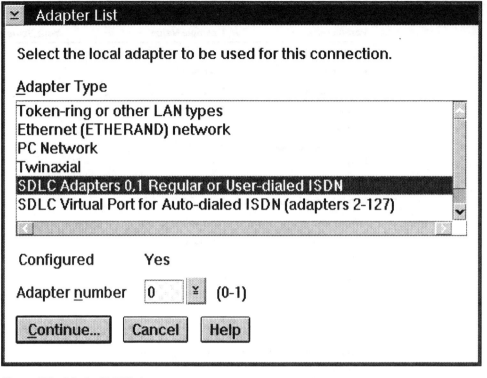

Figure 131. Adapter List Window

You should now go to "Configuring Communications Manager for OS/2 V1.1" on page 212 for DB2 for MVS/ESA or to "Configuring Communications Manager for OS/2 V1.1" on page 236 for DB2 for VM to continue your configuration. Be sure to use the values you are working with in this scenario, rather than changing to the ones in previous scenarios. When you complete the configuration, return here.

Resulting Network Definition File (.NDF)

The Network Definition File shown in Figure 132 on page 269 is the result of following the configuration steps in this section and in "Configuring Communications Manager for OS/2 V1.1" on page 212. The steps above apply to both DB2 for MVS/ESA and to DB2 for VM. The sample .NDF file below is only for a DB2 for MVS/ESA connection. Because the .NDF is automatically generated by following the steps in this section, the .NDF for DB2 for VM is not shown.

```
DEFINE_LOCAL_CP   FQ_CP_NAME(SPIFNET.SYD2100    )
                  DESCRIPTION(Created on 04-01-92 at 10:18a)
                  CP_ALIAS(SYD2100    )
                  NAU_ADDRESS(INDEPENDENT_LU)
                  NODE_TYPE(EN)
                  NODE_ID(X'D2100')
                  HOST_FP_SUPPORT(YES)
                  HOST_FP_LINK_NAME(LINK0001);

DEFINE_LOGICAL_LINK   LINK_NAME(LINK0001)
                      DESCRIPTION(DB2 VIA SDLC)
                      FQ_ADJACENT_CP_NAME(SPIFNET.HOST    )
                      ADJACENT_NODE_TYPE(LEN)
                      DLC_NAME(SDLC)
                      ADAPTER_NUMBER(0)
                      CP_CP_SESSION_SUPPORT(NO)
                      ACTIVATE_AT_STARTUP(YES)
                      LIMITED_RESOURCE(USE_ADAPTER_DEFINITION)
                      LINK_STATION_ROLE(USE_ADAPTER_DEFINITION)
                      SOLICIT_SSCP_SESSION(YES)
                      EFFECTIVE_CAPACITY(USE_ADAPTER_DEFINITION)
                      COST_PER_CONNECT_TIME(USE_ADAPTER_DEFINITION)
                      COST_PER_BYTE(USE_ADAPTER_DEFINITION)
                      SECURITY(USE_ADAPTER_DEFINITION)
                      PROPAGATION_DELAY(USE_ADAPTER_DEFINITION)
                      USER_DEFINED_1(USE_ADAPTER_DEFINITION)
                      USER_DEFINED_2(USE_ADAPTER_DEFINITION)
                      USER_DEFINED_3(USE_ADAPTER_DEFINITION);

DEFINE_LOCAL_LU   LU_NAME(SYD2100A)
                  LU_ALIAS(MYOS2    )
                  NAU_ADDRESS(INDEPENDENT_LU);


DEFINE_PARTNER_LU   FQ_PARTNER_LU_NAME(SPIFNET.NYM2DB2   )
                    PARTNER_LU_ALIAS(DB2PART)
                    PARTNER_LU_UNINTERPRETED_NAME(NYM2DB2  )
                    MAX_MC_LL_SEND_SIZE(32767)
                    CONV_SECURITY_VERIFICATION(NO)
                    PARALLEL_SESSION_SUPPORT(YES);

DEFINE_PARTNER_LU_LOCATION   FQ_PARTNER_LU_NAME(SPIFNET.NYM2DB2   )
                             WILDCARD_ENTRY(NO)
                             FQ_OWNING_CP_NAME(SPIFNET.HOST    )
                             LOCAL_NODE_NN_SERVER(NO);
```

Figure 132 (Part 1 of 2). Network Definition File for DB2 for MVS/ESA Connection

```
DEFINE_MODE    MODE_NAME(MODE0001)
               DESCRIPTION(Created on 04-01-92 at 10:18a)
               COS_NAME(#CONNECT)
               DEFAULT_RU_SIZE(NO)
               MAX_RU_SIZE_UPPER_BOUND(1920)
               RECEIVE_PACING_WINDOW(2)
               MAX_NEGOTIABLE_SESSION_LIMIT(32767)
               PLU_MODE_SESSION_LIMIT(253)
               MIN_CONWINNERS_SOURCE(126);

DEFINE_MODE    MODE_NAME(IBMRDB )
               DESCRIPTION(DB2 MODE)
               COS_NAME(#CONNECT)
               DEFAULT_RU_SIZE(NO)
               MAX_RU_SIZE_UPPER_BOUND(4096)
               RECEIVE_PACING_WINDOW(4)
               MAX_NEGOTIABLE_SESSION_LIMIT(32767)
               PLU_MODE_SESSION_LIMIT(20)
               MIN_CONWINNERS_SOURCE(10);

DEFINE_DEFAULTS  IMPLICIT_INBOUND_PLU_SUPPORT(YES)
               DESCRIPTION(Created on 04-01-92 at 10:18a)
               DEFAULT_MODE_NAME(MODE0001)
               MAX_MC_LL_SEND_SIZE(32767)
               DIRECTORY_FOR_INBOUND_ATTACHES(*)
               DEFAULT_TP_OPERATION(NONQUEUED_AM_STARTED)
               DEFAULT_TP_PROGRAM_TYPE(BACKGROUND)
               DEFAULT_TP_CONV_SECURITY_RQD(NO)
               MAX_HELD_ALERTS(10);

DEFINE_TP   SNA_SERVICE_TP_NAME(X'07',6DB)
               DESCRIPTION(Created on 04-01-92 at 10:18a)
               FILESPEC(C:\SQLLIB\SQLCIAA.EXE)
               CONVERSATION_TYPE(BASIC)
               CONV_SECURITY_RQD(YES)
               SYNC_LEVEL(NONE)
               TP_OPERATION(NONQUEUED_AM_STARTED)
               PROGRAM_TYPE(BACKGROUND)
               RECEIVE_ALLOCATE_TIMEOUT(INFINITE);

DEFINE_TP   SNA_SERVICE_TP_NAME(X'07',6SN)
               DESCRIPTION(Created on 04-01-92 at 10:18a)
               FILESPEC(C:\SQLLIB\SQLCNSM.EXE)
               CONVERSATION_TYPE(BASIC)
               CONV_SECURITY_RQD(YES)
               SYNC_LEVEL(NONE)
               TP_OPERATION(NONQUEUED_AM_STARTED)
               PROGRAM_TYPE(BACKGROUND)
               RECEIVE_ALLOCATE_TIMEOUT(INFINITE);

START_ATTACH_MANAGER;
```

Figure 132 (Part 2 of 2). Network Definition File for DB2 for MVS/ESA Connection

Cataloging DB2 for OS/2 Directory Entries

You should now go to "Cataloging DB2 for OS/2 Directory Entries" on page 222 for
DB2 for MVS/ESA or to "Cataloging DB2 for OS/2 Directory Entries" on page 246 for
DB2 for VM to catalog the database, the workstation (node), and the DCS database.
When you have completed that section, return here.

Configuring the Host

To connect the DB2 for MVS/ESA system in New York to the DB2 for OS/2 system at the Spiffy Retail site, you must add the NCP parameters shown in Figure 133 to the NCP definitions for subarea 23 shown earlier in Figure 49 on page 143. For DB2 for VM, add the NCP parameters in Figure 133 to the NCP definitions for subarea 61 shown in Figure 56 on page 154. The LOCADDR=0 and XID=YES values cause NCP to recognize this DB2 for OS/2 system as a PU 2.1 device.

```
RMTLINE  LINE  ADDRESS=045,NRZI=NO,NEWSYNC=NO, DUPLEX=FULL
RMT1PU   PU    PUTYPE=2,ADDR=C1,MAXDATA=4302,XID=YES
RMTOS2   LU    LOCADDR=0,RESSCB=4,MODETAB=RDBMODES
```

Figure 133. DB2 for VM NCP Parameters for DB2 for OS/2 at Spiffy Retail

Ensure that the CCSID is appropriately assigned at each system.

Chapter 17. DB2 for OS/2 and Multiple Hosts

You can connect DB2 for OS/2 to multiple hosts with a single configuration. The connections can be to multiple DB2 for MVS/ESA systems, to multiple DB2 for VM and VSE systems, to multiple DB2 for OS/400 systems, or to combinations of DB2 for MVS/ESA, DB2 for VM and VSE, and/or DB2 for OS/400. Figure 134 shows a DB2 for OS/2 token-ring connection to two different host systems, DB2 for OS/400 and DB2 for MVS/ESA.

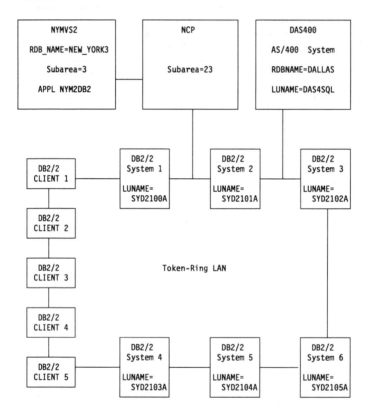

Figure 134. DB2 for OS/2 Token-Ring Connection to DB2 for OS/400 and DB2 for MVS/ESA

If the definitions of the host database systems are in the same subarea network, all you need to do is configure multiple partner LUs (PLUs). From the Create a Connection to a Host window, click on **Define Partner LUs...** for each system PLU.

If the PLUs are not in the same VTAM domain, you must make sure that the network ID is correctly identified for each PLU. From SNA Features, select each partner LU and change the network ID to the correct value. Ignore the warning that comes up.

If the host database systems are not all defined in the same subarea network and are in the same VTAM domain, you need to configure connections to separate nodes.

Because you can only specify one host connection in Communications Manager for OS/2 V1.1, you must specify any additional connections as peer nodes. This requires that you know the **VTAM SSCP name** of the peer node to which you want to connect.

The method for configuring multiple nodes is described in this chapter. This example shows how to connect DB2 for OS/2 to a DB2 for MVS/ESA host and to a DB2 for OS/400 host (see Figure 134 on page 272).

You should read Chapter 1, "Introducing DRDA Connectivity" on page 2 to become familiar with the concepts before you study the examples in this chapter.

Configuring Communications Manager for OS/2 V1.1

To connect DB2 for OS/2 to the host, you should have DB2 for OS/2 and Communications Manager for OS/2 V1.1 installed on your OS/2 workstation. Communications Manager for OS/2 V1.1 must be configured for APPC. The following example shows you how to configure APPC. This example also assumes you have installed the DDCS for OS/2 Multi-User Gateway or Single-User product.

If you have not configured a DLC profile for the connection to the host, you must configure the appropriate DLC profile before configuring the SNA network definitions. For more information on configuring DLC profiles, see *Communications Manager/2 Configuration Guide*.

Getting to the Communications Manager for OS/2 V1.1 Profile List Sheet

Starting from the Communications Manager/2 icon:

1. Click on the **Communications Manager Setup** icon and then the **Setup...** pushbutton.

2. Choose a configuration file name and then click on **OK**. The Communications Manager Configuration Definition window appears.

3. Select **Token-ring or other LAN types** from the Workstation Connection Type list.

4. Select **APPC APIs** from the Feature or Application list.

5. Click on the **Configure...** pushbutton. The Communications Manager Profile List Sheet window appears.

Specifying Local Node Characteristics

At the Communications Manager Profile List Sheet window, select **SNA local node characteristics**, then click on the **Configure....** The Local Node Characteristics window appears (Figure 135 on page 274).

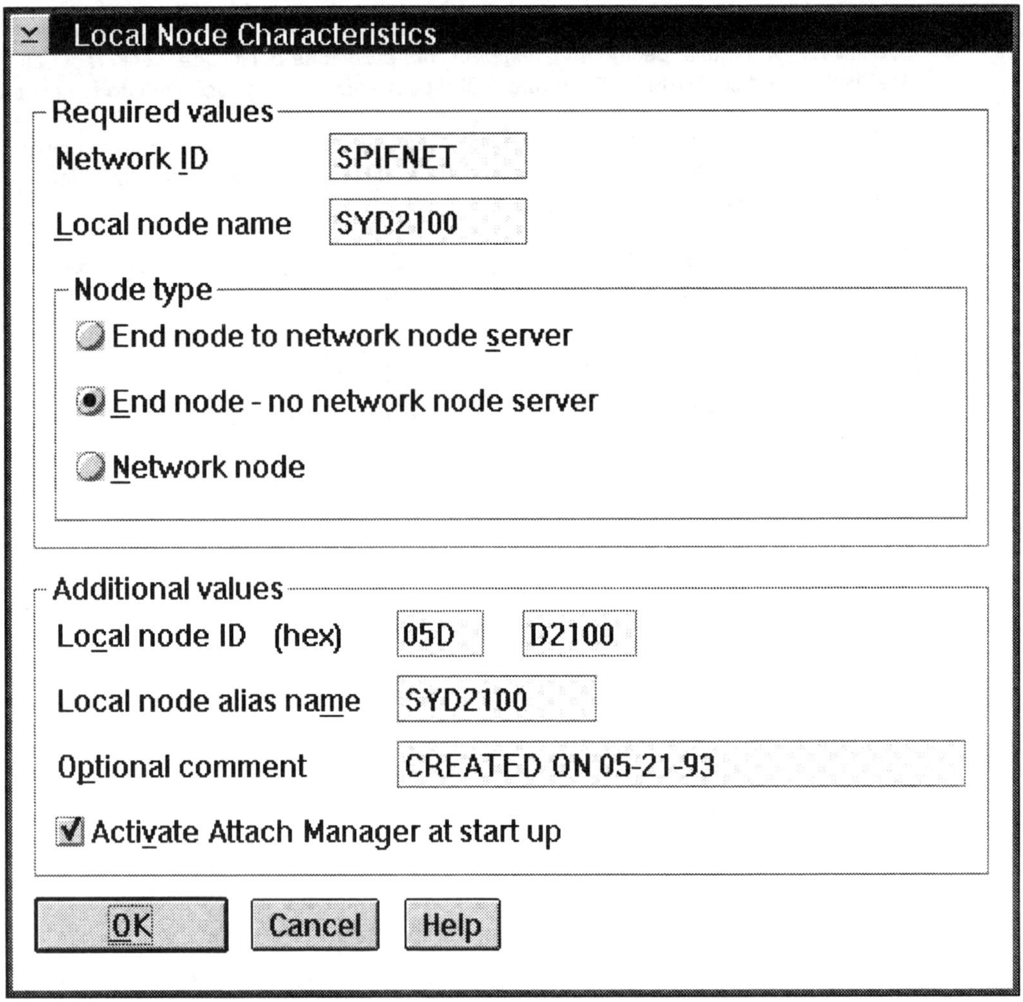

Local Node Characteristics

Required values

Network ID — `SPIFNET`

Local node name — `SYD2100`

Node type

○ End node to network node server

◉ End node - no network node server

○ Network node

Additional values

Local node ID (hex) — `05D` `D2100`

Local node alias name — `SYD2100`

Optional comment — `CREATED ON 05-21-93`

☑ Activate Attach Manager at start up

[OK] [Cancel] [Help]

Figure 135. Local Node Characteristics Window

Specify the network ID, the local node name (also known as the PU/CP name), the local node ID, and the local node alias name. When you are finished, click on **OK**. This returns you to the Communications Manager Profile List Sheet window.

Table 56 gives the sample parameters used for this example and provides a blank column that you can use for your own configuration. You need to get these values from your host administrator.

Table 56. Parameters for Local Node Characteristics

Parameter	Example Value	Your Value	Comment
Network ID	SPIFNET		
Local node name	SYD2100		See the discussion regarding CPNAME and IDBLK/IDNUM in Chapter 19, "DB2 for OS/2 and Other DRDA Servers" on page 304.
Local node ID	D2100		See the discussion regarding CPNAME and IDBLK/IDNUM in Chapter 19, "DB2 for OS/2 and Other DRDA Servers" on page 304.
Local node alias name	SYD2100		

Specifying Connections and Partner LUs

In this scenario, the DB2 for MVS/ESA system is defined as the host, and the DB2 for OS/400 is defined as a peer node.

DB2 Connection

1. At the Communications Manager Profile List Sheet, select **SNA connections**, then click on **Configure....** A Connections List window appears.

2. Select **To host** from the **Partner type** group.

3. To create a new definition, select click on **Create**. To change an existing definition, select a link from the **Link Name** list and click on **Change....** The Adapter List appears.

4. Select **Token-ring or other LAN types** from the Adapter List.

   The **Configured** field shows whether the adapter is configured, and the selections available in the **Adapter number** field change to match the adapter type you selected.

5. Select an adapter number from the **Adapter number** list and click on **Continue....** The Create a Connection to a Host window appears (Figure 136 on page 276).

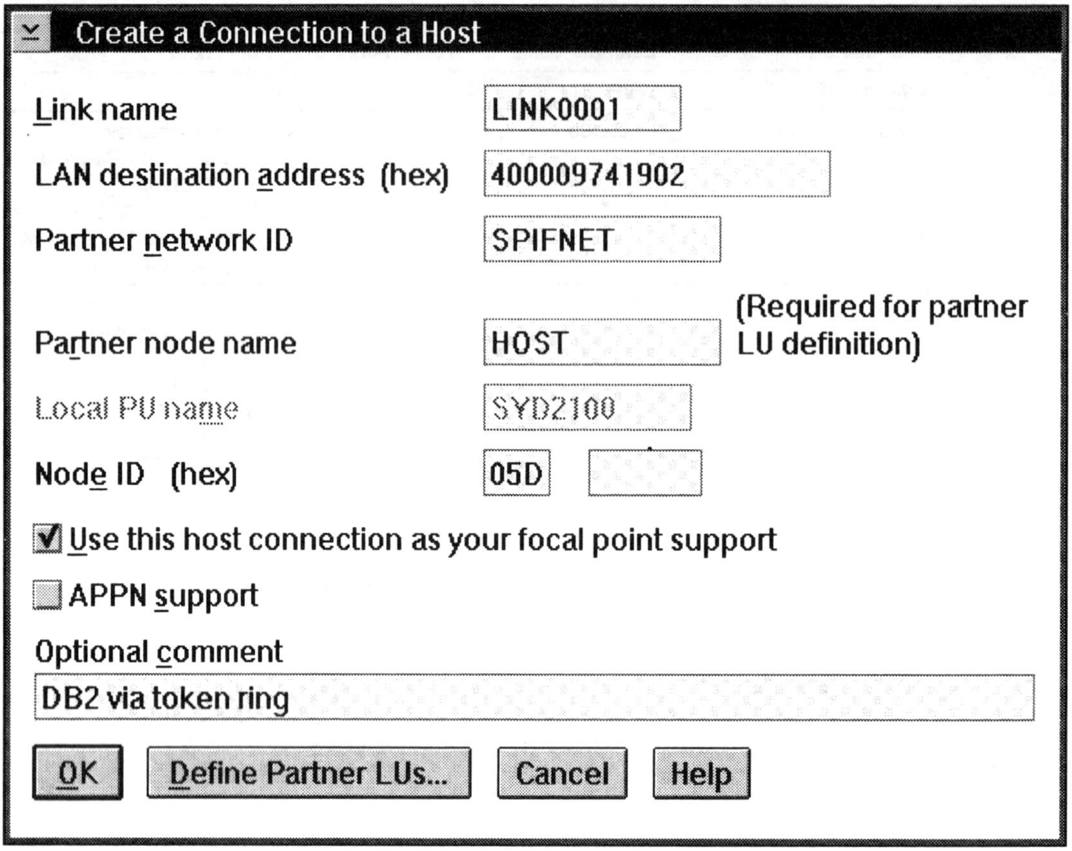

```
┌─────────────────────────────────────────────────────────────────┐
│ ▽  Create a Connection to a Host                                  │
├─────────────────────────────────────────────────────────────────┤
│                                                                   │
│  Link name                    ┌────────────────┐                  │
│                               │ LINK0001       │                  │
│                               └────────────────┘                  │
│  LAN destination address (hex) ┌───────────────────────┐          │
│                               │ 400009741902          │           │
│                               └───────────────────────┘           │
│  Partner network ID           ┌───────────────┐                   │
│                               │ SPIFNET       │                   │
│                               └───────────────┘                   │
│                               ┌───────────────┐ (Required for     │
│  Partner node name            │ HOST          │  partner          │
│                               └───────────────┘  LU definition)   │
│  Local PU name                ┌───────────────┐                   │
│                               │ SYD2100       │                   │
│                               └───────────────┘                   │
│  Node ID  (hex)      ┌──────┐ ┌───────┐                           │
│                      │ 05D  │ │       │                           │
│                      └──────┘ └───────┘                           │
│  ☑ Use this host connection as your focal point support           │
│  ☐ APPN support                                                   │
│  Optional comment                                                 │
│  ┌──────────────────────────────────────────────────────────┐    │
│  │ DB2 via token ring                                        │    │
│  └──────────────────────────────────────────────────────────┘    │
│  ┌─────┐ ┌───────────────────┐ ┌─────────┐ ┌──────┐               │
│  │ OK  │ │ Define Partner LUs...│ │ Cancel │ │ Help │            │
│  └─────┘ └───────────────────┘ └─────────┘ └──────┘               │
└─────────────────────────────────────────────────────────────────┘
```

Figure 136. Creating a Connection to a Host Window

6. Enter a link name and the LAN destination address.

7. Enter the network ID and node name for the partner node. The **Define Partner LUs...** pushbutton is enabled.

Table 57 gives the sample parameters used for this example and provides a blank column that you can use for your own configuration. You need to get the partner network ID and LAN destination address from your host administrator.

Table 57. Parameters for Defining DB2 for MVS/ESA as the Host

Parameter	Example Value	Your Value
Link name	LINK0001	
Partner network ID	SPIFNET	
Partner node name	HOST	
LAN destination address	400009451902	
Comment	DB2 for MVS/ESA via token ring	

8. Click on the **Define Partner LUs...** pushbutton. The Create Partner LUs window appears (Figure 137 on page 277).

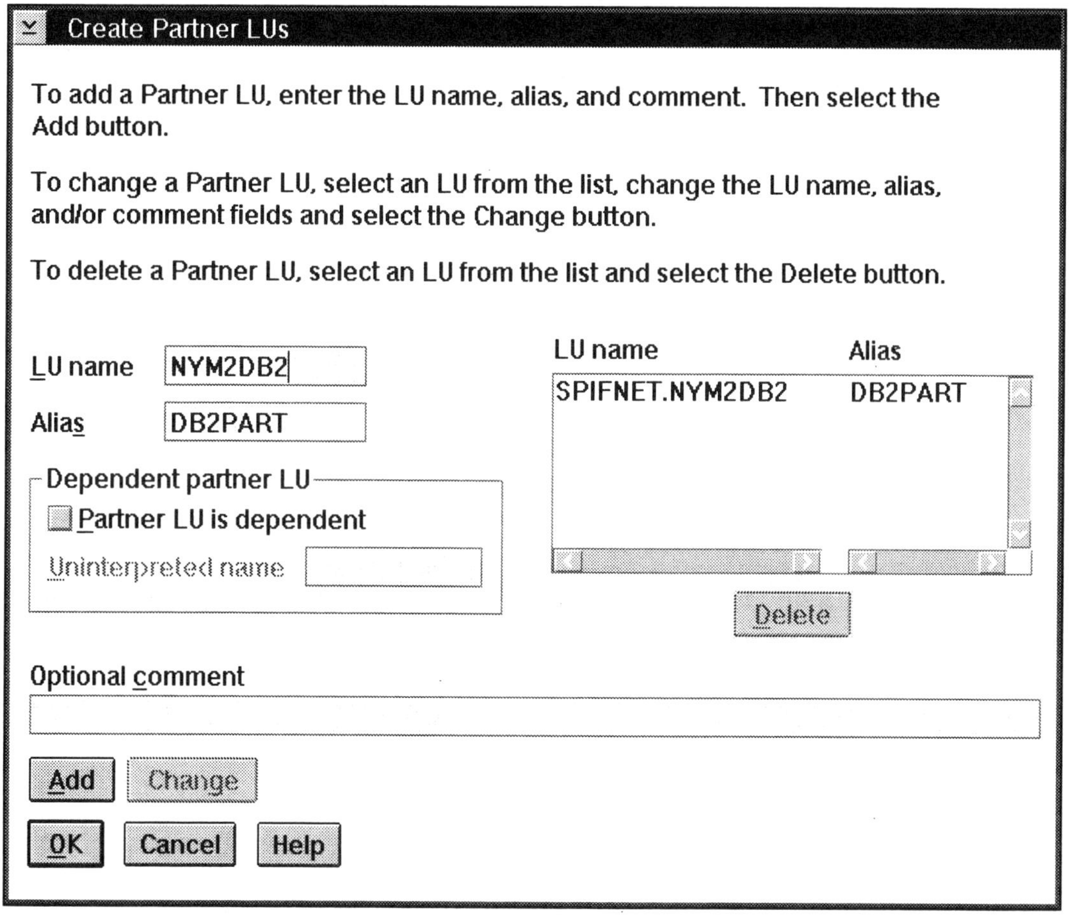

```
┌──────────────────────────────────────────────────────────────────────────┐
│ ⌄  Create Partner LUs                                                      │
├──────────────────────────────────────────────────────────────────────────┤
│                                                                            │
│ To add a Partner LU, enter the LU name, alias, and comment.  Then select the│
│ Add button.                                                                │
│                                                                            │
│ To change a Partner LU, select an LU from the list, change the LU name, alias,│
│ and/or comment fields and select the Change button.                        │
│                                                                            │
│ To delete a Partner LU, select an LU from the list and select the Delete button.│
│                                                                            │
│                                              LU name             Alias      │
│  LU name    [NYM2DB2]                       ┌────────────────────────────┐ │
│                                             │ SPIFNET.NYM2DB2    DB2PART  │ │
│  Alias      [DB2PART]                       │                            │ │
│  ┌─Dependent partner LU─────────┐           │                            │ │
│  │ ☐ Partner LU is dependent     │           │                            │ │
│  │ Uninterpreted name  [       ] │           └────────────────────────────┘ │
│  └───────────────────────────────┘                                         │
│                                                     [ Delete ]              │
│  Optional comment                                                          │
│  [                                                                       ]  │
│                                                                            │
│  [ Add ]  [ Change ]                                                       │
│  [ OK ]  [ Cancel ]  [ Help ]                                              │
│                                                                            │
└──────────────────────────────────────────────────────────────────────────┘
```

Figure 137. Create Partner LUs window

9. Enter an LU name and an alias.

   Table 58 gives the sample parameters used for this example and provides a blank column that you can use for your own configuration. You need to get the LU name from your host administrator.

Table 58. Parameters for Create a Partner LU

Parameter	Example Value	Your Value
LU name	NYM2DB2	
Alias	DB2PART	

10. Click on the **Add** pushbutton.

11. When the partner LU definition is complete, click on **OK**. The Create a Connection to the Host window reappears.

12. Click on the **Cancel** pushbutton. This returns you to the Connections List window where you can configure the second node as a peer node.

OS/400 Connection

Starting at the Connections List window.

1. Select **To peer node** from the **Partner type** group.

2. To create a new definition, click on the **Create** pushbutton. To change an existing definition, select a link from the **Link Name** list and click on the **Change...** pushbutton. The Adapter List appears.

3. Select **Token-ring or other LAN types** from the Adapter List.

   The **Configured** field shows whether the adapter is configured and the selections available in the **Adapter number** field change to match the adapter type you selected.

4. Select an adapter number from the **Adapter number** list and click on the **Continue...** pushbutton. The Create a Connection to a Peer Node window appears (Figure 138).

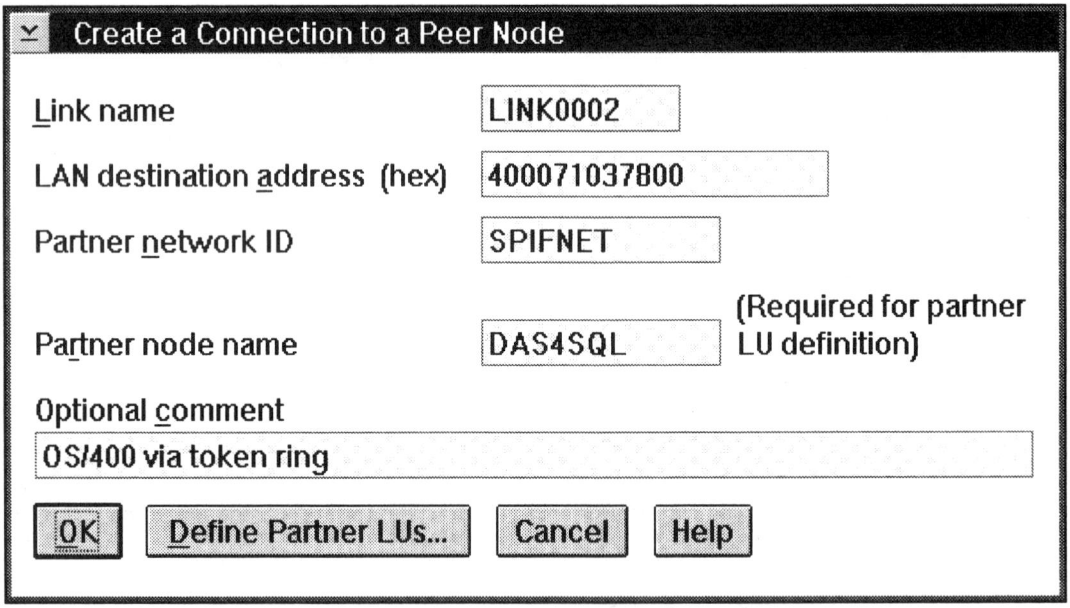

Figure 138. Create a Connection to a Peer Node Window

5. Enter a link name and the LAN destination address.

6. Enter the network ID and node name for the partner node. The **Define Partner LUs...** pushbutton is enabled.

Note the following correspondences for OS/400:

Partner network ID is the local network ID from the OS/400 display network attributes (DSPNETA) command.

Partner node name is the control point name (CP name) from the DSPNETA command.

LAN destination address is the local adapter address from the OS/400 display line description (DSPLIND) command or the work with line description (WRKLINE) command when you display the token ring line description.

Table 59 gives the sample parameters used for this example and provides a blank column that you can use for your own configuration.

Table 59. Parameters for Create a Connection to a Peer Node

Parameter	Example Value	Your Value
Link name	LINK0002	
Partner network ID	SPIFNET	
Partner node name	DAS4SQL	
LAN destination address	400071037800	
Comment	OS/400 via token ring	

7. Click on the **Define Partner LUs...** pushbutton. The Create Partner LUs window appears (Figure 139 on page 280).

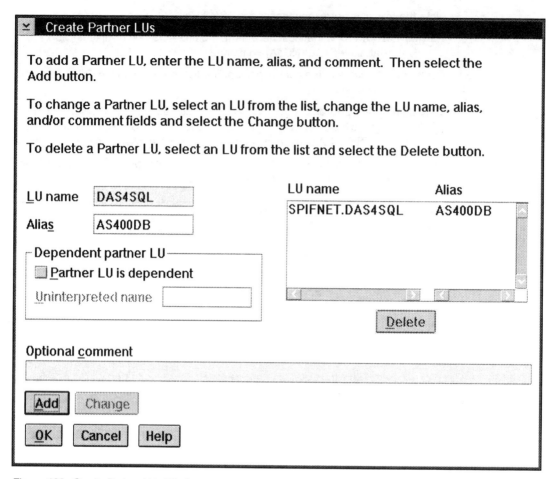

To add a Partner LU, enter the LU name, alias, and comment. Then select the Add button.

To change a Partner LU, select an LU from the list, change the LU name, alias, and/or comment fields and select the Change button.

To delete a Partner LU, select an LU from the list and select the Delete button.

Figure 139. Create Partner LUs Window

8. Enter an LU name and an alias.

   Table 59 on page 279 gives the sample parameters used for this example and provides a blank column that you can use for your own configuration.

Table 60. Parameters for Create a Partner LU

Parameter	Example Value	Your Value
LU name	DAS4SQL	
Alias	AS400DB	

9. Click on the **Add** pushbutton.

10. When the partner LU definition is complete, click on **OK**. The Create a Connection to a Peer Node window reappears.

11. Click on the **Cancel** pushbutton.

12. Select **Close** from the Connections List.

Specifying the Local LU

The following steps define the local LU to connect to DB2 for MVS/ESA. The local LU does not need to be defined for OS/400. OS/400 uses the local node (CP) name as the local LU name.

At the Communications Manager Profile List Sheet window, select **SNA Features**, then click on **Configure....** The SNA Features List window appears. From this window, select **Local LUs** and click on the **Create...** pushbutton. The Create a Local LU window appears (Figure 140).

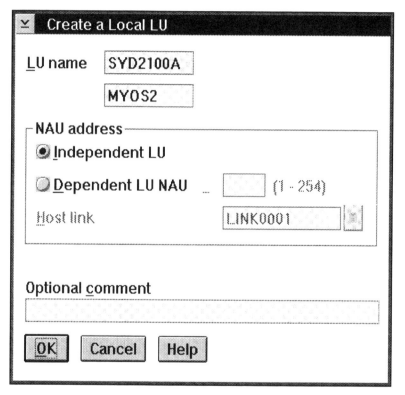

Figure 140. Create a Local LU Window

On this window, specify the local LU name and the local alias and click on **OK**. This returns you to the SNA Features List window.

Note: The LU alias is case sensitive.

Table 61 on page 282 gives the sample parameters used for this example and provides a blank column that you can use for your own configuration. You need to get the LU name from your host administrator.

Table 61. Parameters for Create a Local LU

Parameter	Example Value	Your Value
LU name	SYD2100A	
Alias	MYOS2	

Specifying the Mode

Because both hosts use the same mode name, only one mode needs to be defined. However, you should consider that each host might require different values for session limit, minimum contention winners, receive pacing window, and RU size. This might require that you use different modes.

At the SNA Features List window, select **Modes**. Then click on the **Create...** pushbutton. The Create a Mode Definition window appears (Figure 141).

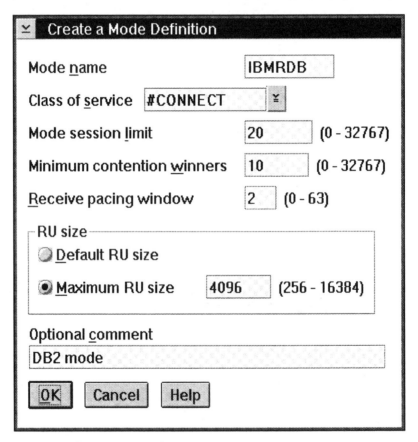

Figure 141. Create a Mode Definition Window

On this window:

1. Specify the **Mode name**.

2. The default values for mode session limit, minimum contention winners, and receive pacing window will work in many cases. However, you should check these with your host administrator.

3. Select **Maximum RU size** and specify the value.

Table 62 gives the sample parameters used for this example and provides a blank column that you can use for your own configuration. You need to consult with your host administrator for the mode name, pacing window size, and RU size.

Table 62. Parameters for Create a Mode Definition

Parameter	Example Value	Your Value
Mode name	IBMRDB	
Mode session limit	20	
Minimum contention winners	10	
Receive pacing window	2	
Maximum RU size	4096	
Comment	DB2 mode	

When you are finished, click on **OK**. This returns you to the SNA Features List window.

Completing the Configuration

After you complete the steps in the previous sections, you are ready to verify and save your updated configuration file. To do this:

1. Return to the Communications Manager Configuration Definition window.
2. Select **Verify configuration** from the **Options** action bar.
3. Select **On**.

Resulting Network Definition File (.NDF)

Figure 142 shows the resulting network definition file.

```
DEFINE_LOCAL_CP    FQ_CP_NAME(SPIFNET.SYD2100  )
                   DESCRIPTION(Created on 04-03-92 at 12:53p)
                   CP_ALIAS(SYD2100 )
                   NAU_ADDRESS(INDEPENDENT_LU)
                   NODE_TYPE(EN)
                   NODE_ID(X'D2100')
                   HOST_FP_SUPPORT(YES)
                   HOST_FP_LINK_NAME(LINK0001);

DEFINE_LOGICAL_LINK  LINK_NAME(LINK0002)
                     DESCRIPTION(OS/400 via token ring)
                     FQ_ADJACENT_CP_NAME(SPIFNET.DAS4SQL  )
                     ADJACENT_NODE_TYPE(LEARN)
                     DLC_NAME(IBMTRNET)
                     ADAPTER_NUMBER(0)
                     DESTINATION_ADDRESS(X'400071037800')
                     CP_CP_SESSION_SUPPORT(NO)
                     ACTIVATE_AT_STARTUP(NO)
                     LIMITED_RESOURCE(USE_ADAPTER_DEFINITION)
                     LINK_STATION_ROLE(USE_ADAPTER_DEFINITION)
                     SOLICIT_SSCP_SESSION(NO)
                     EFFECTIVE_CAPACITY(USE_ADAPTER_DEFINITION)
                     COST_PER_CONNECT_TIME(USE_ADAPTER_DEFINITION)
                     COST_PER_BYTE(USE_ADAPTER_DEFINITION)
                     SECURITY(USE_ADAPTER_DEFINITION)
                     PROPAGATION_DELAY(USE_ADAPTER_DEFINITION)
                     USER_DEFINED_1(USE_ADAPTER_DEFINITION)
                     USER_DEFINED_2(USE_ADAPTER_DEFINITION)
                     USER_DEFINED_3(USE_ADAPTER_DEFINITION);
```

Figure 142 (Part 1 of 3). Network Definition File for Connecting DB2 for OS/2 to DB2 for MVS/ESA and DB2 for OS/400

```
DEFINE_LOGICAL_LINK  LINK_NAME(LINK0001)
                     DESCRIPTION(DB2 via token ring)
                     FQ_ADJACENT_CP_NAME(SPIFNET.HOST    )
                     ADJACENT_NODE_TYPE(LEN)
                     DLC_NAME(IBMTRNET)
                     ADAPTER_NUMBER(0)
                     DESTINATION_ADDRESS(X'400009451902')
                     CP_CP_SESSION_SUPPORT(NO)
                     ACTIVATE_AT_STARTUP(YES)
                     LIMITED_RESOURCE(USE_ADAPTER_DEFINITION)
                     LINK_STATION_ROLE(USE_ADAPTER_DEFINITION)
                     SOLICIT_SSCP_SESSION(YES)
                     EFFECTIVE_CAPACITY(USE_ADAPTER_DEFINITION)
                     COST_PER_CONNECT_TIME(USE_ADAPTER_DEFINITION)
                     COST_PER_BYTE(USE_ADAPTER_DEFINITION)
                     SECURITY(USE_ADAPTER_DEFINITION)
                     PROPAGATION_DELAY(USE_ADAPTER_DEFINITION)
                     USER_DEFINED_1(USE_ADAPTER_DEFINITION)
                     USER_DEFINED_2(USE_ADAPTER_DEFINITION)
                     USER_DEFINED_3(USE_ADAPTER_DEFINITION);

DEFINE_LOCAL_LU  LU_NAME(SYD2100A)
                 LU_ALIAS(MYOS2   )
                 NAU_ADDRESS(INDEPENDENT_LU);

DEFINE_PARTNER_LU  FQ_PARTNER_LU_NAME(SPIFNET.NYM2DB2  )
                   PARTNER_LU_ALIAS(DB2PART)
                   PARTNER_LU_UNINTERPRETED_NAME(NYM2DB2 )
                   MAX_MC_LL_SEND_SIZE(32767)
                   CONV_SECURITY_VERIFICATION(NO)
                   PARALLEL_SESSION_SUPPORT(YES);

DEFINE_PARTNER_LU  FQ_PARTNER_LU_NAME(SPIFNET.DAS4SQL  )
                   PARTNER_LU_ALIAS(AS400DB)
                   PARTNER_LU_UNINTERPRETED_NAME(DAS4SQL )
                   MAX_MC_LL_SEND_SIZE(32767)
                   CONV_SECURITY_VERIFICATION(NO)
                   PARALLEL_SESSION_SUPPORT(YES);

DEFINE_PARTNER_LU_LOCATION  FQ_PARTNER_LU_NAME(SPIFNET.NYM2DB2  )
                            WILDCARD_ENTRY(NO)
                            FQ_OWNING_CP_NAME(SPIFNET.HOST    )
                            LOCAL_NODE_NN_SERVER(NO);

DEFINE_PARTNER_LU_LOCATION  FQ_PARTNER_LU_NAME(SPIFNET.DAS4SQL  )
                            WILDCARD_ENTRY(NO)
                            FQ_OWNING_CP_NAME(SPIFNET.DAS4SQL  )
                            LOCAL_NODE_NN_SERVER(NO);
```

Figure 142 (Part 2 of 3). Network Definition File for Connecting DB2 for OS/2 to DB2 for MVS/ESA and DB2 for OS/400

```
DEFINE_MODE   MODE_NAME(MODE0001)
              DESCRIPTION(Created on 04-03-92 at 12:53p)
              COS_NAME(#CONNECT)
              DEFAULT_RU_SIZE(NO)
              MAX_RU_SIZE_UPPER_BOUND(1920)
              RECEIVE_PACING_WINDOW(2)
              MAX_NEGOTIABLE_SESSION_LIMIT(32767)
              PLU_MODE_SESSION_LIMIT(253)
              MIN_CONWINNERS_SOURCE(126);

DEFINE_MODE   MODE_NAME(IBMRDB )
              DESCRIPTION(Host mode)
              COS_NAME(#CONNECT)
              DEFAULT_RU_SIZE(NO)
              MAX_RU_SIZE_UPPER_BOUND(4096)
              RECEIVE_PACING_WINDOW(2)
              MAX_NEGOTIABLE_SESSION_LIMIT(32767)
              PLU_MODE_SESSION_LIMIT(20)
              MIN_CONWINNERS_SOURCE(10);

DEFINE_DEFAULTS  IMPLICIT_INBOUND_PLU_SUPPORT(YES)
              DESCRIPTION(Created on 04-03-92 at 12:53p)
              DEFAULT_MODE_NAME(MODE0001)
              MAX_MC_LL_SEND_SIZE(32767)
              DIRECTORY_FOR_INBOUND_ATTACHES(*)
              DEFAULT_TP_OPERATION(NONQUEUED_AM_STARTED)
              DEFAULT_TP_PROGRAM_TYPE(BACKGROUND)
              DEFAULT_TP_CONV_SECURITY_RQD(NO)
              MAX_HELD_ALERTS(10);

DEFINE_TP     SNA_SERVICE_TP_NAME(X'07',6DB)
              DESCRIPTION(Created on 04-03-92 at 12:53p)
              FILESPEC(C:\SQLLIB\SQLCIAA.EXE)
              CONVERSATION_TYPE(BASIC)
              CONV_SECURITY_RQD(YES)
              SYNC_LEVEL(NONE)
              TP_OPERATION(NONQUEUED_AM_STARTED)
              PROGRAM_TYPE(BACKGROUND)
              RECEIVE_ALLOCATE_TIMEOUT(INFINITE);

DEFINE_TP     SNA_SERVICE_TP_NAME(X'07',6SN)
              DESCRIPTION(Created on 04-03-92 at 12:53p)
              FILESPEC(C:\SQLLIB\SQLCNSM.EXE)
              CONVERSATION_TYPE(BASIC)
              CONV_SECURITY_RQD(YES)
              SYNC_LEVEL(NONE)
              TP_OPERATION(NONQUEUED_AM_STARTED)
              PROGRAM_TYPE(BACKGROUND)
              RECEIVE_ALLOCATE_TIMEOUT(INFINITE);

START_ATTACH_MANAGER;
```

Figure 142 (Part 3 of 3). Network Definition File for Connecting DB2 for OS/2 to DB2 for MVS/ESA and DB2 for OS/400

Cataloging DB2 for OS/2 Directory Entries

You now need to catalog the database, the workstation (node), and the DCS database for each of the hosts. To catalog the DB2 for MVS/ESA information, see "Cataloging DB2 for OS/2 Directory Entries" on page 222. To catalog the DB2 for OS/400 information, see "Cataloging DB2 for OS/2 Directory Entries" on page 204. Be sure to use the values you are working with in this scenario, rather than changing to the ones in the previous scenarios.

Configuring the Host

Refer to "Configuring the Host" on page 227 and "Configuring the AS/400" on page 209. Be sure to use the values you are working with in this scenario, rather than changing to the ones in the previous scenarios.

Chapter 18. DB2 for OS/2 and DB2 for MVS/ESA or DB2 for VM and VSE via 3174 Controller

Figure 143 shows DB2 for OS/2 systems connected to DB2 for MVS/ESA, using a 3174 control unit and a token-ring LAN. Spiffy Headquarters uses this configuration to give executives access to the Spiffy corporate database systems. In this example, five DB2 for OS/2 clients are attached to a single DDCS for OS/2 Multi-User Gateway workstation (DB2 for OS/2 System 1), which acts as a gateway to the host. The remaining workstations (DB2 for OS/2 System 2 through DB2 for OS/2 System 6) have the Single-User version of DDCS for OS/2 installed, and communicate directly with the host. This example shows the configuration necessary to connect the DDCS for OS/2 Multi-User Gateway to the host.

Note: PU 2.1 support through a local 3174 requires either Configuration Support-C or RPQ 8Q0800, and VTAM 3.4. This example uses Configuration Support-C.

The material in this chapter does not include any VTAM or NCP statements required to connect the machines in question to other parts of the Spiffy network.

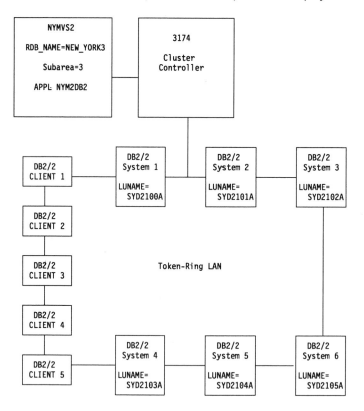

Figure 143. Token-Ring LAN Connected to NCP

You should read Chapter 1, "Introducing DRDA Connectivity" on page 2 to become familiar with the concepts before you use the examples in this chapter.

Independent versus Dependent Logical Unit Configurations

This example shows two configurations, one for independent logical unit (PU 2.1) and another for dependent logical unit (PU 2.0). Emphasis is on the independent configuration because of its ability to support multiple sessions. You can have only one session per partner LU if you use the dependent logical unit. If the LU is a gateway for more than one client, only one can connect at a time. Side notes indicate where changes need to be made to support dependent logical unit configurations.

Configuring Communications Manager for OS/2 V1.1

To connect DB2 for OS/2 to the host, you should have DB2 for OS/2 and Communications Manager for OS/2 V1.1 installed on your OS/2 workstation. Communications Manager for OS/2 V1.1 must be configured for APPC. The following example shows how to configure APPC. This example also assumes you have installed the DDCS for OS/2 Multi-User Gateway product.

If you have not configured a DLC profile for the connection to the host, you must configure the appropriate DLC profile before configuring the SNA network definitions. For more information on configuring DLC profiles, see *Communications Manager/2 Configuration Guide*.

Getting to the Communications Manager for OS/2 V1.1 Profile List Sheet

Starting from the Communications Manager for OS/2 V1.1 icon:

1. Click on the **Communications Manager Setup** icon and then the **Setup...** pushbutton.

2. Choose a configuration file name and then click on **OK**. The Communications Manager Configuration Definition window appears.

3. Select the **Token-ring or other LAN types** from the Workstation Connection Type list.

4. Select **APPC APIs** from the Feature or Application list.

5. Click on the **Configure...** pushbutton. The Communications Manager Profile List Sheet window appears.

Specifying Local Node Characteristics

At the Communications Manager Profile List Sheet, select **Local node characteristics**, then click on the **Configure....** The Local Node Characteristics window appears (Figure 144 on page 290).

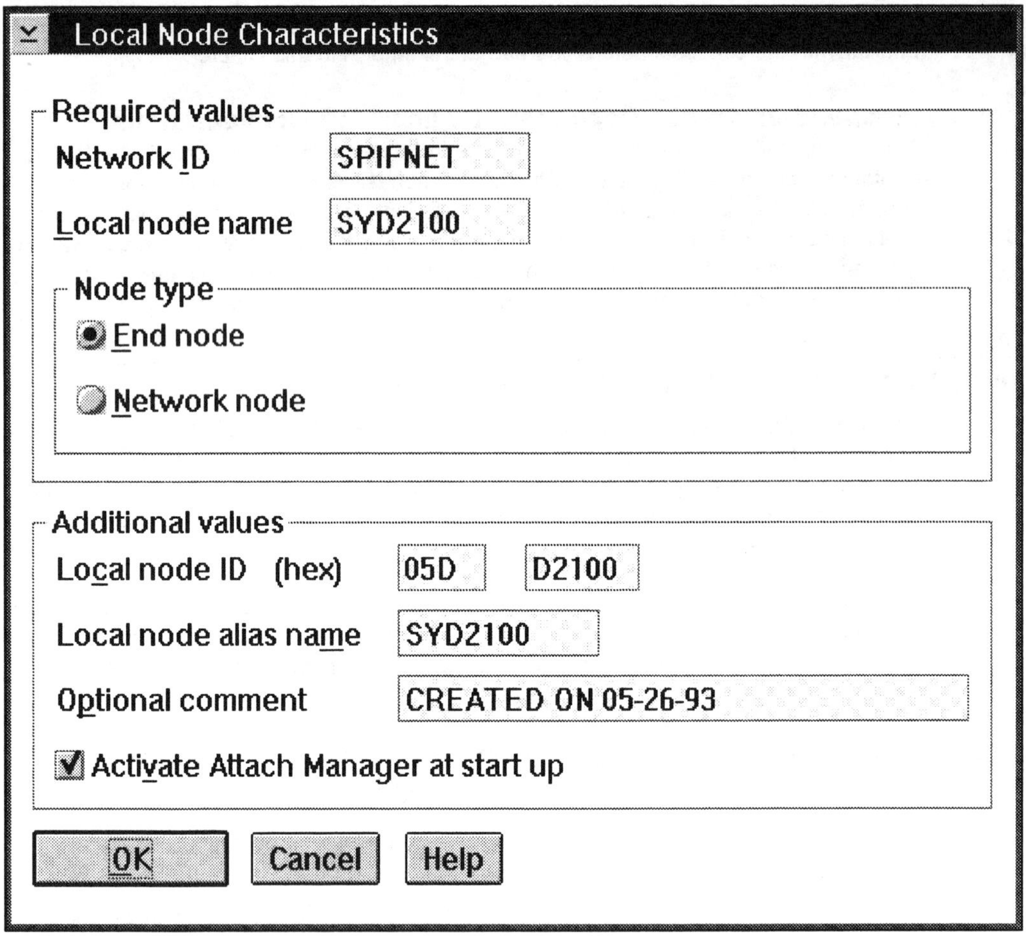

```
 ▼  Local Node Characteristics
┌─Required values──────────────────────────────────────────┐
│  Network ID          │SPIFNET    │                        │
│                                                            │
│  Local node name     │SYD2100    │                        │
│  ┌─Node type──────────────────────────────────────────┐  │
│  │  ◉ End node                                          │  │
│  │                                                      │  │
│  │  ○ Network node                                      │  │
│  │                                                      │  │
│  └──────────────────────────────────────────────────────┘  │
└────────────────────────────────────────────────────────────┘
┌─Additional values────────────────────────────────────────┐
│  Local node ID   (hex)   │05D│   │D2100│                  │
│                                                            │
│  Local node alias name   │SYD2100    │                     │
│                                                            │
│  Optional comment        │CREATED ON 05-26-93          │   │
│                                                            │
│  ☑ Activate Attach Manager at start up                    │
└────────────────────────────────────────────────────────────┘
┌──────────┐   ┌──────────┐   ┌──────────┐
│   OK     │   │ Cancel   │   │  Help    │
└──────────┘   └──────────┘   └──────────┘
```

Figure 144. Local Node Characteristics Window

On this panel, specify the network ID, the local node name (also known as the PU/CP name), the local node ID, and the local node alias name.

Table 63 on page 291 gives the sample parameters used for this example and provides a blank column that you can use to fill in the values for your own configuration. You need to contact your host administrator for these values.

Table 63. Parameters for Local Node Characteristics

Parameter	Example Value	Your Value	Comment
Network ID	SPIFNET		
Local node name	SYD2100		See the discussion regarding CPNAME and IDBLK/IDNUM in Chapter 19, "DB2 for OS/2 and Other DRDA Servers" on page 304.
Local node ID	D2100		See the discussion regarding CPNAME and IDBLK/IDNUM in Chapter 19, "DB2 for OS/2 and Other DRDA Servers" on page 304.
Local node alias name	SYD2100		

When you are finished, click on **OK**. This returns you to the Communications Manager Profile List Sheet.

Specifying Connections and Partner LUs

1. At the Communications Manager Profile List Sheet, select **SNA connections**, then click on **Configure....** A Connections List window appears.

2. Select **To host** from the **Partner type** group.

3. To create a new definition, click on **Create**. To change an existing definition, select a link from the **Link Name** list and click on the **Change...** pushbutton. The Adapter List appears.

4. Select **Token-ring or other LAN types** from the Adapter List.

   The **Configured** field shows whether the adapter is configured and the selections available in the **Adapter number** field change to match the adapter type you selected.

5. Select an adapter number from the **Adapter number** list and click on the **Continue...** pushbutton. The Create a Connection to a Host window appears (Figure 145 on page 292).

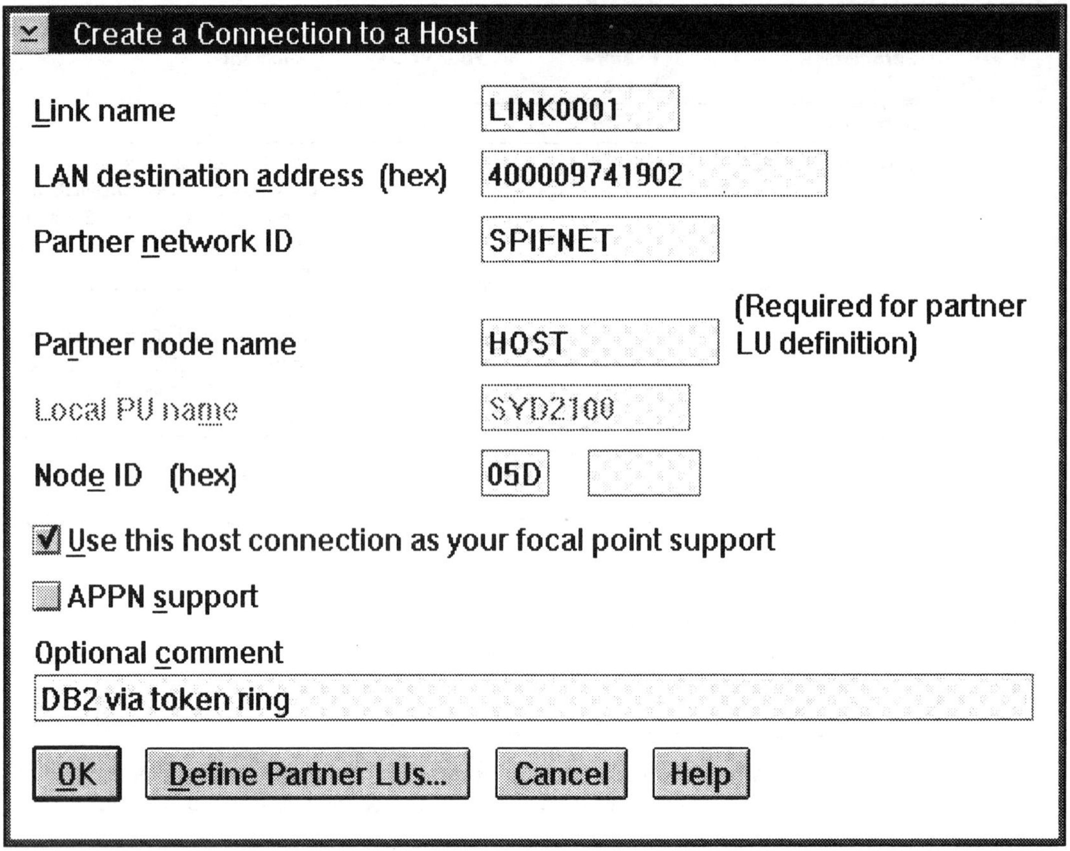

Create a Connection to a Host

Link name	LINK0001
LAN destination address (hex)	400009741902
Partner network ID	SPIFNET
Partner node name	HOST (Required for partner LU definition)
Local PU name	SYD2100
Node ID (hex)	05D

☑ Use this host connection as your focal point support

☐ APPN support

Optional comment

DB2 via token ring

OK	Define Partner LUs...	Cancel	Help

Figure 145. Create a Connection to a Host Window

6. Enter a link name and the LAN destination address.

7. Enter the network ID and node name for the partner node. The **Define Partner LUs...** pushbutton is enabled.

Table 64 gives the sample parameters used for this example and provides a blank column that you can use to fill in the values for your own configuration. You need to coordinate with your host administrator for these values.

Table 64. Parameters for Create a Connection to a Host

Parameter	Example Value	Your Value
Link name	LINK0001	
Partner network ID	SPIFNET	
Partner node name	HOST (see note)	
LAN destination address	400009741902	
Comment	DB2 for MVS/ESA via token ring	

Note: Note for dependent LU: The partner node name must match the VTAM SSCP name.

8. Click on the **Define Partner LUs...** pushbutton. The Create Partner LUs window appears (Figure 146).

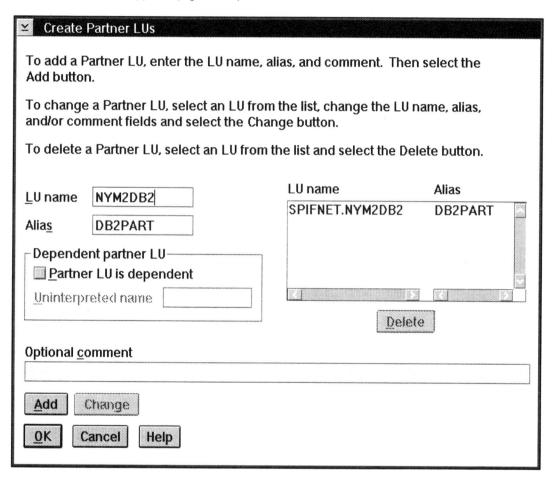

Figure 146. Create Partner LUs Window

9. Enter an LU name and an alias.

Table 65 on page 294 gives the sample parameters used for this example and provides a blank column that you can use to fill in the values for your own configuration. You need to coordinate with your host administrator for the LU name.

Table 65. Parameters for Create a Partner LU

Parameter	Example Value	Your Value
LU name	NYM2DB2	
Alias	DB2PART	

10. Click on the **Add** pushbutton.

11. When the partner LU definition is complete, click on **OK**. The Create a Connection to a Host window reappears.

12. Click on the **Cancel** pushbutton.

13. Click on the **Close** pushbutton from the Connections List.

Specifying the Local LU

At the Communications Manager Profile List Sheet, select **SNA Features**, then click on **Configure....** The SNA Features List window appears.

From this window select **Local LUs** and click on **Create....** The Create a Local LU window appears (Figure 147).

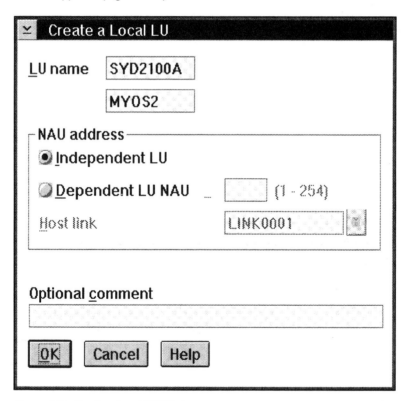

Figure 147. Create a Local LU Window

In this window, specify the local LU name and the local alias and click on **OK**. This returns you to the SNA Features List window.

Note: The LU alias is case sensitive.

Table 65 on page 294 gives the sample parameters used for this example and provides a blank column that you can use to fill in the values for your own configuration. You need to coordinate the LU name and dependent LU NAU with your host administrator.

Table 66. Parameters for Create a Local LU

Parameter	Example Value	Your Value
LU name	SYD2100A	
Alias	MYOS2	
NAU address	Independent LU	—
	Dependent LU NAU (see note)	

Note: Note for dependent LU: The NAU address parameter needs to be specified as Dependent LU NAU. The address you enter must be coordinated with the host administrator.

Specifying the Mode

At the SNA Features List window, select **Modes** and click on **Create....** The Create a Mode Definition window appears (Figure 148).

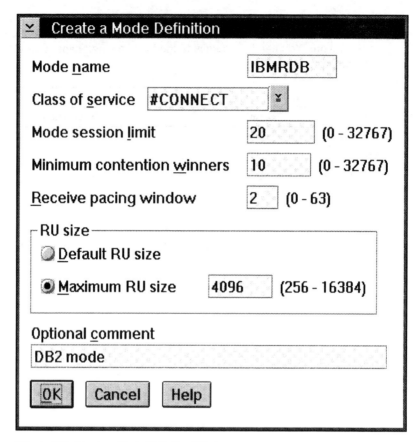

Figure 148. Create a Mode Definition Window

On this window:

1. Specify the **Mode name**.

2. The default values for mode session limit, minimum contention winners, and receive pacing window will work in many cases. However, you should coordinate these with your host administrator. If you are configuring for a dependent LU (see "Specifying the Local LU" on page 294), you should set the mode session limit and minimum contention winners values to 1.

3. Select **Maximum RU size** and specify the value.

Table 67 on page 297 gives the sample parameters used for this example and provides a blank column that you can use to fill in the values for your own configuration. You'll need to coordinate with your host administrator for the mode name, pacing window size, and RU size.

Table 67. Parameters for Create a Mode Definition

Parameter	Example Value	Your Value
Mode name	IBMRDB	
Mode session limit	20	
Minimum contention winners	10	
Receive pacing window	2	
Maximum RU size	4096	
Comment	DB2 mode	

When you are finished, click on **OK**. This returns you to the SNA Features List window.

For dependent LU: The previous example showed an independent LU configuration where parallel session support was assumed. Dependent logical unit configurations only allow single session support.

Completing the Configuration

After you complete the steps in the previous sections, you are ready to verify and save your updated configuration file. To do this:

1. Return to the Communications Manager Configuration Definition window.
2. Select **Verify configuration** from the **Options** action bar.
3. Select **On**.

Resulting Network Definition (.NDF) File

Two examples are given. Figure 149 on page 298 shows the resulting NDF file for an independent logical unit definition. Figure 150 on page 300 shows a dependent logical unit definition.

Independent LU .NDF

```
DEFINE_LOCAL_CP    FQ_CP_NAME(SPIFNET.SYD2100    )
                   DESCRIPTION(Created on 04-01-92 at 10:18a)
                   CP_ALIAS(SYD2100    )
                   NAU_ADDRESS(INDEPENDENT_LU)
                   NODE_TYPE(EN)
                   NODE_ID(X'D2100')
                   HOST_FP_SUPPORT(YES)
                   HOST_FP_LINK_NAME(LINK0001);


DEFINE_LOGICAL_LINK    LINK_NAME(LINK0001)
                       DESCRIPTION(DB2 VIA TOKEN RING)
                       FQ_ADJACENT_CP_NAME(SPIFNET.HOST    )
                       ADJACENT_NODE_TYPE(LEN)
                       DLC_NAME(IBMTRNET)
                       ADAPTER_NUMBER(0)
                       DESTINATION_ADDRESS(X'400009741902')
                       CP_CP_SESSION_SUPPORT(NO)
                       ACTIVATE_AT_STARTUP(YES)
                       LIMITED_RESOURCE(USE_ADAPTER_DEFINITION)
                       LINK_STATION_ROLE(USE_ADAPTER_DEFINITION)
                       SOLICIT_SSCP_SESSION(YES)
                       EFFECTIVE_CAPACITY(USE_ADAPTER_DEFINITION)
                       COST_PER_CONNECT_TIME(USE_ADAPTER_DEFINITION)
                       COST_PER_BYTE(USE_ADAPTER_DEFINITION)
                       SECURITY(USE_ADAPTER_DEFINITION)
                       PROPAGATION_DELAY(USE_ADAPTER_DEFINITION)
                       USER_DEFINED_1(USE_ADAPTER_DEFINITION)
                       USER_DEFINED_2(USE_ADAPTER_DEFINITION)
                       USER_DEFINED_3(USE_ADAPTER_DEFINITION);

DEFINE_LOCAL_LU    LU_NAME(SYD2100A)
                   LU_ALIAS(MYOS2    )
                   NAU_ADDRESS(INDEPENDENT_LU);

DEFINE_PARTNER_LU    FQ_PARTNER_LU_NAME(SPIFNET.NYM2DB2 )
                     PARTNER_LU_ALIAS(DB2PART)
                     PARTNER_LU_UNINTERPRETED_NAME(NYM2DB2 )
                     MAX_MC_LL_SEND_SIZE(32767)
                     CONV_SECURITY_VERIFICATION(NO)
                     PARALLEL_SESSION_SUPPORT(YES);

DEFINE_PARTNER_LU_LOCATION    FQ_PARTNER_LU_NAME(SPIFNET.NYM2DB2 )
                              WILDCARD_ENTRY(NO)
                              FQ_OWNING_CP_NAME(SPIFNET.HOST    )
                              LOCAL_NODE_NN_SERVER(NO);
```

Figure 149 (Part 1 of 2). Network Definition File for Independent LU

```
DEFINE_MODE  MODE_NAME(MODE0001)
             DESCRIPTION(Created on 04-01-92 at 10:18a)
             COS_NAME(#CONNECT)
             DEFAULT_RU_SIZE(NO)
             MAX_RU_SIZE_UPPER_BOUND(1920)
             RECEIVE_PACING_WINDOW(2)
             MAX_NEGOTIABLE_SESSION_LIMIT(32767)
             PLU_MODE_SESSION_LIMIT(253)
             MIN_CONWINNERS_SOURCE(126);


DEFINE_MODE  MODE_NAME(IBMRDB )
             DESCRIPTION(DB2 MODE)
             COS_NAME(#CONNECT)
             DEFAULT_RU_SIZE(NO)
             MAX_RU_SIZE_UPPER_BOUND(4096)
             RECEIVE_PACING_WINDOW(2)
             MAX_NEGOTIABLE_SESSION_LIMIT(32767)
             PLU_MODE_SESSION_LIMIT(20)
             MIN_CONWINNERS_SOURCE(10);

DEFINE_DEFAULTS  IMPLICIT_INBOUND_PLU_SUPPORT(YES)
             DESCRIPTION(Created on 04-01-92 at 10:18a)
             DEFAULT_MODE_NAME(MODE0001)
             MAX_MC_LL_SEND_SIZE(32767)
             DIRECTORY_FOR_INBOUND_ATTACHES(*)
             DEFAULT_TP_OPERATION(NONQUEUED_AM_STARTED)
             DEFAULT_TP_PROGRAM_TYPE(BACKGROUND)
             DEFAULT_TP_CONV_SECURITY_RQD(NO)
             MAX_HELD_ALERTS(10);

DEFINE_TP    SNA_SERVICE_TP_NAME(X'07',6DB)
             DESCRIPTION(Created on 04-01-92 at 10:18a)
             FILESPEC(C:\SQLLIB\SQLCIAA.EXE)
             CONVERSATION_TYPE(BASIC)
             CONV_SECURITY_RQD(YES)
             SYNC_LEVEL(NONE)
             TP_OPERATION(NONQUEUED_AM_STARTED)
             PROGRAM_TYPE(BACKGROUND)
             RECEIVE_ALLOCATE_TIMEOUT(INFINITE);

DEFINE_TP    SNA_SERVICE_TP_NAME(X'07',6SN)
             DESCRIPTION(Created on 04-01-92 at 10:18a)
             FILESPEC(C:\SQLLIB\SQLCNSM.EXE)
             CONVERSATION_TYPE(BASIC)
             CONV_SECURITY_RQD(YES)
             SYNC_LEVEL(NONE)
             TP_OPERATION(NONQUEUED_AM_STARTED)
             PROGRAM_TYPE(BACKGROUND)
             RECEIVE_ALLOCATE_TIMEOUT(INFINITE);

START_ATTACH_MANAGER;
```

Figure 149 (Part 2 of 2). Network Definition File for Independent LU

Dependent LU .NDF

```
DEFINE_LOCAL_CP   FQ_CP_NAME(SPIFNET.SYD2100   )
                  DESCRIPTION(Created on 04-01-92 at 10:18a)
                  CP_ALIAS(SYD2100   )
                  NAU_ADDRESS(INDEPENDENT_LU)
                  NODE_TYPE(EN)
                  NODE_ID(X'D2100')
                  HOST_FP_SUPPORT(YES)
                  HOST_FP_LINK_NAME(LINK0001);

DEFINE_LOGICAL_LINK   LINK_NAME(LINK0001)
                      DESCRIPTION(DB2 VIA TOKEN RING)
                      FQ_ADJACENT_CP_NAME(SPIFNET.HOST   )
                      ADJACENT_NODE_TYPE(LEN)
                      DLC_NAME(IBMTRNET)
                      ADAPTER_NUMBER(0)
                      DESTINATION_ADDRESS(X'400009741902')
                      CP_CP_SESSION_SUPPORT(NO)
                      ACTIVATE_AT_STARTUP(YES)
                      LIMITED_RESOURCE(USE_ADAPTER_DEFINITION)
                      LINK_STATION_ROLE(USE_ADAPTER_DEFINITION)
                      SOLICIT_SSCP_SESSION(YES)
                      EFFECTIVE_CAPACITY(USE_ADAPTER_DEFINITION)
                      COST_PER_CONNECT_TIME(USE_ADAPTER_DEFINITION)
                      COST_PER_BYTE(USE_ADAPTER_DEFINITION)
                      SECURITY(USE_ADAPTER_DEFINITION)
                      PROPAGATION_DELAY(USE_ADAPTER_DEFINITION)
                      USER_DEFINED_1(USE_ADAPTER_DEFINITION)
                      USER_DEFINED_2(USE_ADAPTER_DEFINITION)
                      USER_DEFINED_3(USE_ADAPTER_DEFINITION);

DEFINE_LOCAL_LU   LU_NAME(SYD2100A)
                  LU_ALIAS(MYOS2   )
                  NAU_ADDRESS(01);

DEFINE_PARTNER_LU   FQ_PARTNER_LU_NAME(SPIFNET.NYM2DB2  )
                    PARTNER_LU_ALIAS(DB2PART)
                    PARTNER_LU_UNINTERPRETED_NAME(NYM2DB2 )
                    MAX_MC_LL_SEND_SIZE(32767)
                    CONV_SECURITY_VERIFICATION(NO)
                    PARALLEL_SESSION_SUPPORT(NO);  <<--Changed for dependent LU

DEFINE_PARTNER_LU_LOCATION   FQ_PARTNER_LU_NAME(SPIFNET.NYM2DB2  )
                             WILDCARD_ENTRY(NO)
                             FQ_OWNING_CP_NAME(SPIFNET.HOST      )
                             LOCAL_NODE_NN_SERVER(NO);
```

Figure 150 (Part 1 of 2). Network Definition File for Dependent LU

```
DEFINE_MODE    MODE_NAME(MODE0001)
               DESCRIPTION(Created on 04-01-92 at 10:18a)
               COS_NAME(#CONNECT)
               DEFAULT_RU_SIZE(NO)
               MAX_RU_SIZE_UPPER_BOUND(1920)
               RECEIVE_PACING_WINDOW(2)
               MAX_NEGOTIABLE_SESSION_LIMIT(32767)
               PLU_MODE_SESSION_LIMIT(253)
               MIN_CONWINNERS_SOURCE(126);

DEFINE_MODE    MODE_NAME(IBMRDB )
               DESCRIPTION(DB2 MODE)
               COS_NAME(#CONNECT)
               DEFAULT_RU_SIZE(NO)
               MAX_RU_SIZE_UPPER_BOUND(4096)
               RECEIVE_PACING_WINDOW(2)
               MAX_NEGOTIABLE_SESSION_LIMIT(32767)
               PLU_MODE_SESSION_LIMIT(1)
               MIN_CONWINNERS_SOURCE(1);

DEFINE_DEFAULTS  IMPLICIT_INBOUND_PLU_SUPPORT(YES)
               DESCRIPTION(Created on 04-01-92 at 10:18a)
               DEFAULT_MODE_NAME(MODE0001)
               MAX_MC_LL_SEND_SIZE(32767)
               DIRECTORY_FOR_INBOUND_ATTACHES(*)
               DEFAULT_TP_OPERATION(NONQUEUED_AM_STARTED)
               DEFAULT_TP_PROGRAM_TYPE(BACKGROUND)
               DEFAULT_TP_CONV_SECURITY_RQD(NO)
               MAX_HELD_ALERTS(10);

DEFINE_TP      SNA_SERVICE_TP_NAME(X'07',6DB)
               DESCRIPTION(Created on 04-01-92 at 10:18a)
               FILESPEC(C:\SQLLIB\SQLCIAA.EXE)
               CONVERSATION_TYPE(BASIC)
               CONV_SECURITY_RQD(YES)
               SYNC_LEVEL(NONE)
               TP_OPERATION(NONQUEUED_AM_STARTED)
               PROGRAM_TYPE(BACKGROUND)
               RECEIVE_ALLOCATE_TIMEOUT(INFINITE);

DEFINE_TP      SNA_SERVICE_TP_NAME(X'07',6SN)
               DESCRIPTION(Created on 04-01-92 at 10:18a)
               FILESPEC(C:\SQLLIB\SQLCNSM.EXE)
               CONVERSATION_TYPE(BASIC)
               CONV_SECURITY_RQD(YES)
               SYNC_LEVEL(NONE)
               TP_OPERATION(NONQUEUED_AM_STARTED)
               PROGRAM_TYPE(BACKGROUND)
               RECEIVE_ALLOCATE_TIMEOUT(INFINITE);

START_ATTACH_MANAGER;
```

Figure 150 (Part 2 of 2). Network Definition File for Dependent LU

Cataloging DB2 for OS/2 Directory Entries

You should now go to "Cataloging DB2 for OS/2 Directory Entries" on page 222 for
DB2 for MVS/ESA or to "Cataloging DB2 for OS/2 Directory Entries" on page 246 for
DB2 for VM and VSE to catalog the database, the workstation (node), and the DCS
database. When you complete that section, return here.

Configuring the Host

Figure 151 shows the VTAM definitions necessary to configure the host.

```
LOC300   VBUILD TYPE=LOCAL
*
C0776    PU     CUADDR=300,
                DISCNT=NO,
                ISTATUS=INACTIVE,
                LOGTAB=INTAB,
                MAXBFRU=12,
                MODETAB=MODETAB,
                PACING=0,
                PUTYPE=2,
                SECNET=NO,
                SSCPFM=USSSCS,
                USSTAB=USSTAB,
                XID=YES,
                SYNLU=YES,
                VPACING=2
*
V0776000 LU     LOCADDR=000,DLOGMOD=IBMRDB,USSTAB=ISTINCDT
V9974001 LU     LOCADDR=000,DLOGMOD=IBMRDB,USSTAB=ISTINCDT
DBC0776  LU     LOCADDR=131,DLOGMOD=E3278M2
*
C9974    PU     CUADDR=31B,
                DISCNT=NO,
                ISTATUS=INACTIVE,
                LOGTAB=INTAB,
                MAXBFRU=02,
                MODETAB=MODETAB,
                PACING=0,
                SECNET=NO,
                SSCPFM=FSS,
                USSTAB=USSTAB,
                VPACING=2
*
V9974002 LU     LOCADDR=000,DLOGMOD=IBMRDB,USSTAB=ISTINCDT
V9974004 LU     LOCADDR=004,DLOGMOD=PCMOD2
```

Figure 151. VTAM Definitions for Configuring the Host

The IOBUF size must be an even number.

Table 68 gives the important 3174 configuration questions and the answers needed for this scenario.

Table 68. 3174 configuration values

Question #	Value
215	C0776 (PU ID)
242	1 (PU 2.1)
501	SPIFNET (must be network ID)
510	1 (APPN)
511	CP0776 (CP name)
512	VNET0776
610	1 (can have up to 225 sessions)
611	1
612	1 (wildcard routing)
	CP9974 (network resource name)
	2 (end node)
	1 (token ring)
	40002077631B (workstation address)
	04 (SAP)

Ensure that the CCSID is appropriately assigned.

Chapter 19. Configuring DDCS for OS/2

This chapter describes how you configure the DDCS workstation and the DRDA servers. How you configure each remote client is described in the *DB2 Client Application Enabler User* book for the appropriate platform.

This chapter makes the following assumptions:

- Your network is relatively straightforward.

- None of the DRDA servers are OS/2 or UNIX-based DB2 databases. (to connect to an OS/2 or UNIX-based DB2 database we recommend that you use the Client Application Enablers provided with DB2 and not use DDCS for OS/2.)

- For MVS, VSE, or VM, you have access to a VTAM administrator and a database administrator. For OS/400, you have access to an AS/400 administrator.

- Communications Manager is already installed on the system where DDCS is installed.

- A Token Ring is being used as the communications medium.

Configuring Your DRDA Servers

Before you can use DDCS, you must configure both the DRDA servers and the DDCS system. If you decide to configure the DDCS system before you configure the servers, you must at least get information about how the servers *will be* configured before you configure the DDCS system.

The following worksheets are used for configuring DRDA servers:

- "MVS, VSE, and VM Server Worksheet" on page 324
- "OS/400 Server Worksheet" on page 326.

For each server that you are connecting to, fill in one copy of the appropriate server worksheet. Each worksheet contains instructions for how to use it.

For an MVS, VSE, or VM connection, you should find the local node name of your machine. You can find this by going to the Local Node Characteristics panel.

Figure 152 on page 305 illustrates the correspondence between information specified on the DRDA server system, information specified in the DDCS configuration files, and information specified in the DDCS directories. The instructions in this book and the *DDCS User's Guide* show you how to update these files.

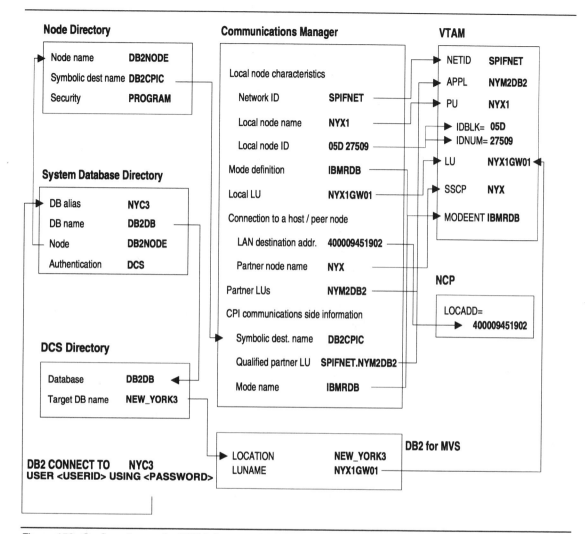

Figure 152. Configuration on the DRDA Server and DDCS Workstation

Planning to Configure Your DDCS System

Fill in a copy of the "OS/2 Configuration Worksheet" on page 327.

For an MVS, VSE, or VM connection, do the following:

1. For Network ID, copy the NETID (item 1) from the server worksheet.
2. For Local node name, copy the PU (item 7) from the server worksheet.
3. For Local node ID, copy the IDBLK and IDNUM (item 8) from the server worksheet.
4. For Mode name, copy the MODEENT (item 3) from the server worksheet.
5. For Local LU name, copy the LU (item 6) from the server worksheet.

6. For Local LU alias, choose an alias. This can be the same as the LU name or different.

For an OS/400 connection, do the following:

1. For Network ID, copy the local network ID (item 1) from the server worksheet.
2. For Mode name, copy the mode name (item 3) from the server worksheet.
3. Leave the other items blank for now.

Planning for Each Server Connection

For each server that you are connecting to, fill in a copy of the "OS/2 Connection to Server Worksheet" on page 328 as follows,

- For Link name, choose a value.

- For LAN destination address, copy item 2 (controller address or local adapter address) from the server worksheet.

- For Symbolic destination name, choose a value.

- For Partner CP name, copy item 4 from the server worksheet. For MVS, VSE, or VM it is an SSCP value; for OS/400 it is a local control point name.

- For Partner LU name for MVS, VSE, or VM, copy item 5 (APPL) from the server worksheet. For OS/400, copy the Partner CP name that you just wrote on this worksheet.

- For Remote transaction program, copy the value from the server worksheet. The default is X'07'6DB for MVS and OS/400 and the RDB_NAME for VSE and VM.

- For Target database name, copy the last item from the server worksheet. This is a LOCATION value (MVS), RDB_NAME (VSE or VM), or relational database name (OS/400).

Planning for Remote Client Support

If you will connect remote clients to the DDCS workstation, fill in a copy of the "OS/2 Configuration for Remote Clients Worksheet" on page 329 as follows,

- For Communication protocols, specify which communication protocols you will use for remote clients. DDCS supports APPC, TCP/IP, IPX/SPX, and NetBIOS. You can specify any combination of these values, separated by commas.

- If you will use APPC, do the following:
  - Choose a TP name.
  - Specify whether you will support connections from DB2 Client Application Enabler Version 1 clients (yes or no).
  - Specify whether you will support connections from DB2 for OS/2 Version 1 clients (yes or no).

- If you will use TCP/IP, do the following:
  - Choose a service name for the connection port.·
  - Choose a service name for the interrupt port.

- Specify which port will be the connection port. The interrupt port must be the next port. For example, if the connection port is 3700, the interrupt port must be 3701.

- If you will use IPX/SPX, do the following:

  - Specify the name of the NetWare file server.
  - Specify a unique object name for the DDCS workstation.
  - Specify a socket for this instance of DDCS. Values from 879E to 87A2 are reserved for DB2 products, including DDCS. The default is 879E.

- For NetBIOS, specify a unique NNAME for the DDCS workstation.

Configuring Your DDCS System

Before using this section, be sure that you have completed the "OS/2 Configuration Worksheet" on page 327.

Note: The boxed numerics correspond with the items located on your worksheet; for example, the symbol **24** would be used to represent the IPX Socket Number. The ***** symbol is used to denote entries that need to be changed but do no have a representation on the worksheet.

Note: The following steps are detailed for those currently using Communications Manager Version 1.1.

Configure your DDCS system as follows:

1. Double-click on the Communications Manager setup icon.

2. Go to the Communications Manager Profile List panel as follows:

   a. Press the Setup pushbutton.
   b. On the Open Configuration panel, specify a configuration name. If you already have a configuration file, you can use the existing name.
   c. On the Communications Manager Configuration Definition panel, press the Configure pushbutton.

   The next several steps begin from the Communications Manager Profile List panel.

3. Update the local node characteristics as follows:

   a. On the Communications Manager Profile List panel, select SNA local node characteristics and press the Configure pushbutton.
   b. For Network ID, type the value that you wrote in item **1** of the worksheet.
   c. The local node name was probably set when Communications Manager was installed. For MVS, VSE, and VM, check that this value matches item **2** on the worksheet. For OS/400, write the local node name in the worksheet now; if no name exists, talk to your LAN administrator.
   d. For Local node ID (hex), type the value that you wrote in item **3** of the worksheet. For OS/400, you can leave the second part of the node ID blank or specify 00000; the first 3 characters are automatically filled in.

   For example, the panel could look like this:

```
┌─────────────────────────────────────────────────────────────┐
│  ╲╱  │  Local  Node  Characteristics                          │
│ ─────┘                                                        │
│                                                               │
│  Network ID                              ┌──────────┐         │
│                                          │ SPIFNET  │         │
│                                          └──────────┘         │
│  Local node name                         ┌──────────┐         │
│                                          │ NYX1     │         │
│                                          └──────────┘         │
│  ┌─Node type──────────────────────────────────────────────┐  │
│  │  ○  End  node  to  network  node  server                │  │
│  │  ◉  End  node  -  no  network  node  server             │  │
│  │  ○  Network  node                                       │  │
│  └─────────────────────────────────────────────────────────┘ │
│                                                               │
│  Your  network  node  server  address  (hex) ┌───────────┐   │
│                                               └───────────┘   │
│  Local  node  ID  (hex)    ┌──────┐  ┌──────────┐            │
│                            │ 05D  │  │ 27509    │            │
│                            └──────┘  └──────────┘            │
│  ┌────┐ ┌──────────┐ ┌──────────────┐ ┌─────────┐ ┌──────┐  │
│  │ OK │ │ Options..│ │ NetWare(R)...│ │ Cancel  │ │ Help │  │
│  └────┘ └──────────┘ └──────────────┘ └─────────┘ └──────┘  │
└─────────────────────────────────────────────────────────────┘
```

    e. Press the `Options` pushbutton and check that the `Activate Attach Manager at Startup` check box is selected.

4. Check the LAN DLC Profile as follows:

    a. On the Communications Manager Profile List panel, select DLC - Token ring or other LAN types and press the `Configure` pushbutton.

    b. If you have not already defined an adapter, you must define at least one now. For Comminications and System Management (C&SM) LAN ID, type the value that you wrote in item **1** of the worksheet.

    For example, the panel could look like this:

```
┌─────────────────────────────────────────────────────────────────┐
│  ╲╱  │ Token  Ring  or  Other  LAN  Types  DLC  Adapter  Parameters │
├─────────────────────────────────────────────────────────────────┤
│                                                                   │
│  Adapter  [0 ▼]          ┌─Window count────────────────────────┐ │
│     ☐ Free unused links  │  Send window count      [4] (1 - 8)  │ │
│     ☐ Send alert for     │  Receive window count   [4] (1 - 8)  │ │
│       beaconing          └──────────────────────────────────────┘ │
│  Maximum link stations          [4    ] (1 - 255)                 │
│                                                                   │
│  Maximum activation attempts    [0    ] (0 - 99)                  │
│                                                                   │
│  Maximum I-field size           [1929 ] (265 - 16393)             │
│                                                                   │
│  Percent of incoming calls (%)  [0    ] (0 - 100)                 │
│                                                                   │
│  Link establishment                                               │
│     retransmission count        [8    ] (1 - 127)                 │
│                                                                   │
│  Retranmission threshold        [8    ] (1 - 127)                 │
│                                                                   │
│  Loacl sap (hex)                [04   ] (04 - 9C)                 │
│                                                                   │
│  C&SM LAN ID                    [SPIFNET  ]                       │
│                                                                   │
│  Connection network                                              │
│     name (optional)             [         ]•[         ]          │
│                                                                   │
│  [OK]   [Delete]   [Cancel]    [Help]                            │
│                                                                   │
└─────────────────────────────────────────────────────────────────┘
```

5. Create a Mode Profile as follows:

   a. On the Communications Manager Profile List panel, select SNA features and press the Configure pushbutton.

   b. Select Modes and press Create.

   c. Define your mode profile. For mode name, use the value that you wrote in item **4** of the worksheet. On the other lines, specify values that match the mode profile defined on your DRDA server systems. If you are using the mode IBMRDB, specify the following values:

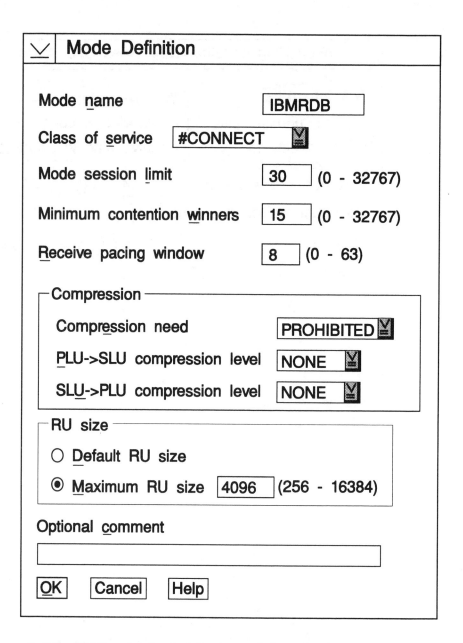

Mode Definition

Mode name   `IBMRDB`

Class of service   `#CONNECT` ▼

Mode session limit   `30`   (0 - 32767)

Minimum contention winners   `15`   (0 - 32767)

Receive pacing window   `8`   (0 - 63)

┌─ Compression ─────────────────────┐

Compression need   `PROHIBITED` ▼

PLU->SLU compression level   `NONE` ▼

SLU->PLU compression level   `NONE` ▼

└──────────────────────────────────┘

┌─ RU size ─────────────────────────┐

○ Default RU size

◉ Maximum RU size   `4096`   (256 - 16384)

└──────────────────────────────────┘

Optional comment

`[                                    ]`

`OK` `Cancel` `Help`

6. If the DDCS workstation is defined as an independent LU, update the Local LU Profile as follows (in most cases, a VTAM administrator on MVS, VSE, or VM would define an independent LU for DDCS; for OS/400, the control point would normally be used instead of an independent LU).

    a. On the Communications Manager Profile List panel, select SNA features and press the `Configure` pushbutton.

    b. Select Local LUs and press `Create`.

c. For LU name, type the value that you wrote in item **5** of the worksheet. For alias, type the value that you wrote in item **6** of the worksheet. For NAU address, select Independent LU.

For example, the panel could look like this:

```
┌──────────────────────────────────────────────────────────────┐
│  ∨ │  Local LU                                                 │
├──────────────────────────────────────────────────────────────┤
│                                                                │
│   LU name        ┌─────────────┐                               │
│                  │ NYX1GW01    │                               │
│                  └─────────────┘                               │
│   Alias          ┌─────────────┐                               │
│                  │ NYX1GW01    │                               │
│                  └─────────────┘                               │
│    ┌─ NAU address ───────────────────────────────────────┐    │
│    │                                                      │    │
│    │   ◉  Independent LU                                  │    │
│    │                                 ┌─────────┐          │    │
│    │   ○  Dependent LU NAU           │         │ (1 - 254)│    │
│    │                                 └─────────┘          │    │
│    │      Host link            ┌────────────┐ ┌──┐        │    │
│    │                           │ HOST0001   │ │▓ │        │    │
│    │                           └────────────┘ └──┘        │    │
│    └──────────────────────────────────────────────────────┘   │
│                                                                │
│   Optional comment                                             │
│   ┌──────────────────────────────────────────────────────┐    │
│   │                                                      │    │
│   └──────────────────────────────────────────────────────┘    │
│   ┌────┐   ┌────────┐   ┌──────┐                               │
│   │ OK │   │ Cancel │   │ Help │                               │
│   └────┘   └────────┘   └──────┘                               │
└──────────────────────────────────────────────────────────────┘
```

Note: In order to use this local LU when the DDCS workstation starts the APPC connection, you can do one of the following:

- Set the OS/2 environment variable APPCLLU to the local LU alias before the APPC connection is started. For example:

  ```
  SET APPCLLU=NYX1GW01
  ```

  When the APPC connection is started, the specified local LU will be used.

- If you are using CM for OS/2 V1.11, when you add the Local LU Profile, check off the box that says "Use this local LU as your default local LU alias". By default, all APPC connections that are started from this DDCS workstation will use this local LU.

- Add an entry to the Communications Manager configuration file (.NDF) directly, to specify the default local LU alias. An entry for DEFAULT_LOCAL_LU_ALIAS is added to the DEFINE_DEFAULTS section of the configuration file (.NDF). For example:

```
DEFINE_DEFAULTS  DEFAULT_LOCAL_LU_ALIAS(NYX1GW01)
```

By default, all APPC connections that are started from this DDCS workstation will use this local LU.

Configuring Each Server Connection

Before using this section, be sure that you have completed the "OS/2 Connection to Server Worksheet" on page 328.

Configure a DRDA server connection as follows:

1. Update the connections as follows:

   a. On the Communications Manager Profile List panel, select SNA connections and press the Configure pushbutton.
   b. On the panel that appears, select either To peer node (normally used for OS/400 connections) or To host (normally used for MVS, VSE, and VM connections) and press Create.

   The Adapter list panel appears:

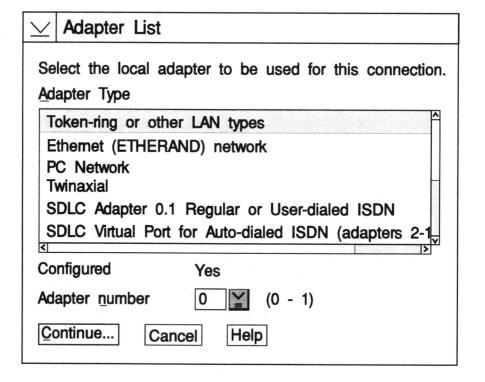

    c. Select adapter type Token ring, or other LAN types, and the adapter number that you specified in the DLC profile. Press the Continue pushbutton.

    d. The Connection to a Peer Node panel or the Connection to Host panel appears.

Change the link name to the value that you wrote in item **7** of the worksheet.

On the Connection to Host panel, change the local PU name to the value that you wrote in item **2** of the worksheet and change the node ID to the value that you wrote in item **3** of the worksheet.

Change the LAN destination address to the value that you wrote in item **8** of the worksheet.

Change the Partner network ID to the value that you wrote in item **1** of the worksheet.

Change the Partner node name to the value that you wrote in item **10** of the worksheet.

For example, the Connection to a Peer Node panel could look like this:

∨ | **Connection to a Peer Node**

Link name   [LINKHOST]   ☐ Activate at startup

LAN destination address (hex)   Address format   Remote SAP (hex)

[400009451902]   [Token Ring ⌄] [04]

Adjacent node ID (hex)   [   ]

Partner network ID   [SPIFNET]

                        (Required for partner

Partner node name   [SYD2101A] LU definition)

Optional comment

[   ]

[OK]   [Define Partner LUs...]   [Cancel]   [Help]

The Connection to Host panel could look like this:

```
┌─────────────────────────────────────────────────────────────────────┐
│ ┌───┐                                                                 │
│ │ ∨ │   Connection to a Host                                          │
│ └───┘                                                                 │
│                                                                       │
│   Link name        ┌──────────────┐      ☐  Activate at startup       │
│                    │ LINKHOST     │                                   │
│   Local PU name    ┌──────────────┐      ☐  APPN support              │
│                    │ NYX1         │                                   │
│   Node ID          ┌─────┐ ┌──────────┐                               │
│                    │ 05D │ │ 27509    │                               │
│                    └─────┘ └──────────┘                               │
│                                                                       │
│   LAN destination address  (hex)   Address format   Remote SAP (hex)  │
│   ┌──────────────────────┐         ┌─────────────┐  ┌──────┐          │
│   │ 400009451902         │         │ Token Ring ∨│  │ 04   │          │
│   └──────────────────────┘         └─────────────┘  └──────┘          │
│   Adjacent node ID (hex)           ┌─────────────┐                    │
│                                    │             │                    │
│                                    └─────────────┘                    │
│   Partner network ID               ┌─────────────┐                    │
│                                    │ SPIFNET     │                    │
│                                    └─────────────┘                    │
│                                                     (Required for     │
│   Partner node name       ┌─────────────┐          partner            │
│                           │ NYX         │          LU definition)     │
│                           └─────────────┘                             │
│   ☐ Use this host connection as your focal point support              │
│                                                                       │
│   Optional comment                                                    │
│   ┌─────────────────────────────────────────────────────────────┐    │
│   │                                                             │    │
│   └─────────────────────────────────────────────────────────────┘    │
│                                                                       │
│   ┌────────┐ ┌────────────────────┐ ┌──────────┐ ┌────────┐          │
│   │ OK     │ │ Define Partner LUs..│ │ Cancel   │ │ Help   │          │
│   └────────┘ └────────────────────┘ └──────────┘ └────────┘          │
└─────────────────────────────────────────────────────────────────────┘
```

e. Press the Define Partner LUs pushbutton.

f. The Partner LUs panel appears.

   For network ID, type the value that you wrote in item **1** of the worksheet.

   For LU name and alias, type the value that you wrote in item **11** of the worksheet.

   For example, the panel could look like this:

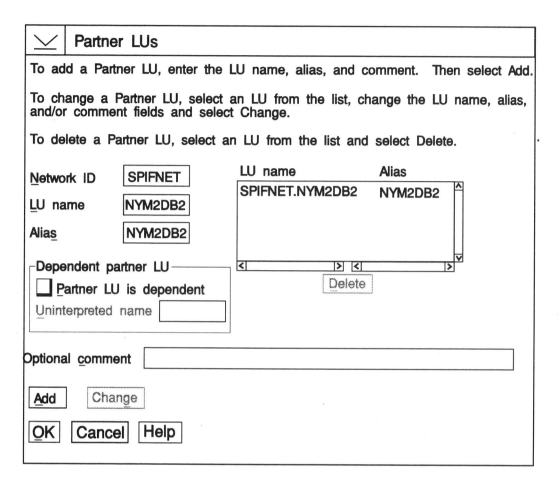

Partner LUs

To add a Partner LU, enter the LU name, alias, and comment. Then select Add.

To change a Partner LU, select an LU from the list, change the LU name, alias, and/or comment fields and select Change.

To delete a Partner LU, select an LU from the list and select Delete.

Network ID   SPIFNET

LU name   NYM2DB2

Alias   NYM2DB2

LU name   Alias
SPIFNET.NYM2DB2   NYM2DB2

Dependent partner LU
☐ Partner LU is dependent
Uninterpreted name [   ]

Delete

Optional comment [   ]

Add   Change

OK   Cancel   Help

    g. Press the Add pushbutton.

2. Update the CPI side information as follows:

    a. On the Communications Manager Profile List panel, select SNA features and press the Configure pushbutton.

    b. Select CPI Communication side information and press the Create pushbutton.

    c. The CPI Communications Side Information panel appears.

       For the symbolic destination name, type the value that you wrote in item **9** of the worksheet.

       Select Fully qualified name, and type the value that you wrote in item **1** of the worksheet followed by the value that you wrote in item **11** of the worksheet.

       In the Partner TP box, specify the remote transaction program name (item **12** of the worksheet). You must specify a value here (in Communications Manager there is no default value). On the DRDA server, the default for MVS or OS/400 is X'07'6DB; the default for VSE or VM is the database name (item **13** in the worksheet). Type the value that you will use in the TP name field. If the value contains hexadecimal data (such as X'07'6DB), also select the Service TP check box.

Select None as the security type (this does not mean that you will have no security, you will specify the security type later, in the node directory).

Note: If you wish to use the APPC security type SAME, the userid to be used for the connection *must* be defined to UPM on the DDCS workstation. For example, if you have a DDCS for OS/2 multi-user gateway, and you wish to use APPC security=SAME at the gateway, all userids that you use must be defined to UPM at the gateway.

For the mode name, select the value that you wrote in item **4** of the worksheet.

For example, the panel could look like this:

```
┌──┬──────────────────────────────────────────────────────────┐
│ ∨│  CPI Communications Side Information                       │
├──┴──────────────────────────────────────────────────────────┤
│                                                              │
│  Symbolic destination name       ┌────────────────┐         │
│                                   │ DB2CPIC        │         │
│                                   └────────────────┘         │
│  ┌Partner LU──────────────────────────────────────────────┐ │
│  │                                 ┌───────────┐ ┌────────┐ │ │
│  │ ⦿ Fully qualified name          │ SPIFNET   │·│NYM2DB2 │ │ │
│  │                                 └───────────┘ └────────┘ │ │
│  │ ○ Alias                         ┌───────────┐┌┐         │ │
│  │                                 └───────────┘└┘         │ │
│  └────────────────────────────────────────────────────────┘ │
│  ┌Partner TP──────────────────────────────────────────────┐ │
│  │ ☑ Service TP                                            │ │
│  │                     ┌──────────────────────────┐       │ │
│  │    TP name          │ X'07'6DB                 │       │ │
│  │                     └──────────────────────────┘       │ │
│  └────────────────────────────────────────────────────────┘ │
│  ┌Security type───────────────────┐   Mode name            │
│  │ ○Same ⦿None ○Program           │   ┌───────────┐┌─┐     │
│  └────────────────────────────────┘   │ IBMRDB    ││∨│     │
│  Optional comment                      └───────────┘└─┘     │
│  ┌────────────────────────────────────────────────────────┐ │
│  │                                                        │ │
│  └────────────────────────────────────────────────────────┘ │
│                                                              │
│  ┌─────────┐  ┌────────┐ ┌──────┐                           │
│  │  OK     │  │ Cancel │ │ Help │                           │
│  └─────────┘  └────────┘ └──────┘                           │
└──────────────────────────────────────────────────────────────┘
```

Configuring DDCS for Remote Clients

Before using this section, be sure that you have completed the "OS/2 Configuration for Remote Clients Worksheet" on page 329.

Note: With this version of DDCS the TP is operator pre-loaded and NOT Attach Manager started. As a result, an OS/2 TP executable file is not required. The previous TP executables - sqlciaa.exe (for database connections), and sqlcnsm.exe (for interrupts), are no longer required and are not provided. If you have existing Transaction Program Definitions for the service transaction programs X'07'6DB and X'07'6SN, please ensure that the operation type in the transaction program definition is changed to queued, operator pre-loaded. Also, since the TP is operator pre-loaded, the OS/2 program path and file name field is not used; however, you must still enter something when you configure the TP since the field is a mandatory input field.

Configure your DDCS workstation for remote clients as follows:

1. If you will use APPC for connections from remote clients, do the following:

   a. On the Communications Manager Profile List panel, select SNA features and press the Configure pushbutton.
   b. Select Transaction program definitions and press the Create pushbutton.
   c. Add the following definition using the value that you wrote in item **15** of the worksheet for TP name.

      This profile will be used for both database connections and interrupts from Version 2 clients, and also for database connections from DB2 Client Application Enabler Version 1 clients.

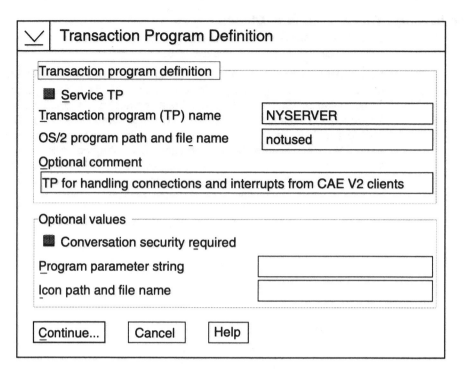

Transaction Program Definition

Transaction program definition

■ Service TP

Transaction program (TP) name   `NYSERVER`

OS/2 program path and file name   `notused`

Optional comment

`TP for handling connections and interrupts from CAE V2 clients`

Optional values

■ Conversation security required

Program parameter string

Icon path and file name

[Continue...]   [Cancel]   [Help]

---

   d. Press the `Continue` pushbutton.

   e. The additional TP parameters panel appears. Specify the following
      parameters:

Additional TP Parameters

Presentation type

  O Presentation Manager

  O VIO-windowable

  O Full screen

  ◉ Background

Operation type

  O Queued, Attach Manager started

  O Queued, operator started

  ◉ Queued, operator preloaded

  O Non-queued, Attach Manager started

[OK]   [Cancel]   [Help]

---

   f. If you will support connections from DB2 Client Application Enabler Version 1
      clients (item **16** on the worksheet), add the following profile. This profile will
      be used for database interrupts from DB2 Client Application Enabler Version 1

clients. You must use the TP name shown in the profile. You must also
specify the additional parameters shown previously.

```
┌─────────────────────────────────────────────────────────────────┐
│ ┌──┐                                                              │
│ │\/│  Transaction Program Definition                             │
│ └──┘                                                              │
│ ┌───────────────────────────────────────────────────────────┐   │
│ │ Transaction program definition                             │   │
│ │ □ Service TP                                               │   │
│ │ Transaction program (TP) name        ┌───────────────────┐ │   │
│ │                                      │ DB2INTERRUPT      │ │   │
│ │                                      └───────────────────┘ │   │
│ │ OS/2 program path and file name      ┌───────────────────┐ │   │
│ │                                      │ notused           │ │   │
│ │                                      └───────────────────┘ │   │
│ │ Optional comment                                           │   │
│ │ ┌─────────────────────────────────────────────────────┐   │   │
│ │ │ TP for handling interrupts from CAE V1 clients      │   │   │
│ │ └─────────────────────────────────────────────────────┘   │   │
│ └───────────────────────────────────────────────────────────┘   │
│ ┌───────────────────────────────────────────────────────────┐   │
│ │ Optional values                                            │   │
│ │ □ Conversation security required                           │   │
│ │ Program parameter string             ┌───────────────────┐ │   │
│ │                                      │                   │ │   │
│ │                                      └───────────────────┘ │   │
│ │ Icon path and file name              ┌───────────────────┐ │   │
│ │                                      │                   │ │   │
│ │                                      └───────────────────┘ │   │
│ └───────────────────────────────────────────────────────────┘   │
│ ┌───────────┐    ┌──────────┐    ┌──────────┐                    │
│ │ Continue..│    │  Cancel  │    │  Help    │                    │
│ └───────────┘    └──────────┘    └──────────┘                    │
└─────────────────────────────────────────────────────────────────┘
```

g. If you will support connections from DB2 for OS/2 Version 1 clients (item **17**
on the worksheet), add the following two profiles.

This profile will be used for database connections from DB2 for OS/2 Version
1 clients. You must use the TP name shown in the profile. You must also
specify the additional parameters shown previously.

Transaction Program Definition

┌─ Transaction program definition ─────────────────────────────────
│ ☑ Service TP
│ Transaction program (TP) name   `X'07'6DB`
│ OS/2 program path and file name   `notused`
│ Optional comment
│ `TP for handling connections from DB2/2 V1 clients`
└──

┌─ Optional values ──
│ ☐ Conversation security required
│ Program parameter string   [   ]
│ Icon path and file name   [   ]
└──

[Continue...]   [Cancel]   [Help]

This profile will be used for database interrupts from DB2 for OS/2 Version 1 clients. You must also specify the additional parameters shown previously.

```
┌─────────────────────────────────────────────────────────────────┐
│ ┌───┐                                                             │
│ │ ∨ │  Transaction  Program  Definition                          │
│ └───┘                                                             │
│ ┌─Transaction program definition──────────────────────────────┐  │
│ │                                                              │  │
│ │  ☑ Service TP                                                │  │
│ │  Transaction  program  (TP)  name    ┌──────────────────┐   │  │
│ │                                       │ X'07'6SN         │   │  │
│ │                                       └──────────────────┘   │  │
│ │  OS/2  program  path  and  file  name ┌──────────────────┐   │  │
│ │                                       │ notused          │   │  │
│ │                                       └──────────────────┘   │  │
│ │  Optional  comment                                           │  │
│ │  ┌────────────────────────────────────────────────────────┐ │  │
│ │  │ TP  for  handling  interrupts  from  DB2/2  V1  clients │ │  │
│ │  └────────────────────────────────────────────────────────┘ │  │
│ └──────────────────────────────────────────────────────────────┘ │
│ ┌─Optional values─────────────────────────────────────────────┐  │
│ │  ☐ Conversation security required                            │  │
│ │                                                              │  │
│ │  Program  parameter  string   ┌────────────────────────┐    │  │
│ │                               └────────────────────────┘    │  │
│ │  Icon  path  and  file  name  ┌────────────────────────┐    │  │
│ │                               └────────────────────────┘    │  │
│ └──────────────────────────────────────────────────────────────┘ │
│  ┌──────────────┐   ┌──────────┐   ┌────────┐                     │
│  │ Continue...  │   │ Cancel   │   │ Help   │                     │
│  └──────────────┘   └──────────┘   └────────┘                     │
└─────────────────────────────────────────────────────────────────┘
```

2. If you will use TCP/IP for connections from remote clients, add entries in the TCP/IP `services` file.

   The first entry consists of the connection service name (item **18** on the worksheet), the connection port (item **20** on the worksheet), and a slash followed by `tcp`

   The second entry consists of the interrupt service name (item **19** on the worksheet), the interrupt port (item **20** on the worksheet plus 1), and a slash followed by `tcp`

   Note: The service names are case-sensitive; type each name exactly as it appears on the worksheet, including uppercase and lowercase letters.

   For example:

   ```
   db2inst1c   3700/tcp
   db2inst1i   3701/tcp
   ```

3. Configure the database manager.

   - For APPC, issue the following CLP command:

     ```
     update database manager configuration using tpname NYSERVER
     ```

     where *NYSERVER* is item **15** on the worksheet.

   - For TCP/IP, issue the following CLP command:

     ```
     update database manager configuration using svcename db2inst1c
     ```

where *db2inst1c* is item ▩18 on the worksheet.

- For IPX/SPX, issue the following CLP command:

```
update database manager configuration using fileserver netwsrv
    objectname db2inst1 ipx_socket 879E
```

where *netwsrv*, *db2inst1c*, and *879E* are items ▩21 , ▩22 , and ▩23 on the worksheet.

- For NetBIOS, issue the following CLP command:

```
update database manager configuration using nname db2inst1
```

where *db2inst1* is item ▩24 on the worksheet.

4. If you will use IPX/SPX for connections from remote clients, register the DB2 server in NetWare as follows:

```
REGISTER [DB2 SERVER] [IN] NWBINDERY USER <userid>
[PASSWORD <password>]
```

where *userid* and *password* are the Novell fileserver login userid and password which must have SUPERVISOR or Workgroup Manager security equivalence.

5. Stop the database manager, if it is running:

```
db2stop
```

6. Set the value of the DB2COMM environment variable to the protocols that you will use (item ▩14 on the worksheet). For example:

```
appc,tcpip,ipxspx,netbios
```

7. Start the database manager:

```
db2start
```

Completing the Configuration

When you have configured your system and all of the server connections, do the following:

1. Stop and start Communications Manager. You can use the Stop Communications Normally icon and the Start Communications icon.

2. Update the node directory, system database directory, and DCS directory. The commands are as follows,

   a. db2 CATALOG APPC NODE DB2NODE REMOTE DB2PIC SECURITY PROGRAM
   b. db2 CATALOG DATABASE DB2DB AS NYC3 AT NODE DB2NODE AUTHENTICATION DCS
   c. db2 CATALOG DCS DATABASE DB2DB AS NEW_YORK3

For details refer to the *DDCS User's Guide*.

To do this, you will need to know the symbolic destination name (item ▩9) and the target database name (item ▩13) from the worksheet.

3. Configure each remote client as described in the *DB2 Client Application Enabler User* book for the appropriate platform.

4. Connect to the DRDA Server and bind the utilities & applications to the DRDA servers, as described in the *DDCS User's Guide*.

Worksheets

This section contains the following worksheets:

- "MVS, VSE, and VM Server Worksheet" on page 324
- "OS/400 Server Worksheet" on page 326
- "OS/2 Configuration Worksheet" on page 327
- "OS/2 Connection to Server Worksheet" on page 328
- "OS/2 Configuration for Remote Clients Worksheet" on page 329.

MVS, VSE, and VM Server Worksheet

Item	Parameter	Example	Your value	Note
1	NETID	SPIFNET		
2	Controller address	400009451902		
3	MODEENT	IBMRDB		
4	SSCP name	NYX		
5	APPL	NYM2DB2		
6	LU	NYX1GW01		1
7	PU	NYX1		1
8	IDBLK and IDNUM	05D 27509		1
9	Remote transaction program	(default)		
10	Database location/name	NEW_YORK3		

Notes:

1. The PU, IDBLK, and IDNUM (items 7 and 8) must be the same for all DRDA server systems that DDCS is connected to. The LU can also be the same.

For the DDCS administrator:

1. If you have already defined a connection to another DRDA server, write the LU, PU, and IDBLK and IDNUM values that you used in the table above.
2. If this is your first DRDA server connection, look at the Local Node Characteristics panel and write the local node name for your machine beside PU in the table above.

For the VTAM administrator:

DDCS gives applications on remote systems (such as OS/2) access to data in your DB2 system. In order to make this possible, you must define DDCS to VTAM as follows:

1. Create an independent LU and a switched major node for the DDCS system. Use the PU value that the DDCS administrator wrote in the table above. If the LU, IDBLK and IDNUM values are already written in the table, use these values also.
2. If the database is not already set up for remote communication in VTAM, set it up.
3. Write the following information for the DDCS administrator in the table:
   - The name of the network (NETID)
   - The locally-administered address or universal address of the communication controller
   - The entry in the mode table (MODEENT) used for communication. We recommend that you use mode IBMRDB.
   - The SSCP name
   - For the database, the APPL value
   - For the independent LU corresponding to the DDCS system, the LU name

- For the switched major node corresponding to the DDCS system, the IDBLK and IDNUM values.
4. Give the worksheet to the database administrator.

For the database administrator:

DDCS gives applications on remote systems (such as OS/2) access to data in your DB2 system. In order to make this possible, you must do the following:

1. Set up the database for remote communication. (For MVS, this includes adding entries to the SYSIBM.SYSLUNAMES and SYSIBM.SYSUSERNAMES tables). As an LU name, use the value written for "LU" in the table.
2. If you are not using the default TP name, write the value that you are using in the table beside Remote transaction program. For MVS systems, the default (defined by DRDA) is X'07'6DB. For VSE and VM systems, the default is the RDB_NAME.
3. For MVS, write the LOCATION value in the last line of the table. For VSE or VM, write the RDB_NAME value in the last line of the table.
4. Give the worksheet to the DDCS administrator.

OS/400 Server Worksheet

Item	Parameter	Example	Your value	Note
1	Local network ID	SPIFNET		
2	Local adapter address	400009451902		
3	Mode name	IBMRDB		
4	Local control point	SYD2101A		
5	Remote transaction program	(default)		
6	Relational database name	NEW_YORK3		

For the AS/400 administrator:

DDCS gives applications on remote systems (such as OS/2) access to data in your DB2 for OS/400 system. In order to make this possible, the DDCS administrator needs the following information:

1. The local network ID. You can get this information by entering **dspneta**.

2. The local adapter address. You can get this information by entering **wrklind (*trlan)**.

3. The mode name. You can get a list of mode names by entering **wrkmodd**. If the mode IBMRDB has been defined on your OS/400 system, we recommend that you use it.

4. The local control point. You can get this information by entering **dspneta**.

5. The remote transaction program name. The default (defined by DRDA) is X'07'6DB.

6. The relational database name. You can get this information by entering **dsprdbdire**.

OS/2 Configuration Worksheet

Item	Parameter	Example	Your value	Note
1	Network ID	SPIFNET		1
2	Local node name	NYX1		2
3	Local node ID	05D 27509		3
4	Mode name	IBMRDB		4
5	Local LU name	NYX1GW01		5
6	Local LU alias	NYX1GW01		

Notes:

1. The Network ID matches item 1 on the server worksheet.
2. For MVS, VSE, or VM, the Local node name matches item 7 (PU) on the server worksheet. For OS/400, any unique node name can be used; in most cases, this value has already been set for you.
3. For MVS, VSE, or VM, the Local node ID matches item 8 (IDBLK and IDNUM) on the server worksheet. For OS/400, you can leave this blank.
4. The Mode name matches item 3 on the server worksheet.
5. The Local LU name matches item 6 (LU) on the MVS, VSE, and VM server worksheet.

OS/2 Connection to Server Worksheet

Item	Parameter	Example	Your value	Note
7	Link name	LINKHOST		
8	LAN destination address	400009451902		1
9	Symbolic destination name	DB2CPIC		
10	Partner CP name	NYX		2
11	Partner LU name	NYM2DB2		3
12	Remote transaction program	(default)		4
13	Target database name	NEW_YORK3		5

Notes:

1. The LAN destination address matches item 2 on the server worksheet.
2. The Partner CP name matches item 4 on the server worksheet.
3. For MVS, VSE, or VM, the Partner LU name matches item 5 (APPL) on the server worksheet. For OS/400, you can use the partner CP name.
4. The Remote transaction program is copied from the server worksheet.
5. The Target database name matches the last item on the server worksheet.

OS/2 Configuration for Remote Clients Worksheet

Item	Parameter	Example	Your value	Note
14	Communication protocols	appc,tcpip,ipxspx,netbios		
	For APPC Connections			
15	TP name	NYSERVER		
16	Back-level DB2 Client Application Enabler V1 clients?	yes		
17	Back-level DB2 for OS/2 V1 clients?	yes		
	For TCP/IP Connections			
18	Connection service name	db2inst1c		
19	Interrupt service name	db2inst1i		
20	Connection port	3700		1
	For IPX/SPX Connections			
21	File server	netwsrv		
22	Object name	db2inst1		
23	Socket	879E		
	For NetBIOS Connections			
24	NNAME	db2inst1		
Notes:				

1. For TCP/IP connections, the interrupt port must be the next port following the connection port. For example, if the connection port is 3700, the interrupt port must be 3701.

Chapter 20. Configuring DDCS for AIX

This chapter describes how you configure the DDCS workstation and DRDA servers. How you configure each remote client is described in the *DB2 Client Application Enabler User* book for the appropriate platform.

Note: If you want to execute applications under CICS for AIX or the AIX Encina Monitor, see Appendix C "Setting up DDCS for CICS for AIX or Encina Monitor" in the DDCS for AIX Installation and Configuration Guide.

This chapter makes the following assumptions:

- Your network is relatively straightforward.

- None of the DRDA servers are OS/2 or UNIX**-based DB2 databases (to connect to an OS/2 or UNIX-based DB2 database, we recommend that you use the Client Application Enablers provided with DB2 and not use DDCS).

- For MVS, VSE, or VM, you have access to a VTAM administrator and a database administrator. For OS/400, you have access to an AS/400 administrator.

- SNA Server for AIX 2.1 is already installed on the system, where DDCS is installed.

- The ASCII or Motif version of **smit** is being used, with SNA Server for AIX 2.1.

- Token Ring is being used as the communications medium.

Configuring Your DRDA Servers

Before you can use DDCS, you must configure both the DRDA servers and the DDCS system. If you decide to configure the DDCS system before you configure the servers, you must at least get information about how the servers *will be* configured before you configure the DDCS system.

The following worksheets are used for configuring DRDA servers:

- "MVS, VSE, and VM Server Worksheet" on page 343
- "OS/400 Server Worksheet" on page 345.

For each server that you are connecting to, fill in one copy of the appropriate server worksheet. Each worksheet contains instructions for how to use it.

For an MVS, VSE, or VM connection, you should find the control point name of your machine. You can find this by entering **smit** and selecting panels in the following order:

1. Communications Applications and Services
2. SNA Server for AIX
3. Configure SNA Profiles
4. Advanced Configuration
5. Control Point

6. Change/Show a Profile.

Figure 153 illustrates the correspondence between information specified on the DRDA server system, information specified in the DDCS configuration files, and information specified in the DDCS directories. The instructions in this book and the *DDCS User's Guide* show you how to update these files.

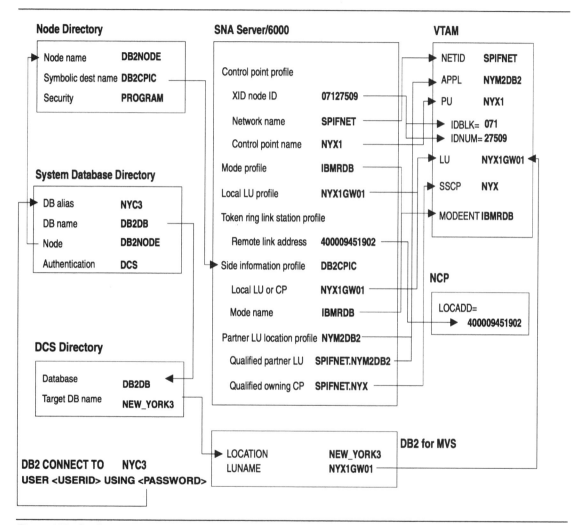

Figure 153. Configuration on the DRDA Server and DDCS Workstation

Planning to Configure Your DDCS System

Fill in a copy of "AIX Configuration Worksheet" on page 346.

For an MVS, VSE, or VM connection, do the following:

1. For XID node ID, copy the IDBLK and IDNUM (item 8) from the server worksheet.
2. For Network name, copy the NETID (item 1) from the server worksheet.
3. For Control point name, copy the PU (item 7) from the server worksheet.
4. Leave the token ring profile name blank for now.
5. For Mode name, copy the MODEENT (item 3) from the server worksheet.
6. For Local LU name, copy the LU (item 6) from the server worksheet.
7. For Local LU alias, choose an alias. This can be the same as the LU name or different.

For an OS/400 connection, do the following:

1. For XID node ID, write an asterisk (*). This means that you will use the default.
2. For Network name, copy the local network ID (item 1) from the server worksheet.
3. For Mode name, copy the mode name (item 3) from the server worksheet.
4. Leave the other items blank for now.

Planning for Each Server Connection

For each server that you are connecting to, fill in a copy of "AIX Connection to Server Worksheet" on page 347 as follows,

- For Link station profile name, choose a value.

- For Remote link address, copy item 2 (controller address or local adapter address) from the server worksheet.

- For Symbolic destination name, choose a value.

- For Partner CP name, copy item 4 from the server worksheet. For MVS, VSE, or VM it is an SSCP value; for OS/400 it is a local control point name.

- For Partner LU name for MVS, VSE, or VM, copy item 5 (APPL) from the server worksheet. For OS/400, copy the Partner CP name that you just wrote on this worksheet.

- For Remote transaction program, copy the value from the server worksheet. The default is X'07F6C4C2' for MVS and OS/400 and the RDB_NAME for VSE and VM.

- For Target database name, copy the last item from the server worksheet. This is a LOCATION value (MVS), RDB_NAME (VSE or VM), or a relational database name (OS/400).

Planning for Remote Client Support

If you will connect remote clients to the DDCS workstation, fill in a copy of "AIX Configuration for Remote Clients Worksheet" on page 348 as follows:

- For Communication protocols, specify which communication protocols you will use for remote clients. DDCS for AIX supports APPC, TCP/IP, and IPX/SPX.

- If you will use APPC, do the following:

  - Choose a TP name.

- Specify whether you will support connections from DB2 Client Application Enabler Version 1 clients (yes or no).
- Specify whether you will support connections from DB2 for OS/2 Version 1 clients (yes or no).

- If you will use TCP/IP, do the following:

  - Choose a service name for the connection port.
  - Choose a service name for the interrupt port.
  - Specify which port will be the connection port. The interrupt port must be the next port. For example, if the connection port is 3 700, the interrupt port must be 3 701.

- If you are using *IPX/SPX*, do the following:

  - Specify the name of the NetWare file server where the DDCS workstation will be registered.
  - Choose an object name that represents the DDCS workstation.
  - Choose a socket number to represent the particular DB2 instance. If you are not using the default 879E select a number in the range of 879E to 87A2, if possible (these numbers are specifically assigned by Novell for DB2).

Configuring Your DDCS System

Before using this section, be sure that you have completed "AIX Configuration Worksheet" on page 346.

Note: The boxed numerics correspond with the items located on your worksheet; for example, the symbol **24** would be used to represent the IPX Socket Number. The **⋆** symbol is used to denote entries that need to be changed but do no have a representation on the worksheet.

Configure your DDCS system as follows:

1. Log on to the AIX machine as *root*.

2. Type **smit** on the command line.

3. Select panels in the following order:

   a. Communications Applications and Services
   b. SNA Server for AIX
   c. Configure SNA Profiles
   d. Advanced Configuration.

   The next several steps begin from the Advanced Configuration panel.

4. Update the Control Point Profile as follows:

   a. Select the Control Point panel.
   b. Select the Change/Show a Profile panel.
   c. Between the square brackets [ ], type the values that you wrote in items 1 and 2 of the worksheet.

The control point name was probably set when the SNA Server for AIX was installed. For MVS, VSE, and VM, check that this value matches item 3 on the worksheet. For OS/400, write the control point name in the worksheet now; if no name exists, talk to your LAN administrator.

To minimize confusion, use the same control point alias and control point name.

For example, the file could look like this:

```
              Change / Show Control Point Profile

*Profile name                                node_cp
 XID node ID                                 [07127509]      1
 Network name                                [SPIFNET]       2
 Control Point (CP) name                     [NYX1]          3
 Control Point alias                         [NYX1]          3
 Control Point type                          appn_end_node
 Maximum number of cached routing trees      [500]
 Maximum number of nodes in the TRS database [500]
 Route addition resistance                   [128]
```

5. Check the Token Ring SNA DLC Profile as follows:

   a. Select the Links panel.
   b. Select the Token Ring panel.
   c. Select the Token Ring SNA DLC panel.
   d. Select the Change/Show a Profile panel.
   e. The profile name and data link device name were probably set when SNA Server for AIX was installed. If you have a reason to change these values, you can do so. If no values appear in the profile, talk to your LAN administrator.

   Write the profile name in item 4 of the worksheet now.

   For example, the profile might look like this:

```
              Add Token Ring SNA DLC Profile

*Profile name                                [tok0.00001]    4
 Data link device name                       [tok0]
 Force disconnect time-out (1-600 seconds)   [120]
 User-defined maximum I-Field size?          no
   If yes, Max. I-Field size (265-30729)     [30729]
```

   f. If you will use APPC for connections from remote clients, make sure that the profile has the following value:

```
 Dynamic link stations supported?                       yes
```

6. Create a Mode Profile as follows:

   a. Select the Sessions panel.
   b. Select the LU 6.2 panel.
   c. Select the LU 6.2 Mode panel.
   d. Select the Add a Profile panel.

e. Define your mode profile. For profile name and mode name, use the value that you wrote in item 5 of the worksheet. On the other lines, specify values that match the mode profile defined on your DRDA server systems. If you are using the mode IBMRDB, specify the following values:

```
*Profile name                                          [IBMRDB]   5
 Mode name                                             [IBMRDB]   5
 Maximum number of sessions (1-5000)                   [30]       *
 Minimum contention winners (0-5000)                   [15]       *
 Minimum contention losers (0-5000)                    [15]       *
 Auto activate limit (0-500)                           [0]
 Upper bound for adaptive receive pacing window        [16]
 Receive pacing window (0-63)                          [8]        *
 Maximum RU size (128,...,32768: multiples of 32)      [4096]     *
 Minimum RU size (128,...,32768: multiples of 32)      [1024]     *
 Class of Service (COS) name                           [#CONNECT]
```

7. If the DDCS workstation is defined as an LU, update the Local LU Profile as follows (In most cases, a VTAM administrator on MVS, VSE, or VM would define an LU for DDCS; for OS/400, control point routing would normally be used instead of an LU).

    a. Select the Sessions panel.
    b. Select the LU 6.2 panel.
    c. Select the LU 6.2 Local LU panel.
    d. Select the Add a Profile panel.
    e. Update three lines using the values that you wrote in items 6 and 7 of the worksheet (use item 6 for the first two lines and item 7 for the third). For example, the file could look like this:

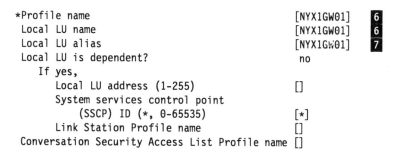

```
                Add LU 6.2 Local LU Profile

*Profile name                                        [NYX1GW01]   6
 Local LU name                                       [NYX1GW01]   6
 Local LU alias                                      [NYX1GW01]   7
 Local LU is dependent?                              no
    If yes,
       Local LU address (1-255)                      []
       System services control point
          (SSCP) ID (*, 0-65535)                     [*]
       Link Station Profile name                     []
 Conversation Security Access List Profile name []
```

Configuring Each Server Connection

Before using this section, be sure that you have completed "AIX Connection to Server Worksheet" on page 347.

Configure a DRDA server connection as follows:

1. Update the Token Ring Link Station Profile as follows:

    a. Select the Links panel.
    b. Select the Token Ring panel.

c. Select the Token Ring Link Station panel.

d. Select the Add a Profile panel.

e. Update the profile, as follows:

- Change the profile name to the value that you wrote in item 8 of the worksheet. For example:

```
*Profile name                         [NYX1LS]      ▉8
 Use Control Point's XID node ID?      yes
```

- Change the SNA DLC profile name to the value that you wrote in item 4 of the worksheet. For example:

```
If no, XID node ID
 SNA DLC Profile name        [tok0.00001]   ▉4
 Stop link station on inactivity?       no
```

- Change the remote link address to the value that you wrote in item 9 of the worksheet. For example:

```
If link_address,
 Remote link address         [400009451902]  ▉9
 Remote SAP address (04-ec)   [04]
```

- If you want to activate the link only when it is needed (rather than activating it when the SNA starts up), update several lines of the profile, as follows:

```
Adjacent Node Identification Parameters
 Verify adjacent node?                     yes        ▉*
 Network ID of adjacent node        -      SPIFNET    ▉2
 CP name of adjacent node                  NYX        ▉11
 XID node ID of adjacent node (LEN node only)  [*]
 Node type of adjacent node                len_node   ▉*

Link Activation Parameters
 Solicit SSCP sessions?                    yes
 Initiate call when link station is activated? yes
 Activate link station at SNA start up?    no         ▉*
 Activate on demand?                       yes        ▉*
 CP-CP sessions supported?                 yes
 If yes,
  Adjacent network node preferred server?  no
 Partner required to support CP-CP sessions?  no
 Initial TG number (0-20)              [1]            ▉*
```

2. Update the LU 6.2 Side Information Profile as follows:

a. Select the Sessions panel.

b. Select the LU 6.2 panel.

c. Select the LU 6.2 Side Information panel.

d. Select the Add a Profile panel.

e. Update the profile, as follows:

- For the profile name, use the value that you wrote in item 10 of the worksheet. This value is case-sensitive; it is recommended that you use uppercase letters.
- For the local LU or control point alias, use the value that you wrote in item 7 of the worksheet (if any) or item 3 of the worksheet.
- For the fully qualified partner LU name, use the value that you wrote in item 2 of the worksheet followed by a period and the value that you wrote in item 12 of the worksheet.
- For the mode name, use the value that you wrote in item 5 of the worksheet.
- For the next two lines, specify the remote transaction program name. You must specify a value here; in SNA Server for AIX, there is no default value. On the DRDA server, the default for MVS or OS/400 is X'07F6C4C2'; the default for VSE or VM is the RDB_NAME.

  Use the value that you wrote in item 13 in the worksheet, or type in the default value. If the value is hexadecimal, specify yes for the second line; otherwise, specify no.

For example, the file could look like this:

```
             Add LU 6.2 Side Information Profile

*Profile name                            [DB2CPIC]           10
 Local LU or Control Point alias         [NYX1GW01]          7  or  3
 Provide only one of the following:
     Partner LU alias
     Fully qualified partner LU name     [SPIFNET.NYM2DB2]   212
 Mode name                               [IBMRDB]            5
 Remote transaction program name (RTPN)  [07F6C4C2]          13
 RTPN in hexadecimal?                     yes                *
```

Note: If you are retrieving information about this server from the DCE Directory, then you do not need to have the Side Information Profile

3. Update the Partner LU 6.2 Location Profile as follows:

   a. Select the Sessions panel.
   b. Select the LU 6.2 panel.
   c. Select the Partner LU 6.2 Location panel.
   d. Select the Add a Profile panel.
   e. Update the profile, as follows:

      - For the profile name, use the value that you wrote in item 12 of the worksheet.
      - For the fully qualified partner LU name, use the value that you wrote in item 2 of the worksheet followed by a period and the value that you wrote in item 12 of the worksheet.
      - For the fully qualified CP name, use the value that you wrote in item 2 of the worksheet followed by a period and the value that you wrote in item 11 of the worksheet.

   For example, the file could look like this:

```
                    Add Partner LU 6.2 Location Profile

*Profile name                                   [NYM2DB2]  12
 Fully qualified partner LU name           [SPIFNET.NYM2DB2]  2.12
 Partner LU location method                      owning_cp
 If owning_cp,
  Fully qualified owning Control Point (CP) name[SPIFNET.NYX]  2.11
  Local node is network server for LEN node?           no
```

Configuring DDCS for Remote Clients

Before using this section, be sure that you have completed "AIX Configuration for Remote Clients Worksheet" on page 348.

Configure your DDCS workstation for remote clients as follows:

1. If you will use APPC for connections from remote clients, do the following:

   a. Select the Sessions panel.
   b. Select the LU 6.2 panel.
   c. Select the LU 6.2 Transaction Program Name (TPN) panel.
   d. Select the Add a Profile panel.
   e. Add the following profile, using the value that you wrote in item 16 of the worksheet for TP name.

   Note: This profile will be used for both database connections and interrupts by Version 2 clients, and also for database connections from DB2 Client Application Enabler Version 1 clients.

   Note: If you are migrating from a previous release of DDCS, you should be aware that the db2acntp, db2aittp and db2cnsm executables have been consolidated into the db2acntp executable.

```
*Profile name                                   [db2v2]    *
 Transaction program name (TPN)                 [NYSERVER]  16
 Transaction program name (TPN) is in hexadecimal? no
 PIP data?                                       no
    If yes, Subfields (0-99)                     [0]
 Conversation type                              basic       *
 Sync level                                      none/confirm
 Resource security level                         none
    If access, Resource Security Access List Prof. []
 Full path to TP executable    [INSTHOME/sqllib/bin/db2acntp]  *
 Multiple instances supported?                   yes         *
 User ID                                         [1918]      *
 Server synonym name                             []
 Restart action                                  once
 Communication type                              signals
    If IPC, Communication IPC queue key          [0]
 Standard input file/device                      [/dev/console]
 Standard output file/device                     [/dev/console]
 Standard error file/device                      [/dev/console]

 Comments                                        []
```

f. If you will support connections from DB2 Client Application Enabler Version 1 clients (item **17** on the worksheet), add the following profile. This profile will be used for database interrupts from DB2 Client Application Enabler Version 1 clients. You must use the TPN name shown in the profile.

```
*Profile name                                    [vlint]          ★
 Transaction program name (TPN)                  [DB2INTERRUPT]   ★
 Transaction program name (TPN) is in hexadecimal?   no
 PIP data?                                           no
    If yes, Subfields (0-99)                      [0]
 Conversation type                                   basic       ★
 Sync level                                          none/confirm
 Resource security level                             none
    If access, Resource Security Access List Prof. []
 Full path to TP executable     [INSTHOME/sqllib/bin/db2acntp]  ★
 Multiple instances supported?                       yes         ★
 User ID                                          [1918]         ★
 Server synonym name                              []
 Restart action                                      once
 Communication type                                  signals
    If IPC, Communication IPC queue key           [0]
 Standard input file/device                       [/dev/console]
 Standard output file/device                      [/dev/console]
 Standard error file/device                       [/dev/console]

 Comments                                         []
```

g. If you will support connections from DB2 for OS/2 Version 1 clients (item **18** on the worksheet), add the following two profiles.

This profile will be used for database connections from DB2 for OS/2 Version 1 clients. You must use the TPN name shown in the profile.

```
*Profile name                                    [db22v1]        ★
 Transaction program name (TPN)                   [07F6C4C2]      ★
 Transaction program name (TPN) is in hexadecimal?   yes          ★
 PIP data?                                           no
    If yes, Subfields (0-99)                      [0]
 Conversation type                                   basic       ★
 Sync level                                          none/confirm
 Resource security level                             none
    If access, Resource Security Access List Prof. []
 Full path to TP executable     [INSTHOME/sqllib/bin/db2acntp]  ★
 Multiple instances supported?                       yes         ★
 User ID                                          [1918]         ★
 Server synonym name                              []
 Restart action                                      once
 Communication type                                  signals
    If IPC, Communication IPC queue key           [0]
 Standard input file/device                       [/dev/console]
 Standard output file/device                      [/dev/console]
 Standard error file/device                       [/dev/console]

 Comments                                         []
```

This profile will be used for database interrupts from DB2 for OS/2 Version 1 clients. You must use the TPN name shown in the profile.

```
*Profile name                                      [db22v1int] *
 Transaction program name (TPN)                    [07F6E2D5]  *
 Transaction program name (TPN) is in hexadecimal? yes         *
 PIP data?                                          no
    If yes, Subfields (0-99)                        [0]
 Conversation type                                  basic       *
 Sync level                                         none/confirm
 Resource security level                            none
    If access, Resource Security Access List Prof.  []
 Full path to TP executable   [INSTHOME/sqllib/bin/db2acntp]    *
 Multiple instances supported?                      yes         *
 User ID                                            [1918]      *
 Server synonym name                                []
 Restart action                                     once
 Communication type                                 signals
    If IPC, Communication IPC queue key             [0]
 Standard input file/device                         [/dev/console]
 Standard output file/device                        [/dev/console]
 Standard error file/device                         [/dev/console]

 Comments                                           []
```

2. If you will use TCP/IP for connections from remote clients, add entries in the TCP/IP services file.

   The first entry consists of the connection service name (item **19** on the worksheet), the connection port (item **21** on the worksheet), and a slash followed by tcp.

   The second entry consists of the interrupt service name (item **20** on the worksheet), the interrupt port (item **21** on the worksheet plus 1), and a slash followed by tcp.

   Note: that the service names are case-sensitive; type each name exactly as it appears on the worksheet, including uppercase and lowercase letters.

   For example:

   ```
   db2inst1c    3700/tcp
   db2inst1i    3701/tcp
   ```

3. Configure the database manager. You must add the TP name (if you are using APPC), the connection service name (if you are using TCP/IP), and the fileserver object name and socket number (if you are using IPX/SPX) to the database manager configuration file. One way to do this is to issue the following CLP command:

```
update database manager configuration using

svcename      db2inst1c    [19]
tpname        NYSERVER     [16]
fileserver    netwsrv      [22]
objectname    db2inst1     [23]
ipx_socket    897E         [24]
```

4. If you will use IPX/SPX for connections to remote clients, you should do the following:

   - For each DB2 instance that will service IPX/SPX connections, register the DB2 instance at the network server. One way to do this is to issue the following CLP command:

     ```
     REGISTER [DB2 SERVER] [IN] NWBINDERY USER <userid>
     [PASSWORD <password>]
     ```

     where *userid* and *password* are the Novell fileserver login userid and password which must have SUPERVISOR or Workgroup Manager security equivalence.

   Note: The register command must be issued from the DDCS workstation. The object name and socket number must be unique per DB2 instance configured on one workstation.

5. Stop the database manager, if it is running:

   ```
   db2stop
   ```

6. Set the value of the DB2COMM environment variable to include one, or more, of the following (If you specify more than one, separate each value with a comma (,))

   ```
   appc
   tcpip
   ipxspx
   ```

   according to which communication protocol or protocols you are using (item [15] on the worksheet).

7. Start the database manager:

   ```
   db2start
   ```

Completing the Configuration

When you have configured your system and all of the server connections, do the following:

1. If your token ring has never before been used for SNA, issue the following command:

   ```
   mkdev -c dlc -s dlc -t tokenring
   ```

2. Choose the Verify SNA Configuration Profiles panel. This checks that all of the required profiles exist on your system and that the information in them does not conflict. You should repeat this step any time you change your configuration, even if you only update one profile.

Verification can take several minutes. For each error message that you receive, correct the error. When you have corrected all the errors, redo the verification.

Note: The verification program does not guarantee that your network parameters are accurate. It verifies only parameters that can be checked within the local system.

3. Stop and start SNA Server for AIX. You can use **smit** or issue the following commands:

```
sna -stop sna
sna -start
```

4. Update the node directory, system database directory, and DCS directory. The commands are as follows:

   a. db2 CATALOG APPC NODE DB2NODE REMOTE DB2PIC SECURITY PROGRAM
   b. db2 CATALOG DATABASE DB2DB AS NYC3 AT NODE DB2NODE AUTHENTICATION DCS
   c. db2 CATALOG DCS DATABASE DB2DB AS NEW_YORK3

(For details refer to the *DDCS User's Guide*).

To do this, you will need to know the symbolic destination name (item 10) and the target database name (item 14) from the worksheet.

5. Configure each remote client as described in the *DB2 Client Application Enabler User* book for the appropriate platform.

6. Connect to the DRDA server and bind the utilities and applications, as described in the *DDCS User's Guide*.

Worksheets

This section contains the following worksheets:

- "MVS, VSE, and VM Server Worksheet" on page 343
- "OS/400 Server Worksheet" on page 345
- "AIX Configuration Worksheet" on page 346
- "AIX Connection to Server Worksheet" on page 347
- "AIX Configuration for Remote Clients Worksheet" on page 348.

MVS, VSE, and VM Server Worksheet

Item	Parameter	Example	Your value	Note
1	NETID	SPIFNET		
2	Controller address	400009451902		
3	MODEENT	IBMRDB		
4	SSCP name	NYX		
5	APPL	NYM2DB2		
6	LU	NYX1GW01		1
7	PU	NYX1		1
8	IDBLK and IDNUM	07127509		1
9	Remote transaction program	(default)		
10	Database location/name	NEW_YORK3		

Notes:

1. The PU, IDBLK, and IDNUM (items 7 and 8) must be the same for all DRDA server systems that DDCS is connected to. The LU can also be the same.

For the DDCS administrator:

1. If you have already defined a connection to another DRDA server, write the LU, PU, and IDBLK and IDNUM values that you used in the table above.
2. If this is your first DRDA server connection, look in the Control Point profile and write the control point name for your machine beside PU in the table above.

For the VTAM administrator:

DDCS gives applications on remote systems (such as OS/2) access to data in your DB2 system. In order to make this possible, you must define DDCS to VTAM as follows:

1. Create an independent LU and a switched major node for the DDCS system. Use the PU value that the DDCS administrator wrote in the table above. If the LU, IDBLK and IDNUM values are already written in the table, use these values also.
2. If the database is not already set up for remote communication in VTAM, set it up.
3. Write the following information for the DDCS administrator in the table:

   - The name of the network (NETID)
   - The locally-administered address or universal address of the communication controller
   - The entry in the mode table (MODEENT) used for communication. We recommend that you use mode IBMRDB.
   - The SSCP name
   - For the database, the APPL value
   - For the independent LU corresponding to the DDCS system, the LU name

- For the switched major node corresponding to the DDCS system, the IDBLK and IDNUM values.

4. Give the worksheet to the database administrator.

For the database administrator:

DDCS gives applications on remote systems (such as OS/2) access to data in your DB2 system. In order to make this possible, you must do the following:

1. Set up the database for remote communication. (For MVS, this includes adding entries to the SYSIBM.SYSLUNAMES and SYSIBM.SYSUSERNAMES tables.) As an LU name, use the value written for "LU" in the table.
2. If you are not using the default TP name, write the value that you are using in the table beside Remote transaction program. For MVS systems, the default (defined by DRDA) is X'07F6C4C2'. For VSE and VM systems, the default is the RDB_NAME.
3. For MVS, write the LOCATION value in the last line of the table. For VSE or VM, write the RDB_NAME value in the last line of the table.
4. Give the worksheet to the DDCS administrator.

OS/400 Server Worksheet

Item	Parameter	Example	Your value	Note
1	Local network ID	SPIFNET		
2	Local adapter address	400009451902		
3	Mode name	IBMRDB		
4	Local control point	SYD2101A		
5	Remote transaction program	(default)		
6	Relational database name	NEW_YORK3		

For the AS/400 administrator:

DDCS gives applications on remote systems (such as OS/2) access to data in your DB2 for OS/400 system. In order to make this possible, the DDCS administrator needs the following information:

1. The local network ID. You can get this information by entering **dspneta**.

2. The local adapter address. You can get this information by entering **wrklind (*trlan)**.

3. The mode name. You can get a list of mode names by entering **wrkmodd**. If the mode IBMRDB has been defined on your OS/400 system, we recommend that you use it.

4. The local control point. You can get this information by entering **dspneta**.

5. The remote transaction program name. The default (defined by DRDA) is X'07F6C4C2'.

6. The relational database name. You can get this information by entering **dsprdbdire**.

AIX Configuration Worksheet

Item	Parameter	Example	Your value	Note
1	XID node ID	07127509		1
2	Network name	SPIFNET		2
3	Control point name	NYX1		3
4	Token ring profile name	tok0.00001		
5	Mode name	IBMRDB		4
6	Local LU name	NYX1GW01		5
7	Local LU alias	NYX1GW01		

Notes:

1. For MVS, VSE, or VM, the XID node ID matches item 8 (IDBLK and IDNUM) on the server worksheet. For OS/400, you can use the default of *
2. The Network name matches item 1 on the server worksheet.
3. For MVS, VSE, or VM, the Control point name matches item 7 (PU) on the server worksheet. For OS/400, any unique control point name can be used; in most cases, this value has already been set for you.
4. The Mode name matches item 3 on the server worksheet.
5. The Local LU name matches item 6 (LU) on the MVS, VSE, and VM server worksheet.

AIX Connection to Server Worksheet

Item	Parameter	Example	Your value	Note
8	Link station profile name	NYX1LS		
9	Remote link address	400009451902		1
10	Symbolic destination name	DB2CPIC		
11	Partner CP name	NYX		2
12	Partner LU name	NYM2DB2		3
13	Remote transaction program	(default)		4
14	Target database name	NEW_YORK3		5

Notes:

1. The Remote link address matches item 2 on the server worksheet.
2. The Partner CP name matches item 4 on the server worksheet.
3. For MVS, VSE, or VM, the Partner LU name matches item 5 (APPL) on the server worksheet. For OS/400, you can use the partner CP name.
4. The Remote transaction program is copied from the server worksheet.
5. The Target database name matches the last item on the server worksheet.

AIX Configuration for Remote Clients Worksheet

Item	Parameter	Example	Your value	Note
15	Communication protocols	appc,tcpip,ipxspx		
For APPC Connections				
16	TP name	NYSERVER		
17	Back-level Client Application Enabler V1 clients?	yes		
18	Back-level DB2 for OS/2 V1 clients?	yes		
For TCP/IP Connections				
19	Connection service name	db2inst1c		
20	Interrupt service name	db2inst1i		
21	Connection port	3700		1
For IPX/SPX Connections				
22	NetWare file server	netwsrv		
23	DB2 for MVS/ESA Object Name	db2inst1		
24	IPX Socket Number	879E (default)		
Notes:				
1. For TCP/IP connections, the interrupt port must be the next port following the connection port. For example, if the connection port is 3700, the interrupt port must be 3701.				

Chapter 21. Configuring DB2 for OS/2 as a DRDA Application Server

This chapter describes how to configure DB2 for OS/2 as a DRDA Application Server.

APPC Support

To use APPC, Communications Manager for OS/2 V1.1 or later must be installed and configured on the DB2 for OS/2 server workstation.

Configuring Communications Manager for OS/2 for the DB2 Server

The following section provides a working example of the profiles configured on a DB2 for OS/2 server to support communications with DRDA Application Requesters (ARs).

Notes:

1. The values provided are for the example only; you must substitute values that are appropriate for your operating environment.

2. Get the correct values from your network administrator.

Only one instance of DB2 can support DRDA AR's which use the default DRDA TP name **X'07'6DB**. The instance is specified by setting the **DB2SERVICETPINSTANCE** environment variable to the instance name.

To use the APPC protocol, you need to create or customize a number of profiles at the server. Assuming a token ring LAN, you must set up the following profiles:

- Local Node Characteristics Profile
- LAN DLC Profile
- Transaction Program Definition Profile(s)
- Mode Definition Profile

Note: The following procedure is using Communications Manager for OS/2 Version 1.11.

Proceed as follows:

1. Double-click on the Communications Manager/2 icon
2. Double-click on the Communications Manager Setup icon
3. Click on the Setup... pushbutton
4. On the Open Configuration panel, specify a configuration name. Enter a new configuration name or select an existing configuration file. Press the OK pushbutton.
5. On the Communications Manager Configuration Definition panel, press the Additional definitions radio button.
6. On the Feature or Application list box, select APPC APIs. Click on the Configure... pushbutton.

APPC APIs through Token-ring

Use the following values:

```
Network ID              SPIFNET
Local node name         NYX1
Node type               End node - no network node server
```

Enter the values and click on **Advanced...** to display the Communications Manager
Profile List panel; all remaining steps start from that screen.

▽ | APPC APIs through Token-ring

Network ID · · · · · · · · · · · · · · · · [SPIFNET]

Local node name · · · · · · · · · · · · · · [NYX1]

┌─Local node type──────────────────────────────┐
│ ○ End node to network node server   │
│ ◉ End node - no network node server   │
│ ○ Network node   │
│   │
│ Network node server address   (hex) [   ] │
└──┘

[OK]   [Advanced...]   [Cancel]   [Help]

Local Node Characteristics

The local node characteristics contains the parameters needed to identify the
workstation to the SNA network.

- Select **SNA local node characteristics**
- Click on **Configure...**
- Enter the values.
- Click on **OK**.

Use the following values:

```
Network ID              SPIFNET
Local node name         NYX1
Node type               End node - no network node server
Local node ID (hex)     05D 27509
```

```
┌─┬─────────────────────────────────────────────────────────────┐
│ ∨│    Local Node Characteristics                               │
├─┴─────────────────────────────────────────────────────────────┤
│                                                                 │
│  Network ID                              ┌─────────┐            │
│                                          │ SPIFNET │            │
│                                          └─────────┘            │
│  Local node name                         ┌────────┐             │
│                                          │ NYX1   │             │
│                                          └────────┘             │
│  ┌─Node type ──────────────────────────────────────────────┐   │
│  │  ○  End node to network node server                      │   │
│  │  ◉  End node - no network node server                    │   │
│  │  ○  Network node                                         │   │
│  └──────────────────────────────────────────────────────────┘  │
│                                                                 │
│  Your network node server address (hex)  ┌──────────┐          │
│                                          │          │          │
│                                          └──────────┘          │
│  Local node ID (hex)    ┌─────┐  ┌───────┐                     │
│                         │ 05D │  │ 27509 │                     │
│                         └─────┘  └───────┘                     │
│  ┌────┐ ┌──────────┐ ┌─────────────┐ ┌────────┐ ┌──────┐       │
│  │ OK │ │ Options...│ │ NetWare(R)...│ │ Cancel │ │ Help │      │
│  └────┘ └──────────┘ └─────────────┘ └────────┘ └──────┘       │
│                                                                 │
└─────────────────────────────────────────────────────────────────┘
```

LAN DLC Profile
The LAN DLC Adapter profile identifies the type of LAN adapter and adapter
characteristics.

- Select **DLC - Token-ring or other LAN types**
- Click on **Configure...**
- Enter the value.
- Click on **OK**.

Use the following values:

```
C&SM LAN ID                         SPIFNET
```

```
┌────────────────────────────────────────────────────────────────┐
│  ∨ │ Token Ring or Other LAN Types DLC Adapter Parameters        │
├────────────────────────────────────────────────────────────────┤
│  Adapter  [0 ⊻]          ┌─Window count ──────────────────────┐  │
│  ☐ Free unused links     │ Send window count      [4] (1 - 8) │  │
│  ☐ Send alert for        │ Receive window count   [4] (1 - 8) │  │
│      beaconing           └────────────────────────────────────┘  │
│  Maximum link stations        [4   ] (1 - 255)                    │
│  Maximum activation attempts  [0   ] (0 - 99)                     │
│  Maximum I-field size         [1929] (265 - 16393)                │
│  Percent of incoming calls (%) [0  ] (0 - 100)                    │
│  Link establishment                                               │
│    retransmission count       [8   ] (1 - 127)                    │
│  Retranmission threshold      [8   ] (1 - 127)                    │
│  Loacl sap (hex)              [04  ] (04 - 9C)                     │
│  C&SM LAN ID                  [SPIFNET    ]                       │
│  Connection network                                               │
│    name (optional)            [          ]•[          ]           │
│                                                                   │
│  [OK]  [Delete]  [Cancel]  [Help]                                 │
└────────────────────────────────────────────────────────────────┘
```

Transaction Program Definitions

The transaction program definition provides the information necessary to start a TP on the local node, and specifies the properties of the TP.

Note: The default TP used by the DRDA AR is **X'07'6DB**. You will need to create a TP definition for this TP, along with TP definitions for any other non-default TPs used by your DRDA AR.

With Version 2 of DB2 the TP is operator pre-loaded and **NOT** Attach Manager started. As a result, an OS/2 TP executable file is not required.

If you have existing Transaction Program Definitions for the service transaction programs X'07'6DB, please ensure that the operation type in the transaction program definition is changed to queued, operator pre-loaded.

Also, since the TP is operator pre-loaded the OS/2 program path and file name field is not used; however, you must still enter something when you configure the TP, since the field is a mandatory input field. See "Additional TP Parameters" on page 354 for more information.

- Select **SNA features**.
- Click on **Configure...**.
- Select **Transaction program definitions**.
- Click on **Create...**.
- Enter the appropriate values for the TPs you are configuring.
- Click on **Continue...**, see "Additional TP Parameters" on page 354 to complete this step.

Default TP for DRDA Database Connections

The following TP definition is used to handle database connections from DRDA Application Requesters using the default TP **X'07'6DB**.

Use the following values:

```
√ Service TP
√ Transaction program (TP) name        X'07'6DB
√ OS/2 program path and file name      notused
√ Conversation security required
```

∨	Transaction Program Definition

Transaction program definition

▨ Service TP

Transaction program (TP) name   X'07'6DB

OS/2 program path and file name   notused

Optional comment

Default TP for DRDA ARs

Optional values

▨ Conversation security required

Program parameter string

Icon path and file name

| Continue... | Cancel | Help |

Non-Default TP for DRDA Database Connections

The following TP definition is used to handle database connections from DRDA
Application Requesters using a non-default value, for example **NYSERVER**.

Use the following values:

```
√ Transaction program (TP) name      NYSERVER
√ OS/2 program path and file name     notused
√ Conversation security required
```

∨	Transaction Program Definition

Transaction program definition

■ **S**ervice TP

Transaction program (TP) name   `NYSERVER`

OS/2 program path and fil**e** name   `notused`

Optional comment

`Non Default TP for DRDA ARs`

Optional values

▨ Conversation security **r**equired

Program parameter string

Icon path and file name

Continue...	Cancel	Help

Additional TP Parameters

The TP definitions should be configured with the following TP parameters.

- Select **Presentation type: Background**
- Select **Operation type: Queued, operator pre-loaded**
- Click on **OK**.

```
┌─────────────────────────────────────────────────────────────────┐
│ ┌───┐                                                             │
│ │ ∨ │  Additional  TP  Parameters                                 │
│ └───┘                                                             │
├─────────────────────────────────────────────────────────────────┤
│ ┌─Presentation type──────────┐ ┌─Operation type─────────────────┐│
│ │                            │ │                                ││
│ │ ○ Presentation Manager     │ │ ○ Queued, Attach Manager started││
│ │                            │ │                                ││
│ │ ○ VIO-windowable           │ │ ○ Queued, operator started     ││
│ │                            │ │                                ││
│ │ ○ Full screen              │ │ ◉ Queued, operator preloaded   ││
│ │                            │ │                                ││
│ │ ◉ Background               │ │ ○ Non-queued, Attach Manager started││
│ └────────────────────────────┘ └────────────────────────────────┘│
│ ┌────┐  ┌────────┐  ┌──────┐                                      │
│ │ OK │  │ Cancel │  │ Help │                                      │
│ └────┘  └────────┘  └──────┘                                      │
└─────────────────────────────────────────────────────────────────┘
```

Mode Definition

You can use an IBM-defined mode, or add a new mode definition that is appropriate for your application.

- Select **Modes**.
- Click on **Create...**.
- Enter the values.
- Click on **OK**.

Use the following values:

```
Mode name                    IBMRDB
Class of service             #CONNECT
Mode session limit               30
Minimum contention winners       15
Receive pacing window             8
Maximum RU size                4096
```

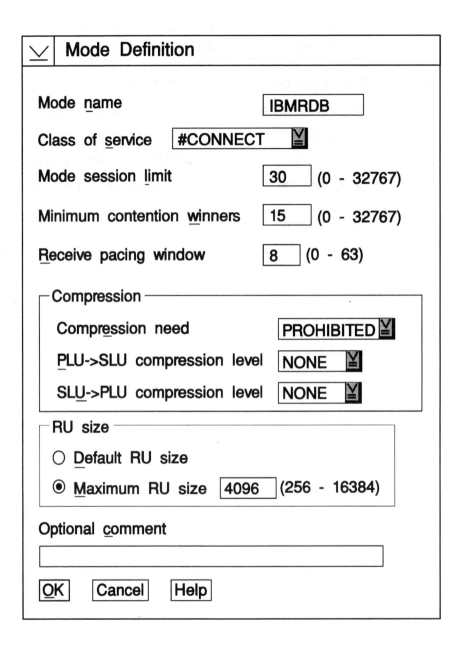

┌───┐
│ ∨ │ Mode Definition   │
├───┤
│   │
│ Mode name   IBMRDB   │
│   │
│ Class of service   #CONNECT   ▼   │
│   │
│ Mode session limit   30   (0 - 32767)   │
│   │
│ Minimum contention winners   15   (0 - 32767)   │
│   │
│ Receive pacing window   8   (0 - 63)   │
│   │
│ ┌─Compression───────────────────────────────────┐   │
│ │ Compression need   PROHIBITED ▼   │   │
│ │ PLU->SLU compression level   NONE   ▼   │   │
│ │ SLU->PLU compression level   NONE   ▼   │   │
│ └──┘ │
│ ┌─RU size───────────────────────────────────────┐   │
│ │ ○ Default RU size   │   │
│ │ ⦿ Maximum RU size   4096   (256 - 16384)   │   │
│ └──┘ │
│   │
│ Optional comment   │
│ ┌───┐ │
│ └───┘ │
│ [OK]   [Cancel]   [Help]   │
└───┘

APPC Security Considerations

Communications Manager for OS/2 should be configured appropriately to accept the type of APPC security requested by the DRDA AR. The APPC security type may be one of the following:

- PROGRAM
- SAME

The following section provides some guidance and examples of how to configure the SNA subsystem at the server to handle each of the security types requested by the DRDA AR. See your Communications Manager for OS/2 documentation for more detailed information on configuring APPC security.

Configuring for APPC Security Type PROGRAM

Do the following:

- Transaction Program Definition

  For the Transaction Program Definition that you are using, **check** the box for "Conversation security required". Communications Manager for OS/2 will check that the userid and password are valid.

  Note: You can configure Communications Manager for OS/2 to use UPM to check the userid and password, or you can have Communications Manager for OS/2 maintain the userids and passwords directly.

Configuring for APPC Security Type SAME

Do the following:

- Transaction Program Definition

  For the Transaction Program Definition that you are using, **check** the box for "Conversation security required".

- Partner LU Definition

  You must create a specific Partner LU Definition for the client partner LU. In the Partner LU Definition, **check** the box for "Conversation security verification".

Tip

If you create a Partner LU Definition, and **check** the box for "Conversation security verification", Communications Manager for OS/2 will actually accept both APPC security type SAME and APPC security type PROGRAM from remote clients.

Updating the Database Manager Configuration File for APPC

If the tpname used by the DRDA AR is something other than the default **X'07'6DB** then you must specify the *tpname* as the value for the **tpname** parameter in the database manager configuration file. *tpname* must be the same as the transaction program name that is configured in the transaction program profile that handles database connections from DRDA ARs.

For DB2 for OS/2 2.1.0, you must set the database manager configuration authentication to client. This setting will result in *NO* authentication at the database level. As a result, it is recommended that Communications Manager for OS/2 V1.1 be configured to use APPC security type **PROGRAM**. This restriction will be lifted with later releases of DB2 for OS/2, once Communications Manager V1.2 becomes available.

The configuration file may be updated using any one of the following:

- The Command Line Processor, documented in the *Command Reference* .

  For example:

  ```
  db2 update database manager configuration using tpname
  NYSERVER
  ```

  ```
  db2 update database manager configuration using authentication
  client
  ```

- The configuration API, documented in the *API Reference*
- The DB2 Database Director

Note

To make this change to the configuration file effective, you must stop and start the database manager.

Setting DB2COMM for APPC

You must set a value of `appc` in the **DB2COMM** environment variable to enable APPC support when a **db2start** command is issued.

Chapter 22. Configuring DB2 for AIX as a DRDA Application Server (DRDA AS)

This chapter describes how to configure DB2 for AIX as a DRDA Application Server.

APPC Support

DB2 provides APPC communication support through the SNA support option (db2_02_01.cs.sna). To use APPC, SNA Server for AIX must be installed and configured on the server workstation; the version should be 2.1.1, using PTF's U435033 and U435034, or higher.

Configuring SNA Server for AIX

The following section provides a working example of the SNA Server for AIX profiles, configured on a DB2 server, to support communications with DRDA Applications Requesters (DRDA ARs).

Notes:

1. The values provided are for the example only; you must substitute values that are appropriate for your operating environment.

2. Get the correct values from your network administrator.

All the configuration steps described below start from the Advanced SNA Configuration Screen.

Login as *root*, execute **smit**, and choose the screens in the following order to reach the Advanced SNA Configuration Screen:

- Communications Applications and Services

- SNA Server for AIX

- Configure SNA Profiles

- Advanced Configuration.

An asterisk (*) in the sample profiles marks the fields that should be updated from the default profiles.

It is a good practice to verify your configuration profiles as you create or change them. Use the **Verify Configuration Profiles** option after you add or change a profile.

Control Point Profile

The Control Point Profile identifies the control point (CP) on the local system. It is created automatically during SNA Server for AIX installation, but can be modified.

Choose the screens in the following order to update the Control Point Profile:

- Control Point

- Change/Show a Profile.

Use the following values:

```
XID node name          07127509
NETWORK name           SPIFNET
CONTROL POINT name     NYX1
CONTROL POINT alias    NYX1
CONTROL POINT type     appn_end_node
```

The resulting profile should look like:

```
               Change / Show Control Point Profile

 Profile name                                      node_cp
*XID node ID                                       [07127509]
*Network name                                      [SPIFNET]
*Control Point (CP) name                           [NYX1]
*Control Point alias                               [NYX1]
*Control Point type                                appn_end_node
 Maximum number of cached routing trees            [500]
 Maximum number of nodes in the TRS database       [500]
 Route addition resistance                         [128]

 Comments                                          []
```

Token Ring SNA DLC Profile

The SNA DLC Profile identifies the adapter device driver and adapter characteristics. The DLC Profile can be automatically created during Initial Node Setup, or can be added manually.

Choose the screens in the following order to update the Token Ring SNA DLC Profile:

- Links

- Token Ring

- Token Ring SNA DLC

- Add a Profile.

Use the following values:

```
Profile name                       tok0.00001
Data link device name              tok0
Dynamic link stations supported?   yes
```

The resulting profile should look like:

```
                 Add Token Ring SNA DLC Profile
 *Profile name                                        [tok0.00001]
 *Data link device name                               [tok0]
  Force disconnect time-out (1-600 seconds)           [120]
  User-defined maximum I-Field size?                  no
      If yes, Max. I-Field size (265-30729)           [30729]
  Max. num of active link stations (1-255)            [100]
      Number reserved for inbound activation          [0]
      Number reserved for outbound activation         [0]
  Transmit window count (1-127)                       [16]
  Dynamic window increment (1-127)                    [1]
  Retransmit count (1-30)                             [8]
  Receive window count (1-127)                        [8]
  Ring access priority                                0
  Inactivity time-out (1-120 seconds)                 [48]
  Response time-out (1-40, 500 msec intervals)        [4]
  Acknowledge time-out (1-40, 500 msec intervals)     [1]
  Local link name                                     []
  Local SAP address (04-ec)                           [04]
  Trace base listening link station?                  no
      If yes, Trace format                            long
 *Dynamic link stations supported?                    yes


  Link Recovery Parameters
      Retry interval (1-10000 seconds)                [60]
      Retry limit (0-500 attempts)                    [20]


  Dynamic Link Activation Parameters
      Solicit SSCP sessions?                          yes
      CP-CP sessions supported?                       yes
      Partner required to support CP-CP sessions?     no


  Dynamic Link TG COS Characteristics
      Effective capacity                              [4300800]
      Cost per connect time                           [0]
      Cost per byte                                   [0]
      Security                                        nonsecure
      Propagation delay                               lan
      User-defined 1                                  [128]
      User-defined 2                                  [128]
      User-defined 3                                  [128]

  Comments                                            []
```

LU 6.2 Transaction Program Name Profile

The LU 6.2 TPN Profile defines SNA and AIX characteristics associated with a target transaction program (TP) on the local node.

The default TP name used by DRDA ARs is **X'07'6DB** (EBCDIC X'07F6C4C2'). You will need to create an LU 6.2 TPN profile for this TP, along with profiles for any other non-default TPs used by your DRDA ARs.

With version 2 of DB2 for AIX, only one TP executable file is provided and configured in the TPN profiles: db2acntp; it is invoked for all APPC connections.

Choose the screens in the following order to update the LU 6.2 Transaction Program Name Profile:

- Sessions
- LU 6.2
- LU 6.2 Transaction Program Name (TPN)
- Add a Profile

Use the following values:

```
Profile names      drdadefault      drdanondefault
TPN                07F6C4C2         NYSERVER
TPN is in          yes              no
  hexadecimal?
Conversation       basic            basic
  type
Path               /db2acntp        /db2acntp
Multiple           yes              yes
  instances
User ID            1918             1918
```

Notes:

1. *NYSERVER* is an arbitrary name that may be replaced by a value that is appropriate for your environment; however, the other name **07F6C4C2** must be specified exactly.

2. The value for User ID (1918 in our example) is the numeric userid (uid) of the instance owner; you can find it with the AIX **id** command.

Default Transaction Program Name Profile

The following TPN profile is used to handle database connections from DRDA ARs, using the default DRDA TPN, **07F6C4C2**.

Add LU 6.2 TPN Profile

```
*Profile name                                          [drdadefault]
*Transaction program name (TPN)                        [07F6C4C2]
*Transaction program name (TPN) is in hexadecimal?     yes
 PIP data?                                             no
     If yes, Subfields (0-99)                          [0]
*Conversation type                                     basic
 Sync level                                           none/confirm
 Resource security level                              none
     If access, Resource Security Access List Prof.   []
*Full path to TP executable                            [INSTHOME/sqllib/bin/db2acntp]
*Multiple instances supported?                         yes
*User ID                                               [1918]
 Server synonym name                                  []
 Restart action                                       once
 Communication type                                   signals
     If IPC, Communication IPC queue key              [0]
 Standard input file/device                           [/dev/console]
 Standard output file/device                          [/dev/console]
 Standard error file/device                           [/dev/console]

 Comments                                             []
```

Non-Default Transaction Program Name Profile

The following TPN profile is used to handle database connections from DRDA ARs, using a non-default DRDA TPN; for example, **NYSERVER**.

```
          Add LU 6.2 TPN Profile

*Profile name                                  [drdanondefault]
*Transaction program name (TPN)                [NYSERVER]
*Transaction program name (TPN) is in hexadecimal?  no
 PIP data?                                      no
    If yes, Subfields (0-99)                    [0]
*Conversation type                              basic
 Sync level                                     none/confirm
 Resource security level                        none
    If access, Resource Security Access List Prof.  []
*Full path to TP executable                     [INSTHOME/sqllib/bin/db2acntp]
*Multiple instances supported?                  yes
*User ID                                        [1918]
 Server synonym name                            []
 Restart action                                 once
 Communication type                             signals
    If IPC, Communication IPC queue key         [0]
 Standard input file/device                     [/dev/console]
 Standard output file/device                    [/dev/console]
 Standard error file/device                     [/dev/console]

 Comments                                       []
```

LU 6.2 Mode Profile

The LU 6.2 Mode Profile is used to specify parameters that can be used to tune throughput, availability, and system resource requirements for sessions that are established between the local LU and partner LU. SNA Server for AIX includes a set of IBM-defined modes. You can choose to use one of these IBM-defined modes, or add a new mode that is appropriate for your application.

Choose the screens in the following order to update the LU 6.2 Mode Profile:

- Sessions

- LU 6.2

- LU 6.2 Mode

- Add a Profile.

Use the following values:

```
Profile name                           IBMRDB
   Mode name                              IBMRDB
   Maximum number of sessions               30
   Minimum contention winners               15
   Minimum contention losers                15
   Receive pacing window                     8
   Maximum RU size                        4096
   Minimum RU size                        1024
```

The resulting profile should look like:

```
                Add LU 6.2 Mode Profile
*Profile name                                      [IBMRDB]
*Mode name                                         [IBMRDB]
*Maximum number of sessions (1-5000)               [30]
*Minimum contention winners (0-5000)               [15]
*Minimum contention losers (0-5000)                [15]
 Auto activate limit (0-500)                       [0]
 Upper bound for adaptive receive pacing window    [16]
*Receive pacing window (0-63)                      [8]
*Maximum RU size (128,...,32768: multiples of 32)  [4096]
*Minimum RU size (128,...,32768: multiples of 32)  [1024]
 Class of Service (COS) name                       [
 Comments                                          []
```

SNA System Defaults Profile

Final Steps

There is an additional step required to set up the DRDA Application Server; you must add trusted group names in the SNA System Defaults profile.

First, determine the group name of INSTHOME/sqllib/adm/db2sysc for every instance; then use **smit** to update the relevant profile.

Choose the screens in the following order to update the SNA System Defaults Profile:

- SNA System Defaults
- Change/Show a Profile

Enter the db2sysc group name(s) in the Trusted Group Names field.

It is a good practice to verify your configuration profiles before you start SNA Server for AIX to activate your new configuration.

You can start and stop SNA Server for AIX using **SMIT**. Select the screens in the following order:

- Communications Applications and Services
- SNA Server for AIX
- Manage SNA Resources.

APPC Security Considerations

The SNA Server for AIX should be configured appropriately to accept the type of APPC security requested by the DRDA AR. The APPC security type may be one of the following:

- PROGRAM
- SAME

The following section provides some guidance and examples of how to configure the SNA subsystem at the server to handle each of the security types requested by the DRDA AR. See your SNA Server for AIX documentation for more detailed information on configuring APPC security.

Configuring for APPC Security Type PROGRAM

Do the following:

- LU 6.2 TPN Profile

  For the LU 6.2 TPN Profile that you are using, set the "Resource security level" to **conversation**. The system will check that the username and password are a valid AIX login username and password.

  Note: You can also set the "Resource security level" to **access**. If so, the system will check that the username and password are a valid AIX login username and password, and if a Resource Security Access List Profile is also specified in the LU 6.2 TPN Profile, the system will also check that the username is contained in the specified resource security access list.

- LU 6.2 Partner LU Profile

  If you have a specific LU 6.2 Partner LU Profile defined for the client partner LU; in that profile, set the "Conversation security level" to **conversation**.

  If you do not have a specific LU 6.2 Partner LU Profile defined for the client partner LU, and your system is set up to support dynamic inbound partner LU definitions (check the SNA Node Profile), your server uses the default LU 6.2 Partner LU

Profile PLUDEFAULT. In that profile, set the "Conversation security level" to **conversation**.

Configuring for APPC Security Type SAME
Do the following:

- LU 6.2 TPN Profile

  For the LU 6.2 TPN Profile that you are using, set the "Resource security level" to **conversation**.

  Note: You can also set the "Resource security level" to **access**. If so, the system will check that the username is a valid AIX login username, and if a Resource Security Access List Profile is also specified in the LU 6.2 TPN Profile, the system will also check that the username is contained in the specified resource security access list.

- LU 6.2 Partner LU Profile

  If you have a specific LU 6.2 Partner LU Profile defined for the client partner LU; in that profile, set the "Conversation security level" to **already_verified**.

  If you do not have a specific LU 6.2 Partner LU Profile defined for the client partner LU, and your system is set up to support dynamic inbound partner LU definitions (check the SNA Node Profile), your server uses the default LU 6.2 Partner LU Profile PLUDEFAULT. In that profile, set the "Conversation security level" to **already_verified**.

Tip

If you specify a "Conversation security level" of **already_verified** in the LU 6.2 Partner LU Profile, SNA Server for AIX will actually accept both APPC security type SAME and APPC security type PROGRAM from remote clients.

Updating the Database Manager Configuration File for APPC
If the tpname used by the DRDA AR is something other than the default **X'07'6DB** then you must specify the *tpname* as the value for the **tpname** parameter in the database manager configuration file. *tpname* must be the same as the transaction program name that is configured in the transaction program profile that handles database connections from DRDA AR.

The configuration file may be updated using any one of the following:

- The Command Line Processor, documented in the *Command Reference* .

  For example:

  ```
  db2 update database manager configuration using tpname NYSERVER
  ```

- The configuration API, documented in the *API Reference*
- The DB2 Database Director

> **Note**
>
> To make this change to the configuration file effective, you must stop and start the database manager.

Setting DB2COMM for APPC

You must set a value of `appc` in the **DB2COMM** environment variable to enable APPC support when a **db2start** command is issued.

Part 3. Network and DRDA Concepts

This part provides general information about communication and distributed relational database concepts. It is assumed that you already have a general understanding of relational database systems. The material in this part builds on relational database concepts and extends them into a distributed database environment.

This part contains:

Chapter 23. SNA Networking: Concepts and Terminology

This chapter describes some of the general concepts of SNA networking. These concepts are important if you are involved in the following activities associated with distributed database systems:

Installation

When you are involved in the installation of distributed database systems, you usually perform tasks associated with the database management system (DBMS), communication subsystem,[11] and operating system. This chapter describes:

- The terminology used to describe tasks associated with defining a distributed database system to the communication subsystem.

- Which publications describe the steps required to connect other products to the distributed database system.

- How to limit the impact a distributed database system can have on an existing SNA network.

- How a distributed database system fits into the rest of the network.

Distributed database system design

This chapter explains:

- The limitations associated with interconnecting distributed database systems in a network.
- The steps you can take to ensure the distributed database network is as reliable as possible.

Problem determination

When you encounter problems using a distributed database system, it is sometimes difficult to isolate database problems from network problems. A general understanding of SNA and distributed database communications helps the database system programmer and network system programmer work together to resolve problems. This chapter explains:

- Distributed database error message descriptions that deal with communication errors.

- How to describe network-oriented problems to communication specialists and IBM support personnel.

- How to read the communication trace information produced by distributed database products.

- How to read and understand the output from network traces and network management products, such as Netview.

---

11 The term communication subsystem is used in this book to generically describe the portion of the operating system responsible for SNA communication. On S/370* and S/390* systems, VTAM is the communication subsystem.

What Is SNA?

Systems network architecture (SNA) is a set of rules that products agree to follow when exchanging information in a network of computers. The role of SNA in a network system can be compared to traffic laws for automobile drivers. If all drivers do not obey the same laws, they cannot drive safely. For example, we must all agree which side of the road to drive on. If everybody drives on the right side of the road, traffic flows smoothly. If some drivers drive on the left side of the road, we have the potential for some very disruptive traffic.

SNA defines many aspects of computer networking. The basic network activities governed by SNA are:

Network activation and deactivation
SNA describes the process used to start or stop the network.

Classifying participants
The SNA network is made up of many diverse participants, for example: terminals, printers, controllers, computers, and programs. Each participant is classified as either a *logical unit* (LU) or a *physical unit* (PU). Logical units and physical units are further classified into *types*. LUs and PUs are discussed in more detail starting on page 377.

For each class of participant, SNA describes what capabilities the network provides and how the participant can interact with other network participants. These SNA-defined interactions allow unlike participants to communicate. For example, SNA allows a computer to send output to a printer.

Activating or deactivating participants
SNA describes how a participant can become an active part of the network, and how the participant can be removed from the network.

Changing the network
SNA describes how to change the network layout. This involves tasks such as adding a new computer to the network, or changing the information associated with existing participants in the network.

Network routing
SNA provides rules for passing information from its source to the final network destination. The network routing protocols in SNA allow multiple routes to be defined, allowing data to be rerouted to avoid network paths that are temporarily inoperative.

Data formatting
SNA defines the content of the messages sent between network participants. For the most part, SNA defines only the header and trailer information in messages. The remaining portion of each message is known only to the sending and receiving participants.

Transmission protocol definition
SNA describes how data messages are broken into packets for transmission. The transmission protocols allow network participants to regulate the rate at which data is transmitted among network participants. They also allow network

participants to break messages into smaller units of information so that
participants with limited capacity can transmit more easily.

Network interconnection protocol definition

Network interconnection protocols allow two SNA networks to interconnect to
pass data between SNA networks. This part of the architecture is referred to as
SNA network interconnection (SNI).

Network management

Network management services define processes to use for informing network
management *focal points* of the status of participants in the network. These focal
points allow the network to be monitored, controlled, and manipulated from a
single location in the network.

Advanced program-to-program communications (APPC)

APPC describes the set of functions to use when two or more network
applications want to exchange data. These functions are of particular interest
because they are used by distributed database products. APPC protocol is
described in greater detail in Chapter 24, "LU 6.2 and APPC: Concepts" on
page 399.

Network Layers

SNA is a layered architecture, where the responsibilities and functions associated with
each layer are clearly defined. There are seven layers in the architecture. Figure 154
shows the functional layers of the system that SNA governs, and how each function is
able to communicate with the function above and below. Each function is also able to
communicate with its peer function in the partner system.

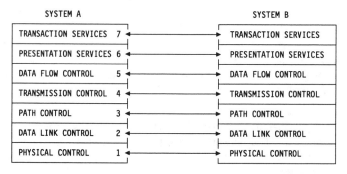

Figure 154. The Seven-Layer Model of SNA

The responsibilities of each layer in the architecture are as follows:

Transaction services

Transaction services provide an application service, such as distributed database
access or document interchange. The end user uses this service.

Presentation services

Presentation services format the data for different media and control the sharing
of devices. You can think of the presentation services as the logic necessary to
display the data on a given device.

Data flow control

Data flow control synchronizes the flow of data within the network, correlates exchanges of data, and groups related data into units.

Transmission control

Transmission control regulates the rate that data is exchanged to fit within the processing capacity of the participants. This layer is also responsible for encryption, when required.

Path control

Path control routes data between source and destination. It controls data traffic within the network.

Data link control

Data link control transmits data between adjacent network nodes.

Physical control

Physical control connects adjacent nodes physically and electrically. This is the hardware part of the connection.

Consider an application program that sends data to a locally attached terminal on an MVS system. The application program formats a screen to be sent. This activity is governed by the transaction services and presentation services layers of SNA. The screen is given to the communication subsystem (VTAM) to send to the terminal. In this case, VTAM handles data flow control, transmission control, path control, and some data link control. The operating system, MVS, controls the actual hardware connection to the terminal controller. Therefore, MVS is also involved in data link control. MVS is responsible for the physical control as well, because MVS owns the channel connected to the terminal controller. The controller then forwards the data to the terminal where it is displayed. In this case, the application is dependent on all seven layers in the SNA model to successfully send the data to the terminal.

To illustrate how the SNA layers communicate with their peer layers in the partner system, consider exchanging data between two applications on the same MVS system. When the first application program sends data to the second application, it uses the transaction services and presentation services layers. The data is passed to VTAM, which determines how to route the data to the second application. In this case, the second application is on the same MVS system, which requires only the data flow control, transmission control, and path control functions. Conceptually, the path control functions on each side of the connection are communicating with each other. There is no need for the data link control and physical control functions, because the connection does not involve any adjacent network nodes.

Elements of Traditional SNA Networking

SNA has been in use for many years. During that time, the nature of computer networks and network technology has changed substantially. To keep pace with this change, SNA has evolved.

In the early days of SNA, SNA networks were made up of mainframes and terminals. The mainframe had absolute control over the terminals, because they were relatively simple devices. As new hardware devices such as minicomputers and personal computers became available, they were added to the SNA network as terminal emulators. Consequently, the traditional SNA network did not view these new network participants as particularly intelligent devices.

However, as personal computers and minicomputers achieved larger memory sizes and faster processing rates, it became apparent that these computers had to be treated differently. This trend led SNA to move toward *peer-to-peer* networking, which resulted in major changes in the SNA architecture. These relatively recent developments are discussed in "Recent Additions to SNA" on page 390.

A traditional view of the SNA network is important to understand for two reasons:

1. Much of the SNA terminology was developed based on the traditional view of networking. It is sometimes difficult to understand why things are defined as they are without this historical perspective.

2. Many existing networks are actually implemented in the traditional SNA network mold, even though the network is filled with intelligent workstations. If your network is implemented in this traditional fashion, there may be constraints on the types of distributed database connections that can be made in your network. This can have implications on the design of your distributed database network, so you need to understand these constraints.

Figure 155 on page 375 gives an overall view of a traditional SNA network. The figure shows host computers connected to communication controllers, terminal controllers, and terminals. The terminal could be either a 3278 terminal or a personal computer emulating a terminal.

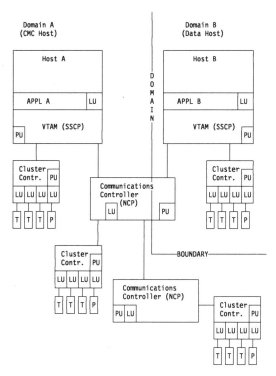

Figure 155. Network diagram showing two domains with system services control points, physical units, and logical units. Logical units connect terminals and printers to the system.

Host

In the traditional SNA network, the network is controlled by the host machine. The term *host* usually describes a mainframe (for example, a 3090*). The host owns all network application programs and is essential in routing data through the network.

Cluster Controller

The cluster controller controls a group of terminals and printers, allowing them to communicate with the host computer. The 3174 controller is an example of a cluster controller. The cluster controller contains the microcode and hardware necessary to control the activities of all the devices to which it is attached.

---
* Trademark of IBM Corporation

In the traditional SNA network, minicomputers commonly emulate a cluster controller. This allows the minicomputer to establish several network connections, but limits it to the operations supported by a cluster controller. For example, the minicomputer can log on to host network applications, but it cannot directly "own" any network applications. Because the minicomputer emulates a terminal controller, the network has no concept of "network applications" on the minicomputer.

Communications Controller

The communications controller is commonly referred to as an NCP, because NCP (Network Control Program) is the name of the IBM software product that runs on the communications controller. The 3705, 3725, and 3745 are all examples of communications controllers.

A communications controller is a special-purpose computer that can control the network connections for the S/370 or S/390 mainframe to which it is attached. It is more powerful than a cluster controller. In some configurations, a communications controller can control one or more cluster controllers.

Originally, the communications controller was almost entirely dependent on the host, which assisted in network operations. The communications controller primarily controlled groups of devices located at a relatively long distance from the host.

As time progressed, the communications controller gained a greater degree of independence from the host. The communications controller can now control network routing on its own. In fact, the communications controller usually continues to operate and route network traffic, even after the host to which it is attached becomes inoperative.

Terminal

This generic term describes a display monitor and keyboard. As stated earlier, personal computers often use software and hardware attachment cards that allow them to emulate terminals. This software can also allow the personal computer to transfer data files to and from the host. However, the host and the network still view the personal computer as a relatively simple device in this configuration. For example, a terminal cannot directly "log on" to a network application residing on a personal computer in the network. Instead, the terminal must first log on to a host application. The host application can then connect to the destination personal computer, with the host application acting as an intermediary for the two "terminals."

IMS/ESA is an example of a host application that can act as an intermediary for two or more terminals. When TERMINALX wants to send a message to TERMINALY, TERMINALX must send the message to IMS. IMS accepts the message and retransmits the message to TERMINALY.

Printer

The network allows output to be routed to a printer connected to a cluster controller.

You should now have a basic understanding of the world of traditional SNA. The following sections explain some of the terminology in more detail.

Virtual Telecommunications Access Method

VTAM is the software product used on mainframe systems to control SNA networks. The VTAM. product supports both VM and MVS operating systems. VTAM provides the system services control point function in the SNA network.

System Services Control Point

A *system services control point* (SSCP) is the portion of ACF/VTAM responsible for managing the resources in a particular section of the network. It performs tasks such as:

- Starting and stopping resources
- Assisting in establishing connections between the LUs
- Reacting to network problems (for example, failure of a cluster controller)

Each SSCP receives a unique name called an SSCPID. The SSCPID allows the SSCPs to identify each other.

Logical Units

A *logical unit (LU)* is a user of the SNA network. It is the source of requests entering the network. It can be:

- An I/O device (a terminal user logged onto an application in the host, such as TSO).

- An output device (a printer).

- An application running in the host (such as IMS/ESA, CICS/ESA, TSO, DB2 for MVS/ESA, VM AVS).

- An application running in the NCP (such as X25NPSI or NPA).

- An application running in a personal computer or minicomputer. Often, a personal computer or minicomputer can be configured to represent several LUs in the network depending on the number of applications running concurrently in the machine.

- A representation of an instance of a distributed relational database management system.

Each of the LUs in the network has a name known as the *LU name*. This name is unique within a single SNA network, allowing SNA to route requests to any given LU within a network. SNA allows connections between SNA networks, which can create a naming problem, because LU names are unique only within a single SNA network.

To identify an LU among several SNA networks, SNA adds a second qualifier to the LU name. When the second qualifier is present, SNA calls the name a *fully qualified* LU name, which takes the form NETID.LUNAME. The first qualifier (NETID) names the SNA network where the LU can be found. The second qualifier identifies the LU within that network.

LU names and fully qualified LU names are used by SNA to route requests between database systems in the network.

LUs are classified by type, according to the kind of network communication that can be accepted or produced by the LU. The following are examples of LU types:

LU Type 0 (LU 0)

This type is reserved for "undefined." "Undefined" means SNA specified a set of communication protocols, but has not associated them with any particular hardware device. LU 0 commonly connects bank teller machines and minicomputers to SNA networks.

LU Type 2 (LU 2)

This type is reserved for terminals. For example, a 3278 terminal is an LU 2 device. A personal computer, with the appropriate software and hardware attachment, can emulate an LU 2 device.

LU Type 6.2 (LU 6.2)

This type is reserved for program-to-program communication. Distributed database systems use this LU type. LU 6.2 is also called *advanced program-to-program communication* (APPC).

Physical Units

A *physical unit* (PU) is not necessarily a physical device. It is the portion of a device (programming, circuitry, or both) that performs control functions for the device. The PU is responsible for controlling one or more LUs. It takes action during:

- Device activation and deactivation
- Error recovery
- Testing

SNA classifies participants in the SNA network into the following types:

- PU type 5 (PU 5)—A host running ACF/VTAM (for example, an ES/3090[*], ES/4381[*], or ES/9370[*]).

- PU 4—A communications controller (for example, a 3745, 3720, or 3725), loaded with a Network Control Program.

- PU 2.0—A cluster controller (for example, a 3174, S/36, S/38, or 8100). This is also referred to as a *peripheral node*. In the traditional SNA network, a personal computer appears as one or more LUs connected to a PU 2.0 device.

  The LUs at a PU 2.0 device are called *dependent LUs* because they depend on the SSCP to establish SNA sessions.

- PU 2.1—A peripheral node capable of connecting directly to other PU 2.1 devices, without assistance from the host. Many network participants are capable of supporting PU 2.1 connections, including S/38, Communications Manager/2 1.1, AS/400, and mainframes. In cases where a communications or cluster controller is

---

[*] Trademark of IBM Corporation

used to connect network participants, PU 2.1 must be supported by the controller as well. If the controller does not support PU 2.1, PU 2.0 must be used, even though the network participants support PU 2.1.

PU 2.1 support is especially useful for LU 6.2 implementations because it provides the most complete support for a true peer-to-peer network connection. PU 2.1 support is described in more detail on page 392.

The LUs at a PU 2.1 device are called *independent LUs* because they can establish sessions without assistance from the SSCP.

It is important to know the PU type of your distributed database system (PU 2.0 or PU 2.1) because the PU type determines the following:

- What products you can connect to your distributed database system
- How many connections you can support
- How many distributed database applications you can support concurrently

Network Control Program

Network control programs route data and control its flow between the communication controller and other network resources. The Advanced Communications Function/Network Control Program (ACF/NCP) is installed on the host and used with *System Services Program* (ACF/SSP) to generate a network control program (NCP) load module. The load module is loaded from the host into a communications controller. IBM Corporation has four communications controllers in general use: 3745, 3720, 3725, and 3705. The NCP controls the lines and devices to which it is attached. It transfers data to and from the devices and handles any errors that occur, including retries after line errors.

A communications controller can be locally attached to a host via a channel, or it can be link-attached to another communications controller that is channel attached. The second case is called a *remote NCP*, as shown in Figure 156.

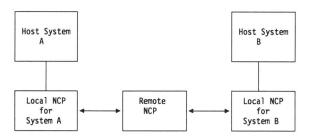

Figure 156. NCP Configurations

Network Addressable Unit

The term *network addressable unit* (NAU) is used to describe any element in the network that can be addressed by other network participants. LUs, PUs, and SSCPs are network elements that are examples of NAUs.

Nodes

The term *node* is used in the two different contexts of SNA and VTAM.

In SNA terms, a node is a physical device. It can be:

- A host processor
- A communication controller
- A cluster controller
- A terminal or printer
- A minicomputer
- An intelligent workstation or personal computer

These nodes vary in capabilities and are divided into the following groups:

Host node
The host node provides an application interface to allow an application access to the SNA network. VTAM acts as a host node.

Boundary node
The boundary node function is supplied by the software in VTAM and NCP. The boundary function allows the connection of the peripheral nodes into the SNA network. It involves converting the headers, added to data sent through the SNA network, into a format acceptable to the devices. It also carries out any pacing required. (Pacing is discussed on page 387.) Both VTAM and NCP can act as boundary nodes.

Peripheral node
A peripheral node provides local control for devices (LUs). Minicomputers, personal computers, and intelligent workstations are examples of peripheral nodes. PU 2.0 peripheral nodes are dependent on the boundary function support in another device in the SNA network. For example, a cluster controller is a PU 2.0 peripheral node. It provides local control for the attached terminals. The boundary function is supplied by VTAM if the controller is locally attached to the host, or by NCP if the controller is physically attached to the communications controller. Without VTAM or NCP, the cluster controller cannot communicate.

PU 2.1 peripheral nodes are less dependent on the boundary nodes in the SNA network, because they are able to directly communicate with other PU 2.1 nodes.

In VTAM terms, a node is any point in a network defined by a symbolic name. These nodes are divided into two groups:

Major nodes
A major node is a set of resources that can be activated or deactivated as a group. The resources are usually grouped by some common function. For example, an application major node can contain multiple CICS/ESA definitions, one for each CICS/ESA region. The major node name is actually a member in the VTAMLST data set, identifying a group of VTAM resource definitions.

Minor nodes

A minor node is a resource that was defined to VTAM within a major node. For example, each CICS/ESA region within the application major node is a minor node.

Subarea Addressing

A *subarea* is a portion of the network that contains a boundary node and any peripheral nodes attached to the boundary node. A host subarea also includes any applications already defined.

Subarea nodes are SSCPs and NCPs.

The resources (for example, PUs and LUs) attached to the subarea node are called *elements* within that subarea. Each element in the subarea is assigned an *element address*.

The element address is important to understand when looking at SNA buffer traces, because the participant is not specified by name, but by address. A network address takes the form: X'00000000 0000'. The first 4 bytes make up the subarea, and the last 2 bytes are the element address in that subarea. For example, an address of X'0000000B 001A' would be element number 26 (X'1A' = decimal 26) in subarea 11 (X'B' = decimal 11).

Domain

A *domain* is the part of a network activated by a particular SSCP. There is only one SSCP to a domain. An NCP residing in a communications controller (for example, 3745 and 3725) can be activated by multiple SSCPs; therefore, it can be in *multiple domains*. The resources on the NCP (the LUs associated with a cluster controller—terminals on a 3174) can be activated by only one SSCP. The domain in which the resource resides depends on the SSCP that activates it.

Often, in a large site, the network is "owned" by one SSCP. This SSCP is referred to as the *Communication Management Configuration* (CMC) host. The other hosts (called *data hosts*) own network applications such as TSO and CICS/ESA. The data hosts can also own resources that are channel attached, such as a local 3174 (PU) with its attached terminals (LUs).

Cross Domain Resource

A *Cross Domain Resource* (CDRSC) is the definition in VTAM of a resource that resides outside this VTAM's domain. For example, a CDRSC is used to define a remote DB2 for MVS/ESA or DB2 for VM and VSE system to VTAM. The CDRSC can be explicitly defined to VTAM, or it can be dynamically created by VTAM when a session to the remote resource is required.

Cross Domain Resource Manager

A *Cross Domain Resource Manager* (CDRM) is a definition in VTAM of the SSCPs in your network. The VTAM system programmer must create a CDRM definition for each remote VTAM system in the network for requests to be exchanged with database systems and users at those remote systems. A CDRM must also be created for the local VTAM system.

SNA Communication Concepts

After you understand the various elements in the SNA network, you are ready to learn the terminology and concepts that deal with communication between network elements.

Sessions

SNA is a connection-oriented architecture. When two network participants (NAUs) need to exchange data, the participants must be logically connected before data can be transmitted. SNA uses the term *session* to describe this logical connection. Depending on the types of NAUs involved in the session, the session fits into one of these categories:

SSCP-to-PU session

This session is established when the SSCP activates the PU. The session must be running before LUs managed by the PU can be activated.

SSCP-to-LU session (for dependent LUs only)

This session is established when the SSCP activates the LU. The session must be running before sessions from this LU can be established with other LUs.

LU-to-LU session

This session is established when two LUs indicate that they would like a session. An LU-to-LU session is used to allow distributed database systems to exchange data.

SSCP-to-SSCP session

This session is set up between two VTAMs (SSCPs) to allow communication between the two hosts. The session must be established before any LU-to-LU sessions between the SSCPs can be created.

The LU-to-LU sessions can be within the same domain where both LUs are "owned" by the same SSCP (both LUs have an SSCP-to-LU session with the same SSCP), or they can be cross-domain, where each LU is "owned" by a different SSCP (each LU has an SSCP-to-LU session with a different SSCP). For example, a cross-domain session allows a distributed database system on one host to communicate with a distributed database system on another host.

When the LU-to-LU session is established, the SSCP-to-LU session for each of the LUs is   still maintained. Therefore, the LU has, in effect, two sessions: one with the SSCP and the other with the LU.

Figure 157 on page 383 shows two VTAM systems connected with an SSCP-to-SSCP session and two LU-to-LU sessions.

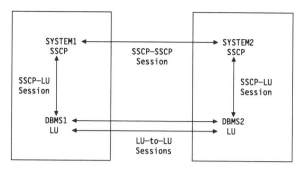

Figure 157. SNA Session Types

PLU and SLU

In an LU-to-LU session, one LU acts as the *primary LU* (PLU) and the other acts as the *secondary LU* (SLU). Both the PLU and the SLU are able to initiate an SNA session, so the LU requesting the session is not necessarily the PLU. Rather than dictating which LU starts the session, the roles of PLU and SLU have more to do with the relationship between the PLU and SLU. For example, a 3278 terminal would act as an SLU when logging onto TSO (the PLU) on the mainframe.

As stated earlier, PUs and LUs are classified by *type*. The PU type describes what capabilities are available to a network participant, especially with regard to the PLU and SLU session roles. A PU 2.1 device can be either a PLU or an SLU, while a PU 2.0 device is always an SLU. Because all non-host machines were PU 2.0 devices in the traditional SNA network, the PLU was always the host machine. This makes clear one of the most fundamental restrictions in a traditional SNA network: a PU 2.0 device (a personal computer or minicomputer) cannot establish a network session with another PU 2.0 device, because a session must have both a PLU and an SLU. Therefore, a distributed database on a PU 2.0 personal computer or minicomputer cannot be accessed by other PU 2.0 personal computers and minicomputers in your network.

This restriction in SNA can be removed, providing you use hardware and software that can support the more recent SNA network configurations (for example, PU 2.1 support). These changes are described in "PU Type 2.1" on page 392.

Before LU 6.2, the PLU controlled the session in a primary/secondary relationship with the SLU. With the introduction of LU 6.2, the relationship between PLU and SLU is less strict. Although there must still be a PLU and an SLU for each LU-to-LU session, the LUs on the session are considered peers where both LUs have very similar capabilities. The distinction between PLU and SLU is further reduced by the PU 2.1 SNA support, which allows an LU to establish multiple sessions with a single partner. Often, an LU is the PLU on some of these sessions and the SLU on the remaining sessions. Thus, in many cases, a given LU is both a PLU and an SLU.

Data Transmission

When you work with distributed database systems, you need to have a basic understanding of the SNA data transmission process. Some instances where this knowledge can be valuable follow:

- When distributed database systems can send a substantial amount of data through the network. Some network software and hardware devices have limitations on the data transmission parameters they accept. Knowledge of the SNA data transmission process is required when defining distributed database connections to ensure your distributed database system does not exceed these transmission limits.

- When you are diagnosing a distributed database problem and need to look at SNA buffer traces. An understanding of the data transmission process is very useful when looking at these traces.

The SNA data transmission process allows an SNA participant (for example, a distributed database system) to transmit an arbitrary amount of data regardless of the transmission capabilities of the devices in the network. If the data being transmitted exceeds the capacity of the devices, SNA breaks the data into smaller units and reassembles it into its original format when it arrives at its final destination.

The network participants sending a message need not be aware of the details of the data transmission process. This is especially true for distributed database systems, because LU 6.2 applications are isolated from the data transmission process. As long as you define your SNA session parameters correctly, a distributed database system can send or receive an unlimited amount of data without exceeding the capacity of devices in the network.

Figure 158 on page 385 shows the data transmission process in SNA. The individual steps in the process and the terms associated with data transmission are described following the figure.

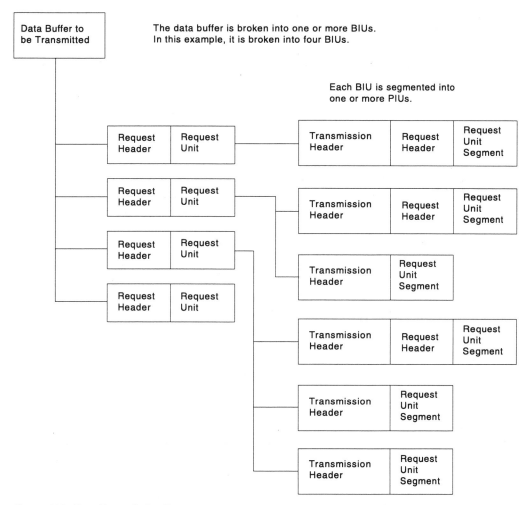

Figure 158. Data Transmission Process

The transmission process involves two basic steps:

The data buffer is broken into *basic information units* (BIUS). Each BIU consists of a *request header* (RH) and a *request unit* (RU). Because the BIU contains an RU, the maximum size of a BIU is dictated by the maximum RU size, which is negotiated when each SNA session is established.

The RH is a 3-byte header that contains the following important information for APPC systems:

- The RU that follows contains user data or SNA data.
- The RU that follows is a request or a response.
- A response is required for this RU.
- The partner requests a reply message at this time.

In the diagram, the RUs contain user-defined data. However, all RUs do not necessarily contain user data. Some RUs contain SNA information, such as the RUs used to initiate SNA sessions.

Some hardware and software products place limits on the size of SNA RUs sent and received. The RU size is limited by the adapter card; for example, Communications Manager for OS/2 V1.1 cannot accept RUs greater than 1920 bytes, when the data is transmitted using a 4Mb token-ring LAN card.

Each BIU can be broken into segments. This occurs when the network hardware or software cannot accept data packets of the size required to handle a complete BIU. For example, the NCP breaks messages into smaller segments when the terminal controller cannot accept a message of the size received by the NCP.

A network *transmission header* (TH) is added to each BIU segment to form a *path information unit* (PIU). The TH portion of each PIU contains the network addressable unit (NAU) addresses for both session partners, allowing the SNA network to route each PIU to the correct destination.

Some hardware and software products do not accept segmented data. For example, Communications Manager for OS/2 V1.1 does not accept segmented data for LU 6.2 applications. For data to be accepted by these products, the RU size specified for the session must be small enough to eliminate the need for segmenting.

SNA Buffer Trace

Essentially, an SNA buffer trace is just a formatted report showing the PIUs observed when the SNA session was being traced. When you read an SNA buffer trace, some of the fields you probably want to examine in each PIU are:

- The origin NAU address in the TH. This describes which network participant sent the PIU. Because the NAU address identifies a particular SSCP, PU, or LU in the network, most SNA buffer trace formatters print the SSCP, PU, or LU name of the origin NAU in the formatted trace output.

- The destination NAU address in the TH. This describes where the PIU is being sent. Most SNA buffer trace formatters also print the SSCP, PU, or LU name associated with the destination NAU in the trace output.

- The RH in each PIU. This contains flags that describe:

  - The type of data contained in the RU portion of this PIU (SNA data or user-defined data).

  - What type of message is being sent: a request or a response.

  - What the partner is expected to do after receiving this message: send a response, send a reply, or continue receiving messages.

- The RU portion of the PIU. This contains the data being sent (either SNA data or user-defined data).

For example, the BIND RU is an SNA message used during SNA session initiation to describe the attributes of the session to be started. If you are trying to diagnose errors during SNA session initiation, you probably want to scan the PIUs in the SNA buffer trace to find the BIND request RU and the BIND response RU.

Pacing

In most of today's network applications, a relatively small amount of data is exchanged in each data transmission operation. Because the data volume is small, it is unlikely that these applications send more data than the network partner can process.

In a distributed database system, the amount of data transmitted in the network can be substantially larger than other network applications. The large data volumes can lead to problems, especially if the sending application is producing data faster than the receiving application can process the data. When this occurs, the network is forced to hold any excess data temporarily. When the amount of data being temporarily stored is very large, it can have an adverse effect on the entire network, because the network buffers used to store the data are shared by all network applications.

When you install a distributed database system, you are probably asked to define pacing parameters. Failure to define pacing properly in a distributed database system can cause severe network problems.

The principle behind SNA pacing is very simple. Pacing allows the receiving application to control the rate at which the sending application transmits data. This is accomplished by defining a *pacing window*, which specifies the maximum number of PIUs that can be transmitted by the sender before the sender must wait for the receiver to process the data. In this way, the receiver can force the sender to transmit a limited amount of data and can thereby consume a fixed amount of the network buffer area.

After the receiver has processed the data, the communication subsystem at the receiver's system automatically notifies the sender, allowing it to resume transmission. This notification is called a *pacing response*. By pacing, the sender can transmit a virtually unlimited amount of data without consuming an excessive proportion of the network buffer area.

Figure 159 on page 388 describes how the communication subsystems at each network node restrict the amount of data being transmitted in the network at any given time. In the figure, a pacing window size of 2 is used to regulate the rate at which data is transmitted from Application 1 to Application 2.

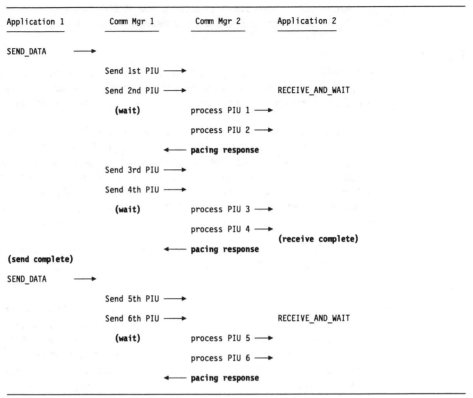

```
    Application 1         Comm Mgr 1         Comm Mgr 2         Application 2
    _____           _____         _____         _____

    SEND_DATA ───────►

                          Send 1st PIU ───►

                          Send 2nd PIU ───►                      RECEIVE_AND_WAIT

                             (wait)         process PIU 1 ───►

                                            process PIU 2 ───►

                                        ◄─── pacing response

                          Send 3rd PIU ───►

                          Send 4th PIU ───►

                             (wait)         process PIU 3 ───►

                                            process PIU 4 ───►
                                                               (receive complete)
                                        ◄─── pacing response

    (send complete)

    SEND_DATA ───────►

                          Send 5th PIU ───►

                          Send 6th PIU ───►                      RECEIVE_AND_WAIT

                             (wait)         process PIU 5 ───►

                                            process PIU 6 ───►

                                        ◄─── pacing response
```

Figure 159. SNA Session Pacing

Some network products are able to support *adaptive pacing*, which allows the network to control pacing dynamically. When using adaptive pacing, the communication subsystem automatically reduces the pacing count when buffer space is constrained. Conversely, the pacing count can be increased when the buffer space is underutilized.

There are two forms of pacing: *session pacing* and *virtual route pacing*. Up until this point, the discussion has focused on session pacing. Virtual route pacing is maintained by the subarea nodes (SSCPs and NCPs). It is used for monitoring and controlling flow through the network. When congestion occurs in any particular part of the network (for example, an NCP buffer shortage), those virtual routes affected are "blocked," so no traffic flows. All sessions on that virtual route are affected. When the congestion clears, the virtual route is unblocked, so traffic can flow again.

Bind

The term *bind* can be confusing if you are familiar with relational database systems, because it is the term used to describe the process of interpreting SQL statements passed from an SQL application program.

In networking terms, *bind* is an SNA request unit that flows from the primary LU (the bind sender) to the secondary LU (the bind receiver). The bind is the first request unit to flow on the LU-to-LU session at session startup. It is via the bind (and bind negotiation) that the two LUs agree on what protocols to use in the session.

The outcome of the bind negotiation determines the:

- Session protocols (LU type is one of these parameters)
- Pacing window size
- Maximum RU size

Some of the information contained in the bind comes from the parameters associated with the mode name for the session.

Mode Name

When establishing an LU-to-LU session, the communication subsystem uses an eight-character string called a *mode name* to identify what SNA session parameters to use. A given pair of LUs may establish sessions using several mode names.

The characteristics taken from the mode name are used to build the bind request that flows between the two LUs. The characteristics associated with the mode name include:

- Pacing
- RU sizes
- Protocols
- Class of service (COS) can also be included depending on the communication product being used

Explicit Route

An *explicit route* (ER) is a physical path through the network between two subareas. It consists of lines (between two NCPs), a channel link (between a host and an NCP), or a channel-to-channel adapter link (between two hosts). Multiple ERs can be defined between two subareas.

Virtual Route

A *virtual route* (VR) is a logical connection within a subarea or between two subareas that need not be adjacent. The VR is mapped along a series of ERs. Up to 16 VRs can be defined between any two subareas. The actual path of the route can vary depending on which ERs are used. Each ER can be mapped to multiple VRs.

Class of Service

Class of service (COS) defines the level of service the session receives and the route over which the session is established.

The level of service is determined by the transmission priority associated with the COS entry. The transmission priority (often called TP) ranges from 0, the lowest priority session traffic, to 2, the highest priority session traffic. Sessions for interactive users generally have a higher priority (and therefore a different COS) than an application doing large file transfers. Transmission priority only affects sessions between two different subareas.

To any particular subarea, there can be multiple paths through the network. The COS entry specifies, in selection sequence, a list of virtual routes over which the session can be established. At session initiation time, the first available VR in the list is selected and used until the session is terminated.

Recent Additions to SNA

As stated earlier, the rapid increase in personal computer and minicomputer memory sizes and CPU rates caused SNA to re-examine how these computers were used within the network. The distinctions between host, minicomputer, and personal computer became vague in many respects. The outcome of these changes is a new influence in SNA called *peer-to-peer* communications. Essentially, this trend is leading to a network where all participants have relatively equal responsibilities. Figure 160 shows a peer-to-peer network.

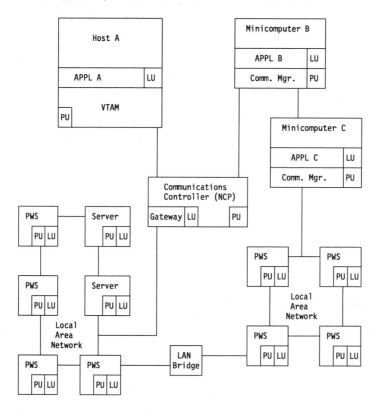

Figure 160. Peer-to-Peer SNA Network

There are a number of differences between the SNA network shown in Figure 160 and the traditional SNA network shown earlier in Figure 155 on page 375:

- The host, minicomputer, and the programmable work station (PWS) are all relatively equal elements.

- Every device in the diagram has both an LU and a PU.

- Any LU can establish a session with any other LU.

- Every device can support a network application program. These network applications are called *servers* because they provide a service to other computers in the network. (A host can also be a server.)

- A LAN bridge can be used to interconnect networks without routing the network traffic through an NCP or a host system.

Local Area Networks

The *local area network* (LAN) is perhaps the most striking change in the SNA network. With the advent of the LAN, computers connected to the LAN are provided an extremely high-speed communication medium. The LAN can be used for a wide variety of tasks. It can:

- Interconnect personal computers, workstations, or minicomputers
- Provide access to special computers that are designated as servers
- Connect to a mainframe in the traditional SNA manner

In most cases, the LAN does not depend on a central mainframe for routing or connection services. Instead, each computer connected to the LAN shares the responsibility for network routing.

When required, individual computers on the LAN can be designated as *gateways*, providing connectivity to other networks. The connection to the traditional SNA host (mainframe) is accomplished through a gateway on the LAN. In some cases, the gateway is simply a personal computer with an adapter card attachment to the host. In other cases, the gateway is actually a communications controller or cluster controller (for example, a 3745 or 3174), which has a special attachment card allowing it to accept data from the LAN.

Each data packet flowing on the LAN has header information identifying the *LAN address* of its intended destination. This LAN address allows the stations on the LAN to route the data packet correctly. For data you want to direct to the mainframe, the LAN address identifies the address of the gateway connecting the LAN to the mainframe.

Computers connected to the LAN can relate to SNA in one of three ways:

PU Type 2.0
> The PU type 2.0 method of connection was described in "Elements of Traditional SNA Networking" on page 373. When defined as a PU 2.0, the computer on the LAN has relatively limited capabilities.

PU Type 2.1
> The PU type 2.1 provides the greatest degree of peer-to-peer function. See "PU Type 2.1" on page 392 for more information.

Server connection
> It is not always necessary to define every computer on the LAN in the SNA network. LANs also provide communication methods outside of the SNA communication techniques. Both SNA and non-SNA communication packets can

be routed within a single LAN. Thus, it is possible to use non-SNA communication techniques from one LAN station to access another LAN station (a server), which in turn can provide any required SNA connectivity (for example, connectivity to the mainframe). There are several reasons to use this approach. For example, the installation may need to minimize the number of LAN stations with direct host SNA connectivity (possibly for security reasons), or allow the LAN server to cache information frequently requested by stations on the LAN.

There are many LAN products on the market today: IBM PC Network, IBM Token-Ring Network, Token-Bus (MAP 3.0), and Ethernet, to name a few. Not all LAN products are currently able to connect to SNA networks using LU 6.2 communication protocols. For example, Communications Manager/2 1.1 limits LU 6.2 communication to the following LAN products:

IBM Token-Ring Network
IBM PC Network
ETHERAND
LANDP

PU Type 2.1

A PU type 2.1 (PU 2.1) is a peripheral node capable of connecting directly to other PU 2.1 devices with or without assistance from a host. In the traditional SNA context, this means that a "terminal" can log on to another "terminal." More importantly, this means a personal computer or minicomputer can establish a session with other personal computers and minicomputers in the SNA network, even when the session is routed through a VTAM network spanning great distances. This allows the PU 2.1 computer to "own" a network application, and, through this ownership, to provide services to hosts and other PU 2.1 devices.

A PU 2.1 device can also establish multiple sessions with a given partner. This capability increases the amount of data that can be sent through the network simultaneously. It also allows the PU 2.1 device to logically separate data traffic in a way the network partner can easily understand, allowing multiple network applications to be supported concurrently.

A personal computer or minicomputer with PU 2.1 capabilities has the potential to support distributed database access by other SNA participants, including multiple concurrent distributed database applications. This was not possible when the personal computer or minicomputer was configured as a PU 2.0 network participant, because two PU 2.0 devices cannot establish an LU-to-LU session. A PU 2.0 device can only be useful in a distributed database environment, when the session partner is a PU 2.1 device. For example, you can connect a large number of existing PU 2.0 devices to a PU 2.1 device that manages a distributed database. Table 69 on page 393 shows the differences between PU 2.0 and PU 2.1 systems.

Table 69. Comparison of PU 2.0 and PU 2.1

PU 2.0 Systems	PU 2.1 Systems
Can be an SLU	Can be an SLU or a PLU
One partner per LU	Multiple partners per LU
One session per partner LU	Multiple sessions per partner LU
Session partner must be PU 2.1 or PU 5	Session partners can be PU 2.0 or PU 2.1
A single active LU 6.2 application per LU	Multiple active LU 6.2 applications per LU

PU 2.0 devices are limited to a single session and a single partner for each LU on the PU 2.0 device. This can be confusing if you are familiar with a system such as Communications Manager/2 1.1, which can be configured as a PU 2.0 system that provides 26 SNA sessions for terminal emulation with S/370 and AS/400 systems. The 26 sessions can be non-coaxial or you may have 5 coaxial sessions with the rest being non-coaxial. See *Communications Manager/2 1.1 Host Connection Reference* for more information. Thus, the system can communicate with multiple partner LUs without implementing PU 2.1.

Some products can be configured as either PU 2.0 or PU 2.1. When a product can support both PU 2.0 and PU 2.1, you are usually asked to pick the desired support. The type of hardware in your network influences your answer to this question. For example, your software can be running on a machine that is limited to PU 2.0, or your machine can be connected to a network control unit restricted to PU 2.0.

Gateway

A *gateway* is used to connect one network to another network. For example, the computer that allows one SNA network to interconnect with another SNA network is called a gateway. Similarly, the computer or controller that allows a LAN (such as token ring) to connect to a mainframe SNA network is also called a gateway.

In general, a gateway provides a mechanism for translating a network address from one network into the corresponding address used in another network. For example, consider the 3174 control unit, which has a gateway feature allowing token-ring LANs to connect to VTAM. When the system programmer configures the 3174, the system programmer defines a series of LAN addresses and their corresponding VTAM addresses. When a work station on the LAN routes a request to the 3174, the microcode in the 3174 uses the requesting work station's LAN address to determine which VTAM address should be presented to VTAM. In this way, the 3174 gateway provides address translation between the token-ring LAN and VTAM. Communications Manager for OS/2 V1.1 is another example of a product that can be configured as an SNA gateway. The Communications Manager for OS/2 V1.1 gateway can accept data from one adapter card (for example, an ETHERAND card) and transmit the data again on another adapter card (for example, a token-ring card). By moving data from one adapter card to another, the Communications Manager for OS/2 V1.1 gateway can be used to route LU 6.2 communications between devices connected using token ring, ETHERAND, PC Network, X25, or SDLC.

LAN Bridge

A *LAN bridge* is used to connect two LANs. For example, a bridge can be used to connect token-ring LANs in two buildings, allowing the LAN stations in the two buildings to communicate as if they are all connected on a single LAN.

Conceptually, a bridge is similar to a gateway. However, bridges and gateways perform protocol conversions at different functions in the SNA architecture. Bridges convert data exchanged at SNA function layer 2 (data link control). Gateways convert data exchanged at SNA function layer 5 or higher (data flow control, presentation services, or transaction services).

Server

As shown in Figure 160 on page 390, a *server* can be a computer on a LAN that provides a service to other computers on the LAN. The computers on the LAN that make use of the service are called *requesters*. The process used by the requester and server is called the *requester/server model*.

LAN servers can provide a wide variety of services:

Sharing files
The most common use of a server is to share files between multiple computers. The server typically controls which LAN stations can update the files and which LAN stations can read the files.

Supporting databases
A LAN server can also support a centralized database, which can be shared with many computers on the LAN.

Access to hardware devices
In cases where a particular hardware device is expensive, bulky, or rarely used, a LAN server can be a convenient way of making the device accessible to many LAN users. For example, a high-speed laser printer or tape drive might be placed on a LAN server.

Running applications
A server can also be used to run a particular application program. The owner of the application can maintain a single copy of the application (because it resides only on the LAN server), while still allowing each LAN user to run the program.

APPN

Advanced peer-to-peer networking (APPN) is a networking technology that makes use of the SNA LU 6.2 and PU 2.1 support. It was originally implemented in the S/3x and AS/400 product lines and is currently available on Communications Manager for OS/2 V1.1.

Important distinctions between APPN and APPC are:

- APPC defines protocols for communicating between network applications, regardless of how network routing is performed.

- APPN defines how the network routing between applications is controlled. Thus, an APPC application can use an APPN network to route data, or it can use a traditional SNA network to route data.

APPN greatly simplifies the tasks associated with defining the network, because APPN network participants are able to dynamically determine network routing information. Thus, the system programmer does not have to "tell" APPN how to route data to a particular destination. APPN dynamically makes that determination. This makes it much easier to change the network configuration or add nodes to the network. Figure 161 shows several APPN network nodes.

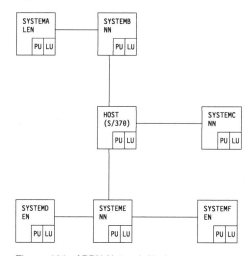

Figure 161. APPN Network Nodes

APPN uses the following terminology for describing the capabilities of computers in the APPN network:

Adjacent Node
An adjacent node is a node directly connected to another node in the APPN network. For example, SYSTEMA and HOST are adjacent nodes to SYSTEMB in Figure 161.

Control Point
An APPN node may contain a control point (CP). The control point performs route selection and directory searches for the APPN network. The directory in each control point allows the APPN network to dynamically build a map of the APPN network topology. The control point is similar to the SSCP in a traditional SNA network.

Control Point Name
A control point name is the unique name given to each APPN node, whether or not the node actually has a control point. In Figure 161, SYSTEMA, SYSTEMB, SYSTEMC, SYSTEMD, SYSTEME, SYSTEMF, and HOST are control point names. The control point name is similar to the SSCPID in the traditional SNA network. When a request is sent to an LU, the APPN directory is searched to determine

which control point name manages the LU. The control point name is used to route the request through the APPN network.

Control Point Session

A control point session is established between two adjacent control points in an APPN network. The control point session is used to exchange information about network links and nodes. For example, the control point session is used to inform adjacent control points when a new network link is activated. The CP-to-CP session is similar to the SSCP-to-SSCP session in a traditional SNA network.

Network Node

A network node (NN) is an APPN node that provides network services to other APPN nodes. The control point in each NN contains a directory that describes the LUs available in the APPN network. Some or all of the directory entries can be defined permanently in the directory so that they are automatically known each time the NN is activated. For example, the NN directory contains the names of all the LUs that run locally on the NN.

Names can also be added dynamically to the directory based on information exchanged between the APPN nodes via the CP-to-CP sessions.

When an NN is contacted to establish a session with a particular LU, the NN performs the following steps:

1. Search the directory on the local NN for the desired LU name.

2. If the LU name matches a known NN control point name, the NN establishes a session with the indicated NN control point.

3. If the LU name matches a directory entry that is not an NN control point name, the NN sends a directed search request to the NN control point identified in the directory to determine which control point owns the requested LU name. The answer to this directed search request is used to establish the requested session.

4. If the LU name is not found in the directory, the NN broadcasts a search request to all adjacent NNs. Each of these NNs searches their directory for the desired LU name until one of the NNs finds a match. The NN that finds the match sends the control point name found in its directory, allowing the local NN to complete the session initiation request.

OS/2 workstations using Communications Manager for OS/2 V1.1 and DB2 for OS/400 systems can connect as network nodes.

Network Node Server

When an APPN node requests network services from an NN, the NN is called a network node server (NNS), to indicate the NN is acting as a network server for the requesting APPN node. In this scenario, the server simply locates other nodes in the network on behalf of the requesting APPN node.

End Node

An end node (EN) is an APPN network node that does not provide any network services to other APPN nodes. In other words, the EN cannot perform network routing on behalf of other APPN nodes. The EN can only participate in the APPN network by using the network services of at least one network node to which it is attached. It can be directly attached to several network nodes.

An EN may or may not include a control point. If the EN does include a control point, the control point is not used to route network requests on behalf of other APPN nodes. The control point can only be used to connect to the NN to register its LU names in the NN's directory and to request sessions. For example, if SYSTEMD in the APPN network diagram (Figure 161 on page 395) contains a control point, SYSTEMD uses its control point to register all its local LU names with SYSTEME (the NN). This allows SYSTEME to route incoming session requests for these network applications to SYSTEMD. OS/2 workstations using Communications Manager and AS/400 systems can connect as end nodes.

Low Entry Node

A low entry node (LEN) is a PU 2.1 node that can support LU 6.2 sessions, but does not have the APPN extensions (for example, the dynamic routing capabilities). An LEN cannot route requests on behalf of other APPN nodes, so it must be at the "ends" of the APPN network. SYSTEMA in the APPN network diagram is an LEN.

An LEN must have all its destination LU names registered in its local communication directory, because the LEN system cannot make use of the dynamic routing capabilities provided by the NN to which it is connected. The AS/400 can connect as an LEN.

Domain

In APPN, a domain consists of a network node and the adjacent nodes controlled directly by the NN (ENs and LENs). For example, SYSTEMD, SYSTEME, and SYSTEMF form one domain in Figure 161 on page 395, because SYSTEMD and SYSTEMF are ENs controlled by SYSTEME.

S/370

Figure 161 on page 395 shows that an S/370 system running VTAM 3.2 (or later releases of VTAM) can participate in an APPN network. VTAM 3.2 allows the S/370 to act as an LEN in the APPN network. Thus, VTAM 3.2 does not support the dynamic routing capabilities of APPN. When an APPN network node routes a request to VTAM, the network applications accessible through the VTAM network appear to be LENs, regardless of their true capabilities.

Figure 161 shows a system named HOST, which is an S/370 machine. SYSTEMC can route requests to all the other APPN network nodes in the diagram by routing sessions through VTAM on the host machine. This allows applications and users on SYSTEMC to connect to other APPN applications.

Because the NN on SYSTEMC has no direct connection to another APPN NN, it has no dynamic routing capabilities at all. This forces SYSTEMC to define all the APPN control point names and LU names in its local directory, because all the other APPN nodes appear as LEN nodes to SYSTEMC. Similarly, SYSTEME views SYSTEMC as an LEN node, because SYSTEME must also route through VTAM to get to SYSTEMC.

Chapter 24. LU 6.2 and APPC: Concepts

Chapter 23, "SNA Networking: Concepts and Terminology," gave you a basic description of the SNA network and the terms used in networking. This chapter describes concepts of advanced program-to-program communications (APPC) and specifically LU 6.2.

LU 6.2

LU 6.2 is an architecture for communication between functionally equivalent LUs (peer-to-peer systems). LU 6.2 is also known as *advanced program-to-program communications (APPC)*. The emphasis on program-to-program communications makes LU 6.2 a natural choice for distributed database systems. LU 6.2 provides a consistent method for:

- Identifying the communication capabilities supported by each application
- Providing the name of the application to be run at the remote site
- Supplying end user security parameters associated with the remote program execution
- Uniquely identifying each instance of a remote program execution
- Reporting and detecting communication errors
- Synchronizing the processing between the applications involved in the communication activity
- Performing coordinated commit processing

Figure 162 shows an LU 6.2 connection between two applications. In general, LU 6.2 is not limited to two applications. The model is able to support applications with multiple partners, and these partners might in turn have partner applications of their own.

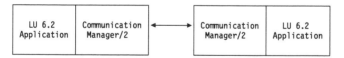

Figure 162. LU 6.2 Communication Model

Transaction Programs

When an APPC application establishes a connection to another LU in the network, it must identify the name of the *transaction program (TPN)* it wants to execute. The *transaction program name (TPN)* is up to 64 characters long, identifying the program in the target LU that receives the message.

The two basic types of TPNs are:

1. *User transaction programs* are application programs that use APPC.

2. *Service transaction programs* provide a service to other application programs. Distributed database support comes in the form of a service transaction program, whose default TPN is X'07F6C4C2'.

Logical Unit Protocol Boundary

For a program to communicate using LU 6.2, the program must have an interface allowing it to route LU 6.2 commands to the communication subsystem. This interface, called the *LU Protocol Boundary* (LU-PB), is shown in Figure 163.

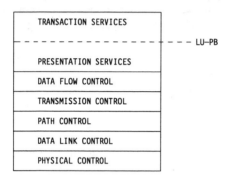

Figure 163. The Seven-Layer Model of SNA Showing the LU Protocol Boundary

The *LU-PB* is a formalized programming interface between the transaction program and the LU. It allows the development of applications that are independent of the underlying communications layers.

LU 6.2 Conversation

An *LU 6.2 conversation* is a logical connection between two transaction programs. It is defined by the beginning and end of a dialog between the two transaction programs (the dialog between the APPC ALLOCATE and APPC DEALLOCATE verbs). When an APPC application issues the ALLOCATE verb, the local LU associates the conversation with an SNA session with the mode name specified on the ALLOCATE verb. If a session already exists, the local LU simply uses it. If a session does not already exist, the local LU attempts to initialize a new session. The transaction program is concerned only with the conversation; it is not involved with the protocols on the session. Figure 164 on page 401 shows one session being used serially by multiple conversations.

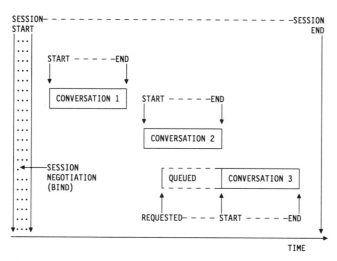

Figure 164. One Session Used for Three Separate Conversations

Sessions tend to last for long periods of time, while conversations tend to last for shorter periods. When a conversation ends, the session it was bound to is available for another conversation.

Sessions are serially reusable by conversations. Multiple conversations can use the same session, though not at the same time. When a conversation is requested and no SNA sessions are available, the conversation is forced to wait for a session to become available. If conversations spend an excessive amount of time waiting for sessions, you might need to increase the session limits so that more sessions are available to process conversations.

A session is required for distributed database access. The number of sessions between two distributed database systems limits the number of SQL applications that can be active between the two distributed database systems at any given time. For example, consider a distributed database system with five sessions available. If each distributed database application requires one session, the system can support up to five applications concurrently. If a sixth application begins execution, the communication subsystem forces the SQL application to wait until one of the other five applications releases an SNA session.

APPC Verbs

The LU protocol boundary is represented to the APPC application as a set of *APPC verbs*. Each of these verbs is mapped to a particular LU 6.2 message sequence. After the resulting LU 6.2 messages are transmitted to the partner, the partner LU maps the content of the messages to APPC return codes, indicators, and messages. This process allows the remote APPC application to correctly interpret the APPC verbs issued by the local APPC application.

The APPC verbs are:

ALLOCATE

Creates a new APPC connection (called a conversation) with another APPC application in the network. The ALLOCATE verb provides the partner LU name, the mode name, the name of the program to be executed in the partner system (TPN), and any security information required to run the program.

DEALLOCATE

Terminates an APPC conversation. The DEALLOCATE verb has options that allow the APPC application to classify the DEALLOCATE action as either *normal* or *abnormal.* The abnormal indication is used to inform the partner LU that the conversation cannot be processed correctly.

SEND_DATA

Transmits data to the partner LU when the buffer is full. The amount of data sent with the SEND_DATA verb is not restricted to the RU size of the underlying SNA session. The communication subsystem is responsible for breaking the data message into RUs before transmitting them to the partner LU.

At the remote site, the communication subsystem reassembles the message before presenting it to the APPC partner application. This allows both APPC applications to be entirely unaware of the RU size and pacing counts chosen by your communications administrator.

PREPARE_TO_RECEIVE

Informs the partner application that you are done transmitting data and are now waiting for the partner to transmit a reply message.

RECEIVE_AND_WAIT

Receives a message from the partner application. The RECEIVE_AND_WAIT verb returns a number of indicators that tell the APPC application:

- The message is complete, or more data coming
- Your partner wants a reply message
- Your partner terminated the APPC conversation after sending the message

SEND_ERROR

Informs the partner that your application has detected an error. This verb places the application in send mode, so that you can use the SEND_DATA verb to send a message describing the error.

CONFIRM

Asks the partner to acknowledge (via the CONFIRMED verb) that the data transmitted to this point was received.

CONFIRMED

The partner uses this verb to respond positively to a CONFIRM verb.

REQUEST_TO_SEND

Informs the partner that your application would like permission to send a reply message.

FLUSH

Forces data sent by the SEND_DATA verb to be transmitted immediately, rather than waiting for the communication subsystem data buffer to be filled.

SYNCPT

Tells the partner application that you want to commit the changes performed to this point (similar to the SQL COMMIT). This verb is part of the *two-phase commit* support in LU 6.2. See "Two-Phase Commit" on page 417 for more information.

BACKOUT

Tells the partner application that you want to perform abort processing for work performed to this point, which is equivalent to an SQL ROLLBACK. This verb is part of the *two-phase commit* support in LU 6.2. See "Two-Phase Commit" on page 417 for more information.

Using APPC Verbs

Figure 165 shows how two programs might use the APPC verbs to implement a telephone directory application.

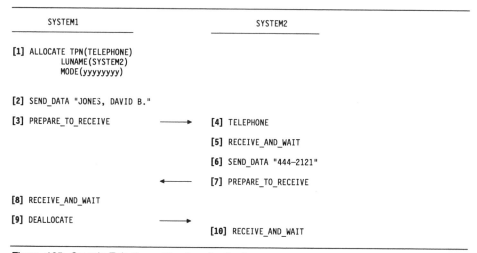

Figure 165. Sample Telephone Directory Application

The sequence of events shown in Figure 165 is as follows:

[1] The application on SYSTEM1 issues the ALLOCATE verb to establish a conversation with the telephone directory application on SYSTEM2. The TPN option on the ALLOCATE verb tells SYSTEM2 which transaction program is to be scheduled. The LUNAME option tells the communication subsystem that the TELEPHONE application resides on SYSTEM2. The MODE option provides the mode name to be used for the conversation.

[2] The application on SYSTEM1 sends the name to be found by the telephone application.

[3] The PREPARE_TO_RECEIVE verb informs the partner application that the message is complete and indicates the SYSTEM1 application is waiting for the answer message.

The PREPARE_TO_RECEIVE verb is optional for LU 6.2 applications. If an LU 6.2 application does not use it, the RECEIVE_AND_WAIT verb transmits the data in the send buffer before waiting for the reply message.

[4] SYSTEM2 receives the request and invokes the TELEPHONE application.

[5] The TELEPHONE program issues a RECEIVE_AND_WAIT verb to receive the name to be found in the directory. It uses the data obtained from RECEIVE_AND_WAIT to search the database for JONES, DAVID B.

[6] The answer message is returned to SYSTEM1 containing the requested phone number.

[7] The TELEPHONE program prepares to receive the next request.

[8] The SYSTEM1 application obtains the desired phone number and is informed that the TELEPHONE program is awaiting a new request.

[9] The SYSTEM1 application terminates the APPC conversation, because no further phone numbers are required.

[10] The TELEPHONE application is notified that the APPC conversation was terminated normally.

SNA Bracket Indicators

APPC sets flags, called the *SNA bracket indicators*, in the SNA request header (RH). Table 70 shows how the bracket indicators are set by SNA to describe the state of an APPC conversation. The partner LU examines the SNA bracket indicators to properly set the completion information returned with the APPC RECEIVE_AND_WAIT verb. It is through this completion information that the partner application is able to determine when the conversation state shifts from send mode to receive mode.

Table 70. Bracket Indicators Set by SNA

Abbrev.	Full Name	APPC Verb	Description
BB	Begin Bracket	ALLOCATE	Marks the beginning of a new APPC conversation.
CD	Change Direction	PREPARE_TO_RECEIVE	Marks the transition from send mode to receive mode. When the partner receives a message marked with CD, the partner is expected to send a reply message or deallocate the APPC conversation.
CEB	Conditional End Bracket	DEALLOCATE	Marks the end of an APPC conversation.

SNA traces and network management products (such as Netview) use bracket indicators to describe the activity on SNA sessions. By understanding the bracket indicators, you can determine what was happening on an APPC conversation at any given time. This is helpful when you're trying to isolate the cause of distributed database network problems. It can be especially important when you're trying to determine which system is the cause of a hung application.

In Figure 166, the SNA bracket indicators are set to control the APPC conversation, using the telephone directory example.

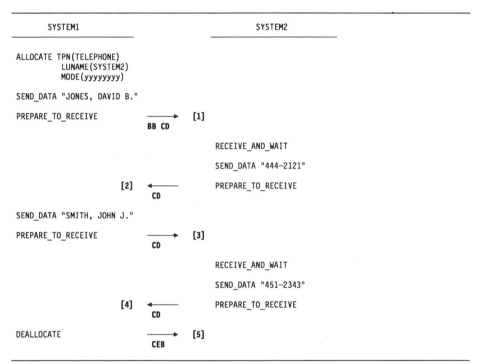

Figure 166. Bracket Indicators with the Telephone Directory Application

The sequence of events shown in Figure 166 is as follows:

[1] The application on SYSTEM1 issues the ALLOCATE and SEND_DATA verbs to establish a conversation with the TELEPHONE application on SYSTEM2. The bracket indicators on the message are BB and CD, indicating a new conversation was initiated and a reply message is expected. After SYSTEM1 sends a message with CD flagged, SYSTEM1 must wait for the reply message before issuing any further SEND_DATA verbs.

In a real distributed database example, the messages can be larger than those shown in the example above. If the first message is too large to fit in a single RU, the communication subsystem breaks the message into multiple RUS. When multiple RUs are transmitted, the first RU is marked with the BB indicator. The last RU is marked with the CD indicator.

[2] The application on SYSTEM2 builds the reply message and prepares to receive another request. In this case, the bracket indicator is CD, which tells SYSTEM1 that

the reply message is complete and that SYSTEM2 is ready for another request on the conversation.

If the reply message requires multiple RUS, only the last RU is marked with the CD indicator.

[3] SYSTEM1 sends another request to SYSTEM2. Only the CD flag is set, because the conversation started in step 1 is still being used.

[4] SYSTEM2 sends the reply message and prepares for another request message. The bracket indicator is CD.

[5] SYSTEM1 terminates the APPC conversation, causing the bracket indicator to be set to CEB. When SYSTEM2 receives this message, the CEB indicator tells SYSTEM2 that the conversation is terminated.

Contention

Contention occurs when two partner LUs want to issue an APPC ALLOCATE verb at the same time on the same SNA session. Contention does not occur after the APPC conversation is established, because APPC does not allow both partners to send data simultaneously. Instead, the APPC protocol forces the partners to take turns sending data. This is referred to as *half duplex protocol* in SNA.

To resolve contention situations, LU 6.2 provides a flag in the bind request unit. During bind negotiation, the PLU and SLU use this flag to agree on which LU is the *contention winner* and which LU is the *contention loser*. When a contention situation is encountered, the contention winner automatically prevails and allocates its conversation. The contention loser must yield control to the contention winner, awaiting permission to allocate a conversation.

For the most part, the contention process is hidden from APPC applications because contention is controlled by the communication subsystem.

Function Management Header

Each SNA RU being transmitted can have an SNA *function management header* (FMH) preceding the user data in the RU. If you are doing problem diagnosis or looking at SNA buffer traces, you should be familiar with these headers.

In LU 6.2, two FMHs of particular importance are:

FMH5

Is called the *attach* header, because it identifies a transaction program to be "attached." When an APPC application issues the ALLOCATE verb, an FMH5 is built by the LU and sent to the partner LU. The FMH5 describes:

- Which transaction program to execute
- The security authentication information for the transaction program
- The logical unit-of-work identifier for the conversation

FMH7

Denotes that an error was detected on the LU 6.2 conversation. The FMH7 contains an SNA *sense data field*, which describes the nature of the error.

LUWID

When a distributed database application issues the APPC ALLOCATE verb, a *logical unit-of-work identifier* (LUWID) is built and sent in the FMH5 header. The LUWID is a string containing the requester's NETID.LUNAME and a unique instance number, which is used by both LU 6.2 partners to identify the LU 6.2 conversation. Distributed database systems often use LUWID values in system commands, system messages, and diagnostic trace records.

LU 6.2 Session

The *LU 6.2 session* is an LU-to-LU session created between two application programs. This is a connection that allows a dialog between the two LUs. In LU 6.2, the applications can have multiple sessions with a given partner LU using a variety of mode names. Multiple sessions between two partner LUs are called *parallel sessions*. As stated earlier, only PU 2.1 devices can support parallel sessions (see "PU Type 2.1" on page 392).

Change Number Of Sessions

Change number of sessions (CNOS) is a special APPC control operator verb. CNOS provides a mechanism allowing both partner LUs to be informed when the number of sessions associated with a given mode name changes. CNOS is used to notify both partners when:

The number of sessions is initially set
Session limits are raised
Session limits are lowered
The number of sessions is set to zero

When CNOS is issued, the action taken depends on the types of PUs involved in the connection:

PU 2.0

A PU 2.0 device is a *single session* device. It cannot support parallel sessions. Thus, the session limits are not negotiable. When CNOS is issued for a PU 2.0 device, the limits are either raised to one or lowered to zero.

If the limit is raised to one, a session is established with the partner using the mode name specified on the CNOS verb. After this session is established, no other session can be established between these partners, because PU 2.0 supports only one session.

If the limit is lowered to zero, the session between the partners is terminated.

PU 2.1

A PU 2.1 device can support parallel sessions. When CNOS is issued for a PU 2.1 device, the following steps are taken:

1. The LU issuing the CNOS verb issues an ALLOCATE verb for a special *CNOS service transaction program*. The mode name used with the CNOS service transaction is SNASVCMG, a reserved mode name in SNA. The SNASVCMG mode supports two sessions at the most, one of which is dedicated to each LU. This allows each LU to issue CNOS service transactions without concern for contention situations. If CNOS is issued in only one direction, only one session is started. If the partner issues CNOS, a second session is started.

   A message sent to the CNOS service transaction program at the partner LU contains the mode name whose limits you want to change and the requested session limit parameters. These session limit parameters contain:

   The minimum number of contention winner sessions
   The minimum number of contention loser sessions
   The maximum number of sessions (both winner and loser sessions)

2. When the CNOS service transaction at the partner LU receives the CNOS request, it returns a reply message containing negotiated session limits. This allows the partner to lower the limits in cases where the initial CNOS limits are unacceptable to the partner.

3. The CNOS reply message is returned to the LU that issued the CNOS verb. This allows both LUs to keep track of the final number of sessions negotiated.

4. Both LUs are now able to establish sessions using the specified mode name.

Figure 167 shows the SNA sessions established after two DB2 for MVS/ESA systems issue CNOS commands for the following mode names:

IBMRDB (2 sessions)
MODE2 (3 sessions)
MODE3 (1 session)

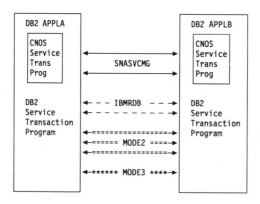

Figure 167. Two DB2 for MVS/ESA Applications with Multiple Sessions and Multiple Mode Names

LU 6.2 Security

In a distributed database environment, security is a critical issue. Networks provide the capability of allowing computers all over the world to access a given database. A poorly protected network provides an opportunity for critical database systems to be penetrated by unauthorized computers in the network.

LU 6.2 provides three major security mechanisms:

Session-level security

Session-level security (also known as *partner LU verification*) allows the communication subsystem to authenticate the partner LU. Session-level security aims at eliminating the opportunity for an unauthorized computer to "masquerade" as one of the known computers in the network. Figure 168 shows how session-level security works.

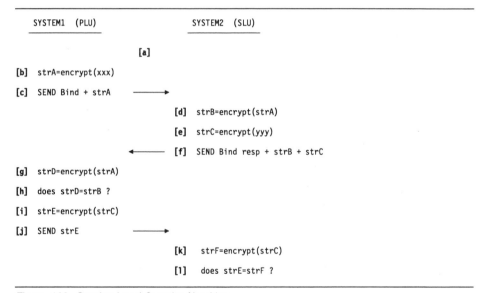

Figure 168. Session Level Security Algorithm

The steps taken to authenticate the partner LU are as follows:

[a] Each authorized LU in the network is given a security encryption key by the network security administrator. Conceptually, this encryption key is similar to a password. At no time is the encryption key transmitted through the network. Thus, if you carefully restrict access to this encryption key, an unauthorized computer cannot obtain the encryption key, even if it is somehow able to monitor your network transmissions.

[b] When the PLU wants to start a session, it creates a random string of data. This random data is encrypted using the encryption key to produce an encoded string (strA).

[c] The encoded data (strA) is added to the bind request and sent to the partner LU (the SLU).

[d] Upon receiving the encoded data, the SLU uses its copy of the encryption key to re-encode the string, producing strB.

[e] The SLU creates a new encoded string, strC, from random data.

[f] The SLU sends strB and strC back to the PLU in the bind response.

[g] The PLU encrypts strA a second time to produce strD.

[h] If the SLU has the correct encryption key, the encoded data sent by the SLU (strB) should match the string (strD) produced by the PLU.

If the strings do not match, you can assume the partner LU does not have the correct encryption key, and therefore is not authorized to make the connection. The session is therefore rejected by the PLU.

If the two strings match, the PLU can safely assume the SLU is authorized to make the network connection.

[i] The PLU must now encrypt the random string chosen by the SLU (strC), which produces yet another encoded string (strE).

[j] The PLU sends the encoded string (strE) to the SLU.

[k] The SLU also encrypts strC to produce strF.

[l] The SLU can now compare strE and strF. If the values match, the SLU can be sure the PLU is also authorized to establish the LU 6.2 session.

If the values do not match, the SLU rejects the session.

The LU 6.2 session-level security algorithm is very rigorous. The algorithm provides several important safeguards:

- Encryption keys are never transmitted over the network.

- Because the algorithm uses random data, a successful exchange between two LUs cannot be "replayed" to gain entry to the system.

- The algorithm allows both LUs to validate the identity of their respective partner, regardless of which LU requests the SNA session.

Session-level security is an optional feature in LU 6.2, so an installation is not necessarily required to use this level of security validation.

Conversation-level security

Conversation-level security authenticates the end user issuing the APPC request. The three supported levels of conversation security are:

1. SECURITY=NONE is used when no security information is transmitted. Distributed relational database architecture does not support SECURITY=NONE.

2. SECURITY=PGM indicates the application program is sending a user ID and password to the partner LU. The partner LU then validates this information

using the local security subsystem. For example, the user ID and password are passed to the RACF product on MVS systems.

3. SECURITY=SAME provides the partner LU with only the user ID. This is also called *already-verified* security because the originating LU is asking the partner LU to accept the user ID at face value without any means of validating the remote user's identity.

   For SECURITY=SAME to be accepted by the partner LU, the partner LU must agree that the originating LU is *trusted*. In other words, the partner LU must agree that the originating LU operates in a secure environment and can be trusted to enforce security operations on its behalf. Session-level security can be used to ensure that the originating LU is properly authenticated.

The security level used on a conversation is specified on the APPC ALLOCATE verb by the application requesting the conversation. If the partner application does not agree with the conversation security level, the user ID, or the password, the partner can reject the conversation with a SECURITY NOT VALID SNA sense code (X'080F6051').

Distributed database systems support only SECURITY_PGM and SECURITY=SAME.

Encryption

The data flowing on LU 6.2 sessions can be encoded so the data being transmitted can only be deciphered by the partner system.

Chapter 25. Distributed Relational Database Architecture

Distributed Relational Database Architecture (DRDA) is the architecture that meets the needs of application programs requiring access to distributed *relational data*. This access requires *connectivity* to and among relational database managers operating in *like* or *unlike* operating environments. Structured Query Language (SQL) is the language that application programs use to access distributed relational data. DRDA is the architecture that provides the needed connectivity. This chapter describes concepts of distributed relational database systems.

DRDA Structure and Associated Architectures

DRDA uses the following IBM architectures:

- Logical unit type 6.2 (LU 6.2)
- Distributed data management (DDM)
- SNA management services architecture (MSA)
- Formatted data object content architecture (FD:OCA)
- Character data representation architecture (CDRA)

DRDA uses LU 6.2, DDM, MSA, FD:OCA, and CDRA as architectural building blocks. The specific form of each of the blocks is specified to ensure that system programmers implement the blocks in the same way for the same situations so all programmers can understand the exchanges. DRDA ties these pieces together into a data stream protocol that supports this distributed cooperation.

DRDA and SQL

SQL is the database management system language. It provides the necessary consistency to enable distributed data processing across like or unlike operating environments. It allows users to define, retrieve, and manipulate data across environments. SQL provides access to distributed relational data among connected systems that can be at different locations.

DRDA supports SQL as the standardized application programming interface for running applications and defines *flows* (logical connections between the application and a database management system) that the program preparation process can use to bind SQL statements for a target relational database management system (DBMS).

An application uses SQL to access a relational database. When the requested data is remote, the distributed database software receiving the application SQL request must determine where the data resides and establish connectivity with the remote relational database system. One method used to make this determination is via the SQL CONNECT statement. The CONNECT statement allows the application program to explicitly identify the name of the relational database system it wants to use. The term that DRDA uses to represent the name of the relational database (RDB) is RDB_NAME. RDB_NAME is a 1- to 18-character name that identifies a database.

Also, SQL includes RDB_NAME as the high-order qualifier of relational database objects managed by the relational database system. For example, an SQL. table named SAN_JOSE.JONES.TABLE5 is managed by the database management system whose RDB_NAME is SAN_JOSE.

For more information on using SQL in a distributed environment, see *Distributed Relational Database Application Programming Guide*.

DRDA Connection Architecture

Connectivity, in support of remote database management system processing, requires a connection architecture to define specific flows and interactions to convey the intent and results of remote database management system processing requests. DRDA provides the necessary connection between an application and a relational database management system in a distributed environment.

DRDA uses appropriate IBM architectures and extensions to these architectures to describe what information flows between participants in a distributed relational database environment.[12] DRDA also describes the responsibilities of these participants and specifies when the flows should occur. DRDA provides the formats and *protocols* required for distributed database management system processing, but DRDA does not provide the application programming interface for distributed database management system processing.

Types of Distribution

There are three types of distribution of database management system function. Each type of distribution has different DRDA requirements. The types of distribution are:

Remote unit of work
Distributed unit of work
Distributed request

Table 71 summarizes the main characteristics of each type of distribution.

Table 71. Types of Distribution of Database Function

Distribution Type	Requests per unit of work	DBMS per unit of work	DBMS per Request	Coordination of Commit
Remote unit of work	Many	One	One	Application controls
Distributed unit of work	Many	Many	One	Synchronization Point Manager controls
Distributed request	Many	Many	Many	Synchronization Point Manager controls

---

12 The terms distributed database and distributed relational database have the same meaning in this manual and are used interchangeably. The term database always means relational database in this manual.

The following sections briefly describe the types of distribution of database management system function. For examples of these types of distribution, see *Every Manager's Guide*.

Remote Unit of Work

Remote unit of work is the first level of DRDA and is described here.

With remote unit of work, an application program executing in one system can access data at a remote database management system using the SQL provided by that remote DBMS. This access can be achieved through the use of a local DBMS, or it can be achieved through software that is able to simply redirect the SQL statements to a remote DBMS. The DRDA architecture does not require a local DBMS at the requesting system for remote unit of work processing.

Remote unit of work does not support two-phase commit. The application is responsible for coordination of updates to local resources (for example, files) and updates to remote database resources. For more information about two-phase commit, see "Two-Phase Commit" on page 417.

If there is a DBMS at the system where the application is executing, data stored in that DBMS is also accessible by applications executing on other remote systems. Remote unit of work supports access to one DBMS within a unit of work.

Within a unit of work, the application can perform multiple SQL statements on distributed data.

Distributed Unit of Work

Distributed unit of work is the second level of DRDA.

With distributed unit of work, an application program executing in one system can access data at multiple remote database management systems using SQL provided by remote DBMSs. This access is achieved using a local DBMS or through software that is able to simply redirect the SQL statements to a remote DBMS. DRDA does not require a local DBMS at the requesting system for distributed unit of work processing. Distributed unit of work supports two-phase commit. The application is responsible for initiating commit, and the synchronization point manager, with the DRDA defined software, coordinates commit across all DBMSs involved in the unit of work. The application may or may not need to coordinate the DBMS resources with the non-DBMS resources (such as files) depending on the synchronization point manager support on all the systems involved in the unit of work and on the software support of the non-DBMS resources involved.

Although distributed unit of work allows access to multiple sites, the objects that are referenced by any single SQL statement must still be at a single DBMS.

Distributed Request

The distributed request level of distribution is a conceptual direction that is currently not fully described in DRDA.

Distributed request removes all data location restrictions. Within a single SQL statement, relational data from many locations can be combined to produce the desired result. Whatever is possible with local data is possible in a fully distributed environment. The distributed database management system looks like one large DBMS.

Distributed request offers the greatest flexibility in terms of distributed data access, as well as offering the fewest application constraints. Each SQL statement can access several distinct objects stored at multiple locations.

DRDA Protocols and Functions

DRDA connects an application process with the application server of a DBMS. In the remote unit of work level of DRDA, the application process is connected with only one application server for the duration of a logical unit of work. In the distributed unit of work level of DRDA, the application process may be connected to multiple application servers for the duration of a logical unit of work.

The DBMS systems that the application process connects to can be *like* systems (two DB2 for MVS/ESA systems, for example), *unlike* systems (a combination of DB2 for MVS/ESA and DB2 for VM and VSE systems, for example), or even a mix of IBM and non-IBM products. As long as all the systems support DRDA, cooperation between DBMSs to provide database services is possible.

DRDA currently provides one connection protocol and two types of functions. The distributed request level of DRDA conceptually introduces one more connection protocol and one more type of function.

The one DRDA connection protocol is *Application Support Protocol*. Application support protocol provides connection between *application requesters* and *application servers*. It allows the application requester and application server to perform remote unit of work transactions.

The application requester supports the application end of the DRDA connection by making requests to the application server, while the application server supports the DBMS end by answering these requests.

The two types of DRDA functions are:

Application Requester Functions
Application requester functions support SQL and program preparation services from applications.

Application Server Functions
Application server functions route requests to database servers and support requests from application requesters.

Distributed request conceptually introduces the following protocol and type of function:

Database Support Protocol

Database support protocol provides connection between application servers and *database servers*. It allows the application server and database server systems to perform distributed unit of work and distributed request transactions.

Database Server Functions

Database server functions support requests that application servers have sent. These can be simply forwarded requests or subrequests that an application server has developed. Database server functions are defined in later levels of DRDA.

Figure 169 shows the two types of connection protocols and three types of functions.

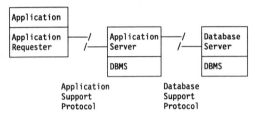

Figure 169. DRDA Network: The three functions and two connection protocols.

A single system may implement all of the functions. Such a system behaves appropriately (differently) according to the role it is playing for any particular request.

This relationship is shown in Figure 170.

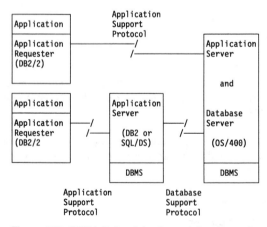

Figure 170. DRDA Network Implementation Example

In this example, the DB2 for OS/2 workstations act as the application requesters and a DB2 for MVS/ESA or DB2 for VM and VSE system acts as the application server. The DB2 for OS/400 system at the right acts as both an application server and a database server at the same time but for different requesters. Any of the DBMSs can be in any position in this figure. Figure 170 shows IBM products, but these can be non-IBM products or a mixture of IBM and non-IBM products.

Packages

A *package* contains the SQL statements and access plan for an application. The operation to create a package is called a bind. You perform a bind at the application requester to create a package at the application server. The application server uses the package to determine which operation to perform when the application is executed on the application requester. Your application can connect to a server and run a package that exists at that server.

With remote unit of work and distributed unit of work, you can bind a package to a remote server. The syntax for creating a package at the application server differs from one application requester to the next. The command or utility used to create the package at the application server is responsible for the following:

- It accepts the SQL statements in the format generated by the precompiler at the application requester. The precompiler usually has an option that allows it to accept SQL statements it does not recognize (because the SQL may be for a different SQL product).

- The SQL statements are converted into DRDA messages recognized by the application server.

- The application server stores the SQL statements in a package, along with any access path selection information the application server generates when it evaluates SQL statements.

For more information, refer to the product documentation for the application requester you are using.

Two-Phase Commit

When two LU 6.2 applications exchange data, certain resources must reflect the changes made on both LUs. In the case of a distributed database, tables are used on both systems with logical interdependencies. These dependencies must be retained regardless of network outages and program failures.

To allow updates to be made consistently on multiple systems, LU 6.2 provides the *sync point tower*, an optional LU 6.2 feature that provides two-phase commit protocols. When an LU implements the sync point tower, the LU can specify one of three values for the SYNC_LEVEL parameter when the LU allocates an APPC conversation.

- SYNC_LEVEL(NONE) is used for conversations that do not support the APPC CONFIRM verb and do not support two-phase commit.

- SYNC_LEVEL(CONFIRM) is used for conversations that support the APPC CONFIRM verb, but do not support two-phase commit.

- SYNC_LEVEL(SYNC) is used for conversations that support the APPC CONFIRM verb and two-phase commit. An LU cannot request SYNC_LEVEL(SYNC) unless both LUs support two-phase commit.

The two-phase commit process is an algorithm that involves exchanging messages in two phases. Breaking the commit process into two phases allows the database system to reconnect and complete the commit processing in cases where a network or system failure occurs. Figure 171 shows the two phases and the steps within each phase.

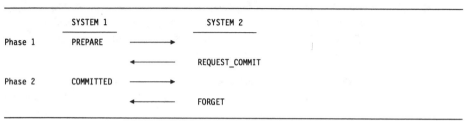

Figure 171. Two-Phase Commit Process

The following SNA messages are used for the two-phase commit process:

PREPARE
> Notifies the partner LU that you are about to commit the database changes for the current unit of work. The partner must write the changes out to its database log, so that a power failure or system failure does not result in the loss of the database updates.

REQUEST_COMMIT
> The partner LU sends this reply message when the database updates are safely recorded on the log. At this point, the partner LU must be able to guarantee that the database changes cannot be lost due to a system outage. However, it must also be able to abort the changes if so instructed by the originating LU. This may be necessary if one of the other databases in the unit of work fails to respond positively to the PREPARE message.

COMMITTED
> Informs the partner that all sites involved in the unit of work have completed phase 1 of the commit process. At this point, each database system is allowed to permanently record the database updates and release any locks.

FORGET
> Informs the receiver that the updates are complete. The log records can now be updated to reflect that the unit of work is committed.

The two-phase commit process can be simplified in some situations. For example, fewer messages can be exchanged when the remote system has no updated database resources. Because these optimizations are not critical to understanding the commit process, they are not discussed here.

The two-phase commit process is used in nondistributed database systems. For example, IMS/ESA and DB2 for MVS/ESA use a two-phase commit process to ensure that changes to IMS/ESA and DB2 for MVS/ESA databases are consistent, allowing application programs to make changes to both IMS/ESA and DB2 for MVS/ESA resources in a single unit of work.

Recovering from Network or System Failures

When the two-phase commit process is interrupted by a network or system failure, one or more of the LUs involved in the two-phase commit process might not know the final outcome of the unit of work. When an LU is waiting for the final outcome of a unit of work, it is said to be *indoubt*. An indoubt unit of work can hold locks in the database, which can cause lock timeouts with other applications in the database system. For this reason, it is important to determine the final outcome for each unit of work in a timely fashion.

The LU 6.2 sync point tower includes a resynchronization protocol (often referred to as *resync*), which provides a mechanism for guaranteeing that the final outcome of each unit of work is transmitted to each of the LUs in the unit of work. LUs that provide two-phase commit automatically perform the LU 6.2 resync process when the network connection can be re-established.

Restrictions on Systems Without Two-Phase Commit

For systems that don't use two-phase commit, there are usually restrictions on the SQL statements issued by the application program. The following are some examples of restrictions that must be enforced:

- Updates are restricted to a single database system. The database management system rejects attempts to update databases at multiple sites, because a network failure could potentially cause inconsistent database updates.

- Updates are restricted to all database systems without two-phase commit. Only systems with two-phase commit are allowed updates, so that the DBMS rejects attempts to update databases on the systems without two-phase commit. This is restricted because a network failure could potentially cause inconsistent database updates.

- When a network or system failure occurs in the middle of a COMMIT operation, the application is responsible for determining whether the database changes were committed or canceled.

These restrictions are designed to ensure that the application always gets a consistent database result. In other words, the changes associated with any COMMIT operation are committed in their entirety, or they are completely backed out of the database.

DRDA Remote Unit of Work Data Flow Protocols

When two DRDA participants exchange relational data, both must be able to understand the SQL statements being executed by the application program. When an SQL statement is issued, a DRDA request message is built and sent to the server. The server is able to correctly interpret the SQL statement being issued by examining various data objects and headers contained in the DRDA request message. These objects and headers tell the server information such as which SQL statement is issued, whether host variables exist, and the values of input host variables.

After the server has interpreted the SQL statement and performed the indicated SQL operation, a DRDA reply message is returned to the requesting system. This reply message contains:

- Completion information for the SQL statement (SQLCODE, for example)
- Data values to return to the application

When SQL query requests and replies are exchanged between two DRDA participants, there must be agreement between the two parties on how the request and reply messages are correlated to the SQL statements they represent. These message correlation rules (or protocols) are divided into two categories: cursor-based FETCH operations and other SQL operations.

Cursor-based FETCH operations

An SQL cursor is used to read and identify the relative position of rows in an SQL result table, where the rows contained in the result table are defined by an SQL SELECT statement. SQL statements that are used to read the result table (OPEN, FETCH, and CLOSE) are called cursor-based SQL operations.

In DRDA, the protocol used to transmit messages relating to cursor-based SQL operations depends on the attributes of the SQL cursor. There are two DRDA message protocols for cursor-based SQL operations:

Fixed row protocol

Fixed row protocol sends a message to the server and returns a reply message from the server for each SQL statement issued by the requester. The fixed row protocol technique is used for cursors that are updateable. For example, fixed row protocol must be used for OPEN, FETCH, and CLOSE operations, when the cursor is the target of an SQL UPDATE WHERE CURRENT OF or DELETE WHERE CURRENT OF statement.

Fixed row protocol may include the return of multiple rows of the SQL answer set to the requester if the application requests multiple rows through the multiple row fetch function in SQL.

Limited block protocol

Limited block protocol transmits the answer set in *blocks*. This means that each SEND_DATA verb issued by the server can prefetch rows of the SQL answer set to the requester in anticipation of the application requesting them later. This is highly desirable for read-only operations, because it greatly reduces the CPU time spent at both the requester and the server. It also greatly reduces the elapsed time used to return the answer set, because fewer network messages and APPC verbs are used to return the answer to the requester. Therefore, network traffic is also reduced.

If the SQL cursor can be updated (for example, it can be the target of an SQL UPDATE or DELETE WHERE CURRENT OF statement), limited block protocol cannot be used to return the results of the SELECT statement. Instead, you must use fixed row protocol.

The CPU and elapsed time required to process a distributed database SELECT statement can vary greatly, depending on whether you use limited block protocol or fixed row protocol. If your SQL application issues dynamic SQL statements, the distributed database system assumes your dynamic SQL may include an SQL DELETE statement with the WHERE CURRENT OF clause for each of your updateable cursors. This means fixed row protocol is the transmission protocol in SQL applications that issue dynamic SQL statements, unless the bind or query overrides the choice of protocol.

You can override the default transmission protocol to improve your application's performance. Some products allow you to override this choice, for example, by specifying the FOR FETCH ONLY clause on your SQL SELECT statement.

The following example shows a DB2 for MVS/ESA SELECT statement that always uses limited block protocol, even when the SQL application issues dynamic SQL:

```
SELECT * FROM TABLE4 FOR FETCH ONLY;
```

In some products, there is an option for binding packages that allows you to specify that limited block protocol should be used to transmit the query answer. See the reference for your product to determine which technique your server requires.

Other SQL operations

SQL operations that are not used to read the rows of an SQL result table (for example, INSERT, UPDATE, or DELETE) use a DRDA message protocol that is similar to the fixed row protocol. For these SQL operations, the application requester sends a message to the server and the server returns a reply message for each SQL statement issued by the requester.

DRDA Remote Unit of Work Examples

This section provides a brief overview of the messages exchanged between the Application Requester and the application server in DRDA. The purpose of this discussion is to give you a basic understanding of how the Application Requester and application server use APPC verbs to perform distributed database communication. In Figure 172 on page 424 through Figure 174 on page 426, a subset of the messages defined in DRDA are exchanged between the Application Requester and the application server. These figures describe the:

- Process used to initialize the Application Requester-to-application server connection
- Messages exchanged to bind an SQL package at the application server
- Messages exchanged to execute SQL statements contained in an SQL package at the application server

The examples in Figure 172 through Figure 174 show several DRDA message exchanges. When you look at the examples, keep in mind that DRDA allows the Application Requester to send some messages in several ways. For example, the

EXCSAT and ACCRDB messages can be transmitted individually, or the two messages can be chained together (possibly with other messages) for transmission purposes. The purpose of this book is to describe the relationship between DRDA and APPC, so the examples simply present the concepts involved in DRDA. The examples do not necessarily present the most efficient implementation of DRDA. For more detailed information about the messages exchanged between DRDA participants, see the *Distributed Relational Database Architecture Reference*. In the examples, the following DRDA messages are shown:

EXCSAT

Exchange Server Attributes allows the Application Requester to identify itself and its capabilities to the application server, including the:

- Application requester's job or task name
- Level of SQL supported
- Application requester's product type

EXCSATRD

Exchange Server Attributes Reply Data is sent by the application server in response to EXCSAT. This response provides the following information to the Application Requester:

- The application server's job or task name
- The level of SQL supported
- The application server's product type

ACCRDB

Access RDB identifies:

- The RDB_NAME the application requester wants to access
- Whether the application requester wants the application server to restrict SQL updates
- The SQL statement and decimal string delimiters
- The application requester's product release level
- The data representation of the application requester (for example, 370, 80X86, AS400) and the coded character set used for character data

ACCRDBRM

Access RDB Reply Message describes the outcome of the ACCRDB command at the application server and identifies the:

- CCSIDs chosen by the application server
- Interrupt token
- Authid of the user as received by the application server
- Application server's product release level
- Data representation of the application requester (for example, 370, 80X86, AS400) and the coded character set used for character data

BGNBND

Begin Bind marks the beginning of a series of SQL statements to be bound into a package at the application server. The package name is one of the values supplied in the BGNBND message.

BNDSQLSTT

Bind SQL Statement sends an individual SQL statement to the application server along with the section number and statement number associated with the SQL statement.

At execution time, the application requester sends the section number and statement number to the application server, which identifies the SQL statement to be executed.

ENDBND

End Bind marks the end of a series of SQL statements that must be bound into an SQL package.

SQLCARD

SQLCA Reply Data returns the result of an SQL operation to the application requester (for example, the SQLCA).

OPNQRY

Open Query is sent to the application server when an SQL OPEN is issued by the application requester.

OPNQRYRM

Open Query Reply Message is sent by the application server to describe the outcome of the OPNQRY message. The OPNQRYRM message also tells the application requester whether the answer set is sent as individual rows (fixed row protocol) or groups of rows (limited block protocol).

QRYDSC

Query Descriptor is sent by the application server to describe the columns that are returned in the answer set associated with an SQL SELECT statement.

QRYDTA

Query Data is sent by the application server to return each row of the answer set associated with SQL cursor SELECT.

CNTQRY

Continue Query is sent by the application requester when the SQL application program issues a FETCH statement, and additional data must be retrieved from the application server to satisfy the FETCH request.

ENDQRYRM

End Query Reply Message is sent by the application server when the answer set associated with the SQL SELECT is exhausted.

The figures that follow explain the communication flows used to establish an Application Requester-to-application server connection. Figure 172 on page 424 shows how the application requester and application server exchange information describing their respective DRDA capabilities, and the RDB_NAMEs that are to be accessed.

```
                                                            Application Server
     SQL Application        Application Requester                  SYSTEM1
     ───────────────        ─────────────────────           ─────────────────

     EXEC SQL
     CONNECT to SYSTEM1


                            AR determines LUNAME
                              for SYSTEM1 is
                              SYS1LU

                            ALLOCATE
                               TPN('07F6C4C2'X)
                               LUNAME(SYS1LU)

                            SEND_DATA  EXCSAT       ────────▶   AS detects new APPC
                                                                conversation
                            RECEIVE_AND_WAIT
                                                                RECEIVE_AND_WAIT

                                                    ◀────────   SEND_DATA   EXCSATRD

                                                                RECEIVE_AND_WAIT

                            SEND_DATA  ACCRDB
                                       SYSTEM1      ────────▶   AS validates the
                                                                RDB_NAME SYSTEM1

                            RECEIVE_AND_WAIT

                                                    ◀────────   SEND_DATA  ACCRDBRM
```

Figure 172. Application Requester to Application Server Initialization Flows

After the Application Requester-to-application server connection is established, you
need to create a package containing the SQL statements you want to execute.
Figure 173 on page 425 shows the DRDA flows used to bind two SQL statements into
a remote package at the application server. The figure does not show the syntax for
performing the bind process, because the syntax is system specific.

```
Application Requester        Application Server
_____            _____


              Initialization Flow

                             RECEIVE_AND_WAIT
SEND_DATA   BGNBND    _____
                      _____\

RECEIVE_AND_WAIT
                      _____   SEND_DATA   SQLCARD
                      _____


                             RECEIVE_AND_WAIT
SEND_DATA   BNDSQLSTT  _____
                      _____\

RECEIVE_AND_WAIT
                      _____   SEND_DATA   SQLCARD

                             RECEIVE_AND_WAIT

SEND_DATA   BNDSQLSTT  _____
                      _____\

RECEIVE_AND_WAIT
                      _____   SEND_DATA   SQLCARD

                             RECEIVE_AND_WAIT

SEND_DATA   ENDBND    _____
                      _____\

RECEIVE_AND_WAIT

                      _____   SEND_DATA   SQLCARD

                             RECEIVE_AND_WAIT
```

Figure 173. Application Requester to Application Server BIND Flows

Now that you have a package at the application server, you need to know the DRDA flows used to call the SQL statements in the package. Figure 174 on page 426 shows the execution of three SQL statements: OPEN, FETCH, and FETCH, where the second fetch returns a +100 SQLCODE. In this case, the SQL SELECT is an updateable cursor and thus uses fixed row protocol.

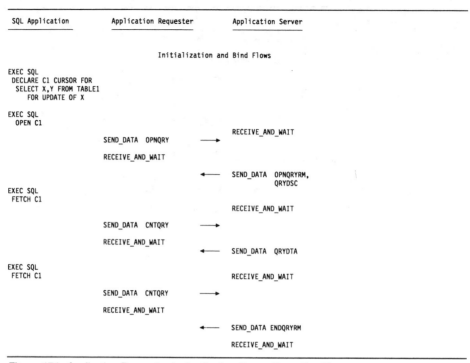

```
SQL Application          Application Requester          Application Server
_____          _____          _____


                            Initialization and Bind Flows

EXEC SQL
 DECLARE C1 CURSOR FOR
  SELECT X,Y FROM TABLE1
    FOR UPDATE OF X

EXEC SQL
 OPEN C1
                                                      RECEIVE_AND_WAIT

                      SEND_DATA  OPNQRY      ———▶

                      RECEIVE_AND_WAIT

                                            ◀———    SEND_DATA  OPNQRYRM,
                                                               QRYDSC
EXEC SQL
 FETCH C1
                                                      RECEIVE_AND_WAIT

                      SEND_DATA  CNTQRY      ———▶

                      RECEIVE_AND_WAIT
                                            ◀———    SEND_DATA  QRYDTA

EXEC SQL
 FETCH C1                                              RECEIVE_AND_WAIT

                      SEND_DATA  CNTQRY      ———▶

                      RECEIVE_AND_WAIT

                                            ◀———    SEND_DATA ENDQRYRM

                                                      RECEIVE_AND_WAIT
```

Figure 174. Application Requester to Application Server Execution Flows

Part 4. Appendixes

427

Appendix A. VTAM Considerations

This appendix gives information you might need to consider about VTAM buffer pools, VTAM pacing, and creating a VTAM mode table. For more information about VTAM, see the VTAM publications listed in the bibliography on page 457.

VTAM Buffer Pools

Distributed database systems have the potential to send and receive a tremendous amount of data through the SNA network. When distributed database systems (DB2 for MVS/ESA and DB2 for VM and VSE) are added to an existing VTAM network, it is very important to examine the impact these systems can have on the network.

VTAM's buffer pools are the area of greatest concern because VTAM needs to store distributed database data temporarily in these buffers. The IO buffer pool (IOBUF) is most affected, because of the large number and size of the RUs sent between distributed database systems.

The VTAM IOBUF pool is a resource shared by all VTAM applications: TSO, IMS/ESA, CICS/ESA, NETVIEW, DB2 for MVS/ESA, and others. It is extremely important to make sure that one application (DB2 for MVS/ESA or DB2 for VM and VSE) does not consume an inordinate amount of the VTAM IOBUF pool. If this occurs, the other VTAM applications experience degraded performance, because they must wait for VTAM IOBUF space to be released before their network requests can proceed.

As part of the distributed database system installation, use the information in this appendix to determine the impact your distributed database system has on the VTAM IOBUF pool.

VTAM Buffer Start Options

The characteristics of the VTAM buffer pools can be specified on the VTAM startup parameters in the ATCSTRxx member of VTAMLST, where the xx portion of the member name is supplied by the LIST=xx option of the VTAM start command. For example, the following command causes VTAM to use the member ATCSTR01 to configure the buffer pools:

```
START VTAM,,,(LIST=01)
```

```
<poolname>=(baseno,bufsize,slowpt,F,xpanno,xpanpt,xpanlim)
```

For example:

```
IOBUF=(320,441,20,F,64,48,768)
```

Figure 175. Buffer Definitions in the VTAM Start Parameters

Figure 175 defines the IO buffer pool for a relatively small system. These values might not be advisable for a production system. The meanings of the parameters, which are positional, are:

baseno   The example specifies 320 buffers to be the base number of buffers in the pool. This is sometimes called the *static area* of the pool. That is, this number of buffers is always allocated. You can configure the VTAM IOBUF pool so that it changes size to meet the needs of peak demand periods. The value for baseno should be close to the number of buffers normally in use in the system. This decreases the frequency of buffer expansion, so that it is only required during peak periods.

bufsize   Each buffer can be 441 bytes long. VTAM modifies this length, increasing it so that a 71-byte control block has a space at the start of each buffer. After the 71-byte header is added to the 441-byte VTAM buffer, a total of 512 bytes (441 + 71) is allocated by VTAM.

slowpt   A slow point of 20 causes VTAM to enter slowdown mode whenever the number of available buffers in the pool drops below 20. In slowdown mode, only priority requests (for example, a read from a channel-attached device) are honored. Normal requests (including normal IO) are queued or rejected. VTAM issues messages to the console when it enters and exits slowdown mode. If this value is set too high, VTAM might be unable to exit slowdown mode.

F   This parameter is used on VTAM buffer specifications to mark a buffer pool as either fixed or pageable. You cannot mark VTAM IOBUF parameters as pageable, because VTAM IOBUF storage is always page-fixed in extended CSA (ECSA).

xpanno   The example defines an expansion number of 64. That is, each time the buffer pool is expanded, 64 more buffers are made available to VTAM.

VTAM allocates storage in 4K increments, so your choice for xpanno should be a multiple of 4096 bytes. In this case, 64 buffers use 8 of the 4K storage increments (64 times 512 is approximately 8 times 4096).

xpanpt   Specifying 48 for the xpanpt requests that the buffer pool be expanded each time the number of available buffers falls to 48 or less.

xpanlim   This parameter specifies the maximum amount of storage the IOBUF pool can use (768K bytes in this case). If you omit this value, the buffer pool can continue expanding as long as required or until ECSA is exhausted. At this stage, messages indicating a storage shortage are issued. If you inadvertently turn off pacing, or you have a very large number of sessions, omission of the xpanlim parameter can cause a large amount of ECSA storage to be claimed. You should specify an upper limit to prevent this from happening.

Tuning VTAM Buffers

When looking at tuning the VTAM IOBUF pool, the system programmer should first monitor the buffer usage for a few days. You can then determine the number of buffers being used, at any one time, during normal load on the network. It is also helpful to have some idea of *normal* usage for comparison purposes, when shortages occur. The buffer pools can be monitored using either the VTAM SMS trace or the VTAM display buffer use command (D NET,ID=BFRUSE).

Expanding the buffer pools takes host processor time and can cause some degradation of performance if the buffer pools are constantly being expanded and contracted. Therefore, a large base allocation is best for processor usage. However, specifying large buffer pools takes up storage. This is particularly important if the buffer pool is fixed in real storage, which is always the case for VTAM IO buffers. See Figure 176.

When tuning the buffer pools, consider the following:

MAXBFRU

This is the maximum buffer usage. It is the number of buffers that VTAM allocates to receive data from the network. MAXBFRU is defined in buffers for receiving data from a local device (including cluster controllers and communications controllers) and in 4K pages when defined for a CTC.

This amount of buffering space should always be available. It is suggested that the expansion point be at least MAXBFRU number of buffers higher than the slow point. This is to avoid pushing VTAM into slowdown when buffers are low. Remember that receiving data from the network (channels, for example) has priority over receiving data from an application. If a buffer request causes VTAM to go into slowdown, and that request comes from an application, it is not honored. If the same request comes from the network, it is honored.

RUSIZE

This is the maximum size for an RU that can be sent on a session. When defining buffer sizes, it is important to keep in mind the size of the RUs that are sent. These RUs vary in size depending on the application. For example, large volume applications like DB2 for MVS/ESA or DB2 for VM and VSE usually use relatively large RUSIZEs, whereas interactive users (such as TSO) usually require only a small RU size (usually enough to hold one screen full of data).

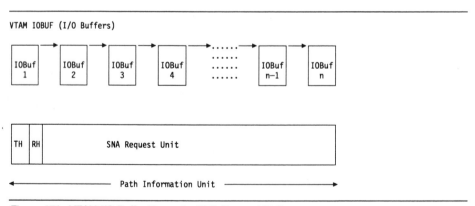

Figure 176. VTAM I/O Buffer Usage by SNA Request Unit

VTAM divides the RU into parts, based on the VTAM buffer size, and chains the buffers together to represent the content of the RU. Each of the VTAM buffers includes a control block header of 71 bytes. A small VTAM buffer size can mean that a relatively large number of buffers is required to send a large PIU. This causes added overhead in VTAM not only in storage (excess number of control block headers), but also in processing (chaining and processing the control blocks and associated data).

4K PAGES

VTAM allocates the buffer pool in 4K pages. To avoid excessive storage waste in each page, select a buffer size that makes most use of the space available on the page.

Figure 175 on page 428 gives a buffer size for the IOBUFs of 441 bytes. A buffer size of 441 bytes is a reasonable compromise between the needs of DB2 for MVS/ESA (large buffers), and terminal-oriented needs (such as IMS, CICS, and TSO). This allows eight buffers per page (remember that by the time VTAM adds its control block the buffer is actually 512 bytes long). If you specify a buffer size of 400 instead, you still have managed to get only eight buffers per page. The extra space is wasted.

Normal usage

The base allocation for the buffer pool should be large enough to cope with *normal* network usage. If it is set too low, an excessive number of expansions might need to be done. This causes added CPU overhead during processing.

Expansion number

This value should be large enough to cope with the largest PIU that can be sent. The pool should not need to be expanded twice to handle any particular PIU. An expansion number that is too small can result in alternating expansions and contractions. This causes excessive processing overhead and should be avoided if possible.

The buffer pool is very dynamic. Buffers are used and released very quickly under normal circumstances. The effect of tuning the buffer pools can be very dramatic. However, take care when adjusting your VTAM buffer pool. Read the "Choosing Buffer Pool Specifications" section in the *VTAM Implementation Guide* before attempting any tuning.

Buffer Expansion Example

The following is an example of how the VTAM buffer definitions interact.

1. Assume that the expansion point was specified as 15, and the expansion number as 10. Normal processing occurs and at this point only 20 buffers available.

2. A request for nine buffers is received. This request is not honored immediately because the request reduces the available buffers below the expansion point (20-9=11, which is less than 15).

3. The request for nine buffers is delayed, and buffer expansion is scheduled. As stated earlier, the buffer expansion acquires 10 new buffers because the buffer expansion number is 10.

4. A request for four buffers is received. This request is honored because the request does not reduce the available buffers below the expansion point. At this point, the buffer pool has 16 buffers available.

5. The buffer expansion operation completes successfully, so now the buffer pool has 26 buffers available. The first request for nine buffers is now honored, so the buffer pool is left with 17 buffers.

6. At this point, only two buffers are available before expansion must occur again. The next time a buffer request is received, a buffer expansion will be scheduled, unless other SEND or RECEIVE requests complete and release their associated buffers back into the pool. This buffer expansion can be avoided (to a certain extent) by increasing the expansion number. For example, an expansion number of 27 can satisfy three requests for nine buffers before requiring another buffer expansion.

Calculating VTAM I/O Buffer Pool (IOBUF) Storage

You can calculate the effect your distributed database system has on the IOBUF pool. Every *path information unit* (PIU) that enters or leaves VTAM resides in one or more IOBUF buffers.

A PIU is composed of a 26-byte transmission header, a 3-byte request/response header, and the request/response unit (RU) that contains VTAM application data. The maximum size of the RU is negotiated during the SNA bind process.

To calculate the maximum number of IOBUF buffers required by your distributed database system, you must do the following:

1. Calculate the number of buffers that each PIU occupies, and call it PIUBUF.

   ```
   PIUBUF = ( 29 + RUSIZE ) / BUFSIZE
   (integer math, rounded up)
   ```

   RUSIZE is the maximum length of the RU in bytes, and an assumption is made that it is the same for both session directions. BUFSIZE is the value you specified on the IOBUF pool definition.

   Assume you have a buffer size of 441 bytes, and an RUSIZE of 4096. With these values, PIUBUF is 10.

2. Calculate the maximum number of IOBUF buffers used by a session, and call it SESBUF.

   ```
   SESBUF = PACECNT • PIUBUF
   ```

   PACECNT is the pacing count for your session. In this calculation, assume that pacing is the same in both directions, and it is the same for all modes.

   If pacing is set to 2, then SESBUF is 20.

3. Calculate the maximum number of sessions that can be active for all modes to all systems, and call it SESCNT.

4. Calculate the maximum number of VTAM buffers used by your distributed database system, and call this TOTBUF. The formula for TOTBUF is based on a worst-case scenario, because it assumes that all sessions are used by concurrent conversations.

   ```
   TOTBUF = SESCNT • SESBUF
   ```

If you assume that the maximum number of sessions that can be active is 50 (SESCNT), then 1000 is the number of IOBUF entries required by your distributed database system in a worst-case scenario.

5. Calculate actual VTAM buffer storage consumption used by your distributed database system, and call it STORAGE.

```
STORAGE = TOTBUF • (BUFSIZE + 71)
```

Each buffer includes 71 bytes for VTAM internal headers.

So, to continue the above example, you can estimate an upper value of real storage of approximately 500K.

If you decide that the amount of storage required to satisfy the calculation is too large, you can adjust the input parameters to arrive at a more reasonable result.

You can change the parameters in the following order:

1. Decrease the session-level pacing count on your distributed database systems.
2. Decrease the number of sessions between distributed database systems.
3. Decrease the RU size on distributed database sessions.

VTAM Pacing

Distributed database systems such as DB2 for MVS/ESA and DB2 for VM and VSE can cause large amounts of data to be sent on the network. Congestion can occur in the network when the data accumulates at a particular part of the network. For example:

- An application is not receiving data from the network. This could occur because:

  The application is looping and is unable to issue the necessary VTAM RECEIVE macro.

  The sending application is in a loop sending huge amounts of data.

  An SQL query has requested a particularly large answer set to be sent on the network.

- A line in the network is having intermittent I/O errors, requiring data to be retransmitted.

- The line capacity between network nodes is insufficient and can no longer keep up with the normal data flow through the network.

In these examples, the data accumulates in one node of the network (SSCP or NCP). This congestion can initially cause degradation in the network response time. If the congestion becomes severe, it can lead to slowdown (out of storage) conditions in either the SSCP or NCP, which should be avoided if at all possible. For more information concerning pacing, see "Pacing" on page 387.

It is very important to specify a pacing window size for your distributed database connections on VTAM-managed networks. This helps prevent your distributed database system from consuming a disproportional share of the VTAM IOBUF pool. It is important to understand the VTAM parameters associated with pacing to ensure that pacing is in fact occurring on your sessions. Pacing can be specified on:

The APPL definition
The MODEENT macro for the bind parameters.

APPL Definition

Two parameters of interest to pacing are:

- AUTH=VPACE or NVPACE

    Specifying NVPACE indicates that, for sessions where this application is PLU, no pacing occurs in the PLU-to-SLU direction. The recommended default is VPACE. This allows pacing to occur in the PLU-to-SLU direction.

- VPACING=<number>

    The value defined here is the pacing window. For sessions where this application is the PLU, this value is used in the SLU-to-PLU direction. For sessions where this application is the SLU, this value is used in the PLU-to-SLU direction. These values interact with the values specified in the MODEENT macro, as discussed later. A VPACING count of 2 is recommended.

MODEENT Parameters

When discussing pacing, much confusion is caused by misunderstanding the use of the terms *secondary send and receive* and *primary receive*. (Here, secondary refers to the SLU and primary refers to the PLU). This is even more complicated for an LU 6.2 application (such as DB2 for MVS/ESA or DB2 for VM and VSE) because it can be both PLU and SLU at the same time on different sessions that use the same mode name. Figure 177 helps to clarify the use of these parameters.

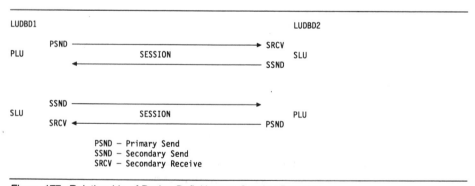

Figure 177. Relationship of Pacing Definitions to Session Direction

In the MODEENT macro of the mode table, you can specify the following pacing values:

- PSNDPAC (primary send pacing count)

    This value has no effect on the pacing values set for an application-to-application session.

- SSNDPAC (secondary send pacing count)

  A zero secondary send pacing count means that no pacing on the session occurs in the SLU-to-PLU direction. A nonzero value causes the pacing window to be taken from the PLU VPACING definition. **Always** specify a nonzero value.

- SRCVPAC (secondary receive pacing count)

  The value specified here determines the PLU-to-SLU pacing window size if it is nonzero, and if the PLU specifies AUTH=VPACING. When the PLU specifies AUTH=VPACING and SRCVPAC is zero, the pacing window is taken from the VPACING definition on the SLU's APPL or PLU definition.

Each of these parameters default to a value of zero.

Figure 178 clarifies the interrelationship of these parameters for the PLU-to-SLU direction on the session.

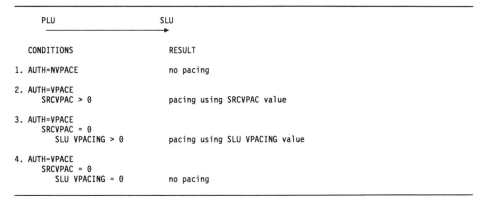

Figure 178. Conditions for Pacing: PLU-to-SLU Direction

Figure 179 clarifies the interrelationship between the parameters for the SLU-to-PLU direction on the session.

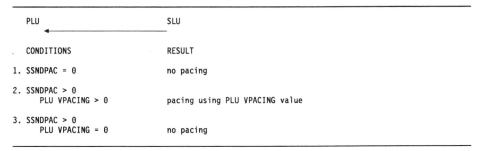

Figure 179. Conditions for Pacing: SLU-to-PLU Direction

Distributed database systems are involved in a peer-to-peer relationship when using sessions. This means they can be the PLU on some sessions and the SLU on other sessions. Because the session role (PLU versus SLU) cannot always be predicted, it might be easier to keep the pacing values the same in both directions on the session.

Control of session pacing can be at either application level or mode name level:

- Application level

  This method causes all the sessions between the two applications to use the same pacing counts, irrespective of the mode name used to establish the session.

  Specifying SRCVPAC=0 and SSNDPAC>0 in the mode entry causes the pacing values to be taken from the PLU and SLU VPACING definitions on the APPL statement. These should each have the same value to ensure the pacing window is the same in each direction.

- Mode name level

  This method causes the primary to secondary pacing window to be controlled by the SRCVPAC definition in the mode name.

  Specifying both SRCVPAC and SSNDPAC greater than zero causes the pacing value for the PLU-to-SLU direction to be taken from the SRCVPAC definition. The SLU-to-PLU pacing window is still taken from the PLU VPACING definition on the APPL macro.

  To have a variety of different pacing values on sessions between the same two VTAM applications, each of the session groups needs a separate mode name specifying the required pacing values.

Because of the large amounts of data being sent by distributed database systems over the network, a pacing count of two is recommended for initial testing.

Virtual Route Pacing

Pacing of the virtual route is controlled by VTAM and NCP. The amount of traffic on each virtual route is continuously monitored and controlled. Virtual route pacing always occurs; however, you can effectively disable it by specifying 255 for both minimum and maximum.

The virtual route pacing window is very dynamic. When mild congestion occurs, the window is decreased by one until the congestion clears. When severe congestion occurs, the window is decreased to its minimum value. Congestion is determined by the number of PIUs waiting to be sent (that is, queued in VTAM or NCP). The severe and mild congestion thresholds can be coded using the ER operand on the PATH statement in the NCP. VTAM only reports severe congestion when buffer shortages are occurring.

Virtual route pacing controls the flow of data between the two ends of the VR. It does not control the flow through any intermediate subareas. Because of this, session pacing is essential to good flow control through the network.

The minimum and maximum virtual route pacing window sizes are defined using the VRPWSxx parameter of the PATH statement, as shown in Figure 34 on page 132.

Creating a VTAM Mode Table

The mode names used by DB2 for MVS/ESA or DB2 for VM and VSE are stored in the VTAM mode table, which is identified with the MODETAB keyword on the VTAM APPL statement. If the VTAM APPL statement does not include the MODETAB keyword, the mode table name defaults to ISTINCLM, which is a VTAM-supplied mode table.

The VTAM mode table is created by assembling and link-editing a table containing:

- A MODETAB macro at the beginning of the table
- One or more MODEENT macros, which define the available mode names
- A MODEEND macro to mark the end of the table

The process for assembling and link-editing the mode table differs, depending on which operating system you are using (VM or MVS). See *VTAM Resource Definition Reference* for more information on how to perform this task in your environment.

The MODEENT macro is used to define the individual mode names. Parameters are specified on the MODEENT macro. The PSNDPAC, SSNDPAC, and SRCVPAC parameters were covered in the discussion of VTAM pacing. The remaining MODEENT parameters are:

LOGMODE   Identifies the mode name associated with this VTAM mode table entry.

COS   Identifies the member in the VTAM Class of Service table used to specify the network priority and virtual routes for this mode name. SNA defines three transmission priorities: 2 (the highest), 1, and 0 (the lowest). By using the COS table, you can assign transmission priorities to your mode names, and thereby prioritize the data transmitted by DB2 for MVS/ESA and DB2 for VM and VSE distributed database applications.

RUSIZES   Specifies a pair of two-digit numbers that describe the send and receive RU sizes. The numbers are in the form mn, where the value represented is $m*[2^n]$. In the IBMDB2LM mode entry in Figure 180 on page 439, both the send and receive RU sizes are coded as 89, which represents 4096 bytes ($8*[2^9]$).

TYPE   Identifies the type of BIND.

FMPROF   Specifies the FM Profile required.

TSPROF   Specifies the TS Profile required.

PRIPROT   Specifies the PRIMARY LU protocols used.

SECPROT   Specifies the SECONDARY LU protocols used.

COMPROT   Specifies the COMMOM LU protocols used.

PSERVIC   Identifies the LU type. (For dependent LUs, use X'122C' for better performance.)

Of these MODEENT parameters, only LOGMODE, COS, RUSIZES, and the pacing values are used by independent LUs. The other parameters may be present, but will be ignored. Dependent LUs require that all listed parameters be defined.

Figure 180 on page 439 defines mode names in a table called RDBMODES:

IBMRDB   This is the default mode name used by remote unit of work conversations. This mode name gives applications a *medium* transmission priority, because it uses the default COS member (SNA transmission priority 1).

IBMDB2LM   This is the default mode name used by DB2 for MVS/ESA-only distributed unit of work conversations. This mode name also gives applications a medium transmission priority, because it uses the default COS member (SNA transmission priority 1).

RDBHIGH   Provides high-priority transmission for distributed database applications that use this mode name, because it tries to use SNA transmission priority 2 (the highest priority).

RDBLOW   Provides low-priority transmission (SNA transmission priority 0).

```
RDBMODES MODETAB

*********************************************************************
*    IBM DISTRIBUTED RELATIONAL DATABASE DEFAULT MODE
IBMRDB   MODEENT LOGMODE=IBMRDB,SSNDPAC=X'02',                       *
                 SRCVPAC=0,PSNDPAC=0,                                *
                 RUSIZES=X'8989',                                    *
                 TYPE=0,                                             *
                 FMPROF=X'13',                                       *
                 TSPROF=X'07',                                       *
                 PRIPROT=X'B0',                                      *
                 SECPROT=X'B0',                                      *
                 COMPROT=X'50A5',                                    *
                 PSERVIC=X'060200000000000000000122F00'
*********************************************************************
*    DEFAULT MODE USED FOR DB2-ONLY DUW CONVERSATIONS
IBMDB2LM MODEENT LOGMODE=IBMDB2LM,SSNDPAC=X'02',                     *
                 SRCVPAC=0,PSNDPAC=0,                                *
                 RUSIZES=X'8989',                                    *
                 TYPE=0,                                             *
                 FMPROF=X'13',                                       *
                 TSPROF=X'07',                                       *
                 PRIPROT=X'B0',                                      *
                 SECPROT=X'B0',                                      *
                 COMPROT=X'50A5',                                    *
                 PSERVIC=X'060200000000000000000122F00'
*********************************************************************
*    MODE FOR HIGH PRIORITY APPLICATIONS   (RDBHIGH COS MEMBER)
RDBHIGH  MODEENT LOGMODE=RDBHIGH,SSNDPAC=X'02',                      *
                 SRCVPAC=0,PSNDPAC=0,                                *
                 COS=RDBHIGH,                                        *
                 TYPE=0,                                             *
                 RUSIZES=X'8989',                                    *
                 FMPROF=X'13',                                       *
                 TSPROF=X'07',                                       *
                 PRIPROT=X'B0',                                      *
                 SECPROT=X'B0',                                      *
                 COMPROT=X'50A5',                                    *
                 PSERVIC=X'060200000000000000000122F00'
*********************************************************************
*    MODE FOR LOW PRIORITY APPLICATIONS   (RDBLOW COS MEMBER)
RDBLOW   MODEENT LOGMODE=RDBLOW,SSNDPAC=X'02',                       *
                 SRCVPAC=0,PSNDPAC=0,                                *
                 COS=RDBLOW,                                         *
                 RUSIZES=X'8989',                                    *
                 TYPE=0,                                             *
                 FMPROF=X'13',                                       *
                 TSPROF=X'07',                                       *
                 PRIPROT=X'B0',                                      *
                 SECPROT=X'B0',                                      *
                 COMPROT=X'50A5',                                    *
                 PSERVIC=X'060200000000000000000122F00'
         MODEEND
         END
```

Figure 180. Example VTAM Log Mode Table

Creating a VTAM COS Table

The VTAM COS table defines the class of service attributes for the virtual routes in
your VTAM network. See Figure 181 on page 440. Because the network transmission

priority is one of the attributes provided by the COS table, the COS table can be used to control the network performance characteristics of your individual mode names.

A COS table contains:

- A COSTAB macro at the beginning of the table
- One or more COS macros, which define the class of service profiles that are available
- A COSEND macro to mark the end of the table

The process for assembling and link-editing the class of service table differs depending on which operating system you are using (VM or MVS). See *VTAM Resource Definition Reference* for more information about performing this task in your environment.

```
*                       COS TABLE ENTRIES
ISTSDCOS COSTAB
**********************************************************************
*    UNNAMED COS ENTRY FOR DEFAULT LIST, USED WHEN NO COS IS SPECIFIED
*       ON THE MODEENT - THIS ENTRY GIVES MEDIUM PRIORITY.
*                                   (TRANSMISSION PRIORITY 1)
         COS VR=((0,1),(1,1),(2,1),(3,1),(4,1),(5,1),(6,1),(7,1),      *
               (0,2),(1,2),(2,2),(3,2),(4,2),(5,2),(6,2),(7,2),        *
               (0,0),(1,0),(2,0),(3,0),(4,0),(5,0),(6,0),(7,0))
**********************************************************************
*    ISTVTCOS ENTRY FOR USE IN SSCP SESSIONS - SSCP TO PU, SSCP-LU
*       AND SSCP TO SSCP - THE SSCP GETS HIGH PRIORITY.
*                                   (TRANSMISSION PRIORITY 2)
ISTVTCOS COS VR=((0,2),(1,2),(2,2),(3,2),(4,2),(5,2),(6,2),(7,2),      *
               (0,1),(1,1),(2,1),(3,1),(4,1),(5,1),(6,1),(7,1),        *
               (0,0),(1,0),(2,0),(3,0),(4,0),(5,0),(6.0),(7.0))
**********************************************************************
*    RDBLOW COS ENTRY FOR SESSIONS THAT DO NOT REQUIRE FAST RESPONSE.
*       THEY HAVE LOW PRIORITY       (TRANSMISSION PRIORITY 0)
RDBLOW   COS VR=((0,0),(1,0),(2,0),(3,0),(4,0),(5,0),(6,0),(7,0),      *
               (0,1),(1,1),(2,1),(3,1),(4,1),(5,1),(6,1),(7,1),        *
               (0,2),(1,2),(2,2),(3,2),(4,2),(5,2),(6,2),(7,2))
**********************************************************************
*    RDBHIGH COS ENTRY FOR SESSIONS THAT REQUIRE FAST RESPONSE.
*       THEY HAVE HIGH PRIORITY      (TRANSMISSION PRIORITY 2)
RDBHIGH  COS VR=((0,2),(1,2),(2,2),(3,2),(4,2),(5,2),(6,2),(7,2),      *
               (0,1),(1,1),(2,1),(3,1),(4,1),(5,1),(6,1),(7,1),        *
               (0,0),(1,0),(2,0),(3,0),(4,0),(5,0),(6,0),(7,0))
**********************************************************************
         COSEND
         END
```

Figure 181. Example VTAM COS Table

VTAM Remote System Connections

Both DB2 for MVS/ESA and DB2 for VM and VSE use VTAM to route requests to remote database systems. When defining remote systems to VTAM, the VTAM and NCP definition statements used depend on how the remote system is physically and logically connected to the local VTAM system. This book describes some of the more common VTAM connections used in distributed database systems. If the material in this book does not cover your hardware configuration, see the *VTAM Network Implementation Guide* for more information. Another good source is the *Advanced Communications Function Products Installation Guide*, which has examples of how to define many of the hardware configurations that are not addressed in this book.

Session-Level Security

In "LU 6.2 Security" on page 409, the algorithm used by SNA to authenticate remote LUs in the network was discussed. VTAM attempts to perform the session-level security algorithm when the VERIFY=OPTIONAL or VERIFY=REQUIRED keyword is specified on the VTAM APPL statement.

To perform the session-level security algorithm, VTAM uses RACF 1.9 (or a similar product) to obtain the session password for the local LU and validate the session password received from the remote LU.

The following steps must be taken to activate session-level security for a VTAM LU:

1. Specify VERIFY=OPTIONAL or VERIFY=REQUIRED on the VTAM APPL statement for the LU on the local VTAM system.

   Session-level security must also be activated by the remote LU. If the remote system is also managed by VTAM, the VTAM APPL statement at the remote system must include the VERIFY keyword as described above. If the remote system is not managed by VTAM, you must activate session-level security using the process provided by the remote LU's communication subsystem.

2. Define a RACF profile for the pair of LUs (the local LU and the remote LU). The following example shows how to establish a session password (SECRET) for the two DB2 for MVS/ESA LUs named SPIFNET.NYM1DB2 and SPIFNET.NYM2DB2.

   At the NYM1DB2 system:

   ```
   RDEFINE  APPCLU  SPIFNET.NYM1DB2.NYM2DB2
            SESSION(SESSKEY(SECRET))
            UACC(NONE)
   ```

   At the NYM2DB2 system:

   ```
   RDEFINE  APPCLU  SPIFNET.NYM2DB2.NYM1DB2
            SESSION(SESSKEY(SECRET))
            UACC(NONE)
   ```

3. Activate the APPCLU class of resources in RACF.

   On each VTAM system:

   ```
   SETROPTS  CLASSACT(APPCLU)
   ```

Appendix B. Setting Up the Interactive SQL Utility to Access Unlike Application Servers

One way to test a DRDA connection is to use the interactive SQL utility of the application requester to access the unlike application server. All of the platforms require some setup for successful interactive sessions. This section summarizes the setup required for an interactive SQL utility specific to each database management system.

DB2 for MVS/ESA: Setting Up SQL Processor Using File Input (SPUFI)

From a DB2 for MVS/ESA application requester, you can use SPUFI to connect and then execute SQL statements at non-DB2 for MVS/ESA application servers. First, you must bind a package for SPUFI on each of those application servers. Use the following commands:

```
BIND PACKAGE (location_name.DSNESPCS) MEMBER(DSNESM68)
          ACTION(ADD) ISOLATION(CS) LIB('DSN310.SDSNSAMP')

BIND PACKAGE (location_name.DSNESPRR) MEMBER(DSNESM68)
          ACTION(ADD) ISOLATION(RR) LIB('DSN310.SDSNSAMP')
```

If the BIND PACKAGE command fails, the package already exists. You can use the existing packages without any change to the package list in the SPUFI plans.

If you want to change the time and date format returned by the existing packages, you must bind new packages with different collection identifiers that have been agreed to by the application server.

For example, if the collection identifiers are PRIVATCS and PRIVATRR, the commands for doing a remote bind are:

```
BIND PACKAGE (location_name.PRIVATCS) MEMBER(DSNESM68)
          ACTION(ADD) ISOLATION(CS) LIB(DSN310.SDSNSAMP')

BIND PACKAGE (location_name.PRIVATRR) MEMBER(DSNESM68)
          ACTION(ADD) ISOLATION(RR) LIB(DSN310.SDSNSAMP')
```

The SPUFI plans at the DB2 for MVS/ESA system must be rebound because the location name parameter (which is usually optional) must be explicitly specified for the remote access functions to construct the correct package name. (SPUFI does not use the SQL statement SET CURRENT PACKAGESET.) The location name entry in the package list must precede any wildcard entry. For example, the package list for the DSNESPCS plan is:

```
location_name.PRIVATCS.DSNESM68
*.DSNESPCS.DSNESM68
```

The package list for the DSNESPRR plan is:

location_name.PRIVATRR.DSNESM68
*.DSNESPRR.DSNESM68

DB2 for VM and VSE: Setting Up Interactive SQL (ISQL) and Database Services Utility (DBSU)

To use the DBS utility on a non-DB2 for VM and VSE application server you must first preprocess the DBS utility package on the non-DB2 for VM and VSE application server and then create the table SQLDBA.DBSOPTIONS on that non-DB2 for VM and VSE application server. This is done on the DB2 for VM and VSE application requester. You must then obtain the necessary program bind and table creation privileges for your authorization ID on the target application server.

Do the following from an DB2 for VM and VSE application server:

1. To establish the non-DB2 for VM and VSE application server as the default application server, run the SQLINIT EXEC against it.

2. To link to the database machine's service disk, enter:

   ```
   LINK machid 193 193 RR
   ```

3. To access the service disk, enter:

   ```
   ACC 193 V
   ```

4. To preprocess the DBS utility, enter:

   ```
   SQLPREP ASM PP (PREP=SQLDBA.ARIDSQL,BLOCK,ISOL(CS),NOPR,NOPU,
       CTOKEN(NO),ERROR) IN (ARIDSQLP MACRO V)
   ```

5. To create the table SQLDBA.DBSOPTIONS, enter the following DBS utility commands:

   ```
   SET ERRORMODE CONTINUE;

   CREATE TABLE SQLDBA.DBSOPTIONS
    (SQLOPTION VARCHAR (18) NOT NULL,
     VALUE     VARCHAR (18) NOT NULL);

   CREATE UNIQUE INDEX SQLDBA.DBSINDEX
    ON SQLDBA.DBSOPTIONS (SQLOPTION,VALUE);

   INSERT INTO SQLDBA.DBSOPTIONS
    VALUES ('RELEASE','3.3.0');

   COMMIT WORK;
   ```

You must now obtain the necessary program bind and table creation privileges for your authorization ID on the target application server.

To make ISQL requests of a non-DB2 for VM and VSE application server, you must load the ISQL package on that application server.

Before you can load ISQL on a non-DB2 for VM and VSE application server, you must first preprocess the DBS utility on the non-DB2 for VM and VSE application server. When the DBS utility is preprocessed on the non-DB2 for VM and VSE application server, ensure that you have the necessary program bind and table creation privileges for your authorization ID on the target application server.

To load ISQL, do the following from an DB2 for VM and VSE application requester:

1. Run the SQLINIT EXEC to establish the non-DB2 for VM and VSE application server as the default application server.

2. To link to the database machine's service disk, enter:

   ```
   LINK machid 193 193 RR
   ```

3. To access the service disk, enter:

   ```
   ACC 193 V
   ```

4. Issue the following CMS command:

   ```
   FILEDEF ARIISQLM DISK ARIISQLM MACRO V
   ```

5. To reload ISQL, issue the following DBS utility command:

   ```
   RELOAD PACKAGE (SQLDBA.ARIISQL) REPLACE KEEP INFILE (ARIISQLM);
   ```

6. Create the table SQLDBA.ROUTINE, and any other *userid*.ROUTINE tables that you want.

   For the CREATE TABLE statement that you use to create SQLDBA.ROUTINE, see the *ISQL Guide and Reference* manual.

Use of ISQL is not supported on DB2 for OS/400.

DB2 for OS/400: Setting Up Interactive SQL and Query Manager/400 (QM/400)

For DB2 for MVS/ESA and DB2 for VM and VSE application servers, the first interactive SQL or QM/400 request initiates a create package request on the unlike application server. The package and the name of the package depends on the OS/400 program preparation options (such as date format and commitment control) and is automatically requested as needed. However, the unlike application server must grant authority to create these packages.

The package name is QSQLabcd where abcd corresponds to numbers that refer to specific program preparation options that are used as follows:

Position	Option	Value
a	Date format	0 = ISO, JIS date format; 1 = USA date format; 2 = EUR date format
b	Time format	0 = JIS time format; 1 = USA time format; 2 = EUR, ISO time format

Position	Option	Value
c	Commitment control decimal delimiter	0 = *CS commitment control period decimal delimiter 1 = *CS commitment control comma decimal delimiter 2 = *RR commitment control period decimal delimiter 3 = *RR commitment control comma decimal delimiter
d	String delimiter default character subtype	0 = apostrophe string delimiter, single byte character subtype; 1 = apostrophe string delimiter, double byte character subtype; 2 = double quote string delimiter, single byte character subtype; 3 = double quote string delimiter, double byte character subtype

For example, a package named QSQL1100 is created from interactive SQL to an unlike application server with the following options: USA date format, USA time format, commitment control level of *CS, a period for the decimal delimiter, an apostrophe for the string delimiter, and a default character subtype of single byte. After a package is created with a particular set of options, all subsequent interactive SQL or Query Manager/400 users running with those same options against that application server will use that package.

For a DB2 for VM and VSE application server, a collection name is synonymous with a user ID. To create the needed packages used with the interactive SQL or QM/400 on a DB2 for VM and VSE application server:

1. Grant authority to create all necessary packages on the DB2 for VM and VSE platforms

2. Create a user ID of QSQL400 on the OS/400

3. Use this user ID on the first interactive request for creating all necessary packages on the DB2 for VM and VSE platforms

Setting Up the Command Line Processor

After the host connection and the gateway workstation are set up and running successfully, you can use the command line processor from the DDCS for OS/2 or DDCS for AIX workstation to issue SQL statements against a host database. The command line processor flows SQL statements to the database name you specify.

Authorization Required on Host

- On DB2 for MVS/ESA, you need BINDADD plus CREATE IN COLLECTION NULLID or SYSCTRL and SYSADM authority.

- On DB2 for OS/400, you need object authority of *CHANGE or higher on the NULLID collection.

- On DB2 for VM and VSE, you need DBA authority.

On the DDCS for AIX Workstation

To use the command line processor, you must do the following:

- Bind the command line processor to the host using the following commands:

```
db2 terminate
export DDCSSETP="-f=NUL -s=e"
db2 connect to <DBNAME> user <USERID> using <PASSWORD>
db2 bind INSTHOME/sqllib/bnd/@ddcsbind.lst blocking all
db2 connect reset
unset DDCSSETP
db2 terminate
```

<DBNAME>, <USERID>, and <PASSWORD> are your specific parameters and INSTHOME is the home directory of the instance you are using. If you do not specify a password, you will be prompted for a password and your entry will not be echoed to the display.

- GRANT EXECUTE (RUN) to PUBLIC or to the appropriate users on the following packages:

  - sqlc23b0
  - sqlc33b0
  - sqlc43b0

- Account for the differences in the way SQL statements are supported by each unlike database management system.

On the DDCS for OS/2 Workstation

To use the command line processor, you must do the following:

- Run the SQLJBIND command to bind the command line processor to the host database.

- GRANT EXECUTE (RUN) TO PUBLIC or to the appropriate users to the following packages for DDCS for OS/2 Version 2.0:

  - SQLAR3Λ0
  - SQLAC3A0
  - SQLAU3A0

- Account for the differences in the way SQL statements are supported by each unlike database management system.

DB2 for OS/400 Requirements

When accessing DB2 for OS/400, you must do the following:

- Create a NULLID collection on the AS/400 to which you are connected.

- Grant CHANGE authority or higher on the NULLID collection to the workstation user ID, as in the following example:

```
GRTOBJAUTH OBJ(QSYS/NULLID) OBJTYPE(*LIB) USER(user ID) AUT(*CHANGE)
```

- Ensure that the SQLCODE mapping file maps +595 to 0. For DDCS for OS/2, this mapping is included in the default mapping files, DCS0QSQ.MAP and

DCS1QSQ.MAP. For DDCS for AIX, this mapping is included in the default mapping file, dcs1qsq.map.

Appendix C. CCSID Values

The following tables describe the CCSIDs and conversions provided by the IBM relational database products.

- For DB2 for MVS/ESA and DB2 for VM and VSE, these tables represent the only CCSIDs and pairs of CCSID conversion tables that are initially supplied in the catalog. A user with administrative authority can add any SBCS CCSIDs and SBCS conversion tables at any time. It is also possible to provide user exit routines that perform SBCS or DBCS conversions.

- For DB2 for OS/400, DB2 for AIX and DB2 for OS/2, these charts represent the only CCSIDs and conversion tables that are available. There is no way to add additional CCSIDs or conversion tables.

The following list defines the symbols used in the IBM relational database product column in the following tables:

X   Indicates that the conversion tables exist to convert from and to that CCSID.

C   Indicates that conversion tables exist to convert from that CCSID to another CCSID. This also implies that this CCSID cannot be used to tag local data, because the CCSID is in a foreign encoding scheme (for example, a PC-Data CCSID such as 850 cannot be used to tag local data in DB2 for OS/400).

T   Indicates that while local data can be tagged with this CCSID, conversion tables are not shipped with the product. Administrators might need to take additional product-specific actions to support tagging with this CCSID.

Table 72. CCSIDs for EBCDIC Group 1 (Latin-1) Countries

CCSID	Description	DB2/MVS	DB2/VM and VSE	DB2/400	DB2/OS2	DB2/AIX
37	USA, Canada (S/370), Netherlands, Portugal, Brazil, Australia, New Zealand	X	X	X	C	C
256	Word Processing, Netherlands	T	T	X		
273	Austria, Germany	X	X	X	C	C
277	Denmark, Norway	X	X	X	C	C
278	Finland, Sweden	X	X	X	C	C
280	Italy	X	X	X	C	C
284	Spain, Latin America (Spanish)	X	X	X	C	C
285	United Kingdom	X	X	X	C	C
297	France	X	X	X	C	C
500	Belgium, Canada (AS/400), Switzerland, International Latin-1	X	X	X	C	C
871	Iceland	X	X	X	C	C

Table 73. CCSIDs for PC-Data and ISO Group 1 (Latin-1) Countries

CCSID	Description	DB2/MVS	DB2/VM and VSE	DB2/400	DB2/OS2	DB2/AIX
437	USA	C	C	C	X	C
819	Latin-1 countries (ISO 8859-1)	C	C	C	C	X
850	Latin Alphabet Number 1; Latin-1 countries	C	C	C	X	X
860	Portugal (850 subset)	C	C	C	X	
861	Iceland			C		
863	Canada (850 subset)	C	C	C	X	
865	Denmark, Norway, Finland, Sweden	C	C	C	X	

Table 74. CCSIDs for EBCDIC Group 1a (Non-Latin-1 SBCS) Countries

CCSID	Description	DB2/MVS	DB2/VM and VSE	DB2/400	DB2/OS2	DB2/AIX
420	Arabic	X	T	X	C	C
423	Greek	T	T	X		
424	Hebrew	X	T	X	C	C
870	Latin-2 Multilingual	X	T	X	C	C
875	Greek	X	X	X		C
880	Cyrillic Multilingual	T	T	X		
905	Turkey Latin-3 Multilingual	T	T	X		
1025	Cyrillic Multilingual	T	T	X		
1026	Turkey Latin-5	X	T	X	C	C
1097	Farsi	T	T	X		

CCSID Values

Table 75. CCSIDs for PC-Data and ISO Group 1a (Non-Latin-1 SBCS) Countries

CCSID	Description	DB2/MVS	DB2/VM and VSE	DB2/400	DB2/OS2	DB2/AIX
813	Greek/Latin (ISO 8859-7)	C	C	C		X
852	Latin-2 Multilingual	C	C	C	X	C
855	Cyrillic Multilingual			C		
857	Turkey Latin-5	C		C	X	C
862	Hebrew	C	C	C	X	C
864	Arabic	C	C	C	X	C
866	Cyrillic			C		
869	Greek		C	C		C
912	Latin-2 (ISO 8859-2)	C	C	C	C	X
915	Cyrillic Multilingual (ISO 8859-5)			C		
916	Hebrew/Latin (ISO 8859-8)	C	C	C	C	X
920	Turkey Latin-5 (ISO 8859-9)	C		C	C	X
1046	Arabic	C		C	C	X
1089	Arabic/Latin (ISO 8859-6)				C	X
row 1098		Farsi			C	
4948	Latin-2 Multilingual			C		
4951	Cyrillic Multilingual			C		
4952	Hebrew			C		
4953	Turkey Latin-5			C		
4960	Arabic			C		
4965	Greek			C		

Table 76. SBCS CCSIDs for EBCDIC Group 2 (DBCS) Countries

CCSID	Description	DB2/MVS	DB2/VM and VSE	DB2/400	DB2/OS2	DB2/AIX
290	Japan Katakana (extended)	X	X	X	C	C
833	Korea (extended)	X	X	X	C	
836	Simplified Chinese (extended)	T	X	X		
838	Thailand (extended)	T	X	X		
1027	Japan English (extended)	X	X	X	C	C
28709	Traditional Chinese (extended)	X	X	X	C	

Table 77. SBCS CCSIDs for PC-Data Group 2 (DBCS) Countries

CCSID	Description	DB2/MVS	DB2/VM and VSE	DB2/400	DB2/OS2	DB2/AIX
874	Thailand (extended)			C		
891	Korea (non-extended)		C	C		
897	Japan (non-extended)		C	C		
903	Simplified Chinese (non-extended)		C	C		
904	Traditional Chinese (non-extended)		C	C		
1040	Korea (extended)		C	C		
1041	Japan (extended)		C	C		
1042	Simplified Chinese (extended)		C	C		
1043	Traditional Chinese (extended)		C	C		
1088	Korea (KS Code 5601-89)	C	C	C		
1114	Traditional Chinese (Big-5)			C		

Table 78. DBCS CCSIDs for EBCDIC Group 2 (DBCS) Countries

CCSID	Description	DB2/MVS	DB2/VM and VSE	DB2/400	DB2/OS2	DB2/AIX
300	Japan - including 4370 user-defined characters (UDC)	X	X	X	C	C
834	Korea - including 1880 UDC	X	X	X	C	
835	Traditional Chinese - including 6204 UDC	X	X	X	C	
837	Simplified Chinese - including 1880 UDC	T	X	X		
4396	Japan - including 1880 UDC	X	X	X	C	C

Table 79. DBCS CCSIDs for PC-Data Group 2 (DBCS) Countries

CCSID	Description	DB2/MVS	DB2/VM and VSE	DB2/400	DB2/OS2	DB2/AIX
301	Japan - including 1880 UDC	C	C	C	X	X
926	Korea - including 1880 UDC		C	C	X	
927	Traditional Chinese - including 6204 UDC	C	C	C	X	
928	Simplified Chinese - including 1880 UDC		C	C		
947	Traditional Chinese (Big-5)			C		
951	Korea (KS Code 5601-89) - including 1880 UDC	C	C		X	

CCSID Values

Table 80. Mixed CCSIDs for EBCDIC Group 2 (DBCS) Countries

CCSID	Description	DB2/MVS	DB2/VM and VSE	DB2/400	DB2/OS2	DB2/AIX
930	Japan Katakana/Kanji (extended) - including 4370 UDC	X	X	X	C	C
933	Korea (extended) - including 1880 UDC	X	X	X	C	
935	Simplified Chinese (extended) - including 1880 UDC	T	X	X		
937	Traditional Chinese (extended) - including 4370 UDC	X	X	X	C	
939	Japan English/Kanji (extended) - including 4370 UDC	X	X	X	C	C
5026	Japan Katakana/Kanji (extended) - including 1880 UDC)	X	X	X	C	C
5035	Japan English/Kanji (extended) - including 1880 UDC	X	X	X	C	C

Table 81. Mixed CCSIDs for PC-Data Group 2 (DBCS) Countries

CCSID	Description	DB2/MVS	DB2/VM and VSE	DB2/400	DB2/OS2	DB2/AIX
932	Japan (non-extended) - including 1880 UDC	C	C	C	X	X
934	Korea (non-extended) including 1880 UDC		C	C	X	
936	Simplified Chinese (non-extended) - including 1880 UDC		C	C		
938	Traditional Chinese (non-extended) - including 6204 UDC)	C	C	C	X	
942	Japan (extended) - including 1880 UDC	C	C	C	X	C.
944	Korea (extended) - including 1880 UDC		C	C	X	
946	Simplified Chinese (extended) - including 1880 UDC		C	C		
948	Traditional Chinese (extended) - including 6204 UDC	C	C	C	X	
949	Korea (KS Code 5601-89) - including 1880 UDC	C	C		X	
950	Traditional Chinese (Big-5)			C		

Appendix D. DB2 for VM Character Conversion Values

The application requester CCSIDs are recognized by the application server when the DRDA support is installed and being used. If DRDA support is not installed, the application requester CCSIDs are not recognized by the application server.

Table 82 shows when the application requester CCSIDs are recognized by the application server. This table applies only to VM systems.

- "NO" indicates that the application requester CCSIDs are not recognized and CCSID conversion is not done between the application server CCSIDs and the application requester CCSIDs.

- "YES" indicates that the application requester CCSIDs are recognized by the application server, and CCSID conversion is done between the application server CCSIDs and the application requester CCSIDs.

- "Not Allowed" indicates that this combination of PROTOCOL parameters is not supported.

- "Non-DB2 for VM" is a non-DB2 for VM application server or application requester that supports the DRDA protocol.

Table 82. CCSID Conversion between Application Server and Application Requester.

Application Requester		Application Server		
		DB2 for VM		Non-DB2 for VM
		DB2 for VM	AUTO	
DB2 for VM	DB2 for VM	NO	NO	Not Allowed
	AUTO	NO	YES	YES
	DRDA	Not Allowed	YES	YES
Non-DB2 for VM		Not Allowed	YES	Not Applicable

Table 83 and Table 84 on page 455 show CHARNAMEs and the corresponding CCSIDs that can be used as DB2 for VM system defaults. Table 83 shows the SBCS CHARNAME CCSIDs, and Table 84 on page 455 shows the mixed CHARNAME CCSIDs, with the component SBCS and DBCS CCSIDs for each mixed CCSID.

Table 83 (Page 1 of 2). SBCS CCSIDs

CCSID	Character Set	Code Page	CHARNAME	Description
37	697	37	ENGLISH	Country extended code pages (CECP): USA, Canada (S/370* system), Netherlands, Portugal, Brazil, Australia, New Zealand
273	697	273	GERMAN	CECP: Austria, Germany
277	697	277	DANISH-NORWEGIAN	CECP: Denmark, Norway

Table 83 (Page 2 of 2). SBCS CCSIDs

CCSID	Character Set	Code Page	CHARNAME	Description
278	697	278	FINNISH-SWEDISH	CECP: Finland, Sweden
280	697	280	ITALIAN	CECP: Italy
284	697	284	SPANISH	CECP: Spain, Latin America (Spanish)
285	697	285	UK-ENGLISH	CECP: United Kingdom
290	1172	290	290	Japanese Katakana, extended host single byte
297	697	297	FRENCH	CECP: France
420	235	420	ARABIC	Arabic (all presentation shapes)
424	941	424	HEBREW	Hebrew
500	697	500	INTERNATIONAL	CECP: Belgium, Canada (AS/400* system), Switzerland, International Latin-1
833	1173	833	833	Korean, extended host single byte
836	1174	836	836	Simplified Chinese, extended host single byte
838	1176	838	THAI	Thai, extended host single byte
870	959	870	870	ROECE Latin-2 Multilingual
871	697	871	ICELANDIC	CECP: Iceland
875	925	875	GREEK	Greek
1027	1172	1027	1027	Japanese Latin, extended host single byte
28709	1175	37	28709	Traditional Chinese, extended host single byte

Table 84. Mixed CCSIDs

Mixed CCSID	Component CCSIDs	Character Set	Code Page	CHARNAME	Description
930	290 (SBCS) 300 (DBCS)	1172 1001	290 300	930	Japanese (Katakana)-Kanji mixed host (including 4370 user-defined characters) extended single byte
933	833 (SBCS) 834 (DBCS)	1173 934	833 834	KOREAN	Korean host mixed (including 1880 user-defined characters) extended single byte
935	836 (SBCS) 837(DBCS)	1174 937	836 837	S-CHINESE	Simplified Chinese host mixed (1880 user-defined characters) extended single byte
937	28709 (SBCS) 835 (DBCS)	1175 935	37 835	T-CHINESE	Traditional Chinese host mixed (6204 user-defined characters) extended single byte
939	1027 (SBCS) 300 (DBCS)	1172 1001	1027 300	939	Japanese (Latin)-Kanji mixed host (including 4370 user-defined-characters) extended single byte
5026	290 (SBCS) 4396 (DBCS)	1172 370	290 300	KATAKANA	Japanese (Katakana)-Kanji mixed host (including 1880 user-defined characters) extended single byte
5035	1027 (SBCS) 4396 (DBCS)	1172 370	1027 300	JAPANESE-ENGLISH	Japanese (Latin)-Kanji mixed host , (including 1880 user-defined characters) extended single byte

For more information about CCSIDs, see the *Character Data Representation Architecture Level 1, Registry*, and the *Character Data Representation Architecture Reference*, SC09-1390.

Bibliography

AS/400 Publications

Communications Configuration (SC41-3401)

Distributed Database Programming (SC41-3702)

Security - Reference (SC41-3302)

CL Reference (SC41-3722)

National Language Support (SC41-3101)

OS/400 APPC Programming (V2R3: SC41-8189, V3R1: SC41-3443)

OS/400 APPN Support (V2R3: SC41-8188, V3R1: SC41-3407)

CICS Publications

CICS/VSE Intercommunications Guide (SC33-0701)

DATABASE 2 for MVS/ESA Publications

IBM DATABASE 2 Version 3 Administration Guide (SC26-4888)

IBM DATABASE 2 Version 3 Application Programming and SQL Guide (SC26-4889)

IBM DATABASE 2 Version 3 Command and Utility Reference (SC26-4891)

IBM DATABASE 2 Version 3 Messages and Codes (SC26-4892)

IBM DATABASE 2 Version 3 SQL Reference (SC26-4890)

DATABASE 2 for AIX Publications

DATABASE 2 AIX/6000 Administration Guide (SC09-1571)

AIX Distributed Database Connection Services/6000 Guide (SC09-1568)

DATABASE 2 for OS/2 Publications

DATABASE 2 for OS/2 Guide (S62G-3663)

Distributed Database Connection Services/2 Version 2.0 Guide (S62G-3792)*

Distributed Relational Database Architecture Publications

Application Programming Guide (SC26-4773)

Problem Determination Guide (SC26-4782)

Reference (SC26-4651)

Evaluation and Planning Guide (SC26-4650)

Every Manager's Guide (GC26-3195)

Communications Manager/2 Publications

IBM Communications Manager/2 Version 1.0 Configuration Guide (SC31-6171)

Communications Manager/2 Workstation Installation and Configuration Guide Version 1.1 (SC31-6169)

Communications Manager/2 1.1 Host Connection Reference (SC31-6170)

---

* Trademark of IBM Corporation

SNA Publications

Systems Network Architecture Technical Overview (GC30-3073)

Systems Network Architecture Transaction Programmer's Reference Manual for LU Type 6.2 (GC30-3084)

Systems Network Architecture Formats (GA27-3136)

Systems Network Architecture Format and Protocol Reference Manual (SC30-3269)

Systems Network Architecture Transaction Programmer's Reference Manual for LU Type 6.2 (GC30-3084)

DB2 for VM and VSE Publications

SQL/Data System General Information for IBM VM System Products (GH09-8074)

SQL/DS Reference for IBM VM Systems (SH09-8087)

SQL/DS System Administration for IBM VM Systems (GH09-8084)

SQL/DS System Administration for IBM VSE Systems (GH09-8096)

SQL/DS Database Administration for IBM VM Systems (GH09-8083)

VM Publications

VM/SP CMS Command Reference (SC19-6209)

VM/SP Connectivity Programming Guide and Reference (SC24-5377)

VM/SP Connectivity Planning, Administration and Operation (SC24-5378)

VM/ESA CMS Command Reference (SC24-5461)

VM/ESA CP Programming Services (SC24-5520)

VM/ESA Connectivity Planning, Administration, and Operation (SC24-5448)

VTAM Publications

VTAM Customization (LY43-0046)

VTAM Network Implementation Guide (SC31-6404)

VTAM Resource Definition Reference (LY43-0060)

VTAM Reference Summary (SC31-6412)

VTAM Multiprotocol Transport Feature Version 3 Release 4.2 for MVS/ESA: APPC over TCP/IP User's Guide (SC31-6488)

VTAM Programming for LU 6.2 (SC30-3400)

AnyNet Publications

IBM AnyNet Product Family (G325-3405)

VTAM AnyNet Feature for V4R2 Guide to SNA over TCP/IP (SC31-6527)

AIX SNA Server/6000 AnyNet Feature: Guide to APPC over TCP/IP (SV40-0212)

AnyNet/2 Version 2 Guide to SNA over TCP/IP (GV40-0375)

VTAM V3R4.2 AnyNet/MVS Implementation (GG24-4066)

Related Publications

NCP, SSP, and EP Resource Definition Guide
(SC30-3447)

DB2–APPC/VTAM Distributed Database Usage Guide
(GG24-3600)

Distributed Relational Database Remote Unit of Work
Implementation DB2–DB2 and DB2–SQL/DS, Volume 1
(GG24-3715)

Distributed Relational Database Remote Unit of Work
Implementation DB2–DB2 and DB2–SQL/DS, Volume 2
(GG24-3716)

Using OS/2 DRDA Client Support with DB2
(GG24-3771)

Setting Up and Usage of SQL/DS in a DRDA
Environment (GG24-3733)

OS/2 DDCS/2 and DB2 V2R3 Distributed Relational
Database Performance: Early Experience (GG24-3926)

Distributed Relational Database Cross Platform
Connectivity and Application (GG24-4311)

Formal Register of Extensions and Differences in SQL
(SC26-3316)

Glossary

This glossary defines terms as they are used for distributed relational database architecture (DRDA). If you do not find a term you are looking for, see the other references listed in "Bibliography" on page 456 about that topic. Also refer to the index of this manual or the *Dictionary of Computing (SC20-1699)*.

A

ACF. Advanced Communications Function.

Advanced Communications Function.. A group of IBM licensed programs, principally VTAM programs, TCAM, NCP, and SSP, that use the concepts of Systems Network Architecture (SNA), including the distribution of function and resource sharing.

Advanced Interactive Executive (AIX). IBM's licensed implementation of the UNIX operating system.

* (APPN)

Advanced Peer-to-Peer Networking. A distributed network and session control architecture that allows networked computers to communicate dynamically as equals. Compare with Advanced Program to Program Communication (APPC).

Advanced Program-to-Program Communication (APPC). An implementation of the SNA synchronous data link control LU 6.2 protocol that allows interconnected systems to communicate and share the processing of programs.

AIX. Advanced Interactive Executive.

alert. An error message sent to the system services control point (SSCP) at the host system.

alias. In DB2 for MVS/ESA, an alternate name that can be used in SQL statements to refer to a table or view in the same or a remote DB2 for MVS/ESA subsystem. In OS/2, an alternate name used to identify an object, a database, or a network resource such as an LU.

already verified. An LU 6.2 security option which allows a logical unit to provide the user's authorization ID when allocating a conversation. The user is not validated by the partner logical unit.

APPC. Advanced Program-to-Program Communication.

API. Application Program Interface.

Application Program Interface (API). The interface that application programs use to request services from some program such as a database management system.

application requester. (1) A facility that accepts a database request from an application process and passes it to an application server. (2) In DRDA, the source of a request to a remote relational database management system.

application server. The target of a request from an application requester. (1) The local or remote database manager to which the application process is connected. (2) In DRDA, the target of a request from an application requester.

application support protocol. The protocol used in DRDA that connects application requesters and application servers.

B

basic information unit (BIU). The unit of data and control information transmitted in an SNA network. Each BIU consists of a request header and a request unit.

bind. In DRDA, the process by which the SQL statements in an application program are made known to a database management system over application support protocol (and database support protocol) flows. During a bind, output from a precompiler or preprocessor is converted to a control structure called a package. (Optionally in DB2 for MVS/ESA, the output may be an application plan.). In addition, access paths to the referenced data are selected and some authorization checking is performed.

---

*　Trademark of IBM Corporation

459

C

catalog. A set of tables maintained by the database management system. These tables contain information such as descriptions of tables, views, and packages.

CCSID. Coded character set identifier.

CDRA. Character Data Representation Architecture.

Character Data Representation Architecture (CDRA). The architecture that defines coded character set identifier values to identify the codes (code points) used to represent characters, and the character data conversion of these codes, as needed, to preserve the characters and their meanings.

CICS. Customer Information Control System.

class of service (COS). In SNA, a designation of the path control network characteristics, such as path security, transmission priority, and bandwidth, that apply to a particular session. The end user designates class of service at session initiation by using a symbolic name that is mapped into a list of virtual routes, any one of which can be selected for the session to provide the requested level of service.

client. A functional unit that receives shared services from a server.

CMS communications directory (COMDIR). A CMS facility used by DB2 for VM and VSE that lets APPC/VM applications establish conversations with remote systems using symbolic destination names. DB2 for VM and VSE uses two levels of directories: the *system communications directory* and the *user communications directory*. CMS user and system communications directories map a *server-name* to a symbolic destination name.

Coded character set identifier (CCSID). A 16-bit number identifying a specific set of encoding scheme identifiers, character set identifiers, code page identifiers, and other relevant information, that uniquely identifies the coded graphic character representation used.

connectivity. The enabling of different systems to communicate with each other. For example, connectivity between a DB2 for MVS/ESA application requester and a DB2 for VM and VSE application server enables a DB2 for MVS/ESA user to request data from a DB2 for VM and VSE database.

control point. In SNA, a physical unit control point or a system services control point.

conversation. A logical connection between two programs over an LU 6.2 session that allows them to communicate with each other while processing a transaction.

conversation-level security. An LU 6.2 security option which allows validation of an authorization ID and password before establishing a conversation.

COS. Class of service.

Customer Information Control System (CICS). An IBM licensed program that enables transactions entered at remote terminals to be processed concurrently by user-written application programs. It includes facilities for building, using, and maintaining data bases.

D

database. A collection of data with a given structure for accepting, storing, and providing on demand data for multiple users. In DB2 for MVS/ESA, a created object that contains table spaces and index spaces. In DB2 for VM and VSE, a collection of tables, indexes, and supporting information (such as control information and data recovery information) maintained by the system. In DB2 for OS/400, all the data files stored in the system. In OS/2, a collection of information, such as tables, views, and indexes.

data integrity. A condition of data in which the data is correct and current. To maintain data integrity, all changes to the data within a unit of work are completed or none of them are.

database management system (DBMS). A computer-based system for defining, creating, manipulating, controlling, managing, and using databases. The DBMS also has transaction management and data recovery facilities to protect data integrity.

database server. (1) In DRDA, the target of a request received from an application server. (2) In OS/2, a workstation that provides database services for its local database to database clients.

database support protocol. The protocol in DRDA used to connect application servers with database servers.

DBCS. Double-byte character set.

DBMS. Database management system.

DDM. Distributed Data Management.

deadlock detection. The process of determining that two or more logical units of work are using resources in such a way that none can proceed to conclusion. The units of work may be waiting for an action by or a response from the other. In DRDA, deadlocks may span RDBs and other resources.

Distributed Data Management (DDM). The protocol architecture that defines access to distributed data. The data may be in files or in relational databases.

Distributed Relational Database Architecture (DRDA). A connection protocol for distributed relational database processing that is used by IBM and vendor relational database products. DRDA comprises protocols for communication between an application and a remote relational database management system (RDBMS), and communications between RDBMSs. DRDA provides the connections for remote and distributed processing.

distributed request. An extension of the distributed unit of work method of accessing distributed relational data in which each SQL statement may access data located at several different systems. This extension supports join and union operations that cross system boundaries and inserts of data selected from other sites. Compare with remote unit of work and distributed unit of work.

distributed unit of work (DUW). A method of accessing distributed relational data in which users or applications can, within a single unit of work, submit SQL statements to multiple relational database management systems, but no more than one RDBMS per SQL statement.

domain. In SNA, a system services control point (SSCP) and the physical units, logical units, links, link stations, and all associated resources that the SSCP has the ability to control by means of activation requests and deactivation requests.

double-byte character set (DBCS). A character set, such as a set of Japanese ideographs, that requires two-byte code points to identify the characters.

DRDA. Distributed Relational Database Architecture.

E

execution thread. A process or task that provides for the execution of a sequence of operations. One operation occurs at a time. Operations are single threaded. Commonly, resources (such as locks) are associated with execution threads, and the thread becomes the anchor point for managing such resources.

F

FDOCA. Formatted Data Object Content Architecture

flow. The passing of messages from one process to another, or the passing of messages of a particular type between processes.

Formatted Data Object Content Architecture (FDOCA). An architected collection of constructs used to interchange formatted data.

G

gateway. A functional unit that connects two computer networks of different network architectures. A gateway connects networks or systems of different architectures, as opposed to a bridge, which connects networks or systems with the same or similar architectures.

H

host. A mainframe or mid-size processor that provides services in a network to a workstation.

host variable. In an application program, a program variable referenced by SQL statements.

L

like. Pertaining to two or more similar or identical IBM operating environments. For example, like distribution is distribution two DB2 for MVS/ESA systems with compatible server attribute levels.

local area network (LAN). (1) Two or more processors connected for local resource sharing. (2) A network within a limited geographic area, such as a single office building, warehouse, or campus.

local identifier (LID). An identifier or short label that is mapped by the environment to a named resource.

logical unit (LU). A port through which an end user accesses the SNA network to communicate with another end user and through which the end user accesses the functions provided by system services control points.

logical unit of work (LUW). The work that occurs between the start of a transaction and commit or rollback and between commit and rollback actions after that. It defines the set of operations that must be considered part of an integral set. See data integrity.

logical unit-of-work identifier (LUWID). A name consisting of a fully qualified LU network name, an LUW instance number, and an LUW sequence number, that identifies a logical unit of work within a network.

Logical Unit type 6.2 (LU 6.2). The SNA logical unit type that supports general communication between programs in a distributed processing environment.

LU. Logical unit.

LU 6.2. Logical Unit type 6.2.

LU protocol boundary. A formalized programming interface between the transaction program and the LU, allowing the development of applications that are independent of the underlying communications layers.

LUW. Logical unit of work.

LUWID. Logical unit-of-work identifier.

M

MSA. SNA Management Services Architecture.

N

NCP. Network Control Program.

network addressable unit (NAU). In SNA, a logical unit, a physical unit, or a system services control point. The NAU is the origin or destination of information transmitted by the path control network.

Network Control Program (NCP). An IBM licensed program that provides communication controller support for single-domain, multiple-domain, and interconnected network capability.

node. In SNA, an endpoint of a link or a junction common to two or more links in a network. Nodes can be distributed to host processors, communication controllers, cluster controllers, or terminals. Nodes can vary in routing and other functional capabilities.

P

pacing. In SNA, a technique by which a receiver controls the rate of transmission of a sender to prevent overrun.

pacing window. A specification of the maximum number of PIUs that are transmitted by a sender in a network before the sender must wait for the receiver to process the data.

package. The control structure produced when the SQL statements in an application program are bound to a relational database management system. The database management system uses the control structure to process SQL statements encountered during statement execution.

partner logical unit. In SNA, the remote system in a session.

partner-LU verification. An LU 6.2 security control for authenticating an LU.

path information unit (PIU). In SNA, a message unit consisting of a message header followed by a basic information unit or basic information unit segment.

peer-to-peer networking. A communication approach in which networked systems communicate as equals. See also Advanced Peer-to-Peer Networking (APPN).

physical unit (PU). In SNA, the component that manages and monitors the resources of a node, such as attached links and adjacent link stations, as requested by a system services control point (SSCP) via an SSCP-to-SS CP session.

PIU. Path information unit.

plan. A form of package where the SQL statements of several programs are collected together during bind to create a plan. Distributed Relational Database Architecture does not support the concept of a plan.

primary logical unit (PLU). In SNA, the logical unit (LU) that contains the primary half-session for a particular LU-to-LU session. See also, logical unit (LU).

protocol. The rules governing the functions of a communication system that must be followed if communication is to be achieved.

R

RDB. Relational database.

RDBMS. Relational database management system.

RDB_NAME. The DRDA globally unique name for a relational database. See also *rdbname*.

rdbname. The name of an RDB. Synonymous with server-name. Also called database name in DB2 for OS/2, dbname in DB2 for VM and VSE, location name in DB2 for MVS/ESA, and RDB_NAME in DRDA.

relational data. Data stored in a relational database management system.

relational database (RDB). (1) A database that can be perceived as a set of tables and manipulated in accordance with the relational model of data. (2) In DRDA, a catalog and all the data described by the catalog.

relational database management system (RDBMS). A computer-based system for defining, creating, manipulating, controlling, managing, and using relational databases.

remote unit of work. (1) The form of SQL distributed processing where the application is on a system different from the relational database and a single application server services all remote unit-of-work requests within a single logical unit of work. (2) A unit of work that allows for the remote preparation and execution of SQL statements.

request header. The part of a basic information unit that precedes a request unit. It contains information about the transmission (for example, whether the data that follows the request header is a request or a response).

request unit. The part of a basic information unit that follows a request header, and contains the data.

RH. Request header.

RU. Request unit.

S

SAA. Systems Application Architecture.

SBCS. Single-byte character set.

secondary logical unit (SLU). In SNA, the logical unit (LU) that contains the secondary half-session for a particular LU-to-LU session. See also logical unit (LU).

session-level pacing. In SNA, a flow control technique that permits a receiving session to control the data transfer rate (the rate at which it receives request units) on the normal flow. It is used to prevent overloading a receiver with unprocessed requests when the sender can generate requests faster than the receiver can process them. See also pacing, virtual route pacing.

session-level security. An LU 6.2 security control for authenticating an LU. Also called partner-LU verification and LU-to-LU verification.

single-byte character set (SBCS). A character set that requires one-byte code points to identify the characters.

SNA. Systems Network Architecture.

SNA Management Services Architecture (MSA). The architecture that provides services to assist in the management of SNA networks.

SSCP. System services control point.

synchpoint tower. The collection of capabilities and protocols defined by SNA to support distributed two-phase commit.

system services control point (SSCP). A focal point within an SNA network for managing the configuration, coordinating network operator and problem determination requests, and providing directory services and other session services for end users of a network.

Systems Application Architecture (SAA). A set of software interfaces, conventions, and protocols that provide a framework for designing and developing applications with cross-system consistency.

Systems Network Architecture (SNA). The description of the logical structure, formats, protocols, and operational sequences for transmitting information units through and controlling the configuration and operation of networks.

T

TP. Transaction program.

TPN. Transaction program name.

transaction. The work that occurs between Begin Unit of Work and COMMIT or ROLLBACK. It defines the set of operations that are part of an integral set.

transaction program (TP). A program that processes transactions in an SNA network. There are two kinds of transaction programs: application transaction programs and service transaction programs.

transaction program name (TPN). The name by which each program participating in an LU 6.2 conversation is known. Normally, the initiator of a connection identifies the name of the program it wants to connect to at the other LU. When used in conjunction with an LU name, it identifies a specific transaction program in the network.

two-phase commit protocol. A protocol used in distributed unit of work to ensure that participating relational database management systems commit or roll back a unit of work consistently.

U

unit of work. (1) A recoverable sequence of operations within an application process. At any time, an application process is a single unit of work, but the life of an application process may involve many units of work as a result of commit or rollback operations. (2) In DRDA, a sequence of SQL commands that the database manager treats as a single entity. The database manager ensures the consistency of data by verifying that either all the data changes made during a unit of work are performed or none of them are performed.

unlike. Pertaining to two or more different IBM operating environments. For example, unlike distribution is distribution between DB2 for VM and VSE and DB2 for MVS/ESA.

user communications directory. In DB2 for VM and VSE, a CMS communications directory that resides in a user's virtual machine. It is used by DB2 for VM and VSE to establish conversations with remote systems.

V

virtual route (VR) pacing. In SNA, a flow control technique used by the virtual route control component of path control at each end of a virtual route to control the rate at which path information units flow over the virtual route. VR pacing can be adjusted according to traffic congestion in any of the nodes along the route. See also, pacing, session-level pacing.

Virtual Storage Extended (VSE). An operating system that is an extension of Disk Operating System/ Virtual Storage. A VSE system consists of (1) VSE/Advanced Functions support and (2) any IBM-supplied and user-written programs that are required to meet the data processing needs of a user. VSE and the hardware it controls form a complete computing system.

VSE. See Virtual Storage Extended.

Index

Special Characters

, (comma) in parameter string   117
,, INTERRUPT_ENABLED   117
,D   117
*IDENT   52

Numerics

3174 controller configuration   288

A

ACCRDB message   422
ACCRDBRM message   422
ACF/VTAM   79
adaptive pacing   388
add relational database directory entry command
  (ADDRDBDIRE)   90
additional TP parameters panel   318
advanced peer-to-peer networking
  See APPN (advanced peer-to-peer networking)
advanced program-to-program communications
  See APPC (advanced program-to-program
    communications)
AGW commands for AVS gateway   137
AIX
  worksheets   346
AIX Encina Monitor   114
ALLOCATE verb
  bracket indicators   404
  contention between LUs   406
  description   402
  SNA session association   400
already-verified security   411
ALREADYV statement   62
AnyNet/MVS   6
APPC
  configuring server   359
  tpname   357, 367
APPC (advanced program-to-program communications)
  concepts   399
  configuring
    DB2 for OS/2 connection using 3174   289
    DB2 for OS/2 to DB2 connection   212
    DB2 for OS/2 to DB2 connection via SDLC   264
    DB2 for OS/2 to multiple hosts connection   273

APPC (advanced program-to-program communications)
  (continued)
    configuring (continued)
      DB2 for OS/2 to OS/400 connection   195
      SQL/DS to DB2 for OS/2 connection   236
    description   372
    distinctions between APPN   394
    verbs
      ALLOCATE   400, 402
      DEALLOCATE   402
      distributed database communication   422
      example   403
      issued by APPC application   401
      LU protocol boundary   401
      PREPARE_TO_RECEIVE   402
      SEND_DATA   402
      using   403
APPC/VM support   51
APPC/VTAM support   50
APPCPASS statement   69
APPL   306, 324, 332, 343
APPL statement
  DB2 example   24
  MODETAB keyword   437
  SQL/DS example   61
  VERIFY= keyword   441
application development   110
application directed access   18
application requester   116
  communication subsystem   8
  components   2
  connection protocol   415
  description, local system   7
  function   415
  network information   7
  remote system   7
application requester, DB2   20—36
  communications subsystem   30
  data representation   36
  local system definition   21
  pacing   31
  remote system definition   27
  RU sizing   31
  security
    database manager   35
    end user names   31
    network   33
    subsystem   36

We'd Like to Hear from You

Distributed Relational Database Architecture
Connectivity Guide

Publication No. SC26-4783-03

Please use one of the following ways to send us your comments about this book:

- Mail—Use the Readers' Comments form on the next page. If you are sending the form from a country other than the United States, give it to your local IBM branch office or IBM representative for mailing.
- Fax—Use the Readers' Comments form on the next page and fax it to this U.S. number: 408-463-4393.
- Electronic mail—
  - Internet: comments@vnet.ibm.com

  Be sure to include the following with your comments:
  - Title and publication number of this book
  - Your name, address, and telephone number if you would like a reply

IBM may use or distribute your comments without obligation.

Readers' Comments

Distributed Relational Database Architecture
Connectivity Guide

Publication No. SC26-4783-03

How satisfied are you with the information in this book?

	Very Satisfied	Satisfied	Neutral	Dissatisfied	Very Dissatisfied
Technically accurate	☐	☐	☐	☐	☐
Complete	☐	☐	☐	☐	☐
Easy to find	☐	☐	☐	☐	☐
Easy to understand	☐	☐	☐	☐	☐
Well organized	☐	☐	☐	☐	☐
Applicable to your tasks	☐	☐	☐	☐	☐
Grammatically correct and consistent	☐	☐	☐	☐	☐
Graphically well designed	☐	☐	☐	☐	☐
Overall satisfaction	☐	☐	☐	☐	☐

Please tell us how we can improve this book:

May we contact you to discuss your comments? ☐ Yes ☐ No

_____   _____
Name   Address

_____   _____
Company or Organization

_____   _____
Phone No.

Readers' Comments
SC26-4783-03

Cut or Fold
Along Line

Fold and Tape   **Please do not staple**   Fold and Tape

BUSINESS REPLY MAIL

FIRST-CLASS MAIL   PERMIT NO. 40   ARMONK, NEW YORK

POSTAGE WILL BE PAID BY ADDRESSEE

Department J58
International Business Machines Corporation
PO BOX 49023
SAN JOSE CA 95161-9945

Fold and Tape   **Please do not staple**   Fold and Tape

Cut or Fold
Along Line

SC26-4783-03